LAND AND SOCIETY
IN COLONIAL MEXICO

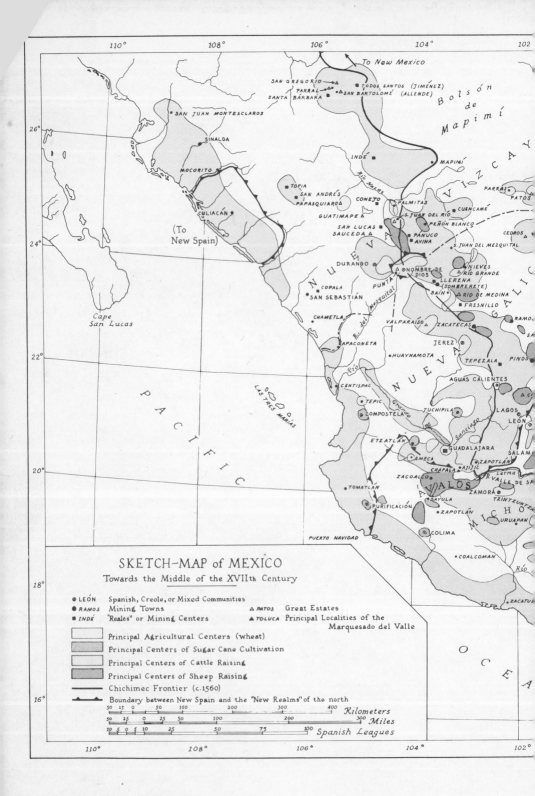

110°   108°   106°   104°   102°

To New Mexico

SAN GREGORIO △
PARRAL ▲ ● △ TODOS SANTOS (JIMÉNEZ)
SANTA BÁRBARA ● ▲ SAN BARTOLOMÉ (ALLENDE)

● SAN JUAN MONTESCLAROS

SINALOA ●

INDÉ ●   ● MAPIMÍ

Bolsón
de
Mapimí

MOCORITO ▲

26°

TOPIA ■   ● PARRAS
SAN ANDRÉS ●   ● PATOS
PAPASQUIARO ■   ● CUENCAMÉ
CULIACÁN ●   CONEJO ●   PALMITAS △
GUATIMAPE ▲   ● S. JUAN DEL RÍO △ ● PEÑÓN BLANCO
SAN LUCAS ■   ● PANUCO   ● CEDROS
SAUCEDA ■   ● AVINA   ● S. JUAN DEL MEZQUITAL

(To
New Spain)

24°

DURANGO ▲   ● NOMBRE DE   △ NIEVES
DIOS   △ RÍO GRANDE
COPALA ●   PUNTA   LLERENA
SAN SEBASTIÁN ●   (SOMBRERETE)
SAÍN ▲   △ RÍO DE MEDINA
CHAMETLA ●   ● FRESNILLO

VALPARAISO △   ● ZACATECAS   RAMO ●

APACONETA ●   JEREZ ●

Cape
San Lucas

HUAYNAMOTA ●   TEPEZALA ●   PINOS ■

22°

CENTISPAC ●   AGUAS CALIENTES ●

LAS TRES MARÍAS   TEPIC ●   TUCHIPILA ●   LAGOS ●
COMPOSTELA ●   LEÓN ●

ETZATLÁN ●   GUADALAJARA ■   SALAM
AMECA ●   ● ZAPOTLÁN
CHAPALA ● AJIJIC ▲   VALLE DE S
ZACOALCO ●   R. Lerma
ZAMORA ●   TZINTZUNTZ
SAYULA ●   MICHO
TOMATLÁN ●   ● ZAPOTLÁN   URUAPAN ●
PURIFICACIÓN ●

20°

P A C I F I C

PUERTO NAVIDAD ●   ● COLIMA

● COALCOMAN   Río

O
C
E
A

18°

SKETCH-MAP of MEXICO
Towards the Middle of the XVIIth Century

● LEÓN   Spanish, Creole, or Mixed Communities
● RAMOS   Mining Towns
■ INDÉ   "Reales" or Mining Centers   △ PATOS   Great Estates
                                               ▲ TOLUCA Principal Localities of the
                                                         Marquesado del Valle

Principal Agricultural Centers (wheat)
Principal Centers of Sugar Cane Cultivation
Principal Centers of Cattle Raising
Principal Centers of Sheep Raising
Chichimec Frontier (c.1560)
Boundary between New Spain and the "New Realms" of the north

Kilometers
Miles
Spanish Leagues

16°

110°   108°   106°   104°   102°

CLOVA
26°
CERRALVO
MONTERREY
CADEREYTA   NUEVO LEÓN
SALTILLO
Río Grande (Bravo)
VALLE DEL PILÓN
PIL   Río de Las Palmas   R San Fernando   24°
TEHUALA
Río de Las Palmas
CHARCAS
EDIONDA
GUADALCÁZAR   HUA   R. Pánuco   22°
S. LUIS POTOSÍ   TAMPICO
RÍO VERDE   SANTIAGO DE   PÁNUCO
DE MATA   LOS VALLES
AN FELIPE   S   L. de Tamiahua
GUANAJUATO   S. LUIS DE LA PAZ   T   R. Pantepec
SAN MIGUEL   SICHÚ   E   TUXPAN
ELAYA   QUERÉTARO   R. San   C   R. Cazones
PASEO   ZIMAPAN   METZTITLÁN   A   R. Tecolutla
SALVATIERRA CADEREYTA   IXMIQUILPAN   R. Nautla   20°
EOS   SAN JUAN DEL   PACHUCA   NAUTLA
ACÁMBARO   RÍO TULA
VALLADOLID   TAXIMAROA   TEZIUTLÁN
ZITÁCUARO   APAN PEROTE
CÁMBARO   LERMA   TEXCOCO   JALAPA
MEXICO   TLAXCALA   LA RINCONADA
TOLUCA   CHALCO   HUAMANTLA   HUATUSCO   VERA CRUZ
CÁMBARO   TINGAMBATO TEPOZTLÁN   HUEJOTZINGO MEDELLÍN
UPÁNDARO   TEMASCALTEPEC ACUERNAVACA CHOLULA   R. Papaloapan   COATZACOALCOS
MIACATLÁN   CUAUTLA OAXTEPEC PUEBLA   CÓRDOBA
SULTEPEC   ATLIXCO   ORIZABA
TAXCO   TAXCO   JOJUTLA   TANTETELCO TENUACÁN   COATZACOALCOS
                      JONACATEPEC   TUXTLA
                                               ULUAPAN   R. Coatzacoalcos
R. Atoyac   CUICATLÁN   18°
MIXTECA ALTA
TIXTLA   NOCHISTLÁN   Río S. Juan
CHILAPA   TLAPA   YANHUITLÁN   VILLA ALTA
PUTLA   ETLA ANTEQUERA DE
MIXTECA BAJA   OAXACA   CHIAPA   SAN
ACAPULCO   CUILAPAN   MITLA   CRISTOBAL
                     EJUTLA NEXAPA
JICAYÁN   MIAHUATLÁN JALAPA IXTEPEC
OMETEPEC   TEHUANTEPEC
HUATULCO   SOCONUSCO
(PORT)   HUAQUECHULA

A T L A N T I C

O C E A N

R. Grijalva

Redrawn by J. Andress 1962

LAND AND
IN

Translated by Alvin Eustis

Edited, with a Foreword, by
Lesley Byrd Simpson

SOCIETY COLONIAL MEXICO

The Great Hacienda

BY FRANÇOIS CHEVALIER

Berkeley and Los Angeles

UNIVERSITY OF CALIFORNIA PRESS 1970

UNIVERSITY OF CALIFORNIA PRESS
BERKELEY AND LOS ANGELES, CALIFORNIA

UNIVERSITY OF CALIFORNIA PRESS, LTD.
LONDON, ENGLAND

THIRD PRINTING, 1970
Translated from *La Formation des grands domaines au Mexique. Terre et société aux XVIe–XVIIe siècles* (Paris: Institut d'Ethnologie, 1952)
PUBLISHED WITH THE ASSISTANCE OF A GRANT FROM
    THE ROCKEFELLER FOUNDATION
STANDARD BOOK NUMBERS: 520-01665-3 PAPER
                    520-00229-6 CLOTH
LIBRARY OF CONGRESS CATALOG CARD NUMBER: 63-20579
PRINTED IN THE UNITED STATES OF AMERICA

FOREWORD

The seventeenth century (from, say, about 1590 to about 1700) was the period of travail and gestation for the "old" Mexico made familiar to us in the works of Lucas Alamán and Alexander von Humboldt—the Mexico of the great landed estate, of the classical hacienda. The period contains few exciting events, few great names, at least in comparison with the Homeric sixteenth century. The military and spiritual conquest had long since come to a halt, except on the remote frontiers. It was a period of shrinking economy and a shrinking or stagnant population. Undistinguished bureaucrats in church and state were slowly molding public life into a suffocating routine, and corruption, nepotism, and time-serving make the records of the day dismal reading. So historians have tended to bypass this dull hiatus and get on to more rewarding times, leaving the impression that little happened in it worthy of note. And yet during that long quietness a new society was forming whose norms of conduct were set by a raw nobility of landed gentry—norms which have persisted to this day. The evolution of this aristocratic society is the theme that François Chevalier has undertaken to explore in his thoughtful and challenging book. Without pretending to have exhausted any one aspect of his subject, he has gathered a massive amount of information from the national and provincial archives of Mexico and the Archives of the Indies at Seville, and presents a boldly conceived and convincing account of a society in the making.

There is little that is startling or unexpected in the book, and, indeed, there could hardly be. The patriarchal "big house" of old Mexico, with its swarms of cousins, *compadres,* huge families, in-laws, vaqueros, priests, retainers, serfs, and hangers-on, is sufficiently well known to eliminate surprises. Chevalier is interested in discovering how that landed aristocracy came into being and what purposes, if any, its members had in mind when they transplanted to the New World the medieval manor of the Old. His approach is philosophical; it gives his book method and architectural coherence. He ignores the silly row between the "scientific" and the "literary" schools of historiography. He marshals a great abundance of evidence, selects what is pertinent to his design, discards the irrelevant, and keeps his exposition within bounds and understandable. He has spared himself no pains in verifying his information, but he allows himself plenty of room for wise and pertinent commentary. In a word, Chevalier has written a book, not just another monograph.

Its plan is conventional enough. Chevalier outlines the familiar human and physical geography of Mexico and Spain, characteristically giving the greater emphasis to culture and social habits. The hacienda, or manorial estate, and the mission, its religious counterpart, were, he thinks, inevitable growths deriving from the ancient traditions of Spaniards and Mexicans.

The Crown and its great agency, the Council of the Indies, were fully aware of the dangers inherent in this New World feudalism and put formidable blocks in the way of those who would acquire the huge holdings necessary to its growth. Land titles bristled with restrictive clauses. Agricultural grants, which were the only ones originally made in fee, seldom exceeded two caballerías (of about 105 acres each) to a grantee. Those made to Indian communities were, moreover, inalienable. Grants of land for stock raising (*estancias de ganado mayor y menor,* of 6.7 and 3 square miles, respectively) were hardly more than permits to graze stock. But Spanish ingenuity was equal to the challenge, and within a century of the conquest a very large part of New Spain was legally in the hands of the cattle and sheep barons—inevitably, for the economy of New Spain had become dependent upon stock raising and its attendant industries, which could not have operated without permanent title. "Les seigneurs de troupeaux," as Chevalier calls them, became, quite literally, lords of the land. In southern Mexico alone, that is, between the Chichimec Frontier (see map) and the Isthmus of Tehuantepec, cattle and sheep estancias covered an estimated 90,000 square miles by 1620. In the enormous empty expanse to the north of that line the great hacienda became the typical and predominant form of landholding.

There were many motives behind its growth. Each mining community (*real de minas*) required a base of supply, and it was the hacienda principally which furnished the necessary food and hides and animals. The miners themselves, in the long depression of the seventeenth century, became hacendados, just as the hacendados had frequently been mine operators, for the crisis in mining, which began to be apparent in the last decades of the sixteenth century, forced the miners to look to the land for a living—and perhaps they needed no forcing. The limited tenure of mining grants, the Crown's monopoly of quicksilver (used in the amalgam process) and the ruinously high prices at which it was sold, the fixed price of bullion, the miners' endemic insolvency, and the scarcity and high cost of labor—all these factors were active in the miners' drift to the land.

The constantly diminishing labor supply, certainly up to the middle of the seventeenth century, also serves to explain the hacendado's preoccupation with stock raising. Without people, the vast, semi-arid stretches of the north could not be farmed and were almost valueless. The northern hacienda was a fortified manor surrounded by a trackless waste. Overgrazing and glut made stock raising frequently an uneconomic activity, but in the great stagnation of the seventeenth century there was little else to which the hacendado could turn his hand.

A curious and, possibly, an equally powerful motive in the formation of the hacienda was purely psychological. Chevalier cites instance after instance of the aggrandizement of estates for the sake of size alone—a mania which at times went to the extreme of the hacendado's buying up land and mines and keeping them out of production. Everyone, it seems, hankered after nobility, a state which required the cachet of land—the more land the more nobility—a phenomenon remarked by Humboldt in 1803, all this regardless of its utility.

The new noblemen had the most diverse and unlikely origins and lacked the patina of antiquity and high birth, but they made out. An important nucleus of the emerging hacendado class was supplied by the "first conquerors" and their descendants, whose services the Crown had rewarded with encomiendas of Indian tributes. They deserve a paragraph to themselves.

Changing conditions and the vanishing native population had reduced the encomenderos' income from tributes and quite early obliged them to look for other means of support. From their ranks came the first line of hacendados. Although the encomienda was not a land title, it should not be inferred that the encomenderos could not hold land. On the contrary, large numbers of grants were made to encomenderos and their descendants, even within the limits of their encomiendas. The encomenderos, to be sure, protected their Indians' land from the encroachments of other Spaniards, for the very good reason that without land the Indians could not pay tributes, a consideration that did not restrain the encomenderos from joining the ranks of the landed aristocracy.

Although the Crown signally failed to prevent the rise of this dangerous feudalism in the New World and thus forged the instrument of its own eventual destruction, there were nevertheless some very real limitations to the growth of the hacienda. In the more densely inhabited agricultural country to the south, the native community, protected by the Crown, the encomenderos, the church, and sometimes effectively by the natives themselves, as in the case of Tlaxcala, kept the hacienda from absorbing all the Indian lands. Another barrier was the Spanish community (the *villa*), whose citizens had been given considerable tracts in the vicinity as an inducement to settling. Some of these citizens sold their land to the hacendados, but probably most of them clung to their holdings and formed the typical communities of, for example, the Spanish Bajío.

The greatest obstacle, however, to the spread of the hacienda was very likely the agricultural estates of the Dominicans and Jesuits, which, in this Dark Age of New Spain, were a necessary source of the urban food supply. The religious orders had several important advantages over the hacendados. The most obvious was tenure: hacendados died; the orders lived on. Besides, they were not interested in holding vast tracts of idle land merely to tickle their vanity, but put it to work raising crops for the market. They made it pay. Their estates were not plastered with mortgages, nor did they have to support the sumptuous town houses that advertised to the world the social prestige of the great families. On the contrary, the orders were soon in a position to lend money, and they made no small part of their income later on by operating the bankrupt haciendas of their rivals. They were not plagued with labor shortages, for the religious, living on the premises, were under no such pressure to sweat their labor as were the hired managers of the haciendas. They were, in short, scientific farmers.

I have tried to give some notion of the scope of M. Chevalier's distinguished book. His timely study of the evolution of the hacienda lifts the dense curtain that hid many aspects of this most significant of Mexican colonial institutions, the recrudescence of which (in other guises, to be sure) is an interesting phenomenon of contemporary Mexico.

In the editing, owing to limitations imposed by cost, I have had to omit the voluminous footnotes and scholarly apparatus, which in any event the specialist will prefer to consult in the original.

The Diego Rivera drawing on the title page appeared originally in *Mexican Maze* (Philadelphia, 1932), by Carleton Beals, who generously gave me permission to reproduce it.

Lesley Byrd Simpson

University of California,
Berkeley

CONTENTS

INTRODUCTION

A seventeenth-century Mexican, no matter how great his interest in his country's growth, would almost certainly have been surprised at the subject of this book. The landed estates of New Spain, for all that, were taking shape before his eyes, and while the phenomenon may have escaped his attention entirely, it is easy for us, a few centuries later, to see that it was destined to dominate the history of Mexico.

From time to time, to be sure, a missionary, a jurist, or an observant traveler would mention the great estates, but always with reference to some occurrence: an injustice done by a powerful landowner, usually to natives, or the seizing of lands and mines by people who neither tilled nor worked them, with resultant losses of revenue for His Majesty. So far as we know, before the second third of the eighteenth century, when the Bourbon dynasty had already left its mark, there are no references made to the great estates as such. Indeed, there was little concern for economic and social problems of any sort, save for practical everyday considerations or remarks by passing travelers, mostly for-

eigners, such as Hawks, Gage, or Gemelli Carreri. It is surprising, for
example, to find no drawings of machinery for refining sugar or extracting silver ore; during the same period, such drawings are far from
rare in the small colonies of England, Holland, or France. And yet we
know that the Jesuits of New Spain, to cite merely one instance, possessed some of the best sugar refineries in the New World.

Although the theme of this work is the evocation of a particular
moment in history, and shows the preoccupations peculiar to our time,
it is not, we feel, an artificial application to the past of a modern point
of view. Our primary purpose is to explain the time in which we are
living and to search for its roots down the past few centuries. Although
the haciendas have been recently broken up, the social conditions to
which they were linked could not disappear overnight. Mexico is evolving today at an ever-increasing pace, but the direct and indirect consequences of former conditions are still to be observed everywhere in
the land.

Why and under what circumstances did the great Mexican estates
come into existence? The problem is not a simple one. On the one hand,
it must be explained how certain individuals or institutions were able
to assemble the huge collections of title deeds which make up the archives of the great haciendas. In a country like Mexico, which in the
beginning was essentially pastoral, what specific rights to the land did
these deeds convey? The grass, in accordance with medieval tradition,
was common property, no matter whether it grew in untilled field,
pasture, or on a right of way.

The question is, therefore, when were the farmers and the cattlemen
able to deny others access to that portion of the soil which henceforth
they intended to exploit for their own profit? Not until they did so can
we speak properly of "great estates."

The land is not the whole problem. There are those who lived off
the land—those who worked it, the peons and day laborers; those who
owned it, the masters dwelling in crenelated strongholds, such as are
still to be seen in the Mexican countryside. What then was the real
bond between the landowners and their people? What survives from
that past and leaves its imprint on modern Mexico?

These questions suggest numerous others and pose so many problems
that it would probably require a team of investigators to solve them

for all this diversified country, with its tropical and temperate zones, its mining, agricultural, and pastoral activities, its peoples encompassing nomadic and sedentary Indians, Spaniards, Creoles, Negroes, mestizos, and mulattoes. Hence we shall often have to admit to gaps in our knowledge. Why not, in that case, limit ourselves to a narrower region or a shorter period of time? In reply, let us observe first of all that the problem's complexity is up to a point not on the same scale as the land area, since in the sixteenth century we find the same Spaniards all over the vast territory, and in the seventeenth the number of actors involved in the drama is never higher than several hundred thousand. In connection with this last observation, we cannot claim to describe the gradual transformations of the indigenous masses as they came into contact with the new arrivals, any more than we can claim to trace the entire social and economic history, crammed with such a variety of incidents, of the conquistadors' "republic." Even if the problem of the great estates is central to New Spain, it remains merely one of many.

Looked at as a whole, Mexico is two different countries. Superficially, it should therefore have been possible to separate the south of the land-tilling Indians, who furnished the Spaniards with so many workers, from the north where fierce nomads roved, the irreducible enemies of all who arrived from the south. In each half of the country, colonization assumed a different guise. The northern zone, however, did come within thirty leagues of Mexico City and included the rich Bajío region. Economically, this wide depression soon became a dependency of the capital; politically, it belonged to New Spain, as did the mines of Guanajuato and San Luis Potosí much farther away in the heart of the nomad country. On the other hand, in New Galicia and New Viscaya, under whose jurisdiction were the other great mines typical of the northern economy, were also to be found a few sedentary peoples who on occasion created an environment comparable to that of the southern zones. It is consequently no easy task to separate the two halves in a study of any scope, particularly as the duality offers profitable opportunities for comparison.

On the contrary, Central America and the West Indies constitute a world apart, or even several, including the peninsula of Yucatan separated from New Spain by impenetrable swamps and forests; from Mexico the peninsula could be reached only by sea, and by virtue of its isolation it will furnish us with only a few illustrations of specific cases. At the other end of the country, New Mexico comprised an "islet of Christians," a lost community beyond the immense deserted, semi-arid plains of the north. New Mexico will develop late. We shall limit our discussion of it to the conditions under which it was settled, because those conditions arose in Mexico proper and exemplify a certain stage in its development.

Within this territory, which thus excludes Central America, the West Indies, and the far north, the Habsburg period offers a clearly visible continuity; it strikes a well-defined contrast with some of the economic and political innovations of the Bourbons. Finally, in the sixteenth and seventeenth centuries Mexico's entire history is dominated by her first big economic cycle, namely, the production of silver, which begins in 1530 or 1550 and comes to a close less than a century later, around 1630–1640, slightly before or slightly afterward, depending upon the region. The following decades show the mines in complete decline; but no other exportable product was developed as exchange that could compare in importance with the precious metals. The country withdrew into itself, and its life seemed to come to a halt at that stage of its evolution; not until the rebirth of the mines in the eighteenth century were conditions to change. It was in the course of this first silver cycle that the great landed estate came into being. Subsequently it was to consolidate its hold and grow into the hacienda; by the end of the seventeenth century, or in isolated instances much earlier, the hacienda had taken on all its essential characteristics.

PART I ▪

The Environment

1. GEOGRAPHIC AND HUMAN BACKGROUND

THE LANDSCAPE

*In that landscape, which was not with-
out a certain aristocratic sterility . . .*
—ALFONSO REYES, *Visión del Anáhuac*

After a naval engagement off Vera Cruz in 1568, a band of English
freebooters ran aground on a deserted strip of the Atlantic coast. Their
ill-fated journey was later recounted by one of their number. Not until
several days had passed did they chance upon a group of wandering
Indians, who robbed and beat them, but who at least showed them the
way to Tampico, described as "a little Spanish city." After ten or
twelve days of tramping through forests and savannas they finally
arrived at the bank of a river, the Pánuco, where they were overjoyed
to hear, at first a gunshot, then a cock crowing—sounds which meant
for them prison, perhaps even hanging; nonetheless, the discovery of an
inhabited place was a kind of deliverance for the famished men, op-
pressed by the unpeopled and endless wilderness.

The early conquistadors, and travelers and missionaries, without exception, dwell upon these interminable marches across the wild mountains, barren plains, and hostile forests. They had to take along supplies

for several weeks, even months. The Pacific coast was uninhabited. Indeed, vastness is the primary characteristic of the New World, especially of New Spain; distances are not on the same scale as in Europe. Except along a few well-traveled roads and in the populated sections of Central Mexico, wayfarers had to know how to navigate limitless wastes just as if they had been sailors on the main. In the north they had to take the elevation of the sun and follow the stars in order to determine their position. The seventeenth-century priest Arregui, who had roamed all over the coasts of New Galicia, relied solely on his astrolabe to give him his latitude. As he phrased it, "there is so much uninhabited space in these realms that I doubt whether Europe's entire population could fill them; not only do they have no known boundaries, but all or nearly all is empty."

In the seventeenth century, heavy carts took three or four months in the dry season to go from Mexico City to the distant mines of Santa Barbara and Parral (present state of Chihuahua), and much longer to reach New Mexico. However, a scant 100 or 150 years after the Conquest, save in the dangerous wilderness which had not yet been brought under control, nearly all the land was already in private hands.

This fact is even more remarkable in that Mexico is, generally speaking, a country of harsh, dry ranges and high plains broken up by countless barrancas, or narrow, deep canyons cut by the waters on their way to the oceans, 2,000 meters below. In the words of Fray Toribio de Motolinía (who, to be sure, was unacquainted with the north), "this country of New Spain is so crowded with mountains that if you stand in the middle of the largest plain and look around you, you will see one or several ranges six or seven leagues away. . . ."

Indeed, the central plateaus, composed of limestone or detritus, are pricked out with volcanic cones the entire length of the nineteenth parallel, from Nevada de Colima to the peak of Orizaba, from Popocatépetl to the numberless craters of Michoacán which mark the southern edge of the highland. In the northwest a seemingly endless Sierra Madre Occidental prolongs the Tertiary folds of the Rockies; in the east, the discontinuous chains of the Sierra Madre Oriental bound the plateaus clear to the Isthmus of Tehuantepec. To the south, finally, the Sierra Madre del Sur extends from the long spine of Baja California to beyond Oaxaca, where all the chains come together in a vast system, although of no great height. The plateau itself is rarely flat, except in the boxed-in lowlands of the far north. It falls off in the basin encompassing the middle stretches of the Lerma, the Bajío, and in the direction of Guadalajara. It becomes uneven as it rises to Toluca or in the Zacatecas area, drops sharply to the east into the Atlantic plains, and slopes more gently southward toward the valley of the Balsas and its tributaries. It does not show up again until one reaches Chiapas and Guatemala.

Furthermore, most of this vast and chaotic landscape receives little water. The rains come usually in summer, with a dry season of five or six months a year. To be sure, huge volcanoes of the plateau, as well as the higher ranges, act as reservoirs that furnish an abundant water supply to the neighboring lowlands, like those of Cuernavaca or Atlixco, for example. Mexico City itself benefits by its proximity thereto. But in this immense country the few such sources are merely local accidents.

Everywhere else cones of middling height or denuded mountain chains are not sufficient to collect clouds and condense moisture. By the end of the dry season all Anáhuac offers the spectacle of "aristocratic sterility" evoked by Alfonso Reyes. The sterility is more apparent than real, however, as in Old Castile, of which these high Mexican plateaus remind one. The naked earth, stripped of trees and grayish yellow in color, rises in large whirlwinds beneath a blistering sun. But then the summer rains bring the countryside back to life and allow the raising of good crops of maize and beans, the traditional foods of Mexico.

In the north, the country gradually loses any trace of moisture, since the precipitation in summer—the only time rain falls—varies from 500 or 600 millimeters a year to 300 or 400. (There are many local variations, of course.) North of the Bajío one finds only high, bare hills and plains covered with cactus, agave, yucca, or the thorny huisaches and mesquites. Toward the west and Los Altos de Jalisco, as well as on the plateau lying at the foot of the two Sierra Madres, the grass is still plentiful and turns green in the rainy season; once it was cropped by large herds of cattle and sheep. Still farther to the north, even the grass grows thin and spotty, and finally disappears completely save where there is a little water. Only cactus and mesquite survive, whose fruit and seed pods comprised almost the entire [vegetable] food supply of the nomad Indians. The soil, which is often chalky and porous, complicates the drought problem; but the barrenness of these northern reaches is not without grandeur. Then come the true deserts of the Bolsón de Mapimí, where the rare streams are lost in the sands and straying travelers would have died of thirst. Nothing but the silver mines could have drawn Europeans into the wastelands where Zacatecas, San Luis Potosí, Mazapil, Cuencamé, and Mapimí were built. In a few favored spots, where water was later to cause protracted wrangling, agricultural centers or missions were established.

Throughout this vast Central Plateau the climate is temperate and healthful; the average mean temperature is between 15° and 18° C., slightly higher in the zones below 2,000 meters, slightly lower in the north and at higher altitudes. In the Zacatecas region the winter is quite cold—in the European sense of the term. However, the general lack of rainfall and above all its marked irregularity in the northern parts inevitably made large expanses of the plateau suitable only for raising cattle, or else as grazing land for the huge flocks of sheep that multiplied and roamed about in the sixteenth and seventeenth centuries.

Even if one does not accept the belief that geographical factors can determine a system of property, such a physical environment must obviously have facilitated the establishment of great estates. A country with slight and intermittent rainfall is not propitious to the small farmer; the risk of going into debt is too great when for a number of years in succession crops fail and cattle waste away for want of water. Crop raising in the same area requires expensive irrigation projects, which cannot be undertaken or maintained except by the rich or by well-organized communities. The emphasis today is on building up the latter; their feeble development during the viceregal period is for the most part attributable to historical reasons. Thus, the legislator's measures and the evolution of society are capable of modifying the situation to a certain extent; but that is not attributable to the geography of the country.

The high plateaus, however, are far from characteristic of all Mexico. Where they descend gradually, transitional zones are formed which resemble them only in part. For example, in the southwest along the great east-west axis of the volcanoes, the state of Michoacán, sloping toward the Pacific, is frequently better watered and wooded; its valleys are better suited to relatively inexpensive farming and perhaps in consequence to medium-sized holdings. In the south the Sierra Madre del Sur and the mountains of Mixteca and Oaxaca have a climate that reminds one of the plateaus, with enough summer rain to sustain the vegetation characteristic of dry prairies. But barring a few fertile basins this part of the country is so broken up that, generally speaking, it is not good for much else than large-scale cattle raising. The country to either side is lower and warmer, but still very hilly; this is the region of squat sierras dotted with curious rock formations resembling pipe organs and candelabra, or covered with thorn bushes. The land is usable when a little more moisture lets the savanna establish itself in low-lying parts. Along the creeks and rivers, woods and thickets break the monotony of a landscape typical of the lowlands along the Balsas River and much of the Pacific coast.

Opposite, the Atlantic coast is much better watered, especially in the low plains of Tabasco, where the tropical forest is well-nigh impassable and few people live today, fewer yesterday. West-northwest there is considerable moisture throughout the coastal zone, which is invaded by lush vegetation. Inland from the dunes in the direction of the fertile-appearing hillocks, it would seem that white men might have lived off small holdings. But in this climate, very hard to bear at times, the white man's initiative appears stifled by a nature so exuberant that wooden houses sprout unless the timber is properly dried. The main reason is that this luxuriant vegetation is scarcely more than camouflage; in reality, as Paul Rivet notes, "tropical soils are poor, rapidly exhausted, and impose harsh conditions on agriculture." Only recently, with bananas and coconuts and coffee, have the resources of this part of the country begun to be properly exploited; it was formerly a grazing or roaming area for the flocks and herds of the great sheep and cattle raisers; besides, the lack of markets and roads did not allow for any other economic policy.

Farther to the north there is less moisture; the coastal plains bear a less tall, less dense kind of tropical forest, where cattle graze at liberty today as they did yesterday. The contrast is brutal, however, in the Huasteca region: Within the distance of a few kilometers one descends from the arid high plateaus to verdant slopes, and then to plains almost entirely covered with woods. Mighty rivers drain the Atlantic regions: those of Tabasco, then the Coatzacoalcos, the Papaloapan—down which the products of Oaxaca used to come all the way to Vera Cruz—the Tuxpan, Tecolutla, and Nautla, the Pánuco. Toward the state of Tamaulipas, not colonized until the eighteenth century, and on the plains of New Leon, which were occupied much earlier, the climate becomes perceptibly much drier; but several rivers coursing down from the Sierra Madre Oriental bring the region a beneficial moisture.

With its present boundaries Mexico is a vast country of two million square kilometers, four times the size of France; for the most part it is hilly or mountainous, although in these latitudes the highlands are cooler and at times covered with useful meadowland, prairies, and woods. It is also a country of contrasts between the low-lying zones, where it is too hot, sometimes damp, and difficult of access, and the temperate, healthful climate of the high plateaus which, because of their extent and the demographic importance of Anáhuac, still constitute the essential part of the land mass; but even so, their climate is often dry, their soil poor, and their moutain ranges numerous and forbidding.

Such characteristics, of which certain are common to other regions of Spanish America, imposed upon New Spain a haphazard pattern of development, an uneconomical colonization thinly spread out over large areas—this, in contrast to the densely populated establishments of the English to the north. But here again, it is difficult to determine the exact degree of influence of purely geographical factors on the one hand, and human, psychological, and historical elements on the other. It goes without saying that differences in climate, soil, and topography alone cannot offer a satisfactory explanation for the dispersal of the Spaniards over the thousands of leagues that lie between Florida and the Straits of Magellan.

THE TWO INDIGENOUS MEXICOS

When the Spaniards arrived, this vast geographical complex, made up of such disparate elements, possessed a small number of useful plants, but it was relatively poor in animal species easy to domesticate. Besides, any such plants or animals were lacking in a large part of the country.

A single cereal was the essential source of food; even, one may say, it was the basis of all sedentary Indian civilizations: maize. Maize was well-adapted to the environment, for its rapid growth in differing climates allows it to make do with a relatively short rainy season. Where there is irrigation it will yield two crops a year. The other indispensable food, frijoles or beans, requires conditions similar to those for maize.

A sort of red pepper, chili, is nothing more than a stimulant, whereas the agave, or maguey, gives an alcoholic drink (*pulque*) as well as fibers used in numerous domestic ways. Cacao, finally, was consumed over a wide area, but it had to be brought inland from the coasts, often far away.

Useful animals were even less numerous, since the most advanced Indians raised nothing for eating except turkeys and tiny dogs, especially fattened for the purpose. In certain regions the Indians hunted red and roe deer. Owing to the absence of livestock, the sedentary Indians utilized only the fertile, well-watered parts of the plateau; this left vast spaces free for the herds of the Spaniards. But since the wooded zones, whose soil was quickly exhausted by crop raising, posed serious obstacles for farmers possessing only the most primitive implements, only the watered plains of Anáhuac offered the right kind of soil for maize and beans. That fact explains the dense population and advanced agricultural civilization in the sufficiently moist parts of the high plateaus, in the grassy valleys and basins of Michoacán or Oaxaca, and on the savannas of certain coastal slopes. On the other hand, cultivation of maize without irrigation was riskier in the central area of the northern plateaus, where primitive nomadic Indians limited themselves to hunting and gathering what nature offered.

From the foregoing some degree of geographical determinism becomes apparent. The single important discrepancy is that the northern limit of the sedentary farmers fails to encompass the Bajío region, where good crops of maize are feasible without irrigation. For the nomadic huntsmen the Bajío was a frontier area into which they penetrated on raids rather than land they considered exclusively theirs. At the height of their expansion they occupied all the territory beyond the Pánuco (Huasteca), Moctezuma, and Tula Rivers, that is, west of Valles, Zimapan, and Jilotepec, north of Acámbaro and the Lerma River, and east of Lake Chapala, Aguascalientes, Zacatecas, Nombre de Dios, Indé, and Santa Barbara. Those are almost exactly the arid zones corresponding to the thin vegetation of the plains, to the thorny cactus and mesquite bushes, or the desert. But the differences are even more marked in population than in vegetation, and for these reasons one can really speak of two distinct Mexicos.

A few groups in the southwest, like the Pamés, had already felt the influence of southern customs originating in the Otomí country. Likewise, in southern Tamaulipas, the "striped people" had a few fixed villages and did some rudimentary farming; but the tribe spread out far to the northwest, in which region they were solely nomadic, like the Guamares, who had joined in a confederation with the Copuces and Guaxabanes, the Guachichiles and the Zacatecos, other powerful groups of the center and west.

These fierce natives were all lumped indiscriminately by the Spaniards under the general name of Chichimecs. They fed on wild berries and roots, especially cactus fruit and mesquite seeds, which they supplemented with a stimulant, peyote (genus *Lophophora*). With bow and arrow they hunted roe deer, hares, rabbits, and other small animals. One particularly important Guachichil center was the great cactus wilderness, El Gran Tunal, of San Luis Potosí, which furnished them with an abundance of prickly pears, or tunas. The men went naked, and the women wore only a strip of leather or a handful of grass hanging from a belt. They roamed incessantly, did not always sleep in a tent or other shelter, and raised no crops. With the exception of the Pamés, they had neither temples nor idols, but did worship the sun.

Far from paying tribute to the Spaniards or furnishing them with labor, these "Chichimec savages" were their implacable enemies. On all sides they attacked travelers, burned merchandise, and perpetrated massacres—sparing only a few missionaries. Consequently, people circulated only in large, armed convoys similar to the fleets which protected them from the corsairs on the seas. Each group, or *cuadrilla*, of fifteen or twenty persons, according to Father Pérez de Rivas in the seventeenth century, had "a wagon made into a fort and reinforced with planks, which was an adequate defence against arrows and also served as a refuge for the ordinary people traveling the roads." Military outposts had been established at long intervals, between which soldiers escorted the convoys. But the fearsome nomads moved about with unbelievable rapidity, particularly after they had captured horses and had quickly become excellent riders. They would suddenly swoop down on the caravans; in 1579, for instance, they attacked and partly destroyed a convoy of 80 wagons on the Guadalajara road. They would hunt cattle with bow and arrow, like game, burn small isolated mines, or wipe out ill-defended estancias "without leaving alive a single dog or cat," writes Captain Vargas Machuca.

To the north of the Lerma River, the Spaniards found themselves in a situation analogous to that which later confronted the pioneers in the United States. Their entire labor force was composed of a few Indians that they had brought along from the south; to a greater extent than elsewhere, they had to take personal charge of their mines or herds. The territory had not been brought under control, and the ruthless war with the Chichimecs meant that there was never any intermarrying. Constantly pushed back and tracked down, the old [Indian] groups tended to disappear; at the same time, however, they were replaced by new bands descending from the north. In this murderous game they were almost destroyed by the eighteenth or nineteenth century.

South of the Lerma the country offered a striking contrast: real villages, maize fields, stable populations of farmers and artisans, even quite complex political and social organizations.

Although to the west the transition was less sudden, the Sierra Madre Occidental and the coasts were inhabited by somewhat primitive natives, cannibals on occasion; but one of their chief resources was still the growing of maize. Probably they hunted and gathered berries and roots in addition, especially in the north; nevertheless, all these independent tribes scattered throughout the sierras were essentially sedentary populations. The Spaniards frequently had trouble making use of them or exacting their tribute. The Coras were not brought under control until the eighteenth century; the Tepehuanes and other tribes rebelled as late as the seventeenth. But in contrast to the nomads, they were not consistently hostile; most of them adapted themselves to the new ways and survive today.

The inhabitants of Anáhuac and the southern regions were by far the richest, most numerous, and the most advanced. There, several organized states of crop-raising and warrior Indians were in existence, the most powerful being that of the Aztecs. The Mexico–Texcoco–Tacuba Federation had succeeded in imposing its law upon vast areas, particularly from the middle of the fifteenth century, that is, very shortly before the Spaniards' arrival. The chief city of the three, Tenochtitlán–Mexico, cramped for space on its island, had expanded by means of its famous floating gardens; then, it had sought new resources in commerce and a little later in wars of conquest.

Under the first Moctezumas and early in the sixteenth century, the Aztec warriors subjugated neighbors who were often as advanced as they. At its height their empire extended from one ocean to the other, from the eastern and southeastern frontier of the nomads to the independent Maya states of Yucatan and Guatemala. Of the most highly evolved sedentary peoples of this area, only the isolated state of Tlaxcala, the states of Metztitlán, the Yopis, Mixtecs of Tututepec, Tarascans of Michoacán, and the tiny political groups to the northwest of the last-named escaped their influence entirely. Some of the conquered peoples kept their own government, merely paying tribute. Cholula, Huejotzingo, Tehuacán, part of Huasteca, part of Mixteca, and the land of the Zapotecos, Chiapas, and Soconusco recognized in varying degrees Mexico City's authority, but they appear to have more or less preserved their autonomy. Sometimes the link was no more than a kind of forced alliance.

These late conquests of the Aztecs made the Spaniards' task easier; the latter found willing accomplices in states defeated or threatened by the Aztecs, so that subsequently to get hold of the tribute or certain lands they merely had to step into the shoes of the former masters. The substitution was all the easier since authority was strongly centralized in the hands of the *tlacatecutli*, Moctezuma II, and his lieutenant, the *cihuacoatl*. This "emperor," as the Spaniards called him, was a sacred personage who enjoyed all religious, judicial, fiscal, and military power. Theoretically elected by a Grand Council, he was always picked from the same family. The political and fiscal centralization of the Aztec empire, and even of some independent states, took the form of a superstructure that the Spanish colonial system was destined to destroy entirely or to supplant. The local and territorial organization, which was characteristic of most of these sedentary cultivators (including particularly important variations, for example in Michoacán), was much more durable.

On the arrival of the Spaniards, the unit of Aztec society was the *calpulli;* although it did not represent a simple clan, the *calpulli* still preserved numerous clannish traits despite a definite evolution, probably fairly recent, away from the clan. The *calpulli* was the geographical quarter or sector of a group of people; at the same time, it was an ancient family: "A quarter belonging to famous people, or of ancient lineage," in the words of the oidor Zurita, who well sums up its two important aspects, territorial and ancestral.

The head of each *calpulli* was an elder, the *pariente mayor*, who considered that he stood *in loco parentis* to all the members of the group, or *macehuales*. He possessed certain religious or military powers and settled internal matters "assisted by other elders." Each of these small units owned a sort of community house, or *calpulco*, where members convened for religious holidays, dances, and ceremonies; for the *calpulco* had its own gods, somewhat similar to the lares of the Roman gens. "He who guards the home": such is the meaning of the word *calpixqui*, which seems to designate the same personage as the *calpullec* in the Aztec civilization proper.

Within the army the members of the group formed a special corps; they also had a kind of private school where youths were instructed in the art of warfare. A centurion (the *macuiltecpanpixqui*) had one hundred men under his orders; they were commanded at lower echelons by five captains of twenty, or *centecpanpixqui*, then by approximately fifteen *tepixquis*. This hierarchy, which the Franciscan Mendieta preserved in each quarter of the evangelized villages, was obviously military in origin and linked to Aztec expansion. The officers mentioned were used to collect tribute.

Although group discipline remained extremely pronounced within the *calpullis*, the clan's original autonomy was much curtailed by the establishment of a central power that from its inception was very strong; autonomy was further weakened by a new and complete governmental system superimposed on the old organization. Thus, in the early sixteenth century the *calpulli* was considerably more important territorially and economically than politically.

Title to the *calpulalli*, or lands as a whole, was vested in the community; the various crop-raising families possessed only the usufruct. Every married man who was a group member, or *macehual*, received an inalienable allotment, the *tlalmilpa*. He had to cultivate it, but none could take it from him as long as he carried out his obligation. If he did not, and after various admonitions, the elder, or *pariente mayor*, could deprive him of his land. The *macehual* was then excluded from the community and usually reduced to hiring himself out to others, becoming a serf, or even selling himself into slavery. Of course, these important restrictions did not normally take effect; lands customarily passed from father to son in the manner of patrimonies. Often it seems as if each piece of land was owned and tilled in common by a sort of patriarchal clan composed of several individual families. In the Tarascan tribe of Michoacán the situation was slightly different: simple peasants as well as notables held "lands in their own right," to quote Zurita.

The allotments were unequal in importance; in 1538, according to Cortés, they ranged from 100 or 200 land measures to 1,000 or 2,000, "depending upon the possibilities enjoyed by the first person to whom they were granted." On the most important estates there was even a kind of tenant farmer, who received a piece of land on which he could build his cabin. In exchange, he paid his debts in kind or in various sorts of tasks. The tenant farmer, of inferior economic position, seems, however, to differ from the *mayeque*, or serf, of whom we shall speak shortly. An allotment, being the property of the entire *calpulli*, could not be sold to another group, but excess lands could be leased. For the latter type of transaction, it appears that the highest lord of the land had to give his authorization.

Finally, all the *calpulallis* (or estates made up of *calpullis*) of a village, town, or district constituted the *altepetlalli*, which might include wooded land and untilled fields that had never been distributed and, in reality, were scarcely ever utilized because of the lack of grazing animals. The town itself was often formed of four *calpulallis*, originally quarters toward the four points of the compass. But the members of the *calpulli*, or *macehuales*, were not merely required to cultivate the individual allotment assigned to them; they were also obliged to work in common other land, which we may call public, although it was perhaps public only in the use to which it was destined.

This sort of land was first of all what was usually called the "estates of Moctezuma," a name that roughly covered the *tlatocatlalli*, or "lord's estates," made up in each village of a great square measuring, according to Ixtlilxochitl, 400 units on each side. The plots of land called *itonal* or *ytunales* were connected with the preceding; the word indicates an eventual utilization of reserve lands, since these latter supplied war materials and food for the soldiers. The same sorts of needs were also filled by the *milchimalli*, which perhaps differed from the others in name only. In addition, the harvest reaped on the *tecpantlalli*, or "palace lands," was intended for the immediate retinue and the court of the "lord"—for his "chamber" (*recámara*). All these different types of land were worked more or less for the direct benefit of the chief lord, who, in the Aztec civilization, embodied the government of the city-state. They were often the best fields, and their yield was collected under the supervision of the *calpixqui.*

There were besides what we may call community lands, which could be leased in part, and certain sectors of which seem to have been set aside for specific purposes, for example to cover the expenses of entertaining travelers. Likewise, the members of the *calpulli* assumed responsibility for cultivating as a group the allotment belonging to their head, the *calpullec;* the temples and priests received the harvest from special estates commonly designated by the Spaniards as "lands of the demons." Sometimes these estates were let or else worked by a kind of serf.

Finally, in conquered territory the Aztecs usually had appropriated lands called *yaotlalli;* these varied in extent—in some instances they were very large—according as the conditions imposed upon the defeated were harsh or mild. Zurita tells us that they were cultivated by the "common herd" of such tributary peoples as a symbol of subjection.

In spite of a certain diversity in the working of the public lands, it can be readily seen that the task fell essentially upon the freemen of the communities. The freemen paid most of their taxes in the form of these personal services, to which were added the *tequío,* or work stint on public utilities, such as roads and buildings. A *tequitlato* appears to have presided over the distribution of the tasks; according to Cortés, he also kept up to date the public register of the inhabitants and land allotments in his quarter. *Tequitlatos* and *tequíos* still survive in remote regions of Mexico.

By the time of the Conquest, however, labor had become much diversified and the original state of society considerably altered in the most advanced civilizations, especially the Aztec. Many men no longer tilled the earth. There were first of all the merchants, who had increased with the development of commerce and with political expansion, the two phenomena being closely linked. Then there were all kinds of artisans, professional hunters or fishermen, musicians and actors who, states Cortés, were not fixed in one quarter, but went wherever they could best earn a livelihood. All these categories seem to have paid taxes in money, unlike the farming *macehuales.*

In the old *calpullis* the evolution and diversification had not stopped at the point mentioned. Besides the traditional allotments and estates devoted to public purposes, there existed other lands, closer, it would seem, to the modern type of individual property. Among the Aztecs a long series of conquests and the military organization of society were certainly not without influence in the creation of a warlike aristocracy, which often owned vast lands distinct from those belonging to the clan.

All sixteenth-century authors carefully differentiate between the *macehuales,* or commoners, and the *pipiltzin-pilli,* or *pille,* whom they call "nobles," "lords," "knights," "notables" (*principales*). Within this latter group, Zurita distinguished various sorts of personages. First the *tlatoques,* or "overlords," who by right of heredity governed provinces over which they had "civil and criminal jurisdiction." There were also the "braves," or *tectecutzin* (plural of *tecuhtli* or *teul*), who occupied for life public positions that were remunerated by the yield of certain lands. These posts were conferred on men who had rendered important services, generally for distinction in war. Even though such honors were not hereditary, they seem to have been bestowed particularly on members of the noble class and on men whose fathers had already merited this type of award. As for the *pilli* themselves, they constituted a true hereditary nobility; for they were *señores,* "not that they possessed a *señorio* or a command," explains Zurita, "but because of their lineage." As in Castile, knights and hidalgos, since they were concerned with war, paid no taxes, but they did make "voluntary contributions." They were the sons or relatives of the overlords, who sometimes entrusted them with private missions.

The economic resources of these *pilli* consisted above all of lands that they owned outright, called *pilalli* or *pilales.* Such lands were numerous by the time the Spaniards came, since the latter point to their existence in many different regions. Completely separate from the lands belonging to the *calpullis,* they constituted at the beginning of the sixteenth century "the patrimonies of the nobles and passed from father to son" (Martín Cortés); also, they could be sold or exchanged. The natives still remembered the origin of these lands; according to native accounts, writes a missionary in 1554, nobles once sold to private parties a portion of those lands, formerly belonging to the communities and quarters, which had subsequently been granted to the nobles, probably as fiefs of sorts. According to the same accounts the purchasers had transmitted the lands to their descendants, "but originally those were the village lands called *altepetlalli* or the quarter lands called *calpulalli*." Thus, in this secondary stage, a kind of private estate, which could be bequeathed or disposed of, had been created at the expense of the old clans and to the benefit of a hereditary nobility.

There is more to the story. These patrimonial estates were often farmed by men who were not absolutely free like the *macehuales*, or members of the *calpulli;* they were the *mayeques*, of lowly condition, bound to the earth they cultivated generation after generation for the master's profit and resembling glebe serfs of medieval Europe. As a consequence, when a noble's estates were divided among his heirs, the *mayeques* were parceled out with the estates. Unlike the *macehuales*, these men paid no taxes to the overlord and took no part in the farming carried out in common, for they owed the masters of the soil a share of their crops, as well as other services that were no doubt more onerous than those required of freemen. Such was the origin of much contention in New Spain, when the caciques likewise claimed that their *mayeques* were exempt from the tribute due to King and encomendero.

The *mayeques* considered nonetheless that the lands they worked were a personal possession; according to the oidor Zurita they owned the "use of them," whereas the masters owned them "outright." Although they had usually been settled on the lands "from time immemorial," according to the same author, it sometimes happened that people recalled their origins, which were perhaps not always so remote. Around the middle of the sixteenth century, the Indians of Chimalhuacán, near Texcoco, were still aware that on the *tecutlalli*, or estates of the lords and judges called *techuhtlis*, men fleeing other tribes or provinces had been taken in; these men had become "the tributaries of the lords" whom they served and obeyed.

When, under cover of the social upheaval that followed the Conquest, caciques were to be observed adding freeman "tyrannically" to their estates, they were probably repeating in a brief period of time a process which had previously developed slowly. The serfs "usurped in this manner" were large in number, according to the oidor Vasco de Puga; "more than a hundred thousand," declares Martín Cortés.

Not only the nobles possessed lands worked by this type of serf; the merchants, or *pochteca,* were also allowed to own landed patrimonies. And especially were there *mayeques* who cultivated government lands linked to certain public functions or offices held during a lifetime, whereas other *mayeques* lived on estates belonging directly to the community.

Different from the *mayeques*, according to Zurita, were the sharecropper Indians, or *renteros*. These would settle for a definite length of time on lands which they rented; but they continued to pay taxes to the overlord and to share in community farming with the other *macehuales*. However, the distinction is not always so clear, since according to accounts that confirm each other, caciques succeeded, as late the sixteenth century, in wresting away community lands and forcing freemen to pay them rent for an indefinite period. If able, they would also arrange for these sharecroppers to be exempted from paying tribute to the King, "stating that they were part of their patrimony." A number of Spanish texts group indiscriminately under the name of *terrazgueros* the former *mayeques*, recent serfs of the type just mentioned, and sharecroppers, and probably many intermediate situations as well.

There were among the Aztecs, finally, numerous slaves used as porters and for various other kinds of work, notably the cultivation of the aristocrats' estates. They were people who had been punished for one reason or another, or who had fallen into poverty; sometimes they would lose their freedom merely through an abuse of power by the lords. Although they could be sacrificed to the gods, their lot was less harsh than that of the former slaves in Europe, for they could own property in their own right, and their masters did not have the power of life and death over them. But the Aztecs frequently handed them over as part of their tribute, thereby allowing the encomenderos to acquire a certain number of them before native slavery was abolished in New Spain.

A kind of recorder's map faithfully mirrored this diversity in the holding of lands, a diversity that was itself the image of a complex society in which the *calpullis* no longer occupied their former place. On the quadrant of the village district the light yellow block that represented the old clan holdings had shrunk, relinquishing a broad purple sector to the private estates which were themselves in proximity to the bright red patch of the fields of Moctezuma and other public lands (Torquemada). The reason was that a landed aristocracy had come into being at the same time the city-state was elaborating a powerful fiscal system; this system consisted of work services carried out on the best community lands.

In the territories under Aztec domination, that is, in the richest fourth of the country, the Spanish missionary state had merely to supplant the native theocracy, while the conquistadors gradually replaced the local nobility. Accordingly both public and private lands were fated to serve the expansion of tillers and colonists. The existence of this vast Mexican empire, with its long social evolution, was to facilitate signally the task of conquerors and settlers. In this part of the New World, finally, the Aztec empire and its highly evolved state would foster the birth and growth of the great European estates in the heart of the native territories.

THE SPANIARDS: CONQUERORS AND SETTLERS

¡A la espada y al compás, y más y más y más y más!
—*Motto of* CAPTAIN BERNARDO DE VARGAS MACHUCA

Upon this central and southern portion of Mexico, whose civilizations had developed without outside influences, the conquistadors descended from across the sea, so unexpectedly that one of their number, who had wandered off from the main body of troops, was taken for a direct descendant of the sun and treated accordingly in the Indian village into which he had stumbled by mistake, half-dead with hunger. Who were these first men off the ship and their successors, these men who would work such an upheaval in the life of the natives and subsequently would mold and thoroughly transform the vast country despite their small number, never more than 100,000 of them in the sixteenth century? Here we need only to become acquainted with the types they represented and their salient features, which were to leave a permanent mark on New Spain, influence the native environment, and then contribute, if only indirectly, to the formation of the large estates characteristic of the Spanish Indies, chiefly Mexico.

There were individuals and there were groups. The individuals were hidalgos or common folk, soldiers at first, soon followed by lawyers and missionaries. Then came the invading groups of relatives or dependents, the communities of the new towns, whose members were often linked together by powerful ties going back to the Middle Ages.

The first arrivals were soldiers, quite often professionals. With the taking of Granada in 1492 the termination of the Reconquest had freed for other service a large number of men; they went off to Italy and elsewhere and finally to the recently discovered Antilles. These same men, or their sons and kin, ended by crossing over to the new continent in search of war and adventure. Many of them were similar to a certain Juan Mogollón, a native of the town of Cáceres in Extremadura, whose father, a squire, had fought at Perpignan, Salses, and Granada. Juan himself had served in the royal armies in Italy, Barbary, the Island of Djerba, and Algiers; then he had taken part in the conquests of Florida, Santa Marta (Venezuela), and Peru. He had finally come to New Spain, long since conquered, in quest of royal favors and probably new expeditions, despite his age. At the time he presented his petition he had been in the King's service 36 years, including 22 in the Indies. If not many soldiers had such a record they had at least already spent some time in the Antilles.

They were natives of the poor regions of the Peninsula, of the sierras of Extremadura, the highlands of León and Asturias, particularly the two Castiles; in other words, from regions that had always furnished soldiers. Many said that they hailed from Seville; but by various tokens it appears that frequently they were Andalusians only by adoption, who had made prolonged stays in Seville, that "mighty Babylon"; the town was thus named because it was the meeting place of all those looking for work, service in the army, expeditions, or a change in luck. Moreover, they did not hesitate to adopt the Sevillian mentality, and it was the thing among the soldiers to pronounce Castilian with an Andalusian accent.

Most of the soldiers claimed to be hidalgos. In point of fact a good number of poor second sons and younger sons of large families did emigrate to the Indies. But among the emigrants were more whose origins were obscure: rustics who had left their villages under a cloud, orphans, children who had left families incapable of supporting them. They all converged on Seville, or wandered off in the wake of companies of soldiers. Charmed by the wonders told of the Indies, and even by deliberate propaganda—as late as the seventeenth century, in the festivals of the people, "the coasts of New Spain [were depicted] as overflowing with nacre, pearls, coral, and fantastically shaped shells" —they would sooner or later throw caution to the winds and embark for Vera Cruz. The first to go certainly needed a large dose of courage; but later the same did not hold true, since in Mexico City any white man was at least sure of his daily bread.

In 1554 Viceroy Velasco complained that the country was populated by "*gente común*" and that there were "very few *caballeros* and *hijosdalgo*." It follows that if most of the Spaniards in the New World were not hidalgos by birth, the important point is that they all considered themselves as hidalgos in comparison with the Indians, who represented the common people and villeins.

The men who shared in the conquest of Anáhuac and in various later expeditions had to prove that they possessed a fantastic amount of energy and endurance, not only during combat, but even more in exhausting marches through a hostile landscape that forced them to endure heat, swamps, mosquitoes, hunger, and thirst. The boldest and most resolute among the soldiers were often the poorest; attracted by the unknown or by golden mirages, they were the ones who wanted to push onward, attempt new ventures, extend conquests.

Legends such as that of the Amazons exerted a powerful attraction on men's imaginations. The ancient myth had been refurbished in *Las Sergas de Esplandián*, an early sixteenth-century romance of chivalry which situated these feminine marvels in a certain Island of California located "to the right of the Indies, near the Garden of Eden." The Amazons fought with weapons of gold; there was no other metal in that fabulous land. The expeditionary leaders themselves, Diego Velázquez, Hernán Cortés, Francisco Cortés, Nuño de Guzmán, Jerónimo López, were all the more inclined to lend credence to the Amazons, since western Mexico was called Cihuatlampa, meaning in Nahuatl "toward the land of women." Also, the natives spoke of the queens of that country, as well as of a great island on that side of Mexico—the *cacica* of Jalisco and the long peninsula to which Rodríguez Cabrillo gave the name of California in 1542. At the same time or slightly later other legends lured these simple untaught soldiers; several expeditions into the boundless north owe their inception to the Seven Cities of Cíbola, the golden bells of mighty Quivira, mountains made of diamonds, fountains of youth, and other wonders.

These heaps of gold, which evoke the alchemist's dream rather than the merchant's solid coin, were, however, far from being the sole attraction for these indefatigable discoverers of uncharted lands. They were frequently aware of their contribution to a task whose magnitude transcended their individual interests; they were doing "great things." "Inquietus est et magna moliens Hispanorum animus," Michael Servetus writes of his countrymen in 1535. In the New World, the conquistadors counted on winning glory and surpassing even Caesar, Pompey, and Hannibal, as Bernal Díaz tells in his charmingly naïve fashion. Menéndez Pidal has seen in this emulation a Renaissance trait on which the soldiers' long stays in Italy were not without effect. Nevertheless, in Spain the Middle Ages survived to a greater extent than elsewhere; feelings shared by all men of the Renaissance were mingled in that country with deep medieval and Iberian currents. Together with the old ideal of chivalry, recently brought up to date by the Amadís cycle of romances, we perceive a keen sense of honor, largely military in nature —Cervantes writes that "he had made that gesture because he was a Spaniard and a knight"—as well as the pride in being the subjects of the puissant King of All Spain, Emperor of Germany, and Lord of many nations. In the Golden Century, pride could even take more aggressive forms, for example, "this arrogance commonly imputed to Spaniards," noted by Cervantes.

These men, finally, were imbued with the religious ideal, closely linked to patriotic feeling during the long centuries of the Reconquest. However large might loom at times the discord and contradictions between this ideal of the soldiers and their conduct, however ignorant and naïve their faith, their faith had deep, living roots. This was particularly apparent in various manifestations of extraordinary devotion to the Virgin, which is typically Iberian and Andalusian before being Mexican, as well as in the worship of certain saints, especially St. James, who is depicted as a knight brandishing his sword. In 1519 one of the chief concerns of the first inhabitants of Vera Cruz was to obtain a papal bull that would absolve of all sins those who might die during the Conquest for the Christian faith. The reason was that by virtue of the bull "everyone will take chances and face up to any kind of danger. . . ." In certain respects the Conquest was a sequel to the crusade against the Moors, "so that Spaniards might fight forever against the infidels and enemies of the Holy Faith of Christ" (Gómara). There is no doubt of the sincere piety of Cortés himself. Astute diplomat that he was, in his ardor and haste to overthrow idols and convert the Indians he committed many imprudent acts whose consequences were serious. The explanation is that not one of these men could conceive of having vassals who were not Christians.

It came about that when the main wars were over and the conquistadors began to settle the country, they and even the colonists, being for the most part professional soldiers, kept their military mentality and habits even in the slightest details of their existence. Bernal Díaz, for example, tells us that long after the Conquest he can sleep only on the hard ground, fully dressed, and a few minutes of the night; "for I must rise," he says, "to see the sky and the stars, and to take a little walk in the cool of the evening." From their wayfaring life these soldiers retained particularly a degree of instability and difficulty in settling down anywhere. The trait is noticeable in many ways. In 1528 two oidores from Santo Domingo show in precise figures that the towns there are being depopulated with unbelievable rapidity. For "everyone is a transient, be it those who have money to travel to Castile or the impecunious who wander from town to town with no intention of stopping permanently or settling any region longer than the Indians last." The oidores go on to say that the experience must be turned to profit in New Spain and an effort made to encourage such people to take up a fixed abode by sending out married farmers. Above all, care must be taken to conserve the Indians, who feed the country.

The islands were emptied for the benefit of the continent, and the situation was only slightly less serious in New Spain. Nevertheless, the same sort of phenomenon is observed there; except Mexico City and perhaps Vera Cruz, all the new towns tended to shrink in population during the years following their establishment. The process was sometimes so rapid or went on for so long that they were wiped out, like the ephemeral town of San Luis, founded in the southern part of the country, or in 1538 the town of Espíritu Santo. Also Colima, established in 1522 by 25 horsemen and 120 soldiers, but containing ten years later no more than 51 inhabitants. For a long time the town was to vegetate; in 1554 a *visitador* found only 38 married citizens, plus ten nonresidents. Of the 48 registered inhabitants only six, including three residents, belonged to the original group; almost all the others were recent arrivals. Likewise, upon its fourth and final founding in 1542 Guadalajara showed 63 citizens; a year later only twenty remained. The number went up to 35 in 1548 and rose thereafter very slowly.

Without exception these men would set off for other regions of whose marvels people were talking; they joined with special enthusiasm any new expedition which came along. Suárez de Peralta writes: "They were all on the verge of depopulating Mexico City" in 1540 to hare off with Vásquez de Coronado's expedition to find the Seven Cities of Cíbola. Many took part, too, in the long series of explorations of Lower California (from 1532), in the Mixtón War which terminated a serious Indian uprising in New Galicia (1541), in the conquest of the Philippines (1542, 1564) and Florida, and later in the New Mexico expedition. In 1548 the discovery of the mines at Zacatecas precipitated a rush to the north, which later repeated itself at San Luis Potosí and other localities.

When there were no wars, discoveries, or particular opportunities for action, these men were "like corks floating on water," in the words of Fray Antonio Tello. Their liking for risks was dissipated in disputes and footling duels, and especially in the gambling fever, which so often symbolizes much wasted energy. Throughout the sixteenth century the authorities issued order after order designed to prohibit or curtail games of chance. In 1529 alone, four royal cédulas devoted to this subject were sent to New Spain, and such bans continued to be plentiful —without much apparent success.

Finally, the civil and religious authorities constantly complained of the wanderlust of Spaniards in the Indies; one of the authorities' chief concerns was to settle them in New Spain and let each one "take root there," writes the *contador* Albornoz. In this respect the establishment of Puebla de los Angeles was a significant success. However, as late as 1549 it was necessary to forbid the men of Mexico to migrate to Peru without permission and just cause. In 1536 Martín Cortés complains of the "infinite number of wanderers" and idlers, who live notably by rustling cattle; countless personages—friars, oidores, prelates, viceroys —write to His Majesty in the same vein. Velasco II asserts that each fleet of ships pours into the country some 800 persons with or without license, "some of whom become merchants—that is not the worst— others, trial lawyers, and mostly wanderers, whence arise great disorder and confusion in the land. . . ." Consequently, he declares, only married farmers, masons, and quarriers should be sent. Whereas forty years or so after the Conquest figures show 3,000 out of a total of 17,000 or 18,000 Castilians with no fixed abode, it is clear that as late as the seventeenth century some whites or mestizos were still leading a truly nomadic life in the vast provinces of the north.

What was called idleness or wandering often constituted merely a deviation of the habits of unemployed soldiers, conquistadors, and discoverers, whose mentality had been slowly forged over the eight centuries of the Reconquest. Perhaps we should even see in such persistent instability the heritage of the Castilians, essentially a people of drovers and shepherds accustomed to journeying between summer and winter pastures; we may contrast with them the French farmer, for example, more closely tied to his own soil. But such a physical and human environment [as that of Mexico] was hardly suitable for anything other than an extensive type of colonization and an exploitation of the soil based upon cattle raising scaled to the size of the country, where the vaqueros led a seminomadic life by preference.

Although the soldiers and like social types left the most significant imprint on the population of the country, from the point of view which interests us, they were far from alone. Among the newcomers were, or soon would be, jurists, theologians, and missionaries, who represented a small minority of the mass of immigrants but whose importance is out of proportion to their number. Some of the conquistadors either had studied or possessed a smattering of law. To begin with, Cortés, the leader, evidenced on various occasions the astuteness of a lawyer and legist; he frequently uses expressions like *paz y amor* or *orden y concierto*, which call to mind the instruction given in the universities of Salamanca and Alcalá. The smallest expeditionary force included a notary to take care of the numerous legal documents, which were accompanied by a series of symbolic and formalistic flourishes, such as the *requerimientos* (inviting the Indians to surrender before a battle) or the taking possession of a region in the King's name—documents of which Cortés bewails the loss in his second letter.

The new towns and their administrations also contained lawyers. As early as 1531 the town of Antequera de Oaxaca went so far as to accuse them of encouraging lawsuits, to the ruin of the inhabitants; the town requested His Majesty not to permit in New Spain "such men of letters, lawyers and attorneys." In Chiapas, Cuidad Real gave voice to similar complaints in 1539. At the beginning, however, the jurists and graduates at law, quite often clerics, were usually royal officials sent out from Spain to see that His Majesty's rights were respected and to impose their will on conquistadors or military men who had organized the country according to their own lights.

Finally, these legists, whatever their rank, left their stamp on Mexican society. In the seventeenth century especially the country—even the Indian villages—was swarming with lawyers, attorneys, and notaries. In spite of considerable destruction of their countless briefs and public documents, what survives gives us an idea of their activity and importance. All had their share in imparting a definitive character to the juridical acts carried out according to traditional formalism, in particular the taking possession of the soil by the Spanish colonists and cattle barons.

Last of all there were the admirable missionaries. The natives had great respect for them, because they owed them the abolition of Indian slavery, as the Protestant Hawks noted in 1572 at the end of a five-year sojourn in Mexico. The friars especially were their natural protectors. The conquistador Jerónimo López accuses them of stirring up the Indians against the encomenderos, of conferring on the Indians titles such as *alcalde* or *alguacil,* teaching them history, science, Latin—in short, of making them the equals of the Spaniards. A certain Díaz de Vargas voices similar complaints: Instead of making them work, the friars teach them all sorts of useless details of polite conduct, even to the scandalous extreme of wearing gloves.

As for the lands belonging to the Indian communities, the sole efficacious defense against the encroachment of the colonists, as we shall see, was to be that offered by the missionaries.

The Spanish tendency to dispersal shown by individuals who had often been uprooted was counterbalanced by the opposite tendency in new groups and later in the reconstituted communities, as might be expected in a society whose robust medieval traditions included a lively collective sense.

The Conquest was carried out by private individuals and armies; it consequently had an economic, even commercial, side, recalling the contracts of "commendam," "society," or "company" utilized by medieval Italian merchants. But associations of capital never reached the degree of freely alienable shares or anonymous stock. These groups are much closer to organizations of men where each brought what little he possessed to the common undertaking; relationship of one man to another always assumes a preponderant place in these sorts of contracts.

The reason is that there were personal bonds between most of the partners, and not always on the same plane, since their contributions were widely discrepant, varying from a sword or provisions to several caravels and large sums of capital. Indeed, we are struck by the number of dependents surrounding the chiefs, either their familiars or those partaking of their bounty. The chiefs were themselves dependents of the *caudillo general,* who might in turn be the dependent of the main capitalist outfitting the expedition; such was the relationship between Cortés and Diego Velázquez.

When an expedition for conquest was impending, or during the expedition itself, these ties seem to have come spontaneously into being among men who were often either solitary individuals or previously unacquainted with one another. In his letters Cortés frequently quotes his own or others' dependents; many of the old conquistadors tried to acquire merit in His Majesty's eyes by reminding him that they had brought along with them numerous dependents and cousins. Blood relatives and relatives by marriage were frequent among influential personages. In the Iberian Peninsula and the Mediterranean countries the peculiar strength of the blood tie, the family relationship, and common ancestry is a well-known fact; the Roman gens and the Corsican feud are the most common examples. Now in the military hosts of New Spain these same ramifying family groups, more or less attenuated, are found again; there were, for example, the "sixteen cousins, brothers, and uncles" of Bachiller Alonso Pérez, who had all had a hand in the storming of Mexico City and the conquest of the country. Especially a few years later relatives swarmed about the former captains, sharing their house and table with other dependents.

Many personages like Juan de Cuevas or Diego Pardo boasted of having a large house in which they sheltered "a great number of hidalgos" as well as a good-sized family. Others stated that they fed numerous cousins and dependents. Alvaro de Bracamonte continually had at least ten or fifteen men, whom he furnished with weapons and mounts, while Antonio de la Cadena "has always had in his house half a dozen Spaniards and has given food both to them and their horses," to serve His Majesty if need arises.

Finally, rich men sometimes kept open house, like Oñate and other miners of Zacatecas, who had a bell rung at mealtimes to invite passersby under their roof. The fact had struck, among other travelers, the English merchant Hawks, who in 1572 reported it to his Queen as an example of munificence. But it was not an isolated instance, and we know that in various towns in the west, the dwellings of the richest encomenderos were, in the words of Father Tello, "like public hostels filled with travelers," with a common board for all comers. In the northern provinces especially the houses of certain "powerful men" were always overflowing with people, a phenomenon that is not completely explained by the requirements of hospitality in an immense, barren country; the origin of the bounteous table for strangers must be sought in the tradition of feeding numerous dependents.

Even ecclesiastics did not always escape such customs; priests and beneficiaries "need many things for themselves . . . and their relatives, friends, and dependents (*allegados*) who live with them, and for the guests and visitors of whom they are never in want," asserts an oidor on several occasions (1584). Doubtless Fray Francisco de Toral is guilty in 1554 of a somewhat hasty generalization in writing to the Council of the Indies that prelates "devote their lives to serving their relatives rather than their flocks," but it is quite probable that some of them at least were, as he indicates, "burdened with nephews and relatives." In fact, most men enjoying any sort of income found themselves in more or less the same situation.

Finally, there were as many kinds of dependents as there were social categories. At the bottom of the scale were poor men who carried out small tasks for someone more affluent than they. They lived under his roof, were called his "hangers-on" (*paniaguados*), shared his bread and water; but for all that they lost none of their personal dignity. They could be, and could consider themselves to be, perfect hidalgos—although the word *paniaguado* seems to have taken on quite rapidly an unfavorable connotation. But personages with these large retinues often owed allegiance themselves to some high official; they were dependents of a superior order who were only occasionally dependents in the proper sense, and they in turn might have a connection with a minister or the King himself. In 1569 the Archbishop of Mexico asked that the viceroy be neither relative nor dependent (*deudo ni allegado*) of a member of the Council of the Indies. To all such, confidential missions were entrusted; their influence and number were evidence of the power possessed by the man on whom they were dependent. In exchange the latter could grant them various favors, without occasion for scandal, since they were the first to receive encomiendas, judicial posts, or large land grants.

On coming from Spain, the rich, the new members of the Audiencias, and the viceroys generally saw to it that they were accompanied by tried men on whom they could bestow positions linked to their own posts. In 1551 two notables who had been appointed as oidores in Mexico City, Dr. Trenado and Antonio Mexía, each received permission to bring with them twelve dependents in addition to Negro slaves. Viceroy Antonio de Mendoza was surrounded by dependents; when he left New Spain and the time came for passing judgment (*residencia*) on his term of office, the only serious accusation that could be made against him was that he had greatly favored his friends and intimates at the expense of others. But for the reasons indicated the accusation did not have the same gravity as it would today: Mendoza went on to become Viceroy of Peru, and he was rightly considered one of the best representatives that His Majesty had ever had in the Indies.

The increasing royal power was, however, opposed to private patronage and family arrangements, since they tended to make some men too powerful and too independent, as the great feudatories had been. Accordingly the second viceroy was forbidden to grant posts to relatives or personal dependents. Luis de Velasco appears to have obeyed, since he formally declared that he had packed off to New Galicia, Peru, or Spain several caballeros and hidalgos whom he had "brought along in his company" to help him carry out his functions in Mexico City. But the custom was too deeply rooted not to reappear a little later in a country as distant and as vast as New Spain. Certain accounts dating from the end of the sixteenth century are filled with allusions to relatives, dependents, and *paniaguados* of the viceroys or oidores. In Guadalajara, around 1602, one oidor is said to have had forty-six such people under his roof.

The fact is that in the seventeenth century the institution seemed more flourishing than ever among officials, despite constantly reiterated orders forbidding them to distribute jobs or favors to their dependents, or to relatives closer than the fourth degree. A lengthy royal cédula, addressed to Mexico City and dated December 12, 1619, is particularly explicit: His Majesty has learned that some of his viceroys, presiding judges, oidores, governors, corregidores, and other officers of the Crown had shown great favoritism to cousins, dependents, and familiars either brought out from Spain or already on the spot; they had granted them or helped them to obtain encomiendas, offices, benefices, prebends. Any such advantages in favor of officials' relatives, even relatives of their wives, sons-in-law, or daughters-in-law, or of their familiars are strictly forbidden. "Familiar" is curiously defined for the occasion:

> Let all those who might be said to have traveled from these realms [Spain] or from one province to another in the company, under the protection, and as intimates, of said viceroys, judges, oidores, governors . . . be deemed their familiars and close friends. Let the same apply to all who might be said to live permanently in the houses of the said persons without being obliged thereto by a lawsuit or specific business, or to escort or serve them, or to be concerned with their private or domestic affairs.

The current conception of public office was not likely to change matters. Throughout the Reconquest offices had been considered as rewards, even as spoils of war, granted the military leaders who distributed them among their followers. Subsequently, to be sure, this characteristic became less marked, especially under Charles V who, in the upper spheres of government at least, strove to hand out offices in accordance with the competence of the individuals concerned. But after his reign a regressive tendency set in attributable to financial difficulties and the sale of public posts, as well as to the weakness of some seventeenth-century administrations.

The system of dependents and family groups went on perpetuating itself among high officials; it was even more logical for it to survive in the lower strata of the settlers, that is, locally in outlying provinces which could be reached only after a journey of several months. Services of mutual aid and protection appeared indispensable in an isolated, often hostile environment; for that reason new bonds were forged among men. To the blood tie was added a religious relationship that, in Mexico, became just as strong and valid: the spiritual link uniting godparents to the father and mother of a christened child. These *compadres*, or "gossips," owed one another reciprocal aid and assistance, if they were of the same social status, or owed loyalty on the one hand and protection on the other, if of different ranks. The fact is that the mighty used their gossips in the same way as their relatives or dependents to establish their influence and power. The Indians went still farther, for they granted an analogous value to the relations between the owner and the "godparent" of a blessed image. Even today blood ties and *compadrazgos*—a significant word—are extremely strong in rural Mexico, where, to a much greater degree than in Corsica, a kind of feud may be carried on for generations. The old institution of dependents appears to survive around certain influential individuals in remote sections of the country.

In sum, this entire social structure tended to create, in the upper ranks, privileged sectors that were qualified to receive public offices and other advantages, notably vast grants of land, and in the lower ranks, several classes of humble folk and protégés who, though they lived like hidalgos, were ordinarily content to be the dependents of richer, more powerful individuals.

Except for the high officials such a society was fundamentally in accord with the concepts of the religious and civil authorities, the jurists and theologians who governed the country. Nearly all were under the influence of the Salamancan Neo-Scholastics and believed in the absolute necessity of a rich and powerful society, of a strongly hierarchical society within a "republic" according to the teaching of St. Thomas Aquinas. These are the sentiments expressed by missionaries like the Dominican Fray Domingo de Betanzos or the Franciscan Fray Toribio de Motolinía. In the seventeenth century and even later such is still the proper state of affairs for jurists as widely read and listened to as Solórzano Pereyra or Castillo y Bobadilla. To choose one example from among several, the Archbishop of Mexico could write to His Majesty in 1570 that "for the tranquillity of the country and to relieve the royal conscience it would be fitting to grant [encomiendas] in perpetuity and to ensure the existence of rich personages well endowed with capital; for not only would they take care of their relatives' needs, but if the occasion should arise they could better serve His Majesty at their own expense."

THE HISTORICAL BACKGROUND

How were these men, a scant few thousand in number, able to occupy New Spain? By what steps? In what regions and in what way did indi-

viduals and groups "populate," as the expression went, the vast conquered territories? What would be the policy of the Spanish state
when confronted with this practically spontaneous taking up of positions? All these questions were to influence the subsequent apportion-
ment of the land.

With their private armies and their archaic personal following
(*mesnadas*), the expeditions or undertakings that culminated in the
occupation of all Mexico appear to us as the last of the great medieval
conquests, following upon that of southern Spain. This is another way
of saying that the first establishments were primarily military in character and that the conquistadors wished to distribute among themselves
the encomiendas and repartimientos traditional in the Iberian Peninsula.
In Andalusia, villages, towns, castles, and lands had been "shared out"
among the knights arriving from the north as alodiums to be held in
perpetuity and with jurisdiction over the inhabitants. Slightly later the
military orders had conferred on certain of their members encomiendas
in conquered territory: They granted cities, lands, and vassals (owing
tribute and personal services), with the stipulation that the beneficiaries
maintain armed forces and support divine worship.

These encomiendas present striking similarities to the later ones in
New Spain; the resemblance is visible even in such details as the word-
ing of the deeds of grant or the ceremonies of investiture. By 1524
the institution seemed clearly fixed: The Spaniards had a right to tribute
and labor from their Indians, whose situation recalled indeed that of
the men in feudal estates (*señoríos de solariego*) after the decadence of
serfdom. In exchange the Spaniards had to maintain their weapons and
a horse, and then evangelize the natives. Finally, they attempted to
obtain grants in perpetuity.

If in theory the encomenderos did not enjoy the right of jurisdiction,
the facts were different, especially in distant regions. Twenty-five
years after the Conquest a royal visitor could write: "Twenty leagues
outside Mexico City there is little or no judicial system, . . . and I
know," he adds, "that in some regions the villagers consider the lords
and encomenderos of the villages as their kings, and they know no
other sovereign. . . ." Accounts agree that certain encomenderos had
their private prisons. They and their proxies, *calpixquis* or "major-
domos," judged and handed down punishments, suspended caciques,
or passed out the position of alcalde in their villages. Only gradually

did the viceroys succeed in gaining control over the entire country.

These encomiendas were quite varied in nature and unequal in size. Some comprised large villages with thousands of tributaries, whereas others were poor hamlets lost in the mountains. In 1532 encomenderos in Colima had only six or ten Indians who, it is made clear on the occasion, were "of no profit" or were even in flight and a state of rebellion. Certain conquistadors possessed nothing at all, while newcomers, who were relatives or dependents of the mighty, were given rich grants. The general lack of stability had further accentuated inequalities; in their haste to push onward new encomenderos would sell, for a few hundred pesos or a little gold, villages whose annual tribute was worth much more; the purchasers who settled down in the country became its wealthiest inhabitants.

However numerous the Indians, the fact that each encomendero customarily received a few hundred "vassals" meant that there was room for only a few Spaniards in any given region. Consequently they scattered themselves throughout the country, at least wherever they did not find the nomads rebellious to any repartimiento or tribute. Small groups of armed encomenderos therefore established themselves at strategic points or in the most thickly populated zones. Each of the new towns was not only a public square, a church, and a few houses, but a person in the legal sense, a corporation in the medieval tradition jealous of its autonomy and its rights.

In the space of a few years corporate communities were founded such as Villa Rica de la Vera Cruz, Espíritu Santo (Coatzacoalcos), and Santiesteban del Puerto (Pánuco) on the Atlantic coast; Zacatula, Colima, Purificación, Compostela, and remote Culiacán on the Pacific slopes; Antequera (Oaxaca), San Ildefonso (Villa Alta), Santiago de las Zapotecas (Nexapa); Villareal (San Cristóbal) in Chiapas; Pátzcuaro and Guadalajara. Most of these cities were separated by hundreds of kilometers—by thousands for the most distant. Accordingly commerce was practically nil. Even the crops were of no significance; the settlers lived essentially off a few herds of swine and especially the tribute, which was paid in maize, slaves, and various sorts of produce, once the Indians' supply of gold was exhausted.

According to one encomendero's account, "The Spaniards then tried to abandon the country, for they said that they certainly were not going to carry off to Castile cotton goods, cacao, or maize, and boats would not come from Castile to fetch such products." In order to buy all that was not to be found on the new continent—weapons, clothes, oil, wine—the Spaniards needed a currency which at that time could only be the precious metals. They therefore put their slaves and tributaries to work washing the gold-bearing sands of the rivers. But the small placers were quickly exhausted. Fortunately around 1532 various silver veins were discovered or reworked, which brought back some degree of tranquillity and stability to the Spaniards, who were on the point of leaving for Peru, as one of their number wrote later. Soon these mines of Taxco, Zumpango, Sultepec, and Pachuca were unable to supply the needs of a constantly expanding "republic of Spaniards," as the Crown was in the process of freeing the Indian slaves and abolishing the labor services due the encomenderos.

This type of economy, founded on tributes and precious metals, consequently gave rise to a need for expansion and discoveries, even when such very small groups of humans were involved. The multiplying herds furnished but a temporary remedy; shortly their real value shrank to that of their hides, which was diminished by the heavy expenses necessary to export them. In New Spain therefore everyone demanded expeditions of conquest. We must occupy new lands so as to create careers for the Spaniards, too numerous in the country (there were scarcely a few thousand score of them); such is the gist of what was constantly being repeated to the King, by Gonzalo de Salazar in 1538, Jerónimo López in 1543, Viceroy Velasco in 1553, Fray Toribio de Motolinía in 1555, and again in 1570 by the Archbishop of Mexico. For some the converting of souls was the primary concern.

Leaving Mexico, the discoverers went to "populate," or to try to do so, Florida, Lower California, the Philippines. Missionaries accompanied them or went before. Then there occurred an event which allowed them to move into the immense northern plateaus. Until that time the absence of sedentary natives, the impossibility of encomiendas, and the existence of fierce, intractable nomads had kept the Spaniards out of those arid wastes. But in 1546 a Basque prospector, Juan de Tolosa, discovered the rich silver deposits of Zacatecas, situated in nomad territory hundreds of kilometers from any Spanish establishment. He went into partnership with two other prominent Basques, Cristóbal de Oñate and

Diego de Ibarra, later with a Castilian, Temiño de Bañuelos, and began to smelt ore. A rush of adventurers and all kinds of men took place; in the desert a city mushroomed, possessing only two years after its birth five churches and fifty-odd refineries. Zacatecas was the second most important city in New Spain, of a new type, since its citizens "are not encomenderos . . . but all miners and merchants," as was noted a few decades later.

Success sent them onward. Francisco de Ibarra, Diego de Ibarra's nephew, and subsequently a few others, discovered, beginning in 1554, the mines of Fresnillo, Saín Alto, San Martín, Mazapil, Aviño, Chalchihuites, Llereno, and Sombrerete. In 1567 (or 1580) Indé commenced operations, then Santa Bárbara, which was to remain for a very long time the extreme tip of colonization, some 700 kilometers beyond Zacatecas and 1,300 or 1,500 from Mexico City. "As soon as each rich deposit is discovered mobs descend upon it from all over America as if they could hear the clink of silver," writes Father Arlegui, and almost everywhere at once the vast northern deserts were spotted with little population centers called *reales de minas*, probably from the name of the flag, or *pendón real*, flown above these camps fortified against nomads.

The advance was much slower east of Zacatecas, especially in the direction of the Gran Tunal. To the south, of course, Guanajuato got its first settlers as early as 1554; but inside the danger zone the *real* of Charcas, founded ten or twenty years later, was wiped out by nomad attacks. Not until around 1592 did the rich deposits of San Luis Potosí attract intrepid pioneers to the proximity of the Tunal; not until 1593–1603 and 1609 were the deposits worked at Sierra de Pino, later still at Ramos. But by these dates the prosperity of the mines had already fallen off. Their decline was scarcely less rapid than their rise. Quite perceptible by 1625, the deterioration was complete fifteen or twenty years later: Total silver production had fallen by then to a very low level and would not rise again before the eighteenth century.

These mines had even so provided the framework for settling the northern provinces, with the result that the Atlantic slope, where there were no mines, was not colonized until late in the seventeenth century, or even the eighteenth in Tamaulipas. The mines constituted the basis of a new expansion which would put the Spaniards ahead of the English and French in the north. Finally, the mines facilitated the advance of the Franciscan and Jesuit missionaries toward the sierras and the western coast with its semi-sedentary populations.

But the mining centers simply could not be self-sufficient, unlike some of the encomenderos' towns, Culiacán for example, which in the seventeenth century subsisted in picturesque isolation. After the invention of the amalgam process in 1555 the refining industry was unable to survive without mercury, which was not to be found on the spot. Situated in unpopulated areas or arid sierras, the mining centers had to see to their food supplies, fetching from a distance maize, wheat, and cattle, as well as the mules indispensable for working refineries. Then the silver extracted had finally to be shipped to Mexico City. Communications were consequently vital, not only for the miners but also the Spanish state, whose chief source of revenue was the Crown's fifth part of all silver produced. The viceroys attempted to secure the roads against nomad raids, especially the roads to Zacatecas and the mines in the northwest, which in the sixteenth century comprised the most important producing center.

To accomplish this the most efficacious means was to settle little nuclei of Spanish colonists along the highways. Since in these dangerous zones there were neither Indians to share out nor precious metals to extract, a third type of population scheme had to be instituted, utilizing farmers and cattle raisers. It was a particularly difficult undertaking. Nevertheless the markets offered by the mining towns, where food brought very high prices, favored these new settlements, whose existence was precarious at the outset. For this purpose Viceroy Velasco founded in 1555 the city of San Miguel on the site of a village of the same name that had been destroyed by nomads, "to put an end," he stated, "to the murders, thefts, and other excesses that have been committed and are still being committed on the plains of San Miguel, on the way to Zacatecas. . . ." Farther north, San Felipe, founded in 1562, played a similar part, as did Silao, Celaya (1571), and León (1576) in the west. In New Galicia, Santa María de los Lagos (1563), Jerez de la Frontera, and Asunción de Aguascalientes (1570 and 1575) were also established. Much farther north Nombre de Dios and Durango (1563), then Saltillo (1577), all three founded by powerful private citizens, had as their chief function the supplying of food to the mines. These towns

contained a few score Spaniards at most, whereas during the same period there were more than 10,000 in Mexico City.

Despite a widely held opinion, the mines, far from having paralyzed
agricultural and pastoral colonization, favored its development, as
Father Arlegui noted long before Humboldt, but the development
was one of small, isolated patches within a vast territory. Nor should
we be amazed at the prodigious drawing power of the mines, "a
lodestone for the Spaniard," wrote Mota y Escobar. If the fact may
be partly explained by the spirit of adventure and a liking for risks,
one must also acknowledge that in a period when the capacity and
tonnage of shipping were absurdly small only a limited quantity of
high-priced goods could be exported, that is, valuable products and
especially the metals constituting the main form of exchange with
Spain. Thus New Spain showed a tendency to withdraw behind her
frontiers when silver production fell off to practically nothing in the
early eighteenth century.

In the same way that the central and southern economy founded
on tribute had distributed the "cities" of the encomenderos among
the native populations, in the north the mining economy dotted the
immense empty spaces with tiny extracting centers lost in the hinter-
land, and a few agricultural communities spread along the endless
roads. Likewise, the necessity of preaching the Gospel carried the missionaries far into the northwest. This is a partial explanation for the
penetration in depth accompanied by a loose-knit sort of occupation
which is so typical of Spanish colonization, for at the end of the sixteenth century New Spain appears to have contained not even 100,000
white men, many of whom were concentrated in the capital city, as
often happens in new countries. Fifty years later there were still only
200,000, plus 50,000 mestizos and 50,000 Negroes and mulattoes, according to Rosenblatt's calculations. The scattered nature of the settlements was emphasized very early by Englishmen like Hakluyt and
Thomas Gage. The latter mentions the contrast with the densely populated colonies of his fellow countrymen, relating particularly the great
astonishment voiced by Spaniards over the English colonists' failure
to penetrate more deeply into North America: "You must be afraid
of the Indians or extremely lazy to prefer a tranquil life and the raising
of a handful of tobacco plants to the conquest of a country paved

with gold and silver." Such are the words Gage attributes to the Castilians.

On the other hand, a certain Spaniard with a business sense was disturbed by this excessive expansion, deeming it unlikely to enrich the King and his subjects—not sound economics, as we should say today. As early as the sixteenth century the Spaniard in question, Pedro de Ledesma, would have liked to see the lagoon of Mexico City drained and the land reclaimed, olive trees and grapevines planted, other crops and weaving developed, and the country settled more intensively. Instead of sending expeditions costing 300,000 to 500,000 pesos to the Molucca Islands, he writes,

> if Your Majesty used but a small portion of those sums in New Spain, the country would become the best in the world and the Crown's revenues would be much increased. For there is no reason why Your Majesty should lose what you have already won in order to seek at such expense what you have never had and consequently have never lost.

And if the King's will is to found cities, spread the Gospel, or find gold and silver, he may do so in the countries already acquired; for there is so much space in them that "even if we sent for all Asia to come there would still be space left over." There is no lack of infidels in them either, and it would be a big enough job in itself to work and populate all the mines of New Spain. Naturally nothing was changed. The heavy engine was already in motion; even at the outset could its course have been altered?

As for the exploiting of the soil resources, that type of colonization could further only extensive cattle raising spread over the entire country; for the herds grew and multiplied almost without care in the vast spaces separating population centers. The rare Spaniards in the country, especially the cattle barons, did not take long to divide up the land. In a "republic" governed by jurists, taking possession of the soil assumed a formalistic, legal, definitive character. The loose-knit type of occupation and extensive cattle raising could not help but create an environment favorable to the rise of vast estates, which moreover were destined to survive unchanged even after population increased and farming became intensive.

The considerable prerogatives granted by the capitulations that the Crown drew up with the conquistadors, it has sometimes been stated, were the origin of the American aristocracy and its large estates. The statement is exact in part only, applying to tardy expeditions and colonizing ventures of the late sixteenth and early seventeenth centuries, particularly in northern Mexico.

At the end of the first decade following the Conquest royal power asserted itself very rapidly in New Spain. The advantages granted in the capitulations were withdrawn or whittled down. Very few among the leaders of the early expeditions founded the great families of the viceroyalty. Even the encomenderos quickly lost their seigniorial characteristics. The monarchy sent its jurists and lawyers to replace the conquistadors, soldiers, and adventurers in all important posts. Four licenciados and a presiding judge, Bishop Ramírez de Fuenleal, formed in 1531–1532 the second Audiencia of Mexico, a kind of supreme court whose political powers were all the greater since Cortés had been ousted from the government. Likewise in 1548 another Audiencia was established in New Galicia, with a permanent seat soon established at Guadalajara.

The appointment of a viceroy in 1535 was the decisive step in strengthening the Crown's power: Antonio de Mendoza revealed himself to be a faithful servant of His Majesty as well as an energetic man of action and a shrewd politician; also he kept an eye on the economic development of the country. His successor, Luis de Velasco (1550–1564), was in turn a remarkable statesman, whose philosophical views led him to protect the Indians and ally himself with the missionaries. Martín Enríquez (1568–1580) was a third valuable viceroy, despite the terrible epidemics that decimated the Indians during his term of office.

Like the *missi dominici* of antiquity, visitors endowed with considerable powers extended the first viceroys' sphere of action into the remotest provinces, ferreting out abuses and imposing royal authority everywhere. After 1530 the corregidores came into existence, and were to multiply in subsequent years. Although only too often their posts appear to be part of the spoils—earlier granted to the soldiers of the Reconquest—the corregidores and alcaldes mayores were the King's direct representatives; they were so to speak local justices with whom the authorities wished gradually to supplant the encomenderos.

In this mighty effort to regain control the Crown could usually count on the powerful support of the Church, especially of the missionaries who saw in the labor services of the encomienda system an intolerable abuse. It is a well-known fact that the Reconquest in the Spanish Peninsula and the war against the infidels had tended to identify the cause of the nation with that of religion, to bind closely together Church and monarchy. Charles V's empire represents the last great attempt of the medieval spirit to establish a *Universitas Christiana:* one God, one faith, one realm. In the minds of Philip II and his successors, their political ideas were inseparable from their religious mission. It is in such an atmosphere and because of this alliance that at the end of the fifteenth and during the sixteenth century the regime of the Patronato was conceived and given shape: The Pope relinquished to the King, together with the tithes, the exclusive right to found missions, churches, and cathedrals, as well as to present for ecclesiastical benefices persons of his choosing; on the other hand, the Crown was responsible for evangelizing the Indians, a mission which became for the Crown a matter of conscience.

Such is the explanation of the rapid consolidation of royal power in New Spain; buttressed by its subjects' loyalty to the monarchy and their deeply religious feelings, the Crown imposed its legists and men of proved loyalty, while its activity was often inspired and supported by theologians and missionaries. Cortés and his lieutenants were removed from power. The famous capitulations creating feudal states of a sort were rendered practically inoperative; as a result those drawn up with Montejo for Yucatan (1526), Cortés for the Pacific expeditions (1529), Páñfilo de Narváez (1526) and Hernando de Soto (1537) for Río de las Palmas and Florida, far from reflecting reality, are valuable only on the plane of juridical theory. Under Philip II the heiress of the Montejo family was still demanding the execution of the clauses stipulated; but the opinion of the royal governor of Yucatan was that she should be given only honorific distinctions with, if so desired, the ten-league-square piece of land provided for by the capitulations, and no Indians, "por ser una pura laja," that is, an area where there was nothing but stones. It appears that she did not even obtain that paltry concession.

In a parallel series of actions the Crown urged its representatives to whittle down the prerogatives of the encomenderos, in order both to restore royal authority and to defend its Indian subjects against the arbitrariness and harsh treatment condemned, at times most violently, by missionaries and theologians. But resistance was strong; in 1537 the first viceroy was able to accomplish reforms only in the personal services required of the Indians. Finally, a series of orders culminated in the famous New Laws promulgated in 1542 under the influence of Las Casas. These laws, the first of a general rather than a fragmentary or local nature, abolished Indian slavery and the encomiendas belonging to officials and prelates, reduced others deemed excessive in size, and levied a tax on the tributes of all encomiendas; especially did they forbid the granting of new encomiendas and made the old ones revert to the Crown on the death of their holders.

These radical measures raised such a storm of protest that their execution had to be suspended; in 1545 the Emperor himself was obliged to revoke the most vital clause: the abolition of the encomiendas following the death of their possessors. Nevertheless this period marks the beginning of a new era in which the encomienda, in practice having remained hereditary, will end up as a simple tribute on which a tax is paid, a kind of trust fund transmitted by certain conquistadors to their descendants.

Native slavery was abolished. Viceroys Mendoza and especially Velasco progressively freed a large number of Indian carriers and slaves. With a few exceptions the Indians remained in bondage only in the remote northern provinces. Tributes were taxed. In 1544 various prelates and high officials were deprived of their encomiendas. Finally, an order of 1549 separated personal services from the encomienda system. Work levies did continue, but they were henceforth regulated by officials who granted them only to possessors of enterprises judged useful to the republic. This important reform seems to have been tried out first in Puebla, then slowly extended to other regions. Thanks to constant vigilance the system went on being improved in subsequent years until in the seventeenth century the work levy was abolished.

Finally, to complete this picture of the control exercised by the Crown and the centralizing activities of its representatives, "cities" were established on the road to the mines by the direct efforts of the viceroy or the Audiencia of New Galicia.

Toward the end of Viceroy Luis de Velasco's term of office (1550–1564) the Crown had consequently regained its authority and begun to impose its authority in all sectors. However, a few disquieting symptoms are to be noted. In 1560 there was the matter of an official, an oidor of Guadalajara, Dr. Morones, to whom the King had given the task of colonizing Chiametla to the south of Culiacán. But, after setting out in great detail the steps to be followed, His Majesty added a condition: "Our will is that in the said establishment no expenses be charged against our treasury." Since in another clause the cédula prohibited encomiendas, and the existence of mines was doubtful, the expedition was practically doomed at the outset. Dr. Morones demanded in vain the 30,000 or 40,000 ducats that he thought indispensable; time went by, and the oidor died without having accomplished anything. This necessary task of settlement was to be entrusted in 1567 to Francisco de Ibarra, a nephew of the rich Zacatecas miner, but this time at his expense and with no outlay from the royal treasury. The example is typical of the financial difficulties that blocked the monarchy's tendency to centralization by allowing private citizens to assume such costs in exchange for economic and political advantage.

Money needs became more and more pressing during the reign of Philip II. The monarch's increasing involvement in endless European wars dictated the necessity of unloading the cost of colonization upon rich personages who received in exchange a few bits and pieces of royal sovereignty. This is apparent in the colonizing laws of 1573, which were promulgated—by a simple coincidence?—shortly after the general uprising in Flanders. These laws revealed a tendency to return to the regime of the governors (*adelantados*), who were again granted exorbitant privileges as at the time of the Conquest and the first capitulations; for example, they were given the right to possess hereditary fortresses, distribute encomiendas, appropriate for themselves a quarter of the land in the district of new towns, and so on. A few articles even seemed to establish for the benefit of the capitalists a seigniorial regime over certain settlers, something contrary to all the ideas of the most humble Spaniard in the Indies. This was a definite regression rendered more or less inevitable by the Crown's lack of money. Such an anachronism had definite practical consequences at the end of the sixteenth and the beginning of the seventeenth century, for it tended to create a new class of powerful personages, especially in the northern provinces.

As early as 1563 Ibarra had founded at his own expense Nombre de Dios and Durango in New Viscaya. In 1573 the King commissioned the presiding judge of the Audiencia of Guadalajara to conclude an agreement (*asiento*) "with some rich man" who would take on the task of settling or resettling danger spots along the Chichimeca frontier; this was accomplished the following year at Tepezala and Charcas. The wars against the nomads were increasingly waged by private individuals, and the laws of 1573 were used as an outline for settlement contracts concluded with capitalists. In certain respects the tendencies to decentralization in fact became more frequent in the seventeenth century under Philip II's weak successors, who were perennially short of money and whose main concern was to unload public outlays upon rich individuals as far as possible.

Besides the capitulations concluded with Oñate for New Mexico, largely modeled on the laws of 1573, a typical case is the foundation of the city of Cadereyta, east of Querétaro in the direction of the Sierra Gorda, this latter being a nomad lair. Around 1641 Captain Alonso Tovar de Guzmán, accompanied by his brother and "other relatives and cousins," carried out the project under conditions deriving from the same laws, notably the grant of a quarter of the land forming the city district to the founder, and the title of *capitán de guerra*, implying both important prerogatives and large military expenses. Three years later in a zone that had long been pacified, a rich man, Gabriel López de Peralta, received authorization to establish the city of Salvatierra on lands donated by him. He dared claim for himself and his descendants the perpetual titles of corregidor and *teniente de capitán general*, with a share in the sales tax (*alcabalas reales*) on the region. But the viceroy temporized, so that it is hard to learn exactly what political advantages were obtained by the López de Peralta family sixty years before they were made Marqueses de Salvatierra.

As if to complete the picture, encomiendas of the original type reappeared in the northern provinces, while the enslavement of Indians taken prisoner during an engagement went on as in the past. Early in the seventeenth century encomenderos living at Saltillo were running their estates with the help of vassal Indians. In New León Governor Zavala was still in 1640 passing out encomiendas of a sort, accompanied by labor services, to men who it appears had already taken them of their own accord and with no justification. A royal cédula of May 26,

1625, had, however, authorized only encomiendas consisting of tax tributes. These seminomadic Indians were furthermore difficult to employ and often rebellious.

The tendency to what amounted in fact to decentralization is one of the aspects of the general recession which accompanied the decline of the mines in the seventeenth century, the relative shrinkage of commerce, and the isolation of the entire country. Despite a considerable increase in the Creole population, shipping diminished. In seventeenth-century Mexico shaky relations with Europe gave rise to an economy lacking large overseas markets. The reason is that the only significant exports were the precious metals, which were easily shipped in boats of small tonnage. But Mexican silver production began to fall off during the early decades of the seventeenth century. It soon reached an extremely low level, and generally speaking did not rise again until the Bourbons reacted late in the next century. Although our knowledge of the rate of metal extraction is very slight, it is an observable fact that many miners were ruined by the high price of mercury—a royal monopoly—and that mining centers as important as San Luis Potosí produced only 22,845 silver marks between the spring of 1690 and that of 1691, in comparison with 120,249 in 1620. At Zacatecas the plunge seems to have come even before that date.

In these circumstances traffic with Spain could not help falling off to a considerable extent for lack of valuable export products and exchange in order to acquire European goods. Without silver, commercial shipping comes to a standstill, notes Veytia Linaje in 1671, and in fact the fleets of New Spain were much less important then than sixty years before. At the end of the seventeenth century the fleets of the Indies had lost during a period of a hundred years three-fourths of their tonnage. The Dutch and English grew bolder in the face of the feeble resistance put up by the Spanish state. In 1628 a fleet was totally destroyed for the first time; the deed would be repeated in the years following, and an English squadron would blockade the coast of Andalusia during the winter of 1655–1656. However, the worst enemy of overseas commerce was not so much corsairs and foreigners as the Spanish state itself, when it authorized the monopoly of overseas trade by a handful of Sevillian merchants interested in keeping it within narrow limits, when it paralyzed any individual initiative by absurd, uselessly irksome regulations, and when on several occasions it seized silver shipments belonging to private individuals. The *avería* tax—a kind of obligatory insurance increasingly supervised by the state—had reached fantastic rates by 1628 and was crushing all commerce.

The monarchy was caught in a vicious circle: The more that shipments of precious metals dropped off and trade languished, the more the state needed silver. Accordingly, the higher it raised taxes or the price of the mercury sold to the miners, the more it tended to confiscate to its benefit the silver of private individuals (who therefore shipped less and less), and the more closely its interests became identified with those of the Sevillian merchants from whom it solicited advances of funds.

In Mexico the marked slowing down of trade had important effects, particularly because the native white population kept on growing. Since on the other hand the Spanish state restricted commerce among its overseas provinces, limited their industrial development, and prohibited certain specialized crops, domestic traffic declined also. With legal currencies scarce and insufficient, and the circulation of products sluggish, prices were static or fell off in the course of the seventeenth century. Finally, each region and even each locality tended to become isolated and self-sufficient and to huddle under the authority of the large landowners or local leaders, who frequently took over the expenses required for maintaining a police force or waging war on the nomads.

To sum up: On the Mexican Plateau the importance of the arid zones with their intermittent rainfall; the rise, long before, of individual estates within the civilized native communites of the center and south; the part played among the newcomers by powerful men with their swarms of relatives and dependents, to whom the penniless Crown very quickly had to cede the right to wage war and colonize in the north; throughout the country the extremely loose-knit, scattered, Spanish form of settlement; and finally the juridical form and definitive character of the cattlemen's seizure of the land—such was the combination of historical circumstances and geographical and social phenomena that created an environment remarkably favorable to the formation and growth of great estates, in which the master's power was to extend strikingly beyond the pattern of economic exploitation.

2. THE SLOW AGRICULTURAL EXPANSION

The first Spaniards' "Republic" was hardly conducive to the development of agriculture, to use a term just then coming into fashion. The soldiers, with their hidalgo mentality and roaming habits, took scant interest in farming. The most enterprising among the encomenderos had limited their activities to washing out a little river gold or raising a few pigs, the only livestock that the conquistadors had brought with them into the country.

The sites of the first garrison towns had furthermore been chosen for their strategic value; they were often useless for agriculture. San Ildefonso de los Zapotecas (Villa Alta), for example, was located in so mountainous and forbidding a region that it could be reached only on foot. The inhabitants themselves said that no business or profit was possible; their sole source of revenue was tribute. Antequera de Oaxaca, in Zapotec territory, had supplanted an Aztec stronghold; although the little town was situated in a fertile valley, the native population was so dense that neither the King nor his representatives would allow the land to be divided among the Spaniards. If they had done so, they would have stripped the Indians of their livelihood.

On the new continent, vegetable and animal resources were meager. During the time that the Spaniards had to live off the country, they discovered little more than maize, beans, and turkeys. Also, since food reserves were limited, they had to exercise caution in taking their share, lest they starve their Indian vassals. The newcomers had no grapevines, olive trees, or even wheat, so that they had to go without the bread that, in Castile or Andalusia, had constituted a staple of their diet. During the Conquest, they had been forced to make do with roasted kernels of maize, or tortillas. But once the fighting and the hardships were over and certain of the conquistadors had become the country's new masters, they looked to their comfort, as the Franciscan Motolinía ironically explains. One of their chief concerns was naturally to taste "Castilian bread" again, and so, to obtain wheat. They were also hungry for familiar vegetables and fruits, such as figs, oranges, pomegranates, quinces, and lemons.

At least with regard to wheat, the Spaniards' first thought was to make the Indians sow it in their small fields alongside their maize. In Mexico, however, wheat raising turned out to be difficult. Unlike the traditional Mexican seed crops (which grow very quickly during the rainy season), wheat was frequently found to require irrigation. Whether because of ignorance or disinclination, the crops obtained by the natives were in general quite poor. In 1550, the quantity of wheat harvested by the Indians was negligible, as Viceroy Mendoza wrote to his successor. In fact, only a trifling fraction of the tribute owed to the royal treasury or to the encomenderos was paid in wheat. A last attempt, by Viceroy Velasco in 1559, was no more successful than the previous ones. He authorized a levy of a small amount of wheat from certain of the Crown's tributaries, but two years later, he was obliged to rescind his order on discovering that the Indians were harvesting practically none and were even buying tribute wheat from outside sources.

If the Spaniards were not going to be satisfied with maize, they would have to grow the other products themselves, as some of them were aware, and set up their own fields and orchards. They did not do the work themselves, of course (that was still left to the Indians); but thenceforth operations were to be directed and closely supervised by a Spaniard. Contemporary drawings depict this personage with his cape flung over his shoulder and his sword hanging at his side. An hidalgo would never put his own hand to the plow—a fact constantly deplored by the viceroys. The wages paid, moreover, though sufficient to feed Indians, were too low to tempt the poorer Spaniards to do the work of which the natives were capable.

HARVEST-LAND GRANTS

The above circumstances led some soldiers and settlers to overcome their initial reluctance and to take an interest in the land, acquiring and running estates and even planting orchards and vineyards. Such activities fell naturally into the framework of the traditional *municipium*, as old as the Reconquest in Spain but newly implanted in the Indies: Each member of a new community receives, in addition to commonage, a plot of land commensurate with his rank.

As if to facilitate this first land distribution in the new towns, which were often located in the midst of native population centers, some fields, as we know, had been legally free since the Conquest. "Your Majesty need have no fear to grant Spaniards reasonable areas of land," writes Ramírez de Fuenleal about 1532, "since in every village there are pieces that were worked for the benefit of the idols or Moctezuma." Around the years 1527–1528, in fact, Mexico City's inhabitants were often given orchards or fields "that used to belong to Moctezuma" or to some native chieftain "killed during the late wars," providing no heirs came forth to make a claim. In 1532, the King requested details of the lands in the city's outskirts which the Oaxaca Indians "had consecrated to, bestowed upon, and set aside for their idols and sacrifices" in order to reply to a petition from the Spanish settlers, who wanted them portioned out. Still, they were not entirely allocated by 1538, although numerous local caciques had appropriated them without leave.

Land allotments were traditionally of two kinds: *peonías* and *caballerías*. The former were for foot soldiers and the latter, five times larger, for those who had fought on horseback. As early as July, 1519, the municipal government of Villa Rica de la Vera Cruz requested the magistrates to authorize land allotments, with full title for the possessors at the end of a two-year period. In 1523, the King recommended to Cortés that he grant the Spaniards in the new towns "their allotments—

caballerías or *peonías*—in accordance with their individual rank"; the grants were to become final after royal confirmation and five years of residence.

However strong the pull of legal tradition, the realities of the American environment soon gained the upper hand. The new arrivals, all hidalgos and caballeros in their own estimation, would have none of the *peonías*, which they identified with inferior rank. (Significantly, the word *peón*, or foot soldier, was never applied except to Indians.) The fact that some new cities and towns were exempted from the commoner's tax—the *pecho*—proves nothing, since in fact no Spaniard ever paid it within the confines of the viceroyalty. Consequently, *peonías* (or *peonerías*) belonging to Spaniards occurred in Mexico only rarely; in 1528, a few did exist in far-off Villareal de Chiapas (San Cristóbal las Casas). Just the same, the judges of the Council of the Indies continued, for fifty years more, to rule on these nearly nonexistent holdings. In 1573, they went so far as to establish down to the last detail the composition of each *peonía*—so much land for wheat, maize, and fruit trees, so many cows, pigs, sheep, mares, and goats—in a series of laws often quoted by historians, but having no practical application whatever.

During the first ten years, few caballerías were brought under cultivation. On drawing up ordinances for two new towns in Honduras, in 1525, Cortés, with experience in the Islands as well as a grasp of practical matters, made provision for only scattered cattle raising. Even in 1524, when his intent was precisely to develop harvest land and plantations, he continued to follow the encomienda system: Spaniards to whom natives had been consigned must plant a thousand grapevines for every hundred Indians and grow wheat, vegetables, and other Castilian produce. The royal jurists, it is true, quickly put an end to this kind of land appropriation by the encomenderos.

It was at Puebla de los Angeles that holdings were first given out in any numbers. At the time, the Crown had reverted to the ideas of Bartolomé de las Casas: The Indies were to be settled by farmers who would be given, not encomiendas, but "a moderate amount of land" that they would work themselves. In the spirit of these early agricultural laws, the Second Audiencia decided to establish a town composed of Spaniards in an uncultivated region near the road to Vera Cruz. (About the same time, an Audiencia judge, Vasco de Quiroga, founded the curious settlement of Santa Fe, part hospital, part village, for free Indian farmers; harvests were held in common, as in Sir Thomas More's *Utopia*.) In 1531–1532, each inhabitant of the new town of Puebla received one or two caballerías, "so that they may be their property and inheritance forever, to clear and to plant them, in conformity with existing and future ordinances passed by the government of this city." The caballería's dimensions not having been fixed for the entire country, each of these allotments measured only "ten fanegadas of grain," that is, six or seven hectares. For once, the holdings were really seeded and planted, notably at Atlixco, a warmer valley slightly to the south. The founding of Puebla had been far from easy: The magistrate Salmerón, bearer of a special commission for the town, had found it impossible to avoid supplying the settlers with Indian laborers, but he was able to limit their number and to set up a new distribution system closely supervised by royal officials.

Barring a few exceptions in Mexico City and elsewhere, the score or so of Spaniards at Puebla were the first farmers in the country. Their farms were for the most part on a modest scale, and although they did not work in the fields themselves, they did live on their land and supervise its working. Since the very large estate did not do as well in Puebla as elsewhere, the small farmers, as their numbers grew, set the pattern for the settlement of the entire region.

The next groups of Spanish farmers did not appear until the second half of the sixteenth century, along the roads leading to the great northern mines. Starting in 1555, settlers in the town of San Miguel were each given a *vecindad*, or allotment, by the viceroy's representative, either in person or in his name. The grant carried with it the title of *vecino*, or burgher, and usually consisted of a building lot, a garden, one or two caballerías of harvest land, and a sheep pasture located within a six-mile square surrounding the town. In exchange, the settlers promised to take up residence on their land, not to sell their grant for at least ten years (later reduced to six), and to maintain a horse and weapons. For a long time the settlement led a precarious existence, not only because of the presence in the region of dangerous bands of nomads, but because the citizens could not get enough Indian laborers; the few they did have had to be brought a long distance from the south. At Santa María de los Lagos, founded in 1563 under the supervision of the Audiencia of New Galicia, similar arrangements were made and similar difficulties encountered; to clear their land and build, the 26 homesteaders could count on only a few Indians settled over a wide area (eight leagues).

Elsewhere, new towns were established in the same way, either by royal officials or by important individuals. Six years after Ibarra's founding of Nombre de Dios, 130 caballerías had been handed out to a few dozen settlers, and not all of the lands were put under cultivation. At San Felipe, the town district was larger and more land was distributed than elsewhere, probably in order to attract colonists to a particularly dangerous region. At Celaya, somewhat later, each of the 32 new settlers received a *vecindad* consisting of 2½ caballerías, to which "two days of water" for irrigation were subsequently added.

Despite various orders reserving the prerogative of distributing land to the King's representatives, communities, once they were established, soon took to giving out *vecindades* themselves, usually within their own district, but sometimes far beyond. Land had little value in the early days and distribution rights seemed of secondary importance; later on, the authorities were relatively lenient, particularly with regard to harvest lands. Mexico City had already begun to apportion *vecindades* on a permanent basis; in 1530, the municipal government specified to one grantee that he could "build in stone and do what he liked" on his allotment, for which he was thereby given a "title deed in due form." In later years, the councilmen of Mexico City were forbidden to make grants of this type, and they were never able to win back the right to initiate them. Few measures were universally applied at the time, however, and conditions were different in other regions.

Although the Crown had not granted Puebla's requests for discretionary powers in 1536–1537, half a century later the city announced to the King that "for over 55 years" it had been exercising the right to distribute orchards and "lands for sowing" and complained on the same occasion of Viceroy Villamanrique's meddling in the matter. In Guadalajara, the very town where the Audiencia of New Galicia met, the local authorities insisted as late as 1563 on continuing to distribute land within the limits of their district, as they had done, they said, "for more than 35 years." The King took no action other than to request his Audiencia to inform him "of the custom that has hitherto been observed and is now being observed in said city concerning lands and commons and other properties, and whether it will be fitting for the municipality to distribute them."

Remote towns naturally had more imperative reasons for behaving in the same way. For many years, the councils of San Felipe, Jerez, and Nombre de Dios granted title deeds that were almost never confirmed by higher authority. Since the important municipal offices quickly fell into the hands of local oligarchies, the lands that were passed out would frequently make the growing haciendas even bigger. The Viceroy received a strongly worded order from Spain in 1589 concerning such encroachments on Crown rights, and thereafter he opposed them in certain cases. For example, Nombre de Dios, an enclave in New Galicia belonging to New Spain, had its grants of harvest lands and pastures nullified in 1595; this did not prevent the grantees from continuing to regard them as valid title deeds and preserving them as such in their archives. By the end of the sixteenth century, however, these municipal grants represented only local incidents in comparison with the number of grants being handed out by the viceroys at the same time.

As soon as the judges of the Second Audiencia arrived in Mexico City to defend the Crown's interests, they were given, by cédulas dated 1530, 1531, 1533, and 1535, a major role in the distribution of land. The prerogative of making land grants was increasing in importance, and in 1535, as a result of a particular instance, it came to be vested in the Viceroy: He was to grant caballerías to those conquistadors and former colonizers who had settled in the country, with the stipulation that they might not make them over to any "church, monastery, or ecclesiastic."

After 1523, by edict, all land grants were theoretically subject to royal approval. In fact, however, the deeds issued by the viceroys were never confirmed by the sovereign except when a grant was made by direct order from Spain. The Crown thus held a heavy juridical weapon in reserve against New Spain's landed proprietors, who, a century later, had to pay out large sums to legalize their irregular titles.

When Viceroy Mendoza began to grant caballerías, he tried to standardize their measurements, which until then had varied from one town to another. In early 1537 he established the dimensions as 552 x 1,104 varas, or a little less than 43 hectares. (Eighty years later in remote

Tabasco, the official dimensions were still unknown and had to be pointed out to the local authorities.)

In accordance with the Castilian custom, stubble fields were by royal decree open to common grazing, "once the harvest is gathered in." From 1565 on, all deeds issued by the viceroys bore this clause. It seems to have been observed in the sixteenth century, inasmuch as landowners were obliged to remove their fences after harvest time. In view of the immense areas readily available for grazing, the regulation had little meaning until considerable land had been brought under cultivation. Whereas in Spain the custom tended to favor the poor and the landless by guaranteeing them grazing rights, in New Spain it opened the natives' fields to the Spaniards' cattle.

In short, the first viceroy distributed gifts of land, called *mercedes*, made up of caballerías (never *peonías*), in His Majesty's name. The legal procedure was never to change. The interested party would make a request specifying what land he wished to cultivate or was already cultivating. If sufficiently powerful, he would back up his request with a royal cédula ordering the grant's execution. The Viceroy would issue a writ, or *mandamiento acordado*, whereby the alcalde mayor or corregidor of the region was empowered to investigate the possibility of making the grant without harm to third parties, particularly Indians. If the final decision was favorable, the petitioner would receive a deed in due form, the *merced*, which was entered in a register. The alcalde mayor would then give possession of the land, following an ancient ceremony held to be essential. The new owner would be led by the hand around his property, pulling up grass, cutting twigs, or throwing stones as he went. Carrying out these ritual gestures ensured an almost definitive title to the land.

Although the first register of *mercedes* to be preserved begins in 1542, we find viceregal deeds to caballerías as early as 1537. Ordinarily, the allotment was given with the proviso that, by the end of the first year, one-quarter or one-fifth of it would be planted in fruit trees or grapevines. Furthermore, it was not to be sold or exchanged for six years; at that time, the grantee entered into permanent possession. The medieval clause prohibiting sale or other disposal for the benefit of "church, monastery, hospital, or other ecclesiastical institution or person," as specified in the royal orders, appears from 1542 onward.

Soon requests were being made for caballerías outside the narrow districts surrounding the Spanish towns, in which all land had been given out at the same time. Encomenderos requested fields near Indian villages where they had their dwelling and some sort of business. There were also miners who needed to grow maize to feed slaves and Indian laborers in regions where that staple was not easily come by. Over a period of years beginning in 1538, for example, the Pérez de Bocanegra family was granted a number of holdings around their encomiendas at Apaseo and Acámbaro, on the northern border of Michoacán, and in 1544, a mine owner, Martín de Pisueta of Sultepec, was given two caballerías alongside his smelter, in the area where he had "cut down a section of forest" and "cleared land in order to sow maize and wheat . . . to feed his slaves and dependents."

Grants were handed out in many cases for reasons other than economic: A keen concern for the country's development did not prevent some viceroys from following the custom that made the *merced* a reward for services rendered, especially when those services were military. The conquistadors, who were to be favored in every way possible, had a right to two caballerías each, regardless of their occupation. Even though this sort of reward could not compare with the deed to an encomienda or with an official appointment, like that of corregidor, a few powerful personages and the members of the viceregal household were in an excellent position not only to obtain such rewards but also to develop the land that they thus acquired. (We shall see how they frequently got hold of grants originally distributed to conquistadors' widows, dowerless girls, or impoverished men; also, how well-to-do Spaniards bought up large quantities of land from the Indians.) Except for several sugar refineries, the grants made by the early viceroys were always on a modest scale, as prescribed by royal decrees. By the turn of the century, however, they had become often very large. The spirit of the decrees was further violated in some cases by the simultaneous issuance of land grants and of authorizations for the sale of the granted properties.

What was most important of all was to have a sufficient labor force, as Viceroy Mendoza had observed. But in the years following the promulgation of the New Laws, Indian slavery was abolished and the services required of the native communities were reduced. Consequently, many allotments lay fallow and farm development fell far behind the issuance of land grants, which continued to multiply.

CROPS OF THE PLATEAU: WHEAT

Constant vigilance was required of the viceroys if they were to keep the Spaniards' Republic supplied with food, particularly wheat. By the middle of the sixteenth century, they were trying to keep the expansion of cattle raising within reasonable limits, while doing their utmost to improve the condition of agriculture, which was still far from flourishing. "It is now up to the Spaniards to grow wheat," Mendoza wrote his successor; "let your lordship support them by granting them land . . ." Wheat of the best quality was harvested on caballerías worked by slaves or Indians owing labor services, either within town limits or slightly beyond, in those areas where fertile, well-watered land was reasonably close to consumer centers, such as Mexico City or a few of the mine towns. Enterprising men like the magistrate Tejada even opened up irrigation canals in the Mexico City and Puebla regions, in which some of the land lacked only water to be productive.

In addition to their white bread, some Spaniards would have liked to have ready at hand their own wine and oil, which had to be shipped at great expense from Spain. In Atlixco, several Puebla residents planted grapevines by the thousands; others wrote to the King proposing the planting of olive groves. The Crown deliberately withheld encouragement of both projects, lest Mexican production reduce trade with Spain, deprive the royal treasury of its export taxes, and weaken the ties between the mother country and overseas possessions. Although it is hard to find the secret instructions that must have been sent to the viceroys on the subject, continual references do exist to prohibitions against planting. These apparently were issued only after several decades had passed. The fact remains that even today, despite a favorable climate and a partially Mediterranean population, the plateaus of Mexico bear few grapes and fewer olives.

Around the middle of the sixteenth century, silk production occupied a considerable place in New Spain's economy. Near Puebla, many mulberry trees were planted; a single estate at Huejotzingo contained 40,000 of them before 1550. Cortés, among others, had large plantations, and in several regions, Mixteca for example, even the Indians began to harvest considerable quantities of silk. According to Viceroy Martín Enríquez, total production reached approximately 20,000 pounds in 1573, supporting an active textile industry that had originated in Puebla. Despite encouragement from the King, this prosperity was short-lived: silk-stuffs from the Philippines undersold the Mexican products, so that by the seventeenth century the industry had completely disappeared.

Fruit trees were planted at Atlixco, Cuernavaca, and elsewhere, furnishing Mexico City with oranges and lemons. The inhabitants of certain regions manufactured *agua de azahar,* or orange-blossom water, and those delicious fruit confections which are even more popular in Mexico than in Spain. The monasteries made a specialty of orchards like the ones, cool and laden with fruit, that Father Alonso Ponce visited with such pleasure in the course of his long travels [in the late sixteenth century].

On the plateaus, however, Spanish farmers grew almost nothing but wheat, in conformity with viceregal policy. A caballería under cultivation and a wheat field were, in the sixteenth century, nearly synonymous in that region. Because of the lack of oxen and agricultural implements, the natives' traditional method for sowing maize was used for wheat: A couple of grains were dropped into a hole drilled by a *coa,* or digging stick. Later, the plow came into general use, and quantities of plow-shares were shipped from Spain—more than 12,000 in 1597 alone. Yet in defiance of the conditions required of grantees, only a small portion of each 43-hectare allotment was seeded, and sometimes not even that, the whole being left to sheep. To a larger extent than in Castile, vast areas lay fallow in districts where Spaniards had been given hundreds of caballerías, each one capable of producing at least 1,000 fanegas of wheat (550 hectoliters), and more when irrigation, as at Atlixco, made two yearly crops feasible.

Whether or not he exploited his caballería, the Spaniard was not satisfied with a single grant, which was worth a mere twenty to fifty pesos in the Mexico City area around 1550. Larger units consequently began to appear near the capital and slightly to the north, in Tacuba, Chalco, Tlalnepantla, Cuautitlán, Tepotzotlán, Huehuetoca, and similar places. They also multiplied along the highway to Vera Cruz, a region in which the needs of travelers, land convoys, and even ships could be easily supplied. The original inhabitants of Puebla extended their activities and holdings first to Atlixco, and then to Huejotzingo, Cholula, Tepeaca, and Tecamachalco, places where abundant Indian labor was available.

Most Spaniards living in these villages were cultivators, either as proprietors, sharecroppers, or bailiffs for rich Mexico City and Puebla citizens. The bailiffs, whether hired managers or tenant farmers, seem to have been more numerous on the estates located north of the capital; in the Puebla–Atlixco region, where hundreds of Spaniards were already settled by the last quarter of the sixteenth century, owner-managers predominated. The narrow Atlixco Valley alone was harvesting about 100,000 fanegas of wheat (55,000 hectoliters) yearly; it was so specialized that the proprietors had banned cattle raising. Travelers like Father Alonso Ponce were amazed to observe sowing, weeding, reaping, and threshing all going on at the same time in adjacent fields. In nearby San Pablo Valley, 60 Spaniards were able to raise 70,000 or 80,0000 fanegas (some 40,000 hectoliters). To be sure, this region was in the sixteenth century by far the richest and best cultivated in all Mexico; it not only supplied the Spanish fleet (whose needs were in excess of 40,000 fanegas, according to Viceroy Velasco II) but exported wheat to Havana and other parts of the Antilles. Sheep raising and even some weaving were carried on in conjunction with the growing of wheat, since sheep were easier to control than cattle and did not endanger the harvest.

In the Mexico City district around 1563–1564, there were 115 farmers, some sowing from 200 to 400 fanegas of grain, but most sowing only 30, 40, or 60. (One caballería required, under normal conditions, 69 fanegas of seed.) In many surrounding Indian villages, especially to the north, Spaniards had settled. In 1569, there were 16 farms, most of them producing crops, others both crops and livestock, in the region of Huehuetoca and two neighboring hamlets. The same year, Tepotzotlán had ten, which were located 1, 1½, or 2 leagues from the village. Ten years later, there were 13 farmers living at Coatepec–Chalco, and so on. In 1602, the judge in charge of labor distribution for Tepotzotlán listed 96 crop-raising haciendas in his district, a large one extending northward from Tlalnepantla to Tepeji and Tula. In the same district, 13,477 fanegas of wheat (some 7,400 hectoliters), 1,952 fanegas of oats, and a little maize were sown—considerably larger amounts, it seems, than 20 or 30 years before. Some of the proprietors were rich residents of Mexico City who had a steward, or sometimes a tenant farmer, in charge; others, of more modest means, appear to have run their estates themselves and to have lived either on their haciendas or near by.

Toward Toluca in the west, in Michoacán near Valladolid, Pátzcuaro, and Zamora, and at Guadalajara, wheat fields were also to be found, but fewer and smaller as the distance from the capital increased. In some of the warm, low-lying zones, wheat was replaced, as we shall see, by sugar plantations and refineries.

Wheat production increased slowly throughout the sixteenth century, but from year to year the crop varied greatly. One of the Viceroys' constant concerns, as has already been mentioned, was therefore to encourage farmers, whose situation was still precarious and of whom there were still too few to supply the country's needs in bad harvest years. In times of crop failure or shortage of native labor, they would abandon farming to raise livestock. They would also become mule drivers, convoy escorts or cattle dealers, or else they would flock back to Mexico City, hoping to find easier living conditions.

Drastic fluctuations in wheat prices point to an economy that is not yet stabilized. To a greater extent than in Europe, a poor crop could send prices sky-high and the lack of transportation could cause them to vary considerably from one region to the next. The whites could always fall back upon the Indians' maize if wheat was lacking, and, in the event of a general shortage, the whites were obviously the last to suffer. Meat was always plentiful; the physician Juan de Cárdenas observed in 1591 that Spaniards of the Indies were well fed and were never exposed to famines as in Europe.

In Mexico City, which was the only large comsumer center, the price of grain and bread, which was controlled, dropped almost steadily from 1529–1531 to about 1542. This must have been due to an increase in the area of land under cultivation, since during the same period prices were mounting in Spain. After that, the price leveled off and even began to climb. After some wavering, between 1550 and 1555 the rise became sharper in spite of price ceilings and requisitions. In 1556, one real no longer bought ten or twelve one-pound loaves of bread, but eight, six, or as few as four. A fanega of grain, which was pegged at three to six reals, jumped to twelve reals at the same period. A number of contemporary accounts offer widely varying explanations for this increase in food prices. Besides a general tendency toward inflation owing to the masses of silver being extracted from the mines, we must mention the serious situation arising from attempts to apply (over the Spaniards' protests) those sections of the New Laws dealing with the abolition of Indian slavery, the reduction in personal labor services, and the like.

It was impossible, too, for Mexico City not to feel the effects—though considerably softened by distance—of the economic chaos then reigning in New Galicia. The discovery of Zacatecas and other rich deposits had occasioned a general stampede to the empty spaces of the arid northwest. Food shortages had resulted in all the new mining communities, accompanied by a fantastic rise of prices in New Galicia. An inspector general's detailed report, dating from 1550 and buttressed by a series of sworn statements, reveals the extent of the calamity even in a fairly fertile region like Guadalajara, 300 kilometers from the closest mine. Licenciado La Marcha, the inspector, seems not to have seen the reasons for the trouble, which emerge clearly enough from his own report. Various witnesses called up for the inquiry mentioned in passing that at Zacatecas prices had risen even more sharply than at Guadalajara. According to one, maize was being sold there for six times what it cost at Guadalajara, where even so its price had increased tenfold in three years. In other words, the price of maize was sixty times higher at Zacatecas in 1550 than it had been at Guadalajara in 1547. Other agricultural products had also risen, but proportionately less; again at Guadalajara, wheat was fetching five times as much as it had three years before.

For a number of years the inflation continued to worsen around the mines located beyond Zacatecas. If we may give credence to Francisco de Ibarra's report of services rendered, a single fanega of maize had sold at the San Martín mines for "48 or 50 pesos"—a fantastic ratio of 1/600 in relation to prices obtaining at Guadalajara seven or eight years before. Actually, evidence is somewhat conflicting except with regard to the exorbitant prices prevalent at the time. They naturally fluctuated wildly in these northern regions, where food had to be brought from "130 leagues" to the south, over roads infested with nomads and impassable in the rainy season.

The incredibly high cost of living finally brought about its own solution, since it incited the Spaniards to resist the lure of the mines, solve the native labor problem, and raise wheat and maize. Some mining outfits were run in conjunction with food-producing haciendas. Ibarra and others were successful in recruiting farmers for the founding of Nombre de Dios and Durango in 1563, followed by Jerez, Saltillo, and other towns. San Juan del Río and San Bartolomé filled up with farmers and cattle raisers who had drifted in more or less of their own free will, because they knew that they could sell their wheat, maize, and livestock at a good profit. Although prices soon returned to a relatively normal level, they remained high in the northern mining regions. Zacatecas became one of the best-stocked towns in the country; its bread, according to Mota y Escobar and other travelers, was all white, of excellent flavor, and made of the finest wheat.

After the above crisis, which did not greatly affect Mexico City, grain prices in the central region became more stable; but they continued to follow an upward trend. In 1576–1578 they spurted again. The fanega, formerly worth 10, 12, or 15 reals, went to 20 and 25. The fact that it stayed so high in the capital tends to prove that more is involved than a simple crop failure, namely, the terrible 1576–1577 epidemic, which wiped out a large number of natives. All the geographical accounts of the years 1579–1580 bear witness to the alarming shrinkage of the Indian population and the farmers' shortage of hands. Seeing that their wheat was lost because there was no one to weed or harvest it, they planted less land; some even abandoned their farms. On several occasions, Viceroy Martín Enríquez reported this gloomy situation to the King.

The white population, on the other hand, was constantly increasing and at the same time, naturally, so was the demand for wheat. In the seventeenth century farmers became more numerous north of Mexico City and south and west of Tlaxcala and Puebla especially, at Atlixco (where 90 haciendas were producing 150,000 fanegas by 1632), at Amozoc, Tepeaca, and so on. They spread to Huamantla, Nopaluca, and San Salvador, and put under cultivation a number of estancias near San Juan de los Llanos, as well as elsewhere in the region. In other areas harvest land was particularly extensive around Zamora, founded by order of Martín Enríquez in 1574, and in the Bajío. The Spaniards there, located as they were between Mexico City and the northern mines, could easily dispose of their wheat and cattle. When the Guanajuato deposits were discovered, these farmers had markets even closer. Early in the seventeenth century grain prices steadied or dropped off. At the same time, large numbers of farmers appeared at Querétaro, Celaya, León, Silao, Irapuato, Salamanca, Guatzindeo (Salvatierra), Valle de Santiago, and other localities. Even without Indian labor allotments, some communities and individuals prospered. Religious orders and a few powerful notables developed large farming haciendas. The Augustinians at San Nicolás, the Pérez de Bocanegra (or Villamayor) family near Apaseo, the Villaseñor, López de Peralta, Ponce de León, Mateos, and (slightly later) Rincón de Gallardo families created estates, many of which were irrigated and highly productive.

During the first decades of the seventeenth century, a single hacienda —San Nicolás, located near Yuriria—harvested a yearly crop of as much as 10,000 fanegas of grain (5,500 hectoliters). The inhabitants of Celaya, on the other hand, raised only 17,000 or 18,000 fanegas in 1580 and 30,000 around 1600. But thanks to more intensive farming, the figure went much higher by 1644–1645, when the settlers there paid His Majesty the generous sum of 20,000 pesos to legalize their title deeds—as much as was paid by all the inhabitants of the rich Atlixco Valley. According to Father Basalenque, whose figures are always extremely precise, by the middle of the seventeenth century 150,000 fanegas (82,000 hectoliters) were being harvested yearly within a radius of eight leagues of Salamanca.

In the order of their importance, the wheat-producing regions were: Puebla–Atlixco–Tepeaca, the wide Bajío Valley and northern part of Michoacán, the areas immediately north and west of Mexico City, and various localities in New Galicia and New Viscaya. "For lack of [nearby] markets," Oaxaca and more distant regions produced only enough wheat for local consumption. When the native white and mestizo populations, great consumers of tortillas and *pulque*, reached certain proportions, maize and maguey took their place beside wheat in the caballerías.

Despite a few bad years, prices in the seventeenth century tended to remain steady. The reasons for this stability may be found in the growing number of *alhóndigas*, or municipal granaries (which prevented hoarding and regulated the amount of grain that could be placed on the market); small, stable groups of whites and mestizos settled throughout the rural areas; and, above all, the gradual formation of the new hacienda economy.

Mexico was even threatened with a surplus of wheat, a rare occurrence at that period of the world's history. In the Bajío, it was at times so plentiful that "If Our Lord does not quickly cause the number of consumers to multiply," Father Basalenque writes around 1640, "farmers will of necessity, given the present rate of production, become even poorer than they are now. And so, I say that Our Lord does not will the establishment of the [projected] water conduit north of Salamanca, because there surely will not be enough people to eat that much more bread." The farmers' poverty and the swelling of their numbers at such a late date coincided with the decline of the great mines; partly abandoned, these could no longer absorb the neighboring regions' produce or afford Spaniards the same financial opportunities as before. Although the decline barely disturbed the areas supplying Mexico City, its effects were clearly visible northward in the Bajío and New Galicia.

This return to the land, associated with impoverishment and a partially closed economy, is one aspect of the general recession affecting the Spanish Indies in the seventeenth century.

A number of questions remain to be answered: Since the Spanish or Creole farmers did not plow, how was the land worked? How did the caballería—tilled by Indian slaves or work gangs—evolve into the hacienda as it existed by the middle of the seventeenth century? What were the stages of the transition, and particularly what were the first rural units—restricted to a few favored regions—in which wheat was grown?

In the second half of the sixteenth century, a new word came into use to designate agricultural enterprises: *estancias,* either *de labor* (plowland) or *de pan llevar* (wheatland). The estancias owed their existence to the native labor services, which after 1549 were taken away from the encomenderos and distributed for the most part among Spanish wheat growers, who were in greater need of laborers than were the cattle raisers, whose flocks roamed at will. The history of the first estancias is consequently almost indistinguishable from that of the repartimientos supplying them with their indispensable native work crews. When the services required of the Indian communities were modified, then reduced, and finally abolished, the almost imperceptible transition had been made to the classical hacienda; a new labor system had replaced the original one.

The repartimiento system undoubtedly brought about improvements in the Indians' working conditions, which were then supervised by officers of the Crown and courts rather than by the employers themselves, who would evade the Indian protection laws when they could. Economically, the repartimientos were also beneficial, since the authorities restricted their labor force to those farmers whose enterprises were judged "useful to the Republic." First tried out in Puebla, the system appears to have spread from there in the second half of the sixteenth century. Theoretically, the force was made up each week of four per cent of the Indians owing tribute in each village. In densely populated regions, consequently, farmers had ample labor, but this was not the case near the nomad zone. Celaya farmers were given a hundred Indian workers, and this small number was cut in 1591 to fifty, who were available only during the two busiest months.

The Crown, however, agreed with the religious orders in wishing to eliminate all forced labor and restore to the Indians the unconditional freedom which philosophers held to be their right. This was one of the Crown's main goals, especially in the last quarter of the sixteenth century. By that time, personal labor services were no longer required anywhere, but on the other hand, the native population had been greatly reduced by epidemics. Acting on the initiative of the Viceroy, Archbishop Moya de Contreras, a council of theologians discussed the matter in 1584. The Jesuits were ready to accept half-measures, but the Franciscans and other orders lashed out at the repartimientos, declaring them to be both illegal and contrary to natural law. They were willing to allow, at the most, temporary labor measures in order to save the Spaniards' estates from ruin while they adjusted to new conditions.

Recognizing the grave abuses to which the system did in fact give rise, the Crown was ready to abolish it. Around 1590–1594, the Council of the Indies carried on a lengthy correspondence with Viceroy Velasco II, urging him to take the first steps in the transition. The plan called for an increase in the employment of free workers called *gañanes* or *naborías*, but the Indians' reluctance to hire themselves out on Spaniards' lands, whatever the wages offered, was a stumbling block. Hence the Viceroy's retort to the Council in 1594: "Inasmuch as Indians and work are natural enemies and they avoid it as far as possible, obviously not one would work if he were not forced to do so and all would be lost." When the Council insisted, he had recourse to the same argument: "The Indians will never work or hire themselves out, even ten per cent of them, unless force is used. The same would be, and is, true for their own holdings beyond their immediate needs and those of their families." At the same time, the Viceroy acknowledged that "the number of Spaniards grows apace each day; the resultant increase in importance of harvest lands and public works and building projects, secular and ecclesiastical, coupled with the alarming shrinkage of the native population, makes it extremely difficult to support so large a structure with so small a labor force."

As a temporary measure, the authorities fell back on lightening the Indians' burden under the obligatory system. The minimum wage was raised from three or four reals, depending on the region, to six. Although Viceroy Villamanrique still did not reduce the number of natives subject to the repartimientos, he did claim, in 1590, that he had limited the call-up to weeding and harvest time. Negro slaves were imported, while native labor was used exclusively for agriculture and in some mines. This measure had been applied earlier in regions like Atlixco, where the demand for farm hands was heavy. In 1599, the sugar refinery repartimientos were abolished entirely, so that a part of the labor thus saved might be set to growing wheat.

A sufficient supply of farm workers was ensured under these new arrangements, but at the expense of the weaving, sugar, and other industries which the state considered less useful or even superfluous. Such a policy, although creditable to the Crown, certainly crippled New Spain's agricultural and industrial development. Perhaps there was also a certain satisfaction in reducing a degree of productivity that was beginning to threaten exports from the mother country.

Further changes followed. On November 24, 1601, an important royal cédula, whose conditions had been under discussion for ten years, replaced the old repartimiento system. Under it the Indians were allocated to landowners by special magistrates, with the simple requirement that natives must hire themselves out, but to employers of their choice. The same rule applied as well to unemployed Spaniards and mestizos. Universal acceptance of so radical a transformation did not come at once. Twenty years later, obligatory services were still in existence around Guadalajara and in various outlying districts. Elsewhere, the methods used by the "judge in charge of hiring" were often indistinguishable from those of the "allocating judge," and so much pressure was exerted in requisitioning labor that it was sometimes hard to tell the new system from the old. The repartimiento's survival was implicitly recognized in 1609, when obligatory services were formally forbidden, except for work in the fields and certain mines. On the other hand, the reform did take effect, though slowly, in a number of heavily populated regions; Indians gathered in the village squares to take service with employers of their choice. The result was a favoring of estates on which natives were well treated.

Starting in 1627, several more royal cédulas were devoted to the problem, recalling the disastrous effects of forced labor on the native population. Viceroy Cerralvo took the final step and abolished all repartimientos (December 31, 1632), save temporarily in the mines. With some measure of success, he and his immediate successor strove for enforcement. After more than a century of unceasing effort, the Crown seemed to be approaching its goal: free working conditions for its Indian vassals.

Without compulsion, however, the Indians showed no greater inclination to work as farm hands. Since the estancias had to have labor, a curious compensatory phenomenon took place. Landed proprietors had found quite early that they could hire a few free workers to increase the number of hands supplied by the authorities. Now they attracted other natives to settle on their estates by diverse means, most often by advancing sums that the Indians could never pay back. Similar practices had been adopted somewhat earlier, as we shall see, in the Bajío and northern districts, where only nomads were available.

Such serfdom through debt became a full-fledged institution in the seventeenth century under the hacienda economy. During the sixteenth century and part of the seventeenth (the length of time depending on the region), the farming estancia was thus marked by the presence of Indian crews who, when it was their turn and the work was the heaviest, would come from neighboring villages under the surveillance of the allocating judge. On each estate, the number of persons impressed varied from a handful to a score or so according to the estate's importance and its owner's influence.

Although each caballería contained 43 hectares, the Spaniards very early acquired more than one. By repeated grants, by purchases from other grantees and caciques, or, even more simply, by taking over unoccupied lands, some of them managed to accumulate estates of three, eight, fifteen or more caballerías. At Tepeaca, for example, a six-caballería farm was in 1600 classified as "average." Wheat and sheep raising were often combined in order to utilize the stubble. In that event, the estancia was called *de labor y ganados* (fields and live-stock) and had added to its caballerías one or more *sitios*, or grazing areas, of 780 hectares each. When agriculture became more intensive, some *sitios* were partly plowed—with or without the authorities' permission. These were the largest farms, for a single *sitio* contained the same land area as eighteen caballerías. Most of the farms destined to grow into great wheat haciendas were officially recorded as being for grazing rather than crop raising. Out of ten estates around Tepotzotlán which were made up exclusively of harvest land, seven possessed in 1569 title deeds as sheep estancias only. Conversely, through negligence or lack of labor, caballerías were sometimes given over to sheep in defiance of existing regulations.

On the estancias, we know that only a small portion of land was cultivated each year. From 50 to 100 fanegas of grain were sown—sometimes, but rarely, as much as 300 or 400—and a crop harvested of twelve or fifteen times that amount. Irrigation, apparently already known to the Aztecs, was developed on a local scale; canals were dug in the vicinity of Mexico City and Atlixco and in parts of the Bajío. Excellent crops were also obtained on virgin land and well-watered sections, but the farming done on the plateau was as a rule far less intensive.

Some of the estancias were not even inhabited the year round. A few Indians or Negro slaves lived on the others, and sometimes (but not always) a family of Spaniards. In 1569, there were only sixty permanent residents on eight estates located near Huehuetoca. The same proportion held for the entire zone north of the capital. The farmers of Tepotzotlán, for example, "come and go . . . , because their place of residence is Mexico City; some live on their estates a couple of years or whatever length of time they feel like spending there." If we may believe contemporary statistics, only 200 Spanish farmers dwelt on the 150 estancias of the archbishopric of Mexico City, in comparison with 8,000 in the capital itself. Many of the country dwellers were actually stewards, tenant farmers, or sharecroppers, since only the poorest owners lived on their land the year around; one, for example, "is in debt and therefore stays in the country," while another states that he is "confined" to his estancia, "not having the wherewithal to own a house in Mexico City."

This situation was peculiar to the region around the capital, the only big town in the country and a center of attraction. Elsewhere, the proportion of farmers living on their estates was always much higher. Six hundred out of 1,200 white and mestizo proprietors in Michoacán were residents; in the Puebla area, "more than 200 Spaniards" were scattered throughout the Atlixco Valley. The fact that they moved into the Villa de Carrión (now Atlixco) when it was founded in 1579 showed that, even in districts which were perfectly safe, community living was invariably preferred.

Except for a few very large estates and sugar refineries, construction outlays consequently went for town houses, at least until well into the seventeenth century. That is why almost no trace remains of estancia buildings. Usually made of adobe, sometimes of stone, they were almost without exception roofed with straw or shingles. The following contract of 1575 between the Marqués del Valle and a Spaniard from Oaxtepec will give an idea of their value and appearance: For a three-year period, the second party was given the use of two un- plowed caballerías, which twenty years before had been bought from the Indians for the considerable sum of 600 pesos. In exchange, he was to "make them into an estate," put the land under cultivation, and build at his expense "a house having an outside gallery and a room 60 by 18 feet; also, a granary with wooden uprights and walls to support it, and a thatch or shingle roof; finally, alongside the threshing floor, a shed 60 by 20 feet and a cattle stockade." This outside gallery, or *portal*, is still typical of many houses in rural Mexico.

TROPICAL CROPS AND SUGAR CANE

In sharp contrast to the temperate plateaus, the deep-cut valleys, the coastal plains, and the terraced slopes above them produce abundantly wherever there is water. Wheat gives way to tropical crops, although it may still grow beside sugar cane halfway down to sea level. Avoid- ing the lowlands, which were often fertile but unhealthy, the Spaniards planted their cane in the cooler inland valleys. Sugar refining was to become New Spain's biggest agrarian industry. A few settlers grew cacao in some areas, as well as indigo, which was principally exported to Spain. Cochineal (*grana*), another export, was a specialty of certain native villages on the plateau.

Quite early, cacao plantations were established and operated on the Pacific slope by encomenderos and inhabitants of the new towns of

Purificación and Colima, and the ports of Zacatula, Huatulco, and Acapulco. They also appeared in various warm regions near Oaxaca, Tabasco, and, especially, Soconusco, toward the Guatemalan border. In other words, these plantations were isolated units, strung out over hundreds of leagues. Crops were all the more lucrative since cacao beans had served the Aztecs as currency, and continued after the Conquest to be accepted "like copper coins in Castile." An attempt was even made to fix the official value of 140 beans to the silver real, or 1,120 to the peso. The value of a load of 24,000 beans ranged from 5 to 25 pesos depending on time and place. Prices were naturally higher on the plateaus than in the producing regions, and in the second half of the sixteenth century they rose rapidly everywhere. Demand was constantly on the increase, especially in Mexico City. Cacao was shipped there in several ways: directly by Indian porter or muleback, or by small coasters that would unload in a port closest to the capital.

Some cacao plantations were operated under the repartimiento system, while others used Negro and Indian slaves. Some raised cotton at the same time, and all prospered until the great epidemics in the last quarter of the sixteenth century, which wiped out a large part of the labor force, particularly in the lowland areas. In 1570, the Englishman John Chilton referred to the few rich planters in distant Soconusco; the region was then exporting annually 4,000 loads worth more than 21 pesos apiece, while on the other side of the Isthmus the port of Santa María de la Victoria shipped some 3,000 loads of cacao beans picked in Tabasco. According to a Guatemalan Audiencia judge writing in 1576, the province of Los Izalcos sold most of its total production of 50,000 loads in New Spain, close by, but some of that figure must have been made up of tributes and the production of native communities.

When the native population dropped off, some cacao plantations were badly crippled, but the demand was greater than ever. Prices moved upward, so that in spite of operating difficulties, some planters and traders, in Colima and other areas, continued to amass fortunes running from 50,000 to 200,000 ducats, according to Father Tello. By the end of the sixteenth century, chocolate had become the Creoles' favorite beverage, and sizeable amounts were being shipped to Spain, where those who had come back after making good in the New World (the "Americans," or *indianos*, as they were called) spread its fame. In seventeenth-century Spain, it was all the rage, to judge by the pamphlets and treatises "In Praise of Chocolate" published at the time. Then, prices plummeted in the face of competition from Peruvian cacao, which came by the shipload from Guayaquil to Acapulco, Seville, and other ports.

Unlike cacao, indigo growing was an entirely Spanish venture. Planted relatively late, this dye became a valuable tender allowing regions without mineral wealth to obtain European products in exchange. It gave a handsome violet-blue that was superior to woad and was in great demand in Spain. A certain Pedro de Ledesma, about 1561, was "its first inventor," in the phrase of Viceroy Martín Enríquez writing to His Majesty. Ledesma was granted a monopoly and soon afterward went into partnership with the Marqués del Valle to develop an industry at Yautepec, near Cuernavaca. Although business looked promising and the Marqués had made nearly 2,000 pesos by 1570, the company was dissolved before 1572. The Viceroy was unwilling to extend the monopoly beyond that date, for, as he explained, indigo appeared to require a large labor force and a single indivdual could not satisfy the demand.

Thereafter, indigo could be grown by anyone and spread rapidly in certain warm areas, especially Yucatan, despite the "violent opposition of the bishop, friars, and Indian commissioner" arising from the strenuous tasks required of the Indians. As early as 1577, "many encomenderos are raising indigo in the villages within their encomiendas and putting their Indians to work at it"; this, in defiance of the abolition of personal services and owing to the lack of Negro slaves. There were in Yucatan at the time more than 48 indigo mills, which had cost as much as 2,000 to 3,000 pesos apiece and were sometimes whole factories on a small scale. Each had its *noria*, or water wheel, turned by mules; one or several boilers for cooking the indigo (later eliminated when it was discovered that the fermenting leaves cooked the mash sufficiently); wheels equipped with blades for beating the paste obtained; settling and drying basins, and so on.

The plants were delicate and required much care. They were a perennial, lasting two or three years, and producing four crops of leaves yearly. In 1576, the first mills produced 600 arrobas of indigo, all of which was shipped to Spain. The industry went on expanding, realizing large profits for the settlers, in spite of royal cédulas in 1579 and 1581 prohibiting repartimientos and the "stubborn opposition" of some ecclesiastics. In 1609, the Vera Cruz fleet sailed away with 11,660 arrobas on board worth 546,562 pesos—for those times an enormous sum.

In spite of many vicissitudes, notably in Yucatan, indigo production (like that of another dye, campeachy wood) was to remain one of tropical Mexico's most important resources. In regions such as lower Michoacán, installations similar to the original ones could still be found until aniline dyes made their appearance in this century.

Sugar cane was, however, the most important of the tropical and semitropical crops grown by the Spaniards. First transplanted from the Canary Islands to the Antilles, it had done well there. The island colonists had grown accustomed to eating sugar as a substitute for wheat, and they quickly recognized its superiority over honey and similar European products. The newcomers naturally planted cane fields very early on the American continent, where demand kept pace with the steadily increasing Creole population.

Estate owners were only too eager to replace their wheat with sugar cane whenever the climate permitted. As early as 1547 or 1548, three rich farmers of Atlixco were denounced to the King by their less affluent neighbors for having done that very thing. By the end of the century, the tendency had gained momentum. Wheat, considered a primary commodity, was subject to price ceilings and requisitions by the authorities which often left producers only a narrow margin of profit; sugar, on the other hand, was a luxury product sold on the open market and fetching high prices because of the growing demand.

Father Acosta noted before 1600 that "the amount of candy and jam consumed in the Indies is absolutely fantastic," even though for years sugar had been going to Seville from Vera Cruz in huge quantities. Even today, probably more sweets are eaten in Mexico than anywhere else. Nevertheless, the authorities kept the European point of view and looked on sugar as an unnecessary indulgence—"good only for superfluous confectionery and drinks," as one viceroy wrote in an attempt to justify the abolition of compulsory labor in the cane fields.

There was another side to the picture. Wheat was grown on estates which required little capital investment and had low operating expenses; sugar refineries were from the start, in New Spain as in the Antilles, huge semi-agricultural, semi-industrial enterprises employing hundreds of Indians and Negroes. Mills were of two kinds: *ingenios*, driven by water wheels, and *trapiches*, utilizing oxen or mules in the absence of sufficient water power. The power was used to set hardwood rollers in motion, which crushed the cane; the juice then flowed into boilers, where it was reduced to molasses. This was treated in various ways before being left to harden in molds or cut into strips in a tank. Some old mills of this sort are still running in Michoacán. Excepting hand-operated mills and similar family undertakings (a few of which also survive), the smallest *trapiche* was a real business in a modest way and needed at least fifteen men to keep it in continual operation during the months that followed cutting time. In addition, cane requires intensive cultivation—constant attention, deep furrows, irrigation—and consequently a large number of hands besides animals and equipment. It took capital, large or small, to be able to own a sugar mill.

As early as the sixteenth century, an extremely detailed inventory (one of the many that the lawyers who ran the country delighted in compiling) gives us a glimpse of operations at the large refinery of Orizaba, with its complete stock of irons, caldrons, kettles, and copper pots; a fully outfitted smithy and woodworking shop for maintenance; the mill itself; the building containing the presses (*casa de prensa*); the boiler house; two refining sheds (*casas de purgar*) with 34 platforms (*barbacoas*) and two tanks; scores of oxen, plows, and carts; two herds of mules (of 37 and 22 head); and especially, as we will see, a number of slaves.

Like the cattle estancias, these sugar mills originated in the Antilles, perhaps even in the Canary Islands. Cortés—always full of new projects —seems to have been the first to plant cane on the continent, at Tuxtla (near Vera Cruz) and later on his domain, where he had several large refineries. Sometime before 1535, Rodrigo de Albornoz, a royal accountant, followed his example, refining sugar on quite a large scale in the Cempoala region; he had also received permission to import two lots of Negro slaves, one of 100, another of 50, to be apportioned among his various enterprises.

About a decade later, Albornoz, wishing to establish a new refinery near Vera Cruz, requested "the amount of land customarily given for this purpose in Española." In consideration of the benefit that the entire country would derive from the refinery, the Viceroy approved the grant in principle, "in the most suitable place." The grant did not involve mere caballerías, but a vast area lying between two rivers in the Jalapa region, which the alcalde mayor of the province picked out. The Indians opposed the grant, however, because of the brutalities visited upon them by the Negroes, "as experience has revealed at said royal accountant's refinery in Cempoala, the province having been entirely laid waste and its population decimated." At about the same time (1543–1544), another powerful notable, Gonzalo de Salazar, who was regidor of Mexico City and later became royal factor, obtained viceregal confirmation of his purchase of twenty caballerías from the Indians of Taximaroa (his Michoacán encomienda), where he intended to install the refinery of San Juan Zitácuaro.

From Spain, instructions were sent Luis de Velasco and Martín Enríquez to promote the growing of sugar cane and distribute land to prospective refinery builders. Although grants were moderate under the two cautious viceroys mentioned, they had grown larger again by the end of the sixteenth century. Always implicitly included, of course, was a repartimiento proportionate to the surface allotted. In 1584, for example, during an interim of Audiencia rule, a licenciado named Luis de Villanueva Zapata, son of a judge of the same name, was given for a refinery not only forty caballerías, together with the water rights, but also four cattle estancias and permission to cut wood for his boilers in adjacent areas, that is, the entire four-league length of the Colontla Valley as well as the surrounding forests. This large landowner, who was also a lawyer, was to protect the Indians' interests in his capacity as viceregal assessor to their tribunal. The same year, two well-to-do men of prominence, Don Luis Ponce de León and Judge Palacio—the latter in the name of his brother, Lope de Palacio—each obtained twenty caballerías for mills.

The large cane grants admittedly went to capitalists and men of influence, but they alone could assume the expense of refinery construction. We know that it cost as much as 50,000 pesos to build one in the sixteenth century and considerably more in the seventeenth. On the Marqués del Valle's domain, where the question of land distribution rights went long unsettled, it was always the same individuals who, on their own responsibility and somewhat irregularly, concluded long-term leases with, or purchases from, the Indians in order to establish refineries.

To compensate for land lost to wheat in warm areas, where farmers had substituted cane, refinery repartimientos were abolished in 1599 and all hands diverted to wheat raising and other ventures classified as indispensable. Prior to this measure, which when it came was to be only partly enforced, sugar refineries had spread rapidly throughout New Spain. South of the capital, a highly favored zone was the Cuernavaca basin, where the Cortés family owned the great refinery at Tlaltenango and a share in the one at Coajomulco. At the beginning of the seventeenth century, there were twelve or fifteen more, belonging to private citizens, around Zacualpan, Cuautla–Amilpas, Oaxtepec, Yautepec, Tlacotepec, and Jojutla, as well as one just outside the Marqués' domain at Malinalco.

Westward, cane was grown in a few sheltered or warm regions of Michoacán, near the Lerma River and Yuriria, in the low-lying central and southern valleys especially. About a dozen large refineries were located at Taximaroa (Ciudad Hidalgo), Zitácuaro, Tingambato, Tacámbaro, Peribán, and so on. There were a few additional ones, smaller and more dispersed, near the Pacific coast and in southern New Galicia, around Juchipila and elsewhere.

To the east, the Marquesado del Valle extended toward Atlixco, and from there all the way to the Atlantic. There were large refineries in some of the particularly well-watered valleys, as for instance at Atlixco and near Huaquechula, Izúcar (Matamoros), Chiautla, and Huehuetlán. Still farther east, on the Atlantic slope, was the huge refinery of Orizaba, belonging to the family of Vivero, later ennobled with the title of count. Other refineries were scattered throughout this warm region, to take advantage of the heavier rainfall. Among them were several near Huatusco.

Lying slightly to the north, but with similar conditions, Jalapa possessed, at the beginning of the seventeenth century, at least a dozen sugar plantations scattered around the provincial capital, as well as at Chicontepec and elsewhere. The Santísima Trinidad, as far as we know the period's largest refinery, belonging to an enormously rich family of farmers, the Hernández de la Higuera, was located there. Isolated refineries were also to be found around Oaxaca and Chiapa.

According to sporadic figures, the refineries' annual sales seem to have varied, in proportion to their importance, from 3,000 or 4,000 arrobas up to as much as 20,000, that is, from 30 or 40 tons to more than 200. If we estimate at fifty or sixty the number of *ingenios* and large *trapiches* in operation throughout New Spain and its Mexican dependencies, we arrive at a yearly figure of between 300,000 and 450,000 arrobas (3,000 to 5,000 tons)—and probably more if we take into account the molasses, liquor, and raw sugar produced by smaller establishments, whose number was on the increase in the seventeenth century. Even though total production cannot have been any larger than that of a single modern refinery, it was no small amount for the period.

Since white sugar sold for one real a pound at Mexico City in 1552, the retail price of the arroba was slightly over three pesos. By 1568, that sum had become the wholesale price of the arroba delivered at Vera Cruz. The price went on rising rapidly for a while and reached six pesos the arroba in 1585, after which, with the increase in the number of refineries, it rose more slowly. During the seventeenth century, it steadied or even dropped off, ranging from place to place and year to year between 2½ and 5 pesos. The reason was that production, most of which was consumed locally, was constantly growing. After the temporary crisis arising from the 1599 labor law, plantations continued to expand. New refineries were built in Huasteca, near Tamazunchale, Valles, and Tantoyuca; in southern New Galicia, at Sayula, Autlán, and Ameca; and around Oaxaca and Santiago Nexapa. They were particularly numerous at Córdoba, as well as toward Cuautla-Yautepec and throughout the rich Marquesado. Also, price stabilization was due to a widespread phenomenon, namely, the establishment of the new hacienda economy.

In the seventeenth century, refineries were often founded by religious orders possessing the necessary capital: Dominicans, Augustinians, the Brothers of St. Hippolytus, and, particularly, the colleges of the Company of Jesus, whose specialty was converting what were already good-sized *trapiches* into large model refineries. By mid-century, some such refineries were able to pay the King, in several installments, 18,000 pesos to regularize their title deeds; others, when they changed hands, commonly fetched 80,000 to 100,000 pesos. The Jesuits were known to have spent 84,000 pesos on the enlarging of a refinery for which they had just paid 89,000. Plant efficiency was more than proportionately increased by the improvements, and their annual production soon exceeded 20,000 arrobas.

The ever-increasing size of the large refinery in the seventeenth century was paralleled, in different areas, by growing numbers of small and medium-sized operations—even of *trapichillos a mano* (tiny, hand-run mills)—which sprang up in the warm valleys of Michoacán and New Galicia, near Cuernavaca and Vera Cruz, and particularly in the districts of new Spanish towns like Córdoba, which, founded in 1616, possessed 33 by the following century.

Around 1670 or 1680, sugar production stood considerably higher then at the turn of the seventeenth century, and it is certain that by then capital investment had risen above the amount represented by the wheat haciendas. During this period of development of the Creole and mestizo population, the consumption of white bread had not kept pace with that of sugar.

The owner of a sugar plantation needed fertile land, ample water, and expensive equipment. Still more, he needed the right kind of labor. Cane growing is a delicate, strenuous operation, and the natives could not stand up to the work involved, either because it was too hard or because it required sustained effort. Experience soon proved that Negroes were more capable of handling the boilers, presses, and other steps in the refining process; besides, the law imposed severe penalties for using Indians.

Slaves came high, however. Demand was greater than supply, since, through fear of uprisings, the authorities kept the slave trade within strict bounds in New Spain. In defiance of the edicts of 1556 and 1561, which had fixed the ceiling price, first, at 120 ducats a head, then 140 (160 for slaves from the Cape Verde Islands), Negroes ordinarily sold for between 200 and 500 pesos—and much more if they were machinists, artisans, or foremen. They were even fought over after the great 1577 epidemic, which did not strike the Negro population until it was already on the wane among the Indians; according to Viceroy Martín Enríquez, numerous Spaniards lost 12, 15, or 20 slaves that year, while others lost many more. At that time, however, there were some 20,000 slaves in all, most of them in the mines or on private estates. The small minority in the sugar refineries was to increase markedly within a short time.

As early as 1549, Martín Cortés had about 60 Negroes of both sexes in his Cuernavaca refinery, in addition to some 120 Indian slaves for the lighter tasks. When, as a result of the general measures taken by the Crown and Viceroy Velasco, the latter were freed, they were replaced by other Negroes, bringing the total, by 1556, to 150, counting men, women, and children. This was one of the largest refineries in New Spain at the time, together with the one at Orizaba which, in 1580, possessed 123 Negro slaves—72 men, 44 women, and 7 children, not counting those in subsidiary undertakings.

In the other *ingenios*, as well as the larger *trapiches*, there were usually fewer slaves, and in some, none at all. However, when the native repartimientos were abolished and the capacity of new refineries continued to increase, the number of Negro workers tended to rise. In the seventeenth century, most establishments had 20, 30, or 40 head, but we begin to find some with as many as 200, for example—as early as 1606—the Santísima Trinidad refinery, near Jalapa, which, together with its vast dependencies, was appraised at 700,000 pesos and brought in an income of 40,000 a year. These were huge sums for a time when a work horse sold for six or seven pesos.

There were rarely enough slaves to keep everything going. For cultivating and harvesting, wood cutting, driving, and other such jobs, owners kept on trying to obtain repartimiento Indians; in the sixteenth century, they were usually successful. In 1551, for example, the factor Salazar was granted, for his refinery at Zitácuaro, "the Indians [from Taximaroa] required solely for cultivating said cane fields, not for tasks within the buildings of said refinery, and this, in consideration of the sum of twelve maravedís a day." It was understood, the Viceroy wrote to the native authorities, that these Indians, recruited "through hiring," would work "of their own free will rather than by the use of force."

With regard to this last point, we have seen how Viceroy Velasco and the Council of the Indies quickly lost their illusions. The Indians rarely hired themselves out of their own free will, and, if the country's entire economy was not to be destroyed, force had to be used. Owners obtained the requisite native labor through the repartimiento system: According to circumstances, they were allotted 10, 20, 40, or 60 men, each paid a weekly wage of four reals (raised to six at the end of the sixteenth century). If we are to believe Viceroy Velasco, the authorities were at least able to prevent their being employed in the boiler house, or as stokers, press workers, or cane carriers. Control over isolated or remote refineries was more difficult.

The great epidemics of the last quarter of the sixteenth century, however, had diminished the native labor supply. At the same time, the theologians and the Crown were maintaining their opposition to the forced labor system. After lengthy discussions, traces of which are preserved in viceregal correspondence between 1559 and 1601, the Count of Monterrey resolved to enact into law the radical decisions made several years before. Considering so much sugar production useless, he abolished all the industry's Indian repartimientos. Fortunately for the planters, there was one royal edict, prohibiting even voluntary Indian services and allowing only Negro labor, which he did not reenact. The same year, he forbade the founding of any new refineries or the planting of any more land to cane without special license. In 1601, finally, all voluntary Indian labor was suspended within the refineries and permitted only in the fields.

After a brief period of grace indispensable under the circumstances, special inspectors, called *veedores,* began to put the orders into execution. Special magistrates "for *ingenios* and *trapiches*" supervised working conditions on a permanent basis. Cane fields continued nonetheless to expand—with or without benefit of license—because fresh Negro slaves partly compensated for the abolition of work services and because the system of *gañanes,* or free Indian laborers (in reality debt peons), developed on the plantations earlier than on the wheat estancias, where a kind of forced labor survived for a long time.

This evolution is one of considerable importance. Thenceforth, the estates which were on the right side of the law would no longer be dependent on "distributing judges," "hiring commissioners," and other royal representatives concerned with Indian workers, but would tend to withdraw, with their slaves, servants, and retainers, behind their own boundaries, where the sole authority was that exercised by the owner, the chaplain, and the handful of Spaniards and mestizos who controlled operations: the bailiff (*mayordomo*), the chief overseer (*mandador*), the refinery director (*maese de azúcar*), and the plantation manager (*cañavero*). On the larger estates this self-sufficiency was also economic, because they included pasture for hundreds of beasts of burden, as well as for the flocks of cattle and sheep which fed and clothed an entire community of Indians and Negroes, who needed great amounts of meat in order to perform the hard tasks at hand. Such estates also had their cultivated fields, which grew the workers' maize. Above all, they had to encompass vast stretches of wooded land, or *montes,* for their great boilers devoured enormous quantities of fuel, even though the fibrous residue of the sugar cane was also burned.

Whereas the wheat estancias of the time could show only a few wretched adobe barns and rudimentary equipment, the great sugar plantations possessed imposing buildings. As early as 1549, the refinery that Cortés had established at Tlaltenango, near Cuernavaca, lodged its machinery "in a large, two-storied dwelling, strongly built of masonry," adjoining another large and sturdy edifice; all around, the servants' huts were clustered. Also among the oldest refineries, the one at Orizaba formed a veritable village in 1580, with the owner's house and the stone church, four big buildings for refining the sugar—"some spanned with two arches . . . and built of masonry with brick vaulting"—its little adobe houses for the Spaniards or Negro foremen, and its cabins for the other slaves and Indians. These huge groups of buildings were to become increasingly common in the course of the seventeenth century. The most important sugar plantations very quickly tended to form communities of a new type, quite distinct from the former native groups and practically self-sufficient. They constituted the first great feudal estates and, as early as the sixteenth century, anticipated the classical Mexican hacienda.

These observations should not lead us to hasty conclusions about the magnitude of the operations. Before the middle or end of the seventeenth century, the agricultural development just described occupied only isolated spots in a vast territory. The land under cultivation, particularly in the hot country, was never more than an infinitesimal fraction of the potential.

Despite their restricted area, however, the cultivated lands might have been able to form centers of resistance to the growth of the great estates. This is what happened, in fact, in some well-irrigated zones, such as the Atlixco Valley and certain districts allotted to communities of modest farmers, which were a patchwork of small and medium-sized holdings. Then, the sugar refineries soon monopolized all the water, pasture, and forests of the warm valleys in which they were isolated.

Elsewhere, however, owing in part to scanty rainfall, the vast cattle estancias tended to annex fields that were cultivated extensively rather than intensively. In short, except for the native communities and a few zones favorable to agriculture, cultivated lands were like tiny islands scattered here and there in the immense spaces which almost from the first the cattle barons had appropriated.

3. THE PREPONDERANCE OF CATTLE RAISING

THE BEGINNINGS

When the Spaniards landed in New Spain, they found that the natives possessed very few domestic animals. The newcomers' only supply of fresh meat in the early days was pork from the pigs that they had imported from the West Indies. Pig raising turned out to be no problem on the mainland; despite little care and almost no swineherds, the scanty droves multiplied rapidly. Around the mines, new towns, and encomienda villages, there was no lack of pasture and wooded land; and no title deeds were required, since grazing rights belonged to all in accordance with ancient Castilian custom. Native tribute furnished an abundance of maize for fattening purposes. The newcomers often had pork to eat while they were still going without bread.

Larger animals increased at a somewhat slower rate. The conquistadors had been able to bring along a very limited number of cattle, which they had to utilize without exception for hauling or plowing. As to horses, there were not enough for transportation and military needs. The island cattlemen, who could have helped out, invoked the death penalty against anyone selling livestock in New Spain; they wished to maintain a monopoly of sorts. Fortunately, growing conditions were unusually favorable. Space alone was required for cattle. Almost no labor was necessary; one or two Indians, a Negro, or a mounted Spaniard could take care of large herds. The occupation, unlike plowing or cultivating, was not regarded as a menial one for white men. At the end of twenty years' time, herds had expanded amazingly throughout Mexico.

In 1523–1524, the tithe for Mexico City's Spaniards was adjudicated at 5,500 gold pesos and the tithes for Medellín and Vera Cruz reached the equivalent of approximately 1,000 pesos. Tithes were collected largely in the form of pigs and sheep. Although there was no large town in Michoacán, tithes there were worth 9,000 pesos in 1530; the increase by a third over the previous year was due to the herds' growth. The same year Tlaxcala diocese yielded fewer than 600 pesos, but Puebla had not yet been founded. By 1531, pigs had become so cheap that stockmen were no longer interested in them; sheep, too, were multiplying rapidly. On the other hand, New Spain was raising fewer than 200 horses a year and cattle slaughtering was still forbidden.

Continental Spaniards could, however, resort to buying in Havana or Santo Domingo; purchases must have been heavy, because a few years later cattle had become plentiful. Prices dropped so low that as early as 1538 cattlemen felt obliged to protest. Some even demanded that explorers set out on new expeditions in order to expand the market, the cattle industry having "grown too large for the country." Beef in Mexico City, officially pegged at 70 maravedís an arrelde (1.840 kilograms) in 1532, was worth only 17 maravedís six years later. A few years more, and prices would plummet again.

During this period, the need arose to found a *mesta*, or cattlemen's association, largely so that owners could recover their strays after they had mingled with other herds. In Mexico City, the organization came into being spontaneously, without official action, on July 31, 1539. The municipality elected its two *mesta* alcaldes in 1538 and 1539, before the statutes were approved either by the Viceroy (April 18, 1539) or by the King (April 4, 1542). Two meetings attended by all stockmen were held each year: at Tepeapulco on February 16 and at Toluca in the last days of August. (These were two valleys in which herds were already numerous.) Other regions soon followed suit, for example, Puebla (1541) and Oaxaca (1543). Michoacán waited until 1563. The 1574 ordinances extended the institution to all of New Spain.

The first viceroy quickly found himself confronted with problems that were the exact opposite of those raised by wheat. Whereas he had tried to encourage wheat farmers, who were only too scarce, he was obliged to stem an invasion by large herds of cattle, which, in certain areas near Mexico City, were threatening to overrun native villages. At the same time, the question of grazing rights became urgent.

Ancient Castilian custom held grass to be a gift of nature; consequently, pastures and untilled fields (*baldíos*) were free and open to all, in the same way as stubble was after the harvest. Called *realengos*, they belonged directly to the Crown. When Ferdinand and Isabella conquered the kingdom of Granada, they distributed much land to their soldiers and retainers; but the beneficiaries were forbidden to establish enclosures (*dehesar*) or "block off [*defender*] grass and other products that the soil bears without cultivation."

In the Spanish Peninsula, however, powerful landowners had been much inclined to fence their grazing lands and keep them for their own flocks. In 1531, the citizens of Antequera de Oaxaca petitioned His Majesty not to allow this sad state of affairs to obtain in Mexico; in Spain, they said, there were too many barriers, too many pastures reserved for the mighty—nobles and other rich men—with the result that the poor often had to buy grass for their cattle from them. These settlers in the New World wanted all grazing land to be held in common. They were obviously afraid that Cortés, having become Marqués del Valle de Oaxaca, might succeed in gaining exclusive rights like the lords of Old Spain.

As an order of 1497 shows, the Crown early opposed any division of grazing land in the Indies. As soon as the King had personal representatives in Mexico City, he determined to settle the question on the basis of all pertinent data. In 1530, the jurists of the Second Audiencia were asked whether it would be advisable to declare all grazing land in New Spain to be commonage, and, barring that, at least the grazing land within a radius of fifteen leagues from each town; "that is the custom and observance in all the cities, towns, and villages of our realms [in Spain]." The replies received were unequivocal. Licenciado Salmerón wrote the next year concerning Puebla and its environs that there as elsewhere pastures, woods, and watercourses should belong to all, "except the properties [*heredades*], commons [*ejidos*], and enclosures which would be allotted to each of said villages." The presiding judge, Fuenleal, was even more categorical: neither individuals nor communities should be granted reserves or zones around towns; everyone should be able to drive flocks wherever desired, since even though enclosures might be beneficial to some, they would be established at the Indians' expense.

Referring as usual to specific cases, a series of royal orders accordingly declared all grazing land in Mexico to be common property. In 1532, His Majesty issued the following instructions: "In the entire district of said city of Antequera and the Oaxaca Valley, on both the King's preserves [unutilized] and private estates, grazing land shall belong to all the inhabitants . . . after the harvest; all may and shall drive their livestock throughout." There was, however, one restriction: "Enclosed pastures, town commons and districts, sheep lanes, and private properties are to be protected by fences." At the same time, and in line with the Audiencia's request, the Marqués del Valle was forbidden the exclusive use of pastures and woods on his estate. In 1538, the right to commonage in the Oaxaca district was reaffirmed for all unenclosed land; this was followed by similar orders in 1538 for the Puebla region and in 1539 for a fifteen-league zone around Mexico City.

As a last step, the Viceroy interpreted as open all pasture land and untilled fields in New Spain. The same held for Santo Domingo and Puerto Rico, where by royal decree shepherds were free to install their cabins and folds wherever they pleased (San Juan, 1541 and 1543). On the books at least, the regulation remained in force in Española until 1550, when it was restricted to a ten-league belt surrounding the towns; cattlemen were authorized to stake out enclosures beyond the belt. As a result of this liberal policy, hardly any of the numerous royal cédulas granting land to individuals, prior to the middle of the sixteenth century, concern pasturage. When the conquistadors requested such land, they were given a dilatory answer. On the other hand, the caballería grants contained a clause reserving the right of way for grazing.

It would seem, in summary, that the Crown, after hesitating initially, wished to avoid the splitting up of pasture to the benefit of individuals and wished to endow New Spain with a general system of common grazing, similar to the one that must have existed in the Spanish Peninsula before its destruction by the erection of numerous barriers.

Commonage, like many medieval ideas, was not always clearly defined, particularly in the sixteenth century, which was a period of transition. The institution reached full development in the *ejido*, or municipal pasture for work and draft animals, as well as in all regions where cattlemen could build pens and cabins without special permission, in conformity with a few laws and the views expressed by certain jurists. Except for the *ejidos*, necessarily limited in area, community ownership of grazing land was anachronistic by the sixteenth century. Local authorities, virtually escaping the Crown's control, and finally even the viceroys, were brought to recognize a much more flexible notion of common pasture; this notion would eventually place the soil in the hands of individual cattlemen.

It was the municipal authorities who, lacking royal approval, took the responsibility of sanctioning the early cattle barons' more or less permanent squatting.

Communities did acknowledge certain of their citizens' rights to fixed sites (*sitios, asientos*), where they could put their sheep and swine out to graze. A new word, *estancia*, was coined in the West Indies and used extensively to designate the point where wanderers and their flocks finally came to rest. Although in the beginning its sense was sometimes vague, it soon came to mean, when used without a modifier, a site for livestock, as Mexico City records show between 1527 and 1530. The word's appearance there coincides with the fixing of several droves, or *hatos*, which until then had grazed freely. Significantly too, the word *hato* soon disappeared in the central portion of New Spain; but it survived alongside *estancia* in other parts of the New World, such as Panama, where to a certain extent livestock raising and even agriculture remained nomadic in nature.

Stockmen were desirous of having their rights to specific grazing lands—and even their exclusive rights—recognized by town councils; the task was not difficult, since the councils were frequently no more than their mouthpieces. The most important council, Mexico City's, began to grant sites and estancias not only around the capital but sometimes far away, in Michoacán or on the Pacific coast. Instead of preceding the stockmen's moving in, such grants would often come after it; or the grants would confirm purchases (or sham purchases) from the Indians. It could be said that the interested parties were attempting to cloak in legal procedures situations that had no foundation in law.

Municipal authorities were aware it was not their right to give title to pasture land. In 1527, the Mexico City council granted a license for some estancias near Zacatula, but the council made clear to the grantee that it was not vesting in him "either property or seigniorial rights." The same year, a man requested "a site [at Chapultepec] on which he was at present pasturing his sheep." The council acceded to his request "in the manner and form consonant with its powers, as it has done for other inhabitants pending delimitation of its prerogatives." In the years following, the council continued to distribute grazing land, but in each instance with some restrictive clause: "of its own free will," "without title being vested," "no buildings allowed" (the opposite was stated in its title deeds for harvest land), "only the usufruct to be enjoyed." All such grants were revocable, notably if the recipient should absent himself; this latter characteristic assimilates them to the *vecindad*, or rights and duties of the burgher.

In the light of the above restrictions, what real advantages and specific rights could the holders expect to derive from these early estancias granted by the town councils? The answer must lie in certain lost ordinances to which a Mexico City grazing license, dated 1530, refers. Since they are not extant, we are obliged to fill in the gap with information from the West Indies, where several decades earlier similar problems had had to be met, and especially from regulations that Cortés laid down for two Honduras towns in an environment similar to Mexico's at the time.

According to these curious ordinances, citizens wishing to raise livestock were to request authorization from the town government, which would grant them a definite site. The grantee could then prohibit any other stockman from establishing the center of a new estancia less than a league away, for cattle or sheep, or less than half a league, for swine. A crop farmer, however, could be authorized to cultivate fields inside one of these overlapping circles, providing he fenced his fields. But stockmen could not settle closer than half a league from land, Spanish or native, already under cultivation. It was naturally quite impossible to prevent flocks and herds from leaving their own areas and mingling; consequently, each stockman had to brand his livestock and register his brand with the town clerk. The custom already existed in pastoral Spain, but it assumed new importance on the American continent, especially at Mexico City, where it is found as early as 1528.

The only right to the land that such regulations gave was a purely negative one: the right to prevent others from establishing on it cabins and pens for tending livestock. The spaces thus set aside (but not enclosed) were vast, measuring about 75 and 20 square kilometers. Although the grass remained common property, probably because the droves could not be separated or fenced in, here, in embryonic form, is the first example of the cattlemen's gradual seizure of the soil. Inasmuch as grazing experiments in the Islands antedated those on the mainland and there were no Spanish precedents, Hernán Cortés, who had raised cattle in Cuba, almost certainly imitated island customs in his regulations. Rather than legislation created *ab ovo*, these 1525 ordinances appear to reflect a previous set of conditions and a spontaneous response to actual needs. The Crown took a long time to recognize the fact.

Circular grants are the rule in the West Indies; they have left few traces in Mexico. In Cuba, the first grant known to us was made by the municipal authorities of Espíritu Santo in 1536; grants went on until the eighteenth century. In Santo Domingo, the King in 1550 allowed, ten leagues outside of each town, the allocation of a circle a league in radius to each drove (*hato*), under conditions identical with those laid down by Cortés 25 years earlier: Common grazing, erection of buildings prohibited for stockmen other than the interested party (but not prohibited for crop farmers).

In New Spain, a land dispute in 1602 revealed that the Crown had formerly possessed near Tlaxcala a cattle estancia circular in form, for "by order of Viceroy Antonio de Mendoza no one else was permitted to establish an estancia within a league's distance round about." The pasture was later sold to private individuals; but for a long time it kept its unusual shape. As late as the seventeenth century, we find a map, drawn up by an alcalde mayor, on which appears a group of three adjacent circular estancias; third parties had laid claim to the intervening space (*blanco*). We may conclude that these first estancias had, as in Honduras and the Islands, a monopoly on the fixed accessories of livestock raising in the sector corresponding to municipal grants; that is to say, unless a stockman could obtain his own estancia from a town council, he could erect no buildings. The observation will be true for New Spain until the end of the sixteenth century, and it would be hard to explain otherwise what advantages would accrue from possessing one of those grazing sites.

The estancias distributed by municipalities were neither identical in size to those that Cortés had defined in 1525, nor were all circular. Diversity in the harvest caballerías before 1537 would make us suspect that even if we did not have more direct proof. Prior to 1539, a New Galicia governor granted a square estancia measuring 5,000 paces on each side; in 1543, the Viceroy issued a reminder that sites for cattle should not exceed 3,000 paces [square] nor those for sheep 2,000 [square], "in conformity with the ordinance passed by the municipal authorities here in Mexico City."

The Mexico City authorities were the first to regulate the heretofore spontaneous growth of the estancias, just as they had drawn up in 1537 the statutes of the first *mesta* in New Spain, which was simply the official body of the cattle barons, themselves members of the town council. Surprisingly enough, there is no mention of estancias either in this 1537 charter composed of twenty-seven articles or in the royal ordinance of the same year fixing the dimensions of the harvest caballería. The reason is that the documents were important legislative measures; the *mesta* statutes had to be approved in Spain. (They were confirmed by the Viceroy in 1539 and by the King in 1542.) And since the Crown still considered the woods and pastures of its overseas possessions to be common and indivisible, the estancias were on the borderline of legality, if not in overt contradiction with it.

A few years later, the ways in which the cattle barons, outdistancing legislation, had already begun to seize land became apparent. The first viceroy's attitude is significant. Realizing that it was impossible to backtrack, and wishing to keep the situation under control at least, he set to apportioning estancias in His Majesty's name—without a trace of royal authorization. Many such grants were made to stockmen already in possession of their land. In 1542, 1543, and 1544, the first grants of which we are aware are frequently for sites on which the recipients' herds had been grazing "for a long time"—8, 12, 15, 16 years, and longer. Such precise quoting of figures would seem to indicate a desire to claim some sort of squatter's rights. At times, the Viceroy's title deeds confirmed grants originally made by the municipalities; much more often, however, the deeds were for pasture seized without anyone's leave.

THE MULTIPLICATION OF CATTLE, AND VICEREGAL CONTROL

During the second decade following the Conquest, cattle, after lagging behind swine and sheep, began to increase on the outskirts of towns. Then, from 1538 or 1540 on, they multiplied at a fantastic rate in the central plateau region.

As a consequence, and despite efforts to peg meat prices at reasonable levels, the bottom dropped out in Mexico City. An arrelde of beef (1.840 kilograms), costing 17 maravedís in 1538, went to 12 in 1539, to 10 the next year, to 7 in 1541, and to 4 in 1542. In other words, the arrelde was worth only one-eighth of a silver real ($\frac{1}{7}$ or $\frac{1}{8}$ its price in Andalusia that same year), in contrast with the high cost of everything else in the Indies. Even so, the Mexico City administration had on several occasions prohibited meat sales at below the fixed price. Then, prices steadied at the lowest level—a proof of the extraordinary abundance at the time. More precisely, prices fluctuated between 4 and 6 maravedís (rising occasionally to 8) and followed with some delay the general upward trend. In 1555, the official price of beef was 4 maravedís plus a 1-maravedí purchase tax, whereas mutton and pork were definitely on the rise.

As a result, Spaniards enjoyed extremely cheap meat. Without a profession or trade, even without working, a white man could always see to his food and creature comfort in New Spain. Low prices made it all the easier for the rich to keep open house and support their numerous retainers. Another consequence of young bulls' selling for a mere two or three pesos a head was to make cattle raising profitable only on a very large scale; that in turn implied considerable investment in cowboys, Negro slaves, and estancias. If ever there had been small stockmen (and it seems there were), they could no longer compete. Cattle raising subsequently took the same course as the other sectors (*grangerías*) of the farming industry and became concentrated "in the hands of the rich and of those possessing Indians under the encomienda system," as the Audiencia prosecutor wrote in 1594.

The sudden multiplication of cattle is one of the most astonishing biological phenomena observable in the New World. According to the prosecutor quoted above, herds nearly doubled in fifteen months; insufficiently guarded, they overran the countryside and destroyed all the Indians' maize. Toluca Valley, twelve or fifteen leagues outside the capital, had been stocked around 1535; less than twenty years later, it contained more than 60 estancias and about 150,000 head of cattle and horses, belonging for the most part to the "rich and mighty, as well as a few of His Majesty's officials." Franciscan missionaries asserted that, on seeing their land invaded, the natives had fled into the mountains. They did no sowing, and a fanega of maize jumped from one-half a real to four. Some stockmen had herds of 10,000 or 11,000 head; according to the missionaries, the authorities appeared powerless in the face of a coalition of cattle barons and Mexico City clerics (living off cattle tithes), who were determined to protect their interests.

The situation was similar near Tepeapulco, twenty miles northeast of the capital; it was perhaps worse in Jilotepec, the same distance to the northwest. There, according to several accounts, huge herds had driven the Indians from their villages and completely depopulated the region. Other regions were also laid waste. In the maritime province of Huasteca, around San Esteban de Pánuco, where originally Nuño de Guzmán had imported livestock from the Islands in exchange for Indian slaves, herds multiplied with the usual rapidity, invading fields and even villages. A viceregal order having remained without effect, an inspector took official cognizance of the havoc in 1553. Damage was so heavy around Oaxaca that Antonio de Mendoza was obliged to abolish all cattle estancias in the "three valleys"; that was a significant act on the part of one so attentive to the country's economic development. "The Spaniards are crying that I have ruined them," he wrote his successor in 1550, "and they are right, for I assure Your Lordship that it is a pity; but I could not do otherwise. May Your Lordship realize that if cattle are allowed, the Indians will be destroyed."

The Viceroy therefore tried to clear the central regions by directing the great herds into less populous districts. From 1542 or 1545 on, cattle spread like the waves of a rising tide over the northern plains and the prairies of the warm zones along the coasts. On the confines of the nomad country, then in the area bounded by Pánuco and Nautla, Vera Cruz and the Grijalva River, "cattle are being born and multiplying unbelievably; you cannot exaggerate their numbers or imagine the spectacle before your eyes," Muñoz Camargo exclaimed. Captured English corsairs, travelers, and newly arrived Spaniards were all amazed to see the multitudes of cattle and to learn that so many Mexicans possessed 10,000, 20,000, 30,000, and even 100,000 head. As late as the end of the century, Samuel de Champlain, who went to "Mechico," was astounded by the "great, level plains, stretching endlessly and everywhere covered with an infinite number of cattle."

Soon after sheep and cattle, horses, too, began to increase rapidly. By the middle of the sixteenth cenutry, mounts could be had for not much more than the trouble it took to break them; numerous Indians obtained the second viceroy's permission to keep pack and even saddle horses. Slightly later, the pasture lands lying between Querétaro and San Juan del Río were sustaining some 10,000 horses (plus many more sheep and cattle); close by Mexico City, the village of Tacuba alone contained 3,000 pack horses used for hauling firewood and maize from the Toluca Valley. As a result of the increase, the humblest mestizo and the poorest Spaniard always possessed his own horse; that simple truth suffices to distinguish Mexican society from all others.

At the time of the mass migrations, cowboys and their masters penetrated into the vast spaces where dangerous nomads lurked. They were the first to chance upon the earliest of the great northern mines, at Zacatecas. Likewise, an estancia had been established at Guanajuato long before the discovery of the famous silver deposits there colonized the land more densely than the cattlemen could have done alone. The increase in sheep particularly gave rise to seasonal migrations wherever lack of water or too large flocks made grazing land insufficient during the dry season. Spain had moreover furnished precedents in the customs of summer and winter pasturing on the one hand and commonage on the other. One writer is obviously thinking of Extremadura when he states that sheep owners drive their flocks "into distant regions, which are called here *agostadero* [summer pasture]." By 1579, and doubtless long before, more than 200,000 sheep from the Querétaro region covered every September the 300 or 400 kilometers to the green meadows of Lake Chapala and the western part of Michoacán; the following May, they would return to their estancias.

Similarly, flocks from Tepeaca and other regions of the plateau would winter near Vera Cruz and on the moist Atlantic slopes. Like migrations took place between other arid zones and the better-watered coasts. In 1632, finally, the discovery by a shepherd of New León's fertile plains started a new seasonal migration; by the middle of the century, and despite the danger from nomads, some thirteen flocks numbering more than 300,000 sheep regularly flowed down from the plateaus on their way to the northeastern pastures.

The ordinances of 1574, which made provision for the opening of *cañadas*, or special sheep lanes, notwithstanding the harm done by the migrating flocks, is not hard to imagine. Untilled land was certainly not wanting; shepherds aimed, however, not for the cactus-studded plains or dry sierras, but the cultivated and watered village zones. Shepherds of course had the right to let their flocks graze in these zones after the harvest, once the King had imposed the obligation of commonage on the entire territory of New Spain. But instead of helping the lowly, as in Spain, the custom worked to the natives' disadvantage; they had no livestock, only fields of maize. Terrible abuses arose not only from the fact that there was no effective opposition to powerful stockmen's gradual appropriation of grazing lands, but also from the fact that they were empowered by law to utilize the stubble in all fields.

Viceroy Velasco, who had just arrived, accordingly settled a dispute between a stockman and the Toluca Indians in the former's favor. Villaseca was permitted to send his flocks into natives' fields to summer pasture (*agostar*) after the maize was harvested, that is, from the end of November to the end of March, a period representing the height of the dry season. The same obligation naturally applied to Spaniards' caballerías, on which enclosures were prohibited; but in the sixteenth century, the caballerías did not count for much in comparison with the large areas under cultivation by the Indians. The second viceroy was not long in estimating the situation and in limiting the right to commonage on community lands.

Winter and summer pasturing, roaming over large areas of stubble, migration to the north or the coasts, seminomadism of flocks in outlying zones: This extremely mobile aspect of Mexican sheep raising offers a curious analogy to the instability of so many Spaniards in the New World.

The rapid increase of cattle and sheep and their overrunning of harvest lands created serious problems for the authorities.

The Crown remained quite reserved in its attitude toward estancias; perhaps it was hoped at court that all pasture land could continue to be held in common, as President Fuenleal had recommended. Whatever may have been the court's intentions, the first viceroy found it necessary to compromise with reality in order not to lose control completely. Mendoza obviously realized that he must distribute estancias in His Majesty's name if he wished to avoid the municipalities' passing them out in accordance with special interests or, still worse, powerful individuals' grabbing land on their own account to the detriment of the native communities. Finally, as stock raising was becoming, next to the mines, the country's main resource, there was some utility in encouraging its development in neglected regions where formal title could be granted to pasture. The same measure would serve to disencumber the overpopulated zones in the country's center.

Since the oldest records have been lost, it is hard to tell at what exact date the Viceroy began to grant official title to estancias. The deeds probably do not go back as far as those to caballerías; the first of which we know are for 1540–1542, dates coinciding with the lowest beef prices in Mexico City. As we have learned, many of the grants merely sanctioned previous occupation and allowed the usurper to hold the estancia "with a better title in His Majesty's name"; such were located either around Mexico City and Puebla, the mines of Sultepec in the west, and Taxco in the south, in Michoacán, and so on, or northward beyond Jilotepec and "among the Chichimecas," on the banks of the Pánuco, and in Huasteca. A few years later, numerous grants were made for estancias near the nomad zones.

Rudimentary property rights are already present in some of the phrases in current use by the Viceroy:

*I ordain that the estancia, once you have entered into possession
of it, shall belong to you and your heirs, successors, and assigns
. . . and that you shall have the right to sell, give, or relinquish
it to whomever you will . . . provided it be not to a church, monastery, or hospital, or to any ecclesiastic, under penalty of breach
of contract . . . and that upon installing your livestock you shall
observe all ordinances regulating the establishment of said estancias
. . . and provided such be not prejudicial to the interests of His
Majesty or any other third party.*

There is no longer anything precarious in such grants, which confer definitive, transmissible property rights guaranteed henceforth by
the King's direct representative. Many a local ordinance passed by a
town government thus acquired a general, official value. Soon Spaniards
were forbidden to possess herds without also possessing estancias; the
latter frequently went on the market. An important step had been
taken toward turning pasture lands into private property, but this
time under viceregal control.

That control did not prevent a few rich individuals from continuing
to grab huge blocks of land; it was probably not considered a crime
anyway. Little importance was attached, it is clear, to the estancia dimensions laid down by Mexico City. They are mentioned only exceptionally, for in so immense a country everyone settled where he
wished and occupied much more than the prescribed 3,000 paces. It
was not unheard of for influential men to be given a large amount of
land at one time; in 1550, Jaramillo obtained eleven estancias and Ruiz
de la Mota seven. They had in fact occupied, even "owned," them "for
a long time" or "for fifteen years." Ruiz de la Mota's seven were within
his encomienda. Likewise, high officials, their relatives, and their retainers somtimes received important grants; Francisco de Velasco, the
second viceroy's son, was given eleven estancias by his father in 1552
and still others in later years. However, grants of this type were infrequent and they might be justified in the sense that they usually lay
along the frontier of the Chichimeca Indians, whose raids had to be
stopped by some means. These grants alone would never have sufficed
to create the great estates; in addition, hundreds of obscure individuals
needed to sell or make over to the mighty the title deeds that they had
just been given.

The Viceroy's most pressing problem was still to keep estancias away from villages and to keep cattle out of the Indians' maize. By 1548, title deeds bore an addition to the clause concerning damage to third parties: The grant has been made only after the approval of the local corregidor, who has consulted the native chiefs and often the encomendero, in order to be certain—the deeds' language is precise—that granting of the estancia will do no harm. Although the inadequate number of royal officials, as well as their complicity with stockmen, frequently nullified the efficacy of such steps, the encomenderos did look with disfavor on third parties settling on their vassals' land; they definitely were not kindly disposed to intruders. Whenever they were not themselves petitioning for an estancia, they were the best champions that the Indians had.

The above measures did not go far in stemming the invasion of harvest land by droves which were not only immense but had also lost a part of their herdsmen through the emancipation of Indian slaves. A few missionaries were the first to sound the alarm, breaking the silence observed by a group of colonists and secular clergy, whose main source of income was the cattle tithe. It so happened that the monks had great influence at court; and in Mexico City they were Viceroy Luis de Velasco's most respected advisers. As early as 1541, the Crown had instructed the Audiencia to protect crop lands against cattle; from 1548–1550 on, royal orders became as numerous as they were urgent. The few measures that Antonio de Mendoza had adopted were deemed timid in Spain (1548), with the result that between 1550 and 1556 at least twenty cédulas were sent requiring that estancias be established far from villages, that those too close should be suppressed, that droves should be better tended, and that traveling judges, or inspectors, should be dispatched to make sure that orders were being complied with at Tlaxcala, Tepeapulco, Toluca, and elsewhere.

It was no easy task to hold back or divert to other regions the sudden enormous expansion. Velasco went to work with a will; the result was that during his term of office the period of anarchy in central Mexico was brought to a close. That did not mean that Indian communities suffered no further hardships, but that damage, thanks to energetic action, was held to a minimum. The settling of Zacatecas and subsequent exploration helped to bring about the migration of many head of cattle into the northern provinces. The Viceroy granted numerous estancias outside of New Galicia in 1550, 1555, and the years following. Contrariwise, Luis de Velasco tried to limit to unused portions of land the expansion on the Mexico City plateau and in densely populated areas.

Like Carolingian *missi dominici*, inspecting judges, who were lawyers and often members of the Audiencia, were sent as plenipotentiaries over the entire country to wipe out abuses and ensure the application of those parts of the New Laws which had been kept in force. From Pánuco and Huasteca to Colima and the Pacific coast, from Michoacán to the Isthmus of Tehuantepec and beyond, these upright, often dedicated men strove specifically to remove estancias endangering villages, obtain satisfactory tending of droves, restore usurped lands to their rightful owners, and force stockmen to observe the various ordinances being issued by the viceroy at the time. The operation, which was carried out in conjunction with the monks, did not neglect purely moral considerations. Velasco, who had gone on the road himself, was vigilant in preventing cowherds and estancia owners from taking concubines; he had apprehended and sent back to Castile men who had left their wives behind.

In remote provinces, as one inspector noted, things sometimes reverted to their former state as soon as the inspector had departed. Also, the situation in some districts was beyond remedy; they had been almost entirely depopulated by cattle invasion, which constituted another national disaster like the great epidemics that had been unknown until then in the New World. Closer to Mexico City, the Viceroy had better success in enforcing his orders; the results accomplished are undeniable. For example, Luis de Velasco, after a personal tour of inspection and "consultation with the monks" at Toluca, decided to construct a barrier between Indian and Spanish holdings. The wall, "more than ten leagues long," was finished by 1555. Then the Crown made the cattlemen pay a tax of 17,000 pesos for its permanent maintenance. The order seems to have been entirely executed by 1561, and the wall was still being kept up in the seventeenth century.

There was also a barrier at Tepeapulco, which in 1551 the authorities wanted to raise and reinforce. The measure was probably inadequate, for the Viceroy decided to clear the area of cattle, which were still doing damage. The cattlemen, all residents of Mexico City, had recourse to the usual delaying tactics: an appeal to the Audiencia (where they doubtless had friends). Velasco, armed with a royal cédula, demanded immediate execution of his orders. After further difficulties, the reform was finally carried out by the Indians who, given backing in high quarters, drove out some 10,000 head of cattle and horses. A new royal cédula is proof that a part of the stock, abandoned by its owners, had returned; but the cédula ordered harsh treatment for the offenders and expulsion by the constabulary of all droves still within the area.

Supported by the Crown and the monks, if not by anyone else, Velasco was usually able to make his authority felt, even if only around Mexico City or Puebla. The Indians were grateful to him; in a touching letter addressed to His Majesty, the inhabitants of Cholula requested that this pious viceroy be kept in office indefinitely, because of "all his acts of pity and kindness" toward them, and especially his having removed "many cattle estancias which were ruining us and putting poor *macehuales* [native farmers] to flight" (1554). The very next year, according to the Franciscan Motolinía, droves were withdrawn from all zones where they could do damage "not for want of sufficient room, but for lack of guarding." Terminal dates were also set for free stubble grazing and summer and winter pasturing.

The ancient right to send herds and flocks into the fields after the harvest had given rise to serious abuses. The Indians received nothing in exchange; livestock raising was exclusively in Spanish hands, and only the richest at that. The Viceroy consequently set about paring down the custom in those zones where the threat was gravest. On much of the plateau stockmen were not allowed to utilize stubble patches except from early January to late February; the dates fixed varied considerably, moreover, depending on region and climate. From 1556 on particularly, a buffer zone was granted numerous native communities; at no time could livestock come closer than a radius of 3,000 paces, or one league, from a village. Subsequently, the distance was often reduced to half a league. The natives, knowing that they had backing, sometimes took it upon themselves to see that the order was observed.

Velasco's successors were not all as zealous as he. A few years after his death, a monk complained bitterly in a letter to the King that droves were invading the Indians' fields before the proper dates and the villages were desolate. "The remedy," the monk went on to say, "is to observe the rules of Viceroy Luis de Velasco's time, when livestock did not enter until a definite date, and then well guarded. Now, livestock wanders in at any time and without enough herdsmen, with the result that everything is laid waste." In 1574, Viceroy Martín Enríquez proclaimed some general rules prohibiting cattlemen from letting their stock out before the beginning of September and after the end of March. However, his orders do not appear to have been as severely enforced as his predecessor's had been.

As a last measure, Viceroy Velasco began to add more restrictions to estancia title deeds. He would often limit the number of head, thereby eliciting vigorous protests from certain cattle barons. He also required owners to have so many mounted herdsmen or to build a fence in an exposed spot. Above all, Luis de Velasco specified, starting in the autumn of 1563, the dimensions of estancias: 3,000 paces [square] for cattle and 2,000 paces [square] for sheep. The first squares consequently measured a Castilian league on each side, or 4,200 meters, and the second ones, approximately 2,500 meters. In this way, Velasco gave official sanction to the custom which previously had been founded on no higher authority than the Mexico City administration. Around the same time, clauses appeared in deeds which forbade sale during the first four years and required stocking within a year. The measures were probably designed to avoid land speculation, the first symptoms of which were appearing at this date.

Viceroy Velasco died in Mexico City in 1564, shortly after having dictated the regulations that were to become so important in future years. He may have been preparing to codify them, since a few months, or less than a year, after the arrival of his successor, the Marqués de Falces, the land ordinances of May 26 and September 19, 1567, were promulgated. Henceforth, grazing lands included in estancia grants must not be closer than 1,000 varas to native villages; the distance was halved for proximity to crop lands (838 and 416 meters). The surface areas of estancias for cattle and for sheep were fixed as before, but with a few supplementary details: squares oriented on an east-west axis measuring on each side either one league (3,000 paces, 5,000 yards) or 2,000 paces (3,333 yards)—approximately 1,750 and 780 hectares, respectively. The dimensions were twice confirmed by Viceroy Martín

Enríquez (1574 and 1580) and once again by the Marqués de Villa-manrique (1589). All title deeds in future referred to those measurements, which were still official in Mexico a few years ago.

The reason for the long delay in issuing the regulations was that no need for them was felt until the estancias had drawn close enough together for contacts and disputes to arise among stockmen. As Martín Enríquez wrote in 1571, "The entire country became dotted [with grants], each person choosing the best land for cattle and sheep, or for wheat or maize or something else. I have taken care that the lands granted and divided up should link the various estates, continuously and without intervening spaces of wasted land." The worst that could be said, he added, was that the Indian villages had been hemmed in, sufficient land not having been left around them. The emphasis placed at the time on measures designed to "avoid lawsuits" shows that in many areas of New Spain the soil was almost entirely taken up; the saturation point was being reached. In this last third of the sixteenth century, pasturage grants are less frequent in the central zones, while deeds make clear that they are for land "on the edge" of existing estancias, "with no wedges in between."

This body of rules and measures is extremely important. By fixing limits and indicating the recipients' rights and duties, the new estancia deeds tended to clarify and circumscribe the raisers' gradual taking over of the land. The years 1563–1567 constitute a point of departure. The estancia was assuming its final shape. That in itself was only a step forward along the way leading to the formation of the hacienda.

THE STABILIZATION OF THE HACIENDA

For half a century, everything had evolved with surprising rapidity in New Spain. The amazing growth of the droves had lasted barely thirty years; then it stopped as suddenly as it had begun. In the boundless north, several decades more were enough to produce the same effect.

In the central and southern regions, numerous accounts testify to the shrinking of the herds before the century's end, around 1565 or 1570. The causes were not always clear to contemporary observers. Massive raids by mounted vagabonds, either rustlers (*abigeos*) or vagrants (*viandantes*), were cited as a possible explanation; but in the raids cattle merely changed hands. Often, it is true, the thieves would kill the animals on the spot in order to sell their hides, which were in great demand in Spain. They would also take the tallow, leaving the remainder of the carcass to the coyotes and buzzards. Also, cattle barons would have huge numbers of cattle slaughtered at one time on their estancias—as many as 1,000 head. Such wholesale destruction perhaps exceeded reproductive capacity. Wild dogs, racing across the plains in large packs and attacking cattle, were also blamed; the Spaniards organized hunts to track them down. Finally, the Chichimeca Indians, who had become excellent horsemen, would shoot cattle with bow and arrow.

Farther south, the sedentary populations had begun to develop a taste for beef (which was cheap), as the existence of butcher shops in purely native villages shows. As early as February, 1560, the Mexico City government claimed that the rise in meat prices was due to the amount being consumed by Indians—a strong possibility—and requested the Viceroy to ban its sale to Indians. The Audiencia, during its interregnum after Velasco's death (1564–1566), did just that. With a few departures from the original text, Viceroy Martín Enríquez confirmed the Audiencia's ordinance on January 3, 1569, and again on January 25, 1574. However, it was plain to see that in 1580 the sale of meat was still being tolerated in a large number of Indian villages.

All these circumstances certainly contributed to checking the herds' expansion. Velasco's stringent limitations also played a part, although no such measure can explain why the same phenomenon should be present in the northern provinces. In 1574, Martín Enríquez added, in the preamble to one of his *mesta* ordinances, so sound a reason that it must be the key one: "Cattle are no longer increasing rapidly; previously, a cow would drop her first calf within two years, for the land was virgin and there were many fertile pastures. Now a cow does not calve before three or four years."

Herds were now reproducing poorly. On his huge estancias located at Tarimoro and near Acámbaro, Jerónimo López the younger admitted that his some 100,000 cows (*hembras de vientre*) gave him a yearly yield of only 6,000 calves for branding and 2,000 steers for market. Though still small, the proportion was somewhat better for horses, which were raised on a smaller scale and with greater care; the same Jerónimo López, possessing 4,000 mares on one estancia, branded 600 colts and sold 300. Nevertheless, the rate must have fluctuated greatly, since in dry years when there was no grass, animals died by the thousand, as Father Alonso Ponce noted for the region in 1586–1587.

The great herds had inevitably exhausted the natural reserves built up over the centuries in this completely untouched pasture land; an equilibrium was reached between the requirements of living creatures and available vegetable resources. It is also possible that lack of new blood brought about a biological exhaustion or degeneration of the species; the hypothesis is plausible in view of the same shrinkage in the north, where grazing land was endless. Finally, there is surely a connection between the shrinkage and the already noted fact that by 1570 or 1580 stockmen had almost entirely occupied the land in many parts of New Spain. It is no accident that from 1563–1567 on, the authorities were greatly concerned with determining and then confirming estancia measurements. Thus a period of stabilization was ushered in; the herds' irresistible thrust and great migrations having come to a close, the estancia took on clearer outlines.

Cattle and meat prices reflected these tendencies, although the general rise at the time must be taken into account. In Mexico City, an arrelde of beef had wavered between four and six maravedís for thirty years. In 1575, it went up to eight or nine maravedís and stayed there; it showed, however, an inflationary trend that the municipal government repressed with great difficulty at the century's end by granting subsidies to the city's meat contractor. At the beginning of the next century, the price rose considerably, reaching twenty maravedís and then settling at seventeen in 1622. At about the same time, steers were fetching at least five or six pesos a head on Michoacán and New Galicia estancias (instead of three or three and a half in 1575) and as much as ten or twelve in Mexico City and at the mines. In inaccessible regions like Tabasco, they were worth not much more than their hides. Horses were cheaper than cattle.

The rise before the turn of the century corresponded to the shrinkage of droves everywhere, no longer merely in the center but also in the north, which had been helping to supply the center for several decades. More than once in 1595, for example, Viceroy Velasco II complained of the situation. He wrote to his successor that meat prices had rocketed and that he had diligently sought a remedy, promulgating new ordinances for stockmen, appointing inspecting magistrates, and prohibiting under grave penalties the slaughter of cows and other female animals. "I cannot see," he added, "that I have been able to cure the evil nor restore droves to their proper size. What is worse is that I do not know what remedy to apply . . . I feel that it is extremely important to enforce the prohibition rigorously and in no wise to allow cows, ewes, or she-goats to be killed. Experience will show to what degree this regulation has been efficacious."

Inspectors and "slaughter judges" (*jueces de matanzas*) traveled over the breadth and depth of the land ensuring the observance of a series of detailed orders. However, it was difficult to exert any influence over so widespread a phenomenon. Interminable reports on the subject have been preserved in Spanish archives, notably petitions from the Guadalajara cathedral chapter, whose main revenue was derived from the cattle tithe. According to Licenciado Paz de Vallecillo, an inspector in New Galicia, the Guadalajara cattlemen, who had branded 23,000 calves in 1594 or 1595, branded only 8,000 in 1602 and 5,000 in 1608, the year in which he was writing. Even in remote Durango, in New Viscaya, as the Guadalajara canons show with detailed statistics, the number of animals branded dropped from 32,746 in 1576 to 25,123 in 1602; the decline in the intervening years, it is true, was far from regular, a characteristic of a still unstable economy.

In the course of the years following, the situation did not improve. Lamentations continued as the competent authorities revealed their inability to cope with a phenomenon going far beyond their strength and the means at their disposal. At all events, the number of cattle seems to have stabilized itself in the course of the seventeenth century, at a much lower level than in the sixteenth. Cattle raising was more and more being combined with crop raising; the transition was taking place between a purely pastoral economy and the mixed hacienda type.

What was the use of these millions of head of sheep and especially cattle when the main meat consumers, namely the Spaniards, mestizos, and Negroes, probably did not number over 200,000 in 1600? Why, after their growth was checked, did the droves shrink so rapidly? Why, finally, was such a chorus of protests raised when the abundance of cattle still seemed to outstrip needs?

Let us first observe that meat was the only cheap product that Mexico had to offer Europeans; as a result, it became a staple of their diet. Droves were so numerous, the King was informed in 1563, that more meat was eaten and more money spent on it in one city in the Indies than in ten in Spain. As in the Spanish Peninsula, a contractor (*obligado*), who was usually at the same time a producer, would agree to supply a town's butcher shops for one year at an adjudicated price. In 1557, Mexico City consumed at least 400 steers a week—16,000 a year, according to a city representative's estimate in 1575. Besides pigs, kids, and poultry, 120,000 sheep were slaughtered in the same period; the figure tended to rise later, whereas beef consumption remained stationary or dropped. Animals were of small size; according to slaughterhouse accounts, the steers killed weighed on an average only 13½ arrobas (150 kg.), gross weight.

An Audiencia judge wrote in 1606: "If the mines have been worked at all, it is thanks to the plentiful and cheap supply of livestock." Only a meat diet could furnish enough energy for such hard work, and many horses and mules were needed to turn machinery and do necessary hauling. For example, cattlemen at Lagos sold their livestock to Guanajuato and San Luis Potosí (whose contractor, Pedro Mateos, was one of their members around 1607). They also supplied the pacified Chichimeca Indians' encampments (who were stuffed with meat as a restraining measure); Michoacán, particularly "the sugar refineries of Tiripitío, Tacámbaro, Vega de Sarria, . . . and others," and Mexico City. At the beginning of the seventeenth century, it was estimated that New Galicia sent to New Spain 20,000 steers on the hoof every year, and sometimes as many as 60,000 or more when a large cattleman sold off a part of his herd.

However important meat consumption may have been in relation to the population, it was only a tiny outlet for the huge herds. Tallow, in short supply moreover, was easily conserved and transported in outlying regions; it was in general use to replace oil in making soap and, of course, candles. Cattlemen were most interested in leather, however, since it was in great demand in Europe, especially for outfitting the great Spanish armies of the time. Silver mines also used many hides, notably for transportation purposes and for raising water.

Hides, used either directly as an export commodity or indirectly in export industries, were consequently a significant item in the Mexican economy, which at the time relied almost entirely on transoceanic trade.

While an average-sized steer in 1575 was worth 26 reals on the estancia, his hide alone brought 11 reals from Mexico City wholesalers. Prices went even higher; ten years or so later hides cost 4 ducats in Spain, or 44 reales. In 1591–1592 hides were a drug on the market in Mexico City, because there was no fleet leaving. On the other hand, the fleet crossing in 1587 had landed nearly 100,000 hides at Seville, 74,352 of them from Mexico. The 1594 fleet carried 196,036 ducats' worth of hides, while the 1598 fleet had on board 150,000 hides. A few years before, a single individual, Juan Nieto, a Mexico City meat contractor, had possessed enough hides to be able to lose 80,000 of them at one blow in a shipwreck.

The heavy European demand and the high prices fetched by hides at the end of the century probably induced cattlemen to sacrifice many animals even at the risk of depleting their herds. Also, rustlers were on the increase, particularly in the vast northern solitudes; they would kill cattle solely for their hides and tallow, which they would then sell for practically nothing at the neighboring mines. The story is set forth at length in the accounts of Audiencia judges and the Guadalajara canons. If we add the fact that the herds' rate of growth had been slowing down for around thirty years, we may understand the essential causes of the evil denounced in so many petitions, notices, and supplications.

In addition to cattle, sheep were extremely numerous on Mexico's dry plateaus. The Jesuits alone owned several hundred thousand in the seventeenth century. Mutton was preferred to beef and, although its cost was higher, Mexico City consumed, in the eighteenth century, almost twenty times more sheep than steers. Wool brought good prices, for after Viceroy Mendoza's innovation flocks were composed of merinos rather than the original coarse-fleeced sheep. Not that large quantities were exported to Spain, however, despite the efforts of the Crown and viceroys like Martín Enríquez, but the fine wool supplied numerous cloth mills, the first industry in the New World.

There were by 1571 more than eighty large textile mills, or *obrajes*, making black and colored cloth, which was used throughout Mexico and exported to Guatemala and Peru. Their numbers increased at the close of the century, because the fleets did not arrive from Seville every year and more and more Indains were adopting Spanish dress.

Despite severe restrictions that the Crown and the authorities imposed on the mills—for ill treatment of native workers—Viceroy Montesclaros drew up in 1604 the following curious list:

MEXICO CITY: *45 mills, including 10 for hats; the largest employing 120 Indian workers whom His Majesty has just ordered freed.*

XOCHIMILCO: *4 mills, plus 2 at Tacuba, others at Coyoacán and Cuautitlán.*

TEXCOCO: *8 mills in operation since 1600, employing a total of 355 Indians.*

PUEBLA: *35 mills employing many Indians [these mills seem to be the largest], plus 6 at Cholula and others in the city of Carrión [Atlixco].*

TLAXCALA: *13 mills, including 2 small ones making coarse cloth [sayal], which the Viceroy has ordered closed.*

TEPEACA: *5 mills for coarse cloth, each employing 50, 60, or 70 Indians, plus others at Tecamachalco.*

CELAYA: *4 mills, and many others at Querétaro, Guatzindeo, and Valladolid, whose mayors have not yet submitted a report.*

The estancia economy, in conclusion, was one that faced outward, dependent as it was on mines that were sometimes far away, on weavers concentrated around Mexico City and Puebla, on Europe, finally, which was a large consumer of American hides. For cattle owners, the result was a widely varying income, with fat and lean years—a large volume of sales followed by a mere trickle. That was due to the irregular fleet crossings and the general unreliability of ocean transport. Sheep owners enjoyed somewhat greater stability, but doubtless more modest earnings, because the market was a domestic one—the *obrajes*—and the latter were hampered by restrictions that the Spanish state had imposed. However, sixteenth- and early seventeenth-century Mexico found compensation for a certain degree of economic insecurity in a livelier circulation of consumer products and some specialization of labor. Both were phenomena foreign to the future hacienda system, which would be characterized by semi-withdrawal into itself.

On the plateau, the estancias were composed of great expanses of plain and brush; in the warm zones, of still larger forests and prairies. All the estancias took in considerably more territory than their legal limits; they had annexed pieces of land that had gone undistributed during the colonization period. Whereas pens and other buildings were supposed to be at least a league or a half-league apart for cattle, they were in fact much farther removed, except near Mexico City, Puebla, and a few other zones more heavily populated by Spaniards.

In the spaces between installations, the various herds and flocks grazed practically untended, each animal bearing its owner's brand. "The pastures of both sorts of estancias are common land; each owner possesses outright only the dwellings, pens, and sheepfolds that he constructs for his animals and his own lodging; strange livestock cannot range without permission on an estancia other than the one belonging to its master," Velasco II wrote His Majesty around 1590. Actually, the Viceroy's reference to commonage was to a certain extent idle, since commonage was considered less an obligation than a convenience and it was impossible to keep cattle on their own estancias. Proof is offered by a 1574 *mesta* ordinance, later confirmed, which prohibited cattlemen from letting livestock loose on their neighbors' estancias: "The ordinance applies to small animals, of course, since it is customary for herds of cattle to mingle."

Some cattlemen went even farther. In 1604, a stockman owning "many estancias" near Chiautla got the Viceroy to deny his neighbors grazing rights within the limits of his estancias, thus converting them into a sort of reserve, or *dehesa*—a word sometimes replacing *estancia* in the sixteenth century. The only reason no fence was put up was that the cost would have been prohibitive for so large an area. Although cattlemen did not yet own the soil, they were beginning to establish their exclusive rights to it. When land was worth the effort, most of them took the final step: By enclosing it, they turned it into a private estate. Seventeenth-century jurisprudence, however, reveals the law's uncertainty and amazing contradictions. The 1574 *mesta* ordinances were often invoked. When disputes arose, the Viceroy was content with merely quoting the old laws declaring all pasture land to be commonage and prohibiting enclosures.

Although there was no general rule restricting the number of animals allowed on each estancia, the number was limited in practice by the group of buildings and the capacity of the pens. Furthermore, jealous neighbors would not have permitted any stockman to go much beyond the normal broad interpretation of his title deeds. Many deeds did specify limitations. On the other hand, the opposite abuse of not having enough cattle was common; grants of the late sixteenth century required stocking inside of a year with 2,000 sheep or 500 head of cattle (sometimes 1,000). Very often an estancia contained 2,000 or 3,000 head of cattle; such numbers implied considerably more grazing land than the 1,750 hectares in the original grant. With the exception of the farming and livestock raising communities in the north central region, cattle barons usually possessed a string of estancias that lay side by side and encompassed areas as vast as "a state in Spain," in a contemporary's words.

Of the two types of estancias, the smaller ones for sheep, although they could be found nearly anywhere on the plateaus, were concentrated in the central zones, north of Mexico City, around Puebla, Tlaxcala, Toluca, and Ixtlahuaca, and particularly toward Huichapa, San Juan del Río, and Querétaro. There were others near Oaxaca (frequently belonging to religious orders), and around most Indian villages, where they made up part of the estates of communities, hospitals, and religious organizations. By the end of the sixteenth century, sheep estancias were frequently operated in conjunction with crop raising, sometimes with textile mills. They required a rather large number of Indian shepherds and, migration of the flocks in the dry season notwithstanding, were linked to the harvest-land economy of some of the most heavily populated regions, as well as to the emerging haciendas.

The cattle estancias were more important and less localized, extending from the torrid zone to the remote northern provinces. They represent an extensive rather than intensive exploitation of the soil and a particularly loose-knit form of colonization. Unlike sheep, cattle and horses lived and multiplied in a half-wild state, with a minimum of care. Although cattlemen had tried to curb them, the animals had grown completely wild in some regions. Contemporary accounts tell of fierce bulls emerging from the tropical forest on moonless nights, in the laguna region of Tampico and Tamiagua. They tell also of splendid mares with flying manes and silky coats, almost impossible to tame even when by a stroke of luck they were taken alive. Only ten leagues away from Mexico City, bands of wild horses roamed the swampy meadows of the Río Lerma, on the road to Toluca, as late as the seventeenth century.

A cowboy's tasks were limited to branding young animals with the owner's iron, sorting out periodically those belonging to each estancia, and separating or killing the ones destined for market. The vaqueros spent their whole life in the saddle; they were remarkable horsemen.

To facilitate the sorting of herds, the rodeo was invented. This typically Mexican procedure was perhaps inspired by a form of Indian hunt. It shows up in the middle of the sixteenth century; Viceroy Enríquez laid down detailed rules for it in his 1574 *mesta* ordinances. The cowboys, mounted on horseback, would fan out in a circle and drive the cattle toward the estancias; or they would make the herds converge upon a fixed point, where they would sort them with the aid of long, iron-tipped poles similar to the *garrochas* of Andalusia. Originally, it seems, rodeos were held on a small scale between Midsummer Day and mid-November, that is, during the rainy season. They soon became a necessity in order to accustom the cattle to men and prevent their growing too wild. Then, after the cattle had moved into the virgin territories in the north and on the coasts, great roundups were held with hundreds of horsemen, spread out in an immense circle, driving the cattle toward a center designated by provincial law officers. There, the cattle were sorted according to their owners. Unbranded animals, or *orejanos*, were divided up among the stockmen, while strays bearing unfamiliar brands were handed over to the King's representatives as *mostrencos*, or animals whose owner was unknown.

Late in the sixteenth century, Suárez de Peralta, a riding enthusiast, tells us how, near Valles, in the hot region of Huasteca Province, "more than 300 horsemen belonging to all the cattle barons" would convene for the great rodeo. Such numbers are not surprising when we remember that in the vast northern stretches some owners had 150,000 head; the author just quoted considered "20,000 . . . a paltry number."

Mesta meetings, presided over by the association heads, also afforded an opportunity for bringing many stockmen together. The latter were supposed to bring along and return to their rightful owners cattle which had strayed upon their estancias. The meetings were held several times a year, generally on fixed dates, in the chief centers under the jurisdiction on each *mesta*. The earliest *mestas* were those of Mexico City, Puebla, and Oaxaca; later, each diocese had its own. So much driving of cattle to and fro elicited complaints from the natives, who sometimes suffered damage; for example, the Nopaluca Indians, in the Puebla–Tlaxcala region, saw the large herds accompanying a general meeting return to their village every year on the feast of St. Peter and St. Paul.

The cattle baron (*señor de ganado*) was usually a rich man from Mexico City, Puebla, or Querétaro; a governor, or a wealthy miner from the "new realms" in the north. But there were also stockmen in more modest circumstances, notably in the Bajío and in the Lagos region.

The *estanciero*, as his name indicates, lived on the estancia. The word is American, and in New Spain is first found in mid-sixteenth century. It often had a derogatory connotation, designating white men at the bottom of the social scale, as well as mestizos, Negroes, and mulattoes (defined as the offspring of a Negro and an Indian woman). The mestizos especially, disowned at the time by both Spaniards and Indians, found their place in the solitary life of the estancia, outside the main stream of the two communities. Contrary to the natives (nomads excepted), the *estancieros* were *hombres a caballo*, or horsemen, like the Spaniards. They worked either for fixed wages or for a share (*a partido*) of the profits; their share could go as high as half the value of the animals sold. These men were independent and usually quite restless; after following the droves displaced by the Viceroy, the habit stuck and they kept on migrating, with frequent changes of employer and location.

To kill the animals, frequently in large numbers, cowboys utilized a crescent-shaped blade mounted on a long pole, called a *desjarretadera*. They would gallop to the side of a bull and cut its hamstrings without dismounting. They acquired such dexterity that to amuse themselves or to sell the hides—sometimes without consulting the owners—they decimated the herds. Although the *mesta* formally banned that dangerous weapon as early as 1574, it continued in general use, especially in the north where the cowboys occasionally wielded it against their fellows.

Throughout the country, these men liked to lead a vagabond's life, free and easy, "especially the mestizos, mulattoes, and free Negroes: they are called saddletree lads [*de fuste*], because their sole possessions are a wretched old saddle, a lightly stepping mare (stolen), and their harquebus or short lance," a New Galicia inspecting magistrate wrote in 1607. "They strike terror to the heart of the population," an inspector declared; "calling themselves vaqueros, they ride about armed with *desjarretaderas* or scythes; they collect in bands and no one dares withstand them." A third licenciado added: "They are agile and hardy. Their breed grows apace, and trouble may well be brewing, for So-and-so is employing 300 of these mounted brigands as cowboys, and most of them are equipped with breastplates, harquebuses, scythes, *desjarretaderas*, and other weapons." On every isolated estancia they had friends or accomplices; if pursued for rustling, they would melt away into the trackless wastes of the northern marches.

Because there simply was no other labor available, stockmen were forced to employ these seminomads, at least for a part of the year and during the big rodeos. If they regretted having hired them, they regretted it more if they did not. The inhabitants of Zacatecas said of the free Negroes: "Their presence is an evil, but their absence is a much greater one."

One must not of course believe that all vaqueros were vagabonds. On the contrary, the stable populations in Celaya, Silao, Irapuato, León, and so on, seem to have included a number of owners who raised their own cattle with the help of a few Indian herdsmen. This was certainly true at Lagos, as well as in several zones of New Viscaya, near San Juan del Río, at Todos Santos (present-day Cordero, in Chihuahua), and even at Durango. There, on small family holdings, *estancieros* branded 200 or 300 calves and harvested a little wheat or maize. They lived on their land and did all the chores with the help of a couple of hands, their sons or sons-in-law. Such modest estancias were nonetheless large estates potentially; they contained thousands of hectares lying around a spring or along a river. Many haciendas sprang from no more than one or two estancia grants, as these were normally expanded in practice. Near the small holdings in the regions listed, members of the Ibarra, Río de Losa, Guerra de Resa, and Urdiñola families occupied areas "as big as states"; they possessed immense herds with their attendant host of hired hands, sharecroppers, farmers, and bailiffs.

All the aforementioned—whites, blacks, mestizos, and mulattoes, seminomad and sedentary populations, *estancieros*, cowboys, and owners—shared a love of horses and bulls which made them astonishingly good riders; even the Andalusians admired their horsemanship, and Cervantes mentioned it in *Don Quixote*. Father Alonso Ponce relates at length the dangerous exploits of a cowboy from the Guadalajara region, "in order to glorify and praise God, who bestows on His creatures such courage, strength, and skill." In his account we recognize various thrusts and feints belonging to *jaripeo*, the game, partly bullfight and partly riding exhibition, at which Mexican rancheros still excel. The Mexican cowboy's influence was so widespread that it impressed his American counterpart in the last century, who took over his rodeo, saddle, stirrups (Andalusian in origin), huge spurs, apparel, and even, in all likelihood, character traits.

The pastoral era of the estancia was thus destined to leave a permanent imprint, first, by furnishing a pattern for the great estate, and second, by creating throughout rural Mexico, except in strictly Indian districts, the environment peculiar to the man on horseback.

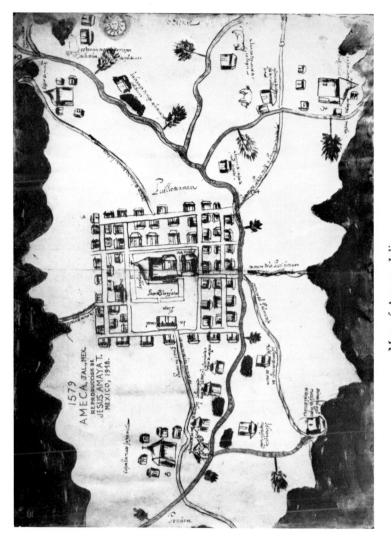

Map of Ameca, Jalisco, 1579.

Fortified bell tower of Augustinian church at Yuriria, Guanajuato,
built in the sixteenth century.

Door of church at Angahua, Michoacán, middle of the
sixteenth century.

Church of the hacienda of Ciénaga de la Mata.

Vaults of the hacienda
of Ciénaga de la Mata.

LITHOGRAPH BY B. H. WARD, LONDON, 1829

Hacienda of Chapingo, now occupied by the School of Agriculture.

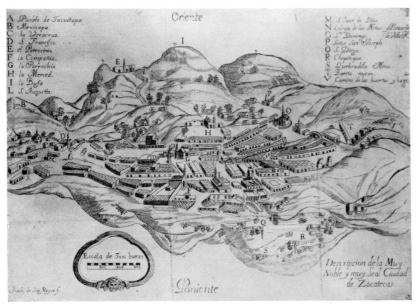

ENGRAVING BY JOAQUÍN DE SOTOMAYOR

Eighteenth-century map of Zacatecas.

Hacienda of San Mateo Valparaíso, Zacatecas.

Patio of the hacienda of Cienaguilla, built by Jesuits
in the seventeenth century.

Water tank at
Teoloyucan, Puebla.

Sugar refinery at Buenavista, built in the sixteenth century.

Ox cart in present-day
Oaxaca.

Town council (*cabildo*) of San Juan Chamula, Chiapas.

The steppes of Zacatecas.

PART II ▣

The First Masters of the Soil

4.CENTRAL AND SOUTHERN MEXICO

ENCOMENDEROS AND ROYAL OFFICIALS

Gold reserves in Mexico were small. Once the spoils had been distributed, conquistadors and settlers (who had already arrived in large numbers) discovered that the country was extremely poor in products that could be exchanged with the mother country or the Islands. Yet everything had to be imported, notably tools and animals needed for farming, transportation, and food. Tributes, though they did not bring in much gold, did supply enough slaves and provisions to allow encomenderos to work a few placer deposits and mines, and hence to obtain capital in the form of precious metals.

Despite the rapid growth of silver production, it remained inferior to the country's needs and the Crown's exactions. Metals flowed out of Mexico and into Spain in torrents, leaving Mexico's financial system in a state of anemia; the sixteenth century is filled with complaints about money troubles. Spaniards found it much harder to earn a little cash than to eat and see to their creature comforts. In this impoverished country, whose economy was unstable regardless of its masses of cattle and horses, the only men to possess capital and steady incomes were the large encomenderos, some of the northern miners, and influential officials whose salaries alone represented big incomes in a country where incomes of any sort were rare. Later, the Church, too, came into considerable capital.

When the Crown, shortly after the middle of the sixteenth century, took back and placed its own moderate tax on the encomiendas of the treasurer Juan Alonso de Sosa, the chief accountant Rodrigo de Albornoz, and the inspector Peralmíndez, it discovered that their tributes still amounted to 6,757, 11,288, and 13,138 pesos, respectively. These were large revenues for the time. Sosa was an important stockman at Jilotepec, though he was not the encomendero; the King denounced his misdeeds in 1553. Albornoz was, with Cortés, among the first to build sugar refineries in New Spain. Peralmíndez induced the King to grant him the exorbitant privilege of buying from the Indians any land he wanted anywhere in the country.

Not to mention the Marqués del Valle's domain, which is a special case, many encomiendas furnished a very adequate income, so adequate that the New Laws of 1542 ordered a reduction [in the size of the encomienda] for certain named individuals. The same laws abolished all personal labor required of the Indians.

Around 1560, there were in New Spain some 480 encomenderos collecting the equivalent of 377,734 pesos (including the Marqués del Valle's tributes). Individual incomes varied greatly. Among the large encomiendas, Jilotepec brought in 17,000 pesos, divided equally between Francisco de Velasco, the second viceroy's brother and Doña Beatriz de Andrade's heir, and Luis de Quesada, Juan Jaramillo's successor. Jaramillo had received from the first viceroy sixteen estancias; some were inside his encomienda district of Jilotepec, on which he possessed vast herds. Velasco owned eighteen estancias near the Chichimeca frontier. Both notables probably had their hands full keeping the nomads in check. Subsequently the two latifundia were combined in one entail.

Also in 1560, Alonso de Avalos, in the province of the same name, and Rodríguez de Orozco at Tututepec, each collected 4,500 pesos. One half of the 13,500 pesos furnished by Metztitlán went to one individual. Two persons shared the 8,100 pesos paid by a region in

Huasteca. Such people as Ortiz de Zúñiga, Hernán Pérez de Bocanegra, Bernardino de Bocanegra, Diego de Ordás, Ruiz de la Mota, and Juan de Sámano received yearly tributes worth several thousand pesos. Most of them were cattle barons, and all the early *mesta* heads were chosen from among them. Other encomenderos, however, received absurd pittances of only twenty pesos or so.

Although the epidemics had considerably thinned out the number of Indians, many encomiendas at the century's close still contained thousands of tributaries paying at least a peso or a peso and a half a head. The heyday was over, however. Tributes were heavily taxed. Petitions and protests availed them nothing; the encomenderos failed in their attempt to have their incomes made perpetual. The Crown reappropriated many encomiendas on the holders' death. In 1642, there were only 140 left, bringing in a total of 300,000 pesos much reduced in value by rising prices. A large part of the sum went to one individual, the Marqués del Valle. Commerce, northern mines, and sugar refineries were by now furnishing considerably larger revenues than the best encomiendas; in the last third of the century, the richest man in Mexico was Alonso de Villaseca, a miner and businessman who had no Indian vassals.

By the seventeenth century, the encomienda had become a negligible source of capital. Its role in providing capital and labor for several decades of early farming and livestock ventures should not, however, be underestimated. As the Audiencia prosecutor wrote in 1544, "all such ventures belong to rich men possessing Indians under the encomienda system; the latter were and still are the industry's wellspring; without the Indians, the industry would perish."

Thanks to the various legal means of gaining title, what was to prevent the encomenderos from seizing all the territory belonging to their tributary villages? At the outset, they were inclined to act like veritable lords. They quickly emulated other stockmen in trying to appropriate pastures that the Crown insisted were common land. If the terrain was favorable, they installed their estancias as a matter of course near Indian villages owing them work services, maize, or silver tribute. As early as 1532, the Audiencia's president, Ramírez de Fuenleal, put the King on guard against pasture enclosures in general and land grabbing by the encomenderos in particular. According to Fuenleal, an encomendero should not be allowed more than one or two caballerías inside his territory; otherwise, "he would shortly own, at any price that he wished to pay, both the master's land and the common folk's, and he would encroach upon other land without paying a cent, as has happened and is happening." Outside the encomiendas, Fuenleal concluded, larger grants of harvest land would be permissible.

As soon as the encomenderos began to feel the weight of viceregal authority, they attempted to legalize their occupation of grazing land by soliciting estancias for themselves and their children, relatives, or dependents. In 1542, for example, Mendoza granted Juan de Villaseñor formal title to three estancias that he had already established within his encomienda at Huango, in Michoacán. They were the nucleus of the rich haciendas on which the family gave such elaborate fiestas that Huango was nicknamed "Petty Court." Around the same time and under the same circumstances, well-known encomenderos like Pedro de Meneses, Antonio de Almaguer, and Maestre de Roa received land grants. In 1550, Jerónimo Ruiz de la Mota was given, at one and the same time, title to seven estancias inside Chapa [de Mota], which was his encomienda; he had already been occupying them "for over fifteen years." That did not prevent him from being a cattle baron at Jilotepec, whose community paid its tribute elsewhere. Ruiz de la Mota's holdings would eventually become part of a great entail.

In the Acámbaro–Apaseo region, a clear-cut example is furnished by the Bocanegra family. In 1557, the tributes from the two encomiendas of Acámbaro and Apaseo brought 4,000 pesos to Hernán Pérez de Bocanegra; his large farms in the same region paid him 6,000 more. The farms were located on the harvest estancia of San Pedro de Apaseo el Bajo, "beside the river . . . , with its dwellings, barns, granaries, livestock pens, threshing floors, and all the caballerías contained within said enclosure of Apaseo, with its watercourses and irrigation canals." Nearby, Hernán Pérez also owned a vineyard, an inn, and three mills at Apaseo el Alto (given him by Mendoza in 1538), plus an impressive string of cattle and sheep estancias in the two territories.

All Bocanegra's holdings had been legalized by grants from the first two viceroys, either in his name or in that of each of his five children. Other grants had been made to third parties, who had sold them to the encomendero. He had also bought various pieces of land from the Acámbaro Indians and their caciques; in 1542, he signed an agreement with their community leaving him the entire Apaseo bank of the river and restricting the Indians to the other bank. Grants and purchases went on throughout the sixteenth century, until a rich entail was formed that almost entirely covered the original encomienda site and spread far into neighboring regions.

In 1544, the agent Gonzalo de Salazar had the King confirm title to twenty cavallerías that he had purchased from the Taximaroa Indians, whose encomendero he was. He intended to build a sugar refinery at San Juan de Zitácuaro, which eventually became one of the biggest in Michoacán. The Oñate and Solís families acquired their refineries in the same way.

Many of these large estates later became entailed; some were even elevated to marquisates. It is not at all surprising that individuals possessing land and tributes, sometimes a noble title like the Bocanegra-Villamayor family, should consider themselves to be the lords of the manor.

The viceroys were constantly handing out land grants to all sorts of people, apparently without drawing a distinction between encomienda villages and those paying tribute directly to the Crown. Besides the natives, only the local encomendero was invited to testify. He was thought to be best qualified to raise possible objections to the grant. His own interests did lead him to defend his vassals against third parties, such as cattlemen, settlers, or merchants, who were quick to invade natives' fields or extort money from them and thereby endanger the tribute.

Sometimes grantees were poor wretches, relatives, or dependents, who hastened to turn their deeds over to their protectors. But others were settlers or capitalists (increasingly numerous after the middle of the sixteenth century) of varying means. There were also encomenderos from other areas interested solely in finding the best spots for their livestock or fields. The vast plains and prairies of Jilotepec furnished sustenance for the droves of not only the two local encomenderos, but also a number of powerful individuals—officials, miners, encomenderos, businessmen, and so on—twenty-nine at least of whom we know by name. Another early instance is Tecamachalco, a certain Alonso Valiente's encomienda, on which no fewer than 56 cattle and sheep estancias were located by 1550, belonging to Spaniards who had been attracted by favorable raising conditions. Stockmen and colonists had settled in many different regions, for example, not far from Tecama-chalco at Tepeaca, which paid its tribute directly to the Crown.

Authorities came to look askance at an encomendero whose estate was on his encomienda, for they feared that he might be tempted to make his vassals work even after the abolition of personal services. Although Viceroy Mendoza sometimes had to compromise in the light of existing conditions, in order to avoid upsetting a nascent economy or offending powerful individuals, Prince Philip ordered him in 1551 to grant a sheep estancia to a Puebla citizen only "providing that you choose a site outside the said Cristóbal Núñez' encomienda." Such estancias were finally forbidden altogether in the seventeenth century.

Even though some encomenderos initially tried to block off pastures for their own use, even though they then were able to obtain title or to acquire by more regular means other lands on their encomiendas, the great estates did not, generally speaking, grow out of the encomiendas—legally or otherwise. Without taking into account the northern zones, where there were no sedentary Indians and hence no true encomiendas, one-third or one-half of New Spain was directly under the Crown's jurisdiction. Also, some of the richest regions paid tribute to the Marqués del Valle; in his territory Spaniards' haciendas had no connection with encomiendas. On the other hand, sugar refineries and different kinds of estates were established on encomiendas. These properties belonged to officials, businessmen, or simple farmers, as well as, and especially, to the Church, which rapidly covered the entire country with its holdings.

The earliest sources of capital in New Spain, besides the encomiendas, were public offices and the law. Silver mines located in the northern provinces developed somewhat later, as did big business.

Next to the Viceroy, who arrived on the scene in 1535, the highest officials were the Audiencia's members in Mexico City: a president, eight judges, four crime commissioners, and two prosecutors, with a chief constable as executive. In addition, a royal finance council of sorts was composed of a treasurer, a chief accountant, and a factor assisted by an inspector, plus local treasurers, lieutenants, and minor officials. Two smaller audiencias relieved the Mexico City body of a part of its work: a Frontier Audiencia in the southwest and one at Guadalajara in the north (1548). In the different provinces, the King was represented by alcaldes mayores, corregidores, and governors. A swarm of officials and lawyers lived off lawsuits and various affairs; their steady incomes and connections with the mighty were eloquent proof of influence.

Until the reforms effected by the New Laws of 1542, certain royal officials were also encomenderos; they were among the biggest ones. In 1544, however, the treasurer's, accountant's, and inspector's encomiendas were replaced with emoluments. At about the same time, the Mexico City judges' yearly salary was 2,400 pesos; it went to nearly 3,000 around 1557, besides providing housing in the *casas reales,* or public buildings. Thirty-three years later, it is true, the salary had not changed, although the cost of living had increased considerably and there was no public housing space. Unlike most of the conquistadors, who were simple, unlettered men, high officials dispatched from Spain were university graduates, licentiates or doctors. Especially, they were well-to-do and even rich; possession of a nest egg on arrival, however modest it might be, was not to be despised in a country where in the early days there was almost no money in circulation. Finally, the influence that went with public office was surely no hindrance to the conduct of private business.

Both the spirit and the letter of the New Laws were opposed, however, to the extraprofessional activities of the King's officials and representatives. As Audiencia judges and chief justice officials were given "decent salaries," they were formally forbidden, in 1549, to own cattle or sheep farms, estancias, harvest land, mines, or commercial enterprises, in partnership or by proxy, directly or indirectly. The royal order was reiterated the next year, then in various wordings throughout the sixteenth and seventeenth centuries, notably in 1558–1575, 1584, 1597, 1607, 1618, and 1619. Actually, no one was ever penalized save a few members of the Mexico City Audiencia; in defiance of regulations which took in their children, many royal officials, particularly in the Treasury, were cattle barons or rich farmers, as were many barristers and lawyers.

Before the New Laws were promulgated—and even afterward— Viceroy Mendoza himself owned a number of estancias and droves in various parts of Mexico, besides a large sugar refinery (which must have been Orizaba). When charges were brought at the end of his term of office, he did not deny the facts; but he did defend himself skillfully and perhaps in good faith. Declaring that he had set an example at a time when not enough interest was being shown in livestock and crop raising, he pointed out that New Spain now possessed the fine wool of the merinos, which he had had imported for his estancias at great expense. A witness asserted in addition that the Viceroy's cattle had allowed him to keep open house "for a large number of caballeros and other needy persons."

The example that Mendoza had set soon bore fruit. In the same period at least two Audiencia judges, the Licenciado Tejada and Dr. Santillán, embarked on a series of highly lucrative farming and business ventures. Having come in 1537 to replace Vasco de Quiroga, Lorenzo de Tejada was particularly active and enterprising. In Mexico City, he built a number of buildings, including a large apartment house which contemporaries described in admiring terms. Tejada was even more a large-scale farmer. He bought land near the capital and, it seems, obtained more from the Viceroy. Then he went into partnership several times, once with Alonso de Mérida, the royal treasurer, and brought water into the area from the sierra of Guaximalpa. With Mendoza's approval, he dug a big canal to irrigate forty-four caballerías, which were soon raising, he claimed, over 10,000 fanegas of wheat.

The same judge also planted mulberry trees, vineyards, and orchards; built several mills, and went into the livestock business. Up to his departure in 1552, he showed unflagging energy; the swarms of Indians who worked for him did not, however, escape unscathed. What he had accomplished on his own initiative, he declared in his defense against charges brought at the end of his term of office, was beneficial to the country; the price of fruit in the capital had been reduced largely because of his efforts, and many Spaniards had imitated him in putting their land under cultivation and beginning to raise livestock. He concluded that he was a good citizen deserving of praise rather than of criticism or penalties. Some people agreed with him. Other witnesses pointed out that he was sailing for Spain with a huge fortune in his pocket; one witness asserted that his lands alone had sold for 100,000 pesos.

Dr. Santillán, too, disposed of considerable property before his departure in 1551: 10,000 sheep, estancias, harvest fields, houses, and mines with their slaves, cattle, and adoining lands. The total amount realized was some 80,000 pesos.

In the provinces, these activities resulted in comic excesses. The little Frontier Audiencia's members, on the Guatemalan border, were all fathers-in-law, brothers-in-law, or sons-in-law of the local royal officials, encomenderos, and planters. One in particular, the secretary Rebolledo, was a "powerful Croesus," in the phrase of the Mexico City Audiencia's clerk; together with a flock of influential relatives he owned "almost the entire region." He was also trying to corner the rich cacao trade. If officials were too zealous, however, they could fall victim to those whose abuses they were denouncing; that happened to the clerk in question. Slightly later, as we shall see, the situation was not much different in the Guadalajara Audiencia.

In Mexico City, Viceroy Luis de Velasco appears to have been a man of integrity. It seems that he spent more than his earnings, went into debt, and died a pauper. He did his utmost to place men of his stamp in key positions. His thirteen years in office (1550–1564) probably represent the best period in Spain's administration of Mexico. On the lower echelons, however, it was hard to combat a medieval notion of public office that went back to the Spanish Reconquest. *Corregimientos* and other minor judicial posts had been handed out to penniless conquistadors as rewards for services rendered. These posts had been given to others as gratifications or pensions, more economical for the Crown than encomiendas. The annual income from such positions being rarely more than a few hundred pesos, the recipients naturally sought to turn their influence into cash by acquiring land, raising livestock, or conducting business in areas under their control. An inspecting judge remarked in 1545: "If it should please His Majesty to order that those married conquistadors and colonizers who, because of the scarcity of Indians, have corregimientos [rather than encomiendas] should be assured of their livelihood in some other way, great evils would cease." Nearly a century later, Viceroy Cerralvo said of his royal officials that "[we must] either raise their salaries or close our eyes [to their personal activities]." The financial crisis at the end of the sixteenth century and the attendant upsurge in the sale of high offices caused corruption to spread to the upper echelons.

After Velasco's death, the King was requested to make provision for more frequent visits of inspection in the provinces; the purpose was to prevent justice officials, corregidores, and alcaldes mayores from appropriating, either directly or through dummies, so many fields, estancias, and mills. It was specifically recommended that the abuses of which a number of Audiencia officials were guilty should be brought to a stop. The officials were occupying the natives' fields to such an extent that the latter were "hemmed in and shut up in their villages," especially in the Mexico City region. No one had dared to protest. Dr. Villanueva, an Audiencia judge, established a large farm at the very gates of Cuyotepec. He later sold it for 10,000 ducats. Other offenders were the secretaries Juan de la Cueva and Sancho López, the factor Ortuño de Ibarra, various lawyers, and the chief constable's lieutenant. Some villages were completely cut off from their lands.

Penalties were sometimes imposed, however. Notwithstanding his eminence, a learned member of the Audiencia, Diego García de Palacio, doctor of canon law and author of scientific works still read and reprinted today (*Diálogos militares* and *Instrucción náutica*, published at Mexico City in 1583 and 1587), was suspended for nine years in 1589 by the Royal Council and given a heavy fine. The chief accusations against him involved acquisitions of land by bringing pressure to bear on Indians, humble folk, and justices and other minor officials. Diego García had obtained a number of grants for a brother, a son, an uncle, cousins, other relatives, and dependents, all of whom were his proxies. Under the same disguise, he had forced Indians to sell many fields, often for trifling sums.

This high official was an extremely active man, astute and enterprising; he was a great capitalist full of personal business schemes, whose like could still be found in Mexico a few years ago. He established four harvest estancias and a big mill in the Mexico City area, promoted livestock in various regions in the south, built an important refinery in Michoacán comprising twenty-four caballerías for raising sugar cane, imported cows from Tabasco by ship, and mares from Chiapas (prices being very low there), and founded a hacienda and a fishery in Yucatan. All these undertakings were his own creation and his own property, for the sundry title holders—relatives and dependents—obviously, as the prosecution stated, "do not have the capital to maintain [them]."

García de Palacio was punished because the much-feared Philip II was still on the throne. In subsequent years, the same type of infraction continued to be committed. It could hardly be otherwise as long as the Spanish state, on the verge of bankruptcy, was selling an increasingly large number of public offices and cutting salaries.

It is difficult to determine from the information we possess what limits were set, on the one hand, to the sale of offices, and on the other, to the prohibition of private property and businesses; a corollary would be how strictly the prohibition was enforced. A fact that speaks for itself is that some seventeenth-century viceroys granted their private secretaries a considerable amount of land—and permission for immediate sale. A few years previously, the Count of Monterrey had issued a series of operating ordinances for a sugar refinery belonging to Gordián Casasano; the latter's official title was Magistrate-Accountant of the Public Treasury of New Spain. Near Cuautla (Morelos) the village of Casasano on the refinery's site perpetuates this great royal accountant's name; otherwise he is completely forgotten today. After his death in 1603, an Audiencia inquiry contained this declaration: "He was one of the most faithful, painstaking, honest, and honorable ministers to serve Your Majesty since the discovery of the Indies." Was there connivance?

THE CASE OF THE MARQUÉS DEL VALLE

One great encomendero and capitalist of New Spain stands out above all others: Hernán Cortés. Immediately after the Conquest, Cortés possessed the biggest fortune in the New World. In addition, by virtue of a royal cédula dated July 9, 1529, he was given "upwards of 23,000 vassals"; they far exceeded that figure and were still paying him in 1560, even after sharp reductions, the sum total of 36,862 pesos [annually].

Cortés could legitimately boast of being more than a very rich encomendero. When he was granted the title of Marqués del Valle de Oaxaca, he received, together with tributary towns and villages, "[the regions'] lands, hamlets, and districts; vassals; civil as well as criminal jurisdiction over capital and petty offenses; revenues; offices; taxes and assessments; woods, meadows, and watercourses"—all with hereditary rights in perpetuity. He had chosen himself the regions indicated in the royal cédula, namely the best portions of New Spain. There, practically the only prerogatives left to the King were courts of appeal, mines, and mintage. The territory was very large and was divided into five or six segments, one of the most important being the broad depression encompassing Cuernavaca and the modern state of Morelos. Also included were several localities close to the capital (Tacubaya and Coyoacán), together with the Toluca Valley to the west; also, the far-off zone of the "four cities" in the southeast around Antequera and Oaxaca, which joined up with the Isthmus of Tehuantepec. In 1535, the territory was made an entail, indivisible and inalienable.

Within his "state," as it was called, the Marqués appointed administrators and justice officials. Just as if he were a king, he claimed as his due the exercising of *jus patronatus*, which he had been awarded by a pontifical bull. He began a palace at Cuernavaca, where he perhaps intended to establish his capital. His son wished to seal his letters with *Martinus Cortesius primus hujus nominis, Dux Marchio secundus*. A large feudal state, a distant replica of the Duchy of Burgundy in Europe, had sprung up in the heart of New Spain.

No sooner had the royal jurists published the famous 1529 cédula than they began to realize just how much they had given away. Making use of typical lawyer-like methods, they set about whittling down, undermining, and restricting the grant in every possible manner. As a result, the first Marqués gave vent to furious rages and the second entered into a conspiracy that was put down with great harshness—the estate was sequestered for many years. A flood of orders, cédulas, provisos, and measures limited Cortés' prerogatives and placed them under strict supervision. One of the earliest orders took Spaniards from under his jurisdiction; they were no longer to be considered his vassals. The measure merely assimilated Castilians in the Marquesado to Peninsular hidalgos, who were under the King's direct jurisdiction when resident on lords' estates. The measure had far-reaching consequences in that the marqueses were careful to found no towns for Spaniards, since such towns would have placed a curb on their jurisdictional rights.

As early as 1531, the new Audiencia's licenciado had denounced Cortés' claiming as his private reserve (*coto suyo*) the woods and pastures on his estate; the King, they stated, did not have it in his power to alienate "something so public." In spite of the original grant's text, the Empress finally accepted this interpretation, declaring that "woods, pastures, and water must be shared by all Spaniards"; therefore, the Marqués could not restrict them to his exclusive use (1533). The question was long to be a bone of contention between two opposing groups of jurists: Did grazing lands and untilled fields (*baldíos*) on the estate belong to the King, or did they belong to the marqueses, as the 1529 cédula implied? The question became of more immediate interest when the Crown, relinquishing commonage throughout New Spain, let the viceroys distribute pasture to private citizens.

No general or definitive solution was found for over a century. The granting and the entering into possession of the various parcels of land followed different rules, depending on locality, period, and individuals. They are all the more significant since in the Cortés state-within-a-state, haciendas developed under peculiar conditions.

Cortés had a better head for business than most of the Spaniards around him. That could already be observed in the Islands, where he had made money in livestock and business. On the continent, he rapidly acquired the biggest principal and the biggest income in the New World. It stood to reason that so dynamic a man would not be satisfied with collecting his tributes or using his resources for risky or ill-fated expeditions, like those to the Pacific. He wanted to increase his fortune by less brilliant but more certain means, in livestock and agriculture, particularly sugar refineries; his refineries were the first and foremost in the country.

Would the Marqueses del Valle, like the encomenderos, solicit grants from the Viceroys, their detested successors at the government's helm? Or did they need to, already having a right to uncultivated land on their estate, in conformity with the 1529 cédula, which, to be sure, had been greatly reduced in scope in 1533? Cortés was a shrewd lawyer (he had studied at Salamanca); instead of availing himself of viceregal grants, he proceeded on his own, but with all the caution that Antonio de Mendoza's energetic stand made advisable. Out of all the first two marqueses' sizable rural domains, only one estancia, Atengo, near Toluca, which was qualified as inalienable and manorial, was definitely held under no title other than its founder's fierce will; around 1556 Martín Cortés was engaged in litigation with His Majesty's prosecutor over it. A different type of appropriation had the advantage of reserving future manorial rights and at the same time furnishing indisputable title to the land in use.

Citing as their authority a 1535 cédula allowing purchases from the Indians in order to expand agricultural production, Cortés and his administrators bought up fertile land cheaply, with which they constituted their best estates. Such is the origin of the great sugar plantation at

Tuxtla, composed of "much excellent land bought from the Indians." Likewise, the estancias and fields at Oaxaca and Etla were bought for 100 pesos in 1543 and sold less than fifty years later for 8,002. The sugar refinery at Tlaltenango, near Cuernavaca, was originally the most important in Mexico; around 1556, it was producing for market year in and year out 8,000 arrobas of white sugar at three pesos the arroba. Fifteen years later, it was still being leased out for 9,000 pesos, and the refinery at Tuxtla for 5,000, despite their being sequestered. The refinery site at Tlaltenango was assessed at the modest rate of 12 pesos per year, while the cane fields were rented for sums usually paid six years in advance. Cortés' precautions did not hinder the Viceroy from appointing a special commissioner in 1550 to restore to the Cuernavaca Indians the lands that the Marqués had "usurped."

The origin of the vast estancias in the Isthmus of Tehuantepec is more difficult to determine. One of them was *cercada,* or enclosed. They raised purebred horses, supplied Oaxaca butcher shops with beef, and, equipped with a tannery, shipped leather as far as Peru. The Marqués in all likelihood took possession of that land on his own authority. He was probably referring to such direct appropriation in his will, when he requested verification of the Indians' having escaped harm, "because in a few localities of my estate lands were seized to plant orchards and vineyards." Usually, however, the first Marqués acted with a wariness that certain of his descendants failed to emulate.

After Cortés' death, those descendants continued to buy land from the Indians, especially in the rich lowlands east of Cuernavaca. Then, compromised in the 1566 conspiracy (a revolt of the aristocrats, whose chief was Martín Cortés) and punished by a long sequestering of their property, the second and third marqueses seem to have accepted the Viceroy's authority as an accomplished fact. We find them requesting and being granted estancias like ordinary citizens. In 1589, they obtained from Viceroy Villamanrique six estancias near the mouth of the Alvarado, and in 1597 two in the Isthmus of Tehuantepec. They showed no inclination to be anything more than wealthy encomenderos and landowners; they seemed to have none of the first Marqués' great creative activity, and at a time when sugar refineries were springing up all over their state, they founded no new ones of their own. The two original refineries were to remain the main items in the entail's list of possessions.

Don Pedro Cortés Ramírez de Arellano, fourth Marqués del Valle, attempted to reimpose his authority. Although the first two marqueses had been clever enough to play down their pretensions in times of crisis, they had refused from the beginning to relinquish certain of their rights. Hernán Cortés had granted, in his town of Cuernavaca, a piece of land to a retainer, his majordomo Bernardino del Castillo, "together with its trees, stones, and water." Did the land belong to the Marqués by Indian purchase, or did he simply arrogate to himself the right to give it away? In any event, the form of the title deed recalls the grants made in His Majesty's name.

Martín Cortés had no lingering doubts either, with the result that he fell afoul of the Viceroy when his alcalde mayor started handing out estancias and caballerías in Tehuantepec. In 1555, Luis de Velasco forbade all such grants without the King's or his express approval. The Viceroy for his part was doubtless not too sure of his ground, since, instead of invoking the real reason for a measure making grants a royal prerogative, he merely claimed that the Marqués' grants had harmed the Indians. Besides, owing to the Isthmus' importance for maritime communications with Peru, His Majesty's representatives kept it under close scrutiny.

The first two viceroys had already begun to grant a few estancias and caballerías to Spaniards inside the Marquesado, near Toluca and elsewhere. Subsequent to the scandal caused by Martín Cortés' conspiracy and to the sequestering of his territory (1566–1567), viceregal grants became more numerous and widespread, as if to emphasize the Crown's rights within its rebel vassal's principality. In 1567 the grants increased in Tehuantepec and other regions. A last vestige of scrupulosity appears to have made the viceroys spare the Cuernavaca district; in that city were located the state palace and administration, with a governor and a minister of justice, a chief accountant, and other officials whom the Marqués appointed.

Happy to be reinstated in his rights, the third Marqués ventured nothing. But the fourth, Don Pedro Cortés, who became head of the family in 1602, acted differently. Philip II was no longer on the throne; a less firm hand and serious financial difficulties favored Don Pedro's undertaking. For several decades he was to make freer with his lands than any of his predecessors, not excepting the title's first bearer. The very year he became head of the family, he instructed his "governor and administrator . . . to establish in my said state cattle and sheep estancias in all the places, parts, and sites that he will deem most suitable." Having been given this advance authorization, the agent needed merely to pick out of the whole Marquesado the choicest pastures for his master's droves.

Don Pedro did not stop there. Instead of waiting for reactions like Velasco's to Martín Cortés, when the latter had distributed land, the fourth Marqués took the offensive by denouncing to His Majesty the "interference" of various viceroys, particularly Montesclaros (1603–1607), who had dared to grant inside his state "caballerías, woods, estancia sites, mills and fulling mills, enclosures, meadows, and other lands." Also, Don Pedro must have thought it less profitable to establish new enterprises than to place permanent assessments on land being exploited or to be exploited by Spaniards. He sold his caballería and estancia grants at public auction; then, in exchange for annual rents of 10, 20, 50, 80, or more pesos, he delivered formal title deeds whose main clauses were drawn up in this style:

> *Let all who may see this letter know that I, Don Pedro Cortés, Marqués del Valle de Oaxaca, lord of the cities of Toluca and Cuernavaca, and of the fourteen villages of Tlalnagua, patron and permanent administrator of the hospital of Our Lady of the Immaculate Conception in Mexico City, knight of the Order of Santiago, and member of His Majesty's Council, etc. . . . inasmuch as . . . [X], inhabiting my said city of . . . , has requested me to lease to him in perpetuity [such and such estancias and caballerías] . . . and as, for the customary investigation to be carried out, I have despatched a writ to . . . [Y], my alcalde mayor, who has carried it out, and as from his official report . . . it appears that the land in question is unoccupied and virgin and may be leased to said . . . [X], and as the grant will not harm Indians or other third parties, and as I have communicated the results of said investigation to Dr. . . . [Z], a lawyer of the Royal Audiencia, . . . who . . . was of the opinion that the land requested might be leased in perpetuity . . . , by these presents I grant and acknowledge that of my own free will and in my heirs' and successors' name I do lease in perpetuity to said . . . [X] said land.*

The Marqués' alcalde mayor placed recipients in formal possession of their grants.

A large number of similar deeds, drawn up in terms recalling vice-regal grants in some respects, were distributed over a period of more than thirty years—until 1628 at least. Sometimes the Marqués leased an area to a stockman for a limited time only. Spaniards who had received grants from the viceroys had to come to terms with Don Pedro by promising to pay him permanent rent; some of them protested.

As the marqueses had avoided founding Spanish communities that would have escaped their jurisdiction, they could rest assured that there were no alods or other independent territories within their state. Don Pedro Cortés had turned the Marquesado into one immense domain whose land was directly exploited by him, leased to Spanish hidalgos, or worked by his Indian vassals and tributaries.

The government reacted through its spokesman, the Audiencia's prosecutor, who charged the fourth Marqués with "usurping what belonged by right to the royal patrimony, the treasury, and the chamber." He had dared to conclude sales, leases, and other contracts for lands, untilled fields, and woods of his state and manor, whereas his only rights were jurisdiction and tributes. This counterattack by the prosecutor was a clever one; together with other sorts of ownerless property (*bienes mostrencos*), the patrimony of persons dying without an heir went by right to the Crown. The Indian population having shrunk in the last quarter of the sixteenth century, many untilled or unoccupied fields constituted property abandoned by hamlets that had disappeared; official documents often mention this fact. When the Marqués leased out territory of that category, he was exceeding manorial rights and encroaching upon his suzerain's, according to ancient Castilian custom. In as different an environment as the Indies, the rule was to be sure open to many interpretations.

Suit had been brought in 1610. The Marqués appealed the Audiencia's verdict, and in 1612 the case came before the Council of the Indies. That body first recognized the Crown's rights to vanished communities' lands, as well as to other possessions of those dying heirless. Then, it settled the essential point in litigation by forbidding the Marqués to distribute any unoccupied land or common pasture (1627). On June 2, 1628, a royal writ of execution charged an Audiencia judge with carrying out the verdict. The countersuit filed by the Marqués' agent was not rejected until 1634, and the executor's death delayed the order's execution until 1642–1644.

Such slowness and lack of vigor in the centralizing monarchy's reactions were a sign of the times. In point of law, the marqueses had, however, been worsted. Also in fact, their situation was rendered precarious by the state's having passed, on Don Pedro's death in 1629, to two women in succession, who did not even live in Mexico: Doña Estefanía, Marquesa del Valle and the Duke of Terranova's wife, and Doña Juana, the Duke of Monteleone's wife. Doña Juana was succeeded by Don Andrés, at one and the same time Marqués del Valle and Duke of Terranova and of Monteleone (1653–1691). All three resided in Spain or especially in Italy, leaving the administration entirely in agents' hands.

The marqueses, in conclusion, could no longer freely dispose of their state; and the royal treasury recovered the rents that Don Pedro Cortés had collected from untilled lands. Finally, the viceroys set about collecting fees for confirming in His Majesty's name the title deeds granted by the Marqués, declaring them inadequate. The Marquesado kept its autonomous judicial system, however, with the result that the Marqués' alcaldes mayors and other representatives maintained some sort of check on viceregal grants.

THE LAND GRABBERS

Elsewhere than in the Marquesado, the customary method of acquiring land or grazing rights was to obtain caballería and especially estancia grants, which were being distributed on a large scale.

Although the viceroys at times showed favoritism to the great conquistadors and encomenderos who were the "country's backbone," in the sixteenth century they hardly ever handed out the vast concessions that would become so frequent later, particularly in the northern provinces. On the contrary, one is struck by the multitude and diversity of grantees, often in one region or even one locality. What can be the explanation, then, of the huge estates and vast entails? Why, and how, did the lands of so many quickly fall into the hands of so few?

Many estancia deeds were made over or sold as soon as they were received, the reason being that the idea of territorial grants still contained traditional and medieval notions condoning trafficking to a certain extent. A grant was a *favor* made in His Majesty's name, a kind of reward for meritorious service to the Crown, especially in the army. In the same manner as the position of corregidor was regarded as a pension for those deserving well of the King rather than as a function requiring certain aptitudes, an estancia grant, on a lower plane, was often considered at least as much a reward as a means of colonizing and developing the country. In some respects grants were a part of the "territorial and bureaucratic spoils" mentioned by Sánchez Albornoz, similar to the spoils that the kings of Castile had distributed throughout the centuries of the Reconquest. As Velasco II wrote around 1590, grants were made at first to encourage livestock raising; then they were also given

as a reward for their services to former colonizers and a few poor conquistadors, as well as to their children and grandchildren; some worked their grants, while others, lacking ready money, sold them to those that could work them and used for their personal needs the sums received in exchange. Thus, many estancias are now in the possession of persons who bought them from recipients of grants made in His Majesty's name by the viceroys and governors.

There is consequently nothing surprising in grantees' having been enabled to turn into immediate cash, favors just bestowed on them. They took full advantage of the opportunity. With or without official permission, girl orphans and poor conquistadors' daughters thus obtained a modest dowry; fatherless children or penniless widows acquired money to live on. Men without the means to stock the land, others lacking initiative or in need of money, and still others by agreement with a patron on whom they were dependent, all sold their deeds for a few hundred pesos to those in a position to buy them.

When harvest land was involved, the Viceroy's primary concern was to provide the country with food; wheat was always in short supply, and sometimes maize. Despite the clause in the deeds forbidding sale during the first six years, many caballerías were ceded as if they had been estancias. Trafficking and speculation started. In 1561–1562 the Franciscan Mendieta recommended that "no one be given [harvest] land or an estancia without the stipulation that for a certain time and during so many years the land should be improved and developed, under penalty of losing it for breach of contract." Viceroy Velasco adopted the recommendation in 1563 and extended to estancia deeds the no-sale clause for the first three years.

The new clause was no more respected than the old ones, at least under viceroys like the Marqués de Falces or the Count of Coruña and during periods of interim rule by the Audiencia. In 1567, for example, a certain Gómez Triguillos de Silva wrote a letter to the King denouncing the "thousand turpitudes and thousand sales and resales" in land grants. A barber, a blacksmith, a tinker, or some such person, Gómez Triguillos went on to say, providing he had a connection with an Audiencia judge or the Viceroy, could obtain, with six witnesses willing to do him a favor by serving as straw men, the promise (*acordada*) of an estancia and three or four caballerías. "Before ever taking out his title deed, he has sold the promise for 300, 500, or 1,000 pesos, even for 2,000, 3,000, or 5,000." Others, more ingenious, would spend 50 or 100 pesos on a few cabins and pens; then they would add 8,000 or 10,000 sheep purchased at a low price and sell out for an enormous profit. "What has been going on," he concludes, "and is still going on, is a sport and a mockery"; large fortunes had been made in this kind of operation alone. The author's tone is aggressive and some of his figures are exaggerated, but an attentive examination of title records proves that he has invented nothing.

Another individual, Gómez de Cervantes, later described in the same vein the methods that viceroys' or Audiencia judges' relatives and retainers used to corner the best lands. Putting their influence to good purpose, they had caballerías, estancias, and mills granted to conquistadors' poorest descendants; the latter were delighted to transfer title immediately to their powerful protectors.

Matters grew steadily worse. Around 1588, Viceroy Villamanrique showed an inclination to take cognizance of the selling of recently issued deeds; he began to honor in the breach clauses forbidding transfer during an initial four- or six-year period. His first dispensations went mostly to poor widows or indigents; but in a few he regularized powerful men's purchases. In the following century, title deeds were frequently issued wth a license authorizing immediate sale, a practice that led inevitably to all sorts of subterfuges. In 1607, a slave was granted land, which he transferred on the spot. Deeds eventually found their way into strongboxes that never let them out again, because they had become either Church property or part of an entail—most land grabbers were building up entails for their children. Under such circumstances, many grants were purely fictitious and their recipients thinly disguised proxy holders for a relatively small number of capitalists, rich farmers, or cattle barons.

We often suspect trickery, and it is even flagrant at times. Some poor wretches confess to it quite naïvely in the act of transfer. Around 1580–1585, for example, Baltasar de Obregón, a small encomendero in need of money, repaid the "kind services, help, and benefactions" of a rich Vera Cruz curate by obtaining several grants, which he at once made over to the curate.

> *I do so because Licenciado Gaspar Ruiz de Cabrera has shown me the estancia's site and because I have requested said grant in his name and for his sake. I have pledged my word to cede and transfer it to him if successful. Moreover, the aforementioned has paid the fees for the grant and the petition, as well as expenses; for my trouble and the steps that I have had to take in said affair he has given me seventy gold pesos, with which sum I declare myself to be paid to my satisfaction . . . For the above reasons I transfer title to him.*

Others among the licenciado's dummies admitted in all innocence to having received the kind of small favors that dependents had a right to expect from their protector. "Since the above-mentioned licenciado has given me fifty pesos to buy a suit, pointed out to me the estancia site (of which I was completely ignorant), requested said writ himself, paying all costs, and since I owe him many kindnesses, I deed to him . . ." Many other beneficiaries joined like considerations to their transfers. Most of the title deeds prohibited sale or cession for four years; but having been promised to the licenciado in advance, they were turned over to him a few days or a few months after issuance. Before the influential curate from Vera Cruz had done, he had assembled thirty-three cattle estancias, thirteen caballerías, a mill, and other land. With these properties he constituted, first, the Santa Fe hacienda and, finally, an entail in favor of his brother, who was himself a big cattle baron.

Nearly all private archives of any importance, including those of most entails, contain many title deeds that were transferred or sold in a manner like the Vera Cruz licenciado's. The viceroys shut their eyes, as Velasco the younger's declaration about grants to poor conquistadors' heirs shows. It would probably have been extremely difficult to ban the practice in a society where large groups of relatives and dependents gravitated around a few powerful men.

The concentration of deeds in the hands of a few was not to be restricted to woods and pastures in thinly populated zones, where the cattle barons had found no difficulty in obtaining estancias by the score. But land had first become valuable in those areas where new towns had been founded and a relatively dense Spanish population had settled. Hence the machinations at an early date of individuals in the Puebla region, where the Second Audiencia had succeeded in settling a few score farmers by 1532; these had increased rapidly. The individuals were Diego de Ordás, a rich encomendero and a nephew of the famous conquistador who had been Cortés' retainer, and Antonio de Almaguer, who claimed to hold in readiness for the King's service "eight or ten horses, retainers, and weapons" at a time when mounts were dear. There were others, including Alonso Martín Partidor, a Spaniard of humble origin, it seems, who soon became Almaguer's intimate; at Puebla he had a land-distributing position which he used for personal ends. After opposing the Audiencia's colonizing measure as a threat to the encomiendas, most of these individuals had hastily acquired interests in the settlement when there was no longer any doubt that it would survive.

The surest way to obtain lands and other advantages was to have a place in the Puebla city government, which was in control of grants. The King himself had recommended in 1532 the placing in office of "the richest and most influential men" as alcaldes and regidores, "preferably married conquistadors." The individuals in question had consequently acquired the position of permanent councilmen, eight such having been authorized in 1537–1538. Twenty years later, Viceroy Velasco passed through Puebla and asked to see the municipal registers. "It has become apparent to me and I have verified," he said to the councilmen, "that your conduct in office has been most irregular; you have committed grave excesses in sharing out to the town's inhabitants, and *mainly to yourselves as councilmen*, a large number of caballerías, allotments, gardens, and building lots, thus harming the community's interests" and leaving nothing for new arrivals. It was, however, practically impossible for the Viceroy to undo the mischief; he merely voided the grant of a part of the municipal pasture to the chief constable and certain councilmen.

Diego de Ordás was one of the busiest. He had requested of the King no fewer than "three leagues of land" in the area for plowing and planting, since, he declared, he intended to settle there permanently. A cédula in 1538 ordered the Viceroy to give him a "good piece of land" with full property rights. At that date, however, large grants were not in favor and instructions were not to distribute lands "to excess" (1535) and even, at Puebla, to give "moderate-sized pieces, not whole caballerías" (1543). Mendoza delayed four years before granting Ordás in principle an area "a quarter of a league square." But the Indians opposed the grant, and the authorities did not appear very eager to put it through.

Councilman Ordás probably felt that a more reliable method of adding to his already large holdings was to annex his neighbors' fields. In the Atlixco Valley alone, he had picked up at least *twenty-six* lots (*suertes*) and blocks of lots by 1547. Since 1536, the municipality had been distributing land in this area to Puebla inhabitants; some of them, in defiance of the no-sale clause, turned their grants over to Ordás before the ink was dry on the deeds. Ordás' next step was to get his colleagues—who did not demur—to commission a surveying magistrate to establish his properties' official boundaries. With the royal corregidor's approval, he took possession, pulling up grass and flinging stones in conformity with the ancient juridical formalities that conferred definitive rights to the soil. He must have already turned the various properties into one estate, because he also took possession of "some buildings that he had put up on said land," with "no one gainsaying." In 1550, he persuaded Viceroy Mendoza, who was leaving, to grant him the entire estate in the King's name.

These first land grabbers' activities aroused the opposition of their neighbors—mostly small farmers—for Puebla was a large, well-organized community. The chief constable complained in the city's name that "one" Diego de Ordás, Pedro de Meneses, and Antonio de Almaguer (all three big encomenderos) "had assembled much individual land originally distributed to the citizens for orchards or wheat fields and were intending to plant sugar cane on it." That, the alguacil mayor declared, would take flour away from the country and the Islands, throw modest millers and bakers out of work, and deforest and depopulate the entire region. In 1548, His Majesty turned the matter over to the Audiencia.

A few years previously, Puebla had leveled even more serious charges at Alonso Martín Partidor, a *vecino* who

> *owns much land, consisting of caballerías and orchards, which the municipal government has granted him or which, he says, he has purchased from individuals. It is a large amount of land; he has usurped it and occupied it with irregular title deeds and no right, because the real owners could not sell it to said Alonso Martín. They did not have the right, had not owned it long enough to receive final title, and had not worked it. Besides, he has occupied the land on his own authority, without owning it.*

Such protests are unusual for the times; elsewhere, immense estates were created unbeknown to contemporaries. Puebla was a unique region, where modest owners farming their own land reacted, successfully, against the big land sharks. By the middle of the sixteenth century, these small farmers had prevented them from occupying more land than their deeds justified and had got the authorities to restore to its rightful owners land held in excess. They had also had restricted to work animals the livestock that cattle barons were doubtless attempting to bring into the valley.

Although the Puebla region offers the first instances of such activities, the land grabbers did not stop there, but spread to all areas under cultivation, or susceptible of cultivation owing to sufficient population, fertility, and proximity to consumer centers. If Cortés is to be believed, Viceroy Mendoza had entrusted one of his retainers with the delicate task of distributing land grants: "An individual desiring much land takes a number of people to see him [the retainer]; the retainer points out caballerías to them in the area desired by the individual . . . , and afterwards the individual buys up the lot." The title deeds of entails and large haciendas furnish many examples of such transfers.

The phenomenon took place much later in the small towns of the Bajío; but the first symptoms may be observed by the end of the sixteenth century, notably toward Celaya, where several miners from San Luis and Guanajuato were already at work and a son of Pérez de Bocanegra, Luis Ponce de León, owned many more irrigation rights than did the other inhabitants. In León a few well-to-do farmers built up large estates. In 1603, New Salamanca, seeking funds to build a badly needed water system, was authorized to sell thirty lots in its district without requiring residence in the title deeds (*30 vecindades sin asistencia*); the purchasers could only have been capitalists and big landowners from Mexico City or elsewhere.

In 1585, an Audiencia judge wrote the King from Guadalajara that

> *estancia founders have striven, either by grant or purchase, to corner all the surrounding sites; some stockmen own estancias for eight, ten, or twenty leagues beyond the one which they have stocked, and stocked inadequately. The other inhabitants are seriously inconvenienced and misused; they cannot find a single site left, owing to the quantity of land occupied, or rather, usurped, in a manner contrary to all reason.*

"Exactly" the same held true for the mines, which were being monopolized by individuals who refused to work them. This lack of calculated interest in earnings, perhaps also this liking for excesses, seems to reflect the psychology of the Spanish Golden Age. Both traits will be exacerbated in the boundless north.

One clear case among many is Ameca, in western New Spain, which paid its tribute to the King. Between 1540 and 1656, the valley of the same name, more than 500 square kilometers in extent, was divided almost in its entirety into at least thirty-three grants, which originally were distributed by the governor, Vásquez de Coronado, or the Guadalajara administration, and later by the viceroys. The recipients were, in addition to the prosecutor's four children, a number of conquistadors and town inhabitants, among others a certain Luis de Ahumada, who received six caballería or estancia grants between 1561 and 1612.

A map, dated 1579 and appended to the geographical description of the locality, shows at that time six cattle domains and four farms belonging to various individuals. Although the region was fertile and had ample water, people had begun to leave, owing to the decimation of the Indian village of Ameca in the last great epidemic; lack of hands had forced five out of eight farmers to "abandon their crops and property and go elsewhere." One man, Ahumada, began to buy up the land of those departing, cheaply, although he did not fail to obtain a few additional grants by the usual tricks. One of his acquisitions, from Pedro

Cabezón, was an estancia that was to become the center of his estates and the nucleus of the vast Cabezón hacienda; a village on the site bears his name today. His descendants carried on his work, buying two native hamlets in the valley: Jayamitla and Santa María, the latter abandoned. By 1658, Luis de Ahumada's three grandchildren (one of whom was named after him) possessed an entail consisting of some thirty-seven estancias, including ten for sheep, and forty-three caballerías, or nearly the whole of the great valley whose other proprietors had been eliminated progressively. This slow formation of a latifundium which seven families eventually owned in common ended in division in 1697. The huge Cabezón estate was destined to outlive any family or individual.

Elsewhere the same situation frequently appears to have prevailed, to judge especially by the archives of the great haciendas; they show title deeds to modest establishments that were purchased twenty, forty, sixty, or more years after issuance of the deeds. The impetus acquired by the expansion of those in power resulted in their cornering also all land still unoccupied in their areas. As Viceroy Martín Enríquez had explained, there were many stray bits and pieces (*baldíos, realengos*) left in the gaps between concessions, which had been granted helter-skelter in accordance with petitioners' wishes. Even in the sixteenth century, viceroys had occasionally dispatched justice officials to force certain owners to hand back annexed lands that were many times larger than those to which they had a right. In the center and south, a large number of haciendas were formed from the private estates of caciques in debt, and even from Indian communities, when communities sold off the lands of natives dying without heirs in order to pay tribute arrears or other obligations.

The King legalized such irregular possession in the course of the seventeenth century, once the interested parties had paid their adjustment (*composición*). The royal cédulas of 1591 are an important departure in the final constitution of the haciendas. However, execution of the cédulas started rather late and reached a peak in 1643–1645 throughout central Mexico.

If we add that at the end of the sixteenth century viceroys began to make increasingly large grants, which encompassed in the following century as many as eight or twelve estancias at one time, particularly in the coastal areas, we are in possession of all the circumstances that ushered in the great estates. Except for a few outlying zones where colonization was delayed, few of the Mexican haciendas' main title deeds—whether by grant or by purchase—are more recent than the seventeenth century; some go back to the sixteenth. On the other hand, the great estates were rarely split up in later centuries; when they were not entailed, they had some sort of lien—a perpetual rent, a mortgage, or an endowment for saying masses—that made them indivisible.

Another question concerns the identity of the hacendados, who were often officials or encomenderos, the latter becoming less numerous as the century advanced. Apart from a few rich encomenderos, who quickly became big landowners, the only descendants of the conquistadors to prosper were either the ones who married to advantage, particularly into Audiencia judges' and viceroys' immediate families, or those who obtained municipal offices, knew how to launch business schemes, and created new sources of income for themselves. Those most active and best able to adapt to new conditions were not always the sons of prominent individuals or of those making the most auspicious start.

Good examples of self-made men are Jerónimo López and his son. Arriving in 1521, the father had a part in the last phase of the Conquest. Starting out as a quite modest encomendero, he became a Mexico City councilman and one of the earliest stockmen in the country. His letters are full of complaints about the drop in cattle prices, Indian workers' laziness, his encomienda's smallness, and lack of consideration shown farmers like him.

The son followed in his father's footsteps, but with the initial advantage of a position of importance. Also a councilman, enterprising and intelligent, he was a big wheat and cattle promoter; he was the city's indispensable counselor for pegging the price of bread, awarding meat contracts, or organizing the municipal granary (*alhóndiga*). He quickly ran up the family fortune by obtaining a number of land grants and especially by buying many estancias (in one instance from an Audiencia judge). He became one of the great landowners in the viceroyalty and took as his second wife the niece of Viceroy the Marqués de Falces. In 1586, he received authorization to found a first entail, but, his wealth growing apace, he founded three in 1608. Gabriel López de Peralta (the heir of his eldest son, who had died in the meantime) received some forty estancias at Tarimoro, in the Acámbaro region, together with over 100,000 head of cattle and 500 saddle horses for the cowboys, a large farm with 200 plow oxen, and still other estancias containing 30,000 sheep. The whole entail was appraised at 294,000 pesos; it yielded an annual income of 24,920 pesos. The second and third entails, also large, were formed chiefly of landed property and droves. A century later, the elder branch of the family was elevated to the peerage.

A few encomenderos did not scruple to go into trade, for example, Francisco de Solís, a son of the conquistador Pedro de Solís. An Audiencia judge's son-in-law, twice alcalde ordinary of Mexico City, he acquired land, operated a small sugar refinery, and was "reputed to be rich." He was censured, however, for having made his money in "vile trade." Others preferred to marry rich merchants' daughters. Nonetheless, many a conquistador's descendant, stiff-necked because he was an hidalgo and contemptuous of business, was reduced by the end of the sixteenth century to begging favors of His Majesty and converting viceregal grants into immediate cash.

Money and property thus tended to flow into merchants' and miners' coffers. The miners' prosperity collapsed, though, in the first decades of the seventeenth century. The wheel of fortune was turning more rapidly in Mexico than anywhere else; for sixty or a hundred years at least, conditions would remain quite unsettled. However, it is significant that in the last quarter of the sixteenth century the richest man in Mexico was presumably Alonso de Villaseca, a miner and businessman who owned no encomiendas, but who became one of the largest landowners in the country. A native of a hamlet in the province of Toledo, this scion of the petty nobility—or so he claimed—had reached New Spain late. The delay did not hinder him from making a colossal fortune; his income was estimated to be 150,000 ducats. His mines and lands and huge droves and farms were scattered all over the region north of Mexico City: Pachuca, Jilotepec, Ixmiquilpan, Metztitlán, Huasteca, and Zacatecas. He settled an entail valued at over a million pesos on his only daughter, who married a certain Agustín Guerrero. The fortune rapidly declined in the course of the seventeenth century.

At about the same time, the new realms in the north were colonized by miners, who established huge estates there. Many merchants became landed proprietors, for real estate was a safe investment in their eyes and they could draw closer to the rural aristocracy with whom they would have liked to mix. As a result, the electoral lists of the merchants' guild included many hacienda owners, even great cattle barons, such as the prior of the merchants' guild, Cristóbal de Ontiveros, or rich refinery owners like Diego Caballero.

In each diocese tithe collecting was farmed out for a fixed sum; it usually left collectors a good margin of profit. This was another source of rural capital, particularly, it seems, in a rich area like Puebla. At the close of the sixteenth century, complaints began to be voiced over the invasion of the best lands by ecclesiastical mortmain; clerics and vicars enjoying benefices often became well-to-do proprietors.

In the coastal zones, which were colonized somewhat later, fewer large encomenderos acquired land and established haciendas than did men of varied incomes: miners, merchants, businessmen. In the last quarter of the sixteenth century, or a little later, we find, south of Vera Cruz and Alvarado and toward the lower stretches of the Papaloapan, the Marquesado del Valle, of course, with probably the earliest continental sugar refinery at Tuxtla. But near by, the Marquesado's former bailiffs and alcaldes mayors had begun to link estancias and form estates. Merchants from Vera Cruz and Mexico City especially obtained grants and acquired land there, as they had done in other regions closer to the capital; there were, for example, three electors of the Mexico City guild, Diego López de Montalbán, Diego de Cepeda, and Francisco Pacho. Or there was Jerónimo Pérez de Aparicio, who was both a merchant and a small encomendero; his son Juan and later descendants put together the huge Zapotal domain (Atezcalco). On the other hand, none of the large encomenderos of the region, such as Jorge de Alvarado, were among the landowners.

The Rivadeneira family belonged to the aristocracy; its members grew rich in the Pachuca mines, although they had arrived late in New Spain. They soon acquired land in the Papaloapan region, through proxies, it seems. In 1610, Don Fernando had forty-six estancias surveyed, which were to give rise to the great hacienda later known as La Estanzuela. A modest conquistador's descendants founded in 1610–1612 the big entail of Estrada–Carbajal with fifty-seven estancias (and thirty-eight Negro slaves) grouped around Uluapan and alongside, but not within, the family's small encomienda. In that family, the biggest land collector was a prebendary who had been given the tithe farm for the region; his profits were without doubt the source of most of the

capital invested in the holdings. A century later, the entail became
the Marquesado de Uluapan.

To sum up, the new masters of the soil sprang from widely divergent
origins: a few encomenderos or conquistadors who had made their
money in various ways, sometimes even in trade; miners (a noble profession); and also many merchants who, after patiently amassing their
good ducats, were thinking about forsaking their shops and mingling
with the aristocracy.

The vast estates and enormous droves should not lead the reader
to the conclusion that the country and its Spanish inhabitants were
rich; that would be an illusion until well into the seventeenth century.
Horses, cattle, and sheep were worth very little for lack of markets;
an inadequate labor supply made crop raising not very productive. A
modest Andalusian farm, with its carefully tended olive trees and
fields, brought in as much as, if not more than, an immense Mexican
hacienda.

The dwellings of the first masters of the soil, poorly built of stone
and adobe, have almost disappeared today. Their household inventories
usually reveal crude furnishings; the only luxuries were silver dishes,
relatively common in Mexico, and horsemen's gear. Save for a few
score individuals and even families by this date (large encomenderos,
miners, merchants, and lawyers, who were all landed proprietors if
they intended to remain in the country), and save also for money-
lenders beyond the pale, there were not in early seventeenth-century
New Spain the same wealthy classes as in Seville or various Mediterranean and Flemish cities, if we speak only of the Spanish empire.
Mexico's capital city was at best no more important in this respect than
the average such city.

It was nevertheless by far the greatest city in the viceroyalty. Most
of the cattle barons and big farmers, except those in remote provinces,
resided there or in Puebla, where they had their manor houses. Barring
the north, few owners remained on their haciendas all year; most left
them in charge of bailiffs. As a result, Mexico City represented a concentration of most of the wealth in central Mexico.

The reason was that much of the wealth was being drained from the
country: by the King, first of all, who drew off huge sums in the form
of heavy taxes; then by certain high officials, who sold out on return-

ing to Spain; and finally by the many Spaniards who went home after making their fortune. That is why the new rich of the Indies must be sought in Seville and Spain in general as often as in Mexico City or Lima; Spanish comedies and novels of the Golden Age frequently portrayed these returning *indianos* and *peruanos*.

Regarded from several centuries' distance, the importance of these early estates cannot be measured merely in terms of the modest incomes furnished the first masters of the soil. Their importance also resides in the future possibilities and potential value that they would acquire as soon as an increase in the white, native, and mestizo population could offer them new prospects and more intensive exploitation. Their boundaries would remain unchanged, however; in a country administered by lawyers, land once distributed was distributed for good. In the first decades of the seventeenth century, the frame was still partially empty but the main lines of the picture were already drawn.

5. THE NORTH: "MEN RICH AND POWERFUL"

In reports of Guadalajara magistrates and bishops on tours of inspection, in royal officials' and ordinary citizens' letters, and in descriptions of the region, the expressions that recur most frequently are: *poderosos vecinos* and *hombres ricos y poderosos*. Indeed, the presence of a group of "rich and powerful" men, etched in sharp outline against a contrasting background, is one of the northern marches' most striking features. Making up the background were poor men, miners, and colonizers with itching feet, as well as soldiers of fortune, mounted vagabonds, and cattle thieves—the scum, but at the same time the vanguard, of a society shifting northward.

By this time, all regions had their influential men, of course, particularly provinces somewhat removed from Mexico City. The situation was different, however, from the one obtaining in the north. Men in the nearer provinces were not separated from the capital and the Viceroy by great distances that took several months to cross.

They usually did not have cavalrymen under their orders, indispensable in the north to ward off the fearsome Chichimecas' onslaughts. And they had confronting them solid native communities, protected by numerous missionaries, in addition to a multitude of corregidores and lawyers whose interests were often not identical with theirs.

In the north, on the contrary, there was nothing standing in the way of bold spirits and leaders. Some of them made their fortune. With the exception of a few miners and merchants, however, they were not extremely wealthy, for all their huge droves—far less so than most of the Mexico City entail builders. Nevertheless, they had adequate money to be regarded as all-powerful in provinces as bare as they were vast. Perhaps they were "rich" in the medieval sense of *ricos homes*, or grandees. If so, that would not be the only archaism or throwback to the Middle Ages to be encountered in this period of the New World's history.

In the south, the era of the great captains, Cortés and his lieutenants, had been of relatively short duration. Once the country was pacified, the military's exclusive reign could no longer be justified. The King had sent his legists to regain control of the government and public affairs. Innumerable inspecting magistrates had been dispatched far and wide to track down abuses and inroads on royal sovereignty. The encomenderos, caught in the toils of the law, had been forced to abandon their schemes for feudal estates and to live on a fixed income.

The northern reaches were inaccessible to this evolution toward a strong central authority. There, most of the rich and influential, regardless of their occupation or office, would be military men for a long time to come. Every *estanciero*, whether Spaniard or mestizo, had to be always on the alert, ready to seize his harquebus or hasten into his tiny stronghold; nomad Indians and bandits of many hues were a constant menace. The King, to be sure, had placed over the military a new Audiencia whose circuit of appeals was supposed to include New Viscaya. In 1548 it settled at Compostela, far to the southwest in a region of sedentary Indians and away from normal communication routes. A 1550 order requiring two of the four magistrates to be "on the road" and the Audiencia's transfer to Guadalajara in 1560 were measures insufficient in themselves to consolidate its authority north of Zacatecas. In that part of the country, as the Audiencia had observed itself, it was hardly ever obeyed. Furthermore, this small tribunal's customary behavior, by the century's end, was most independent; often its members, working through proxies, were the richest miners, landowners, and businessmen in the entire circuit.

In all New Galicia at the beginning of the next century, there were only twenty-six encomenderos, owing to the small Indian population; most of them were poor and concentrated in the southwest, on New Spain's border. The general poverty was offset by huge fortunes springing from the discovery of rich deposits at Zacatecas, Fresnillo, Sombrerete, and, somewhat later, San Luis Potosí, Ramos, and elsewhere. The first governors of New Viscaya, New Mexico, and New León were chosen from among the rich miners and military men, so that they could maintain order at their own expense and by their own means. Some relinquishment of royal authority had become apparent by the end of Philip II's reign; these northern provinces were to reap the benefit. As the 1573 colonizing laws revealed, the hard-pressed monarchy was unloading a share of its responsibilities upon rich private citizens. With the exception of the Bajío plains, close to Mexico City, the northern zone was therefore to be *the* zone of powerful individuals, large family circles, housefuls of dependents, and huge estates.

Groups of small independent farmers did settle in some spots without opposition from the mighty; the latter's interest was to colonize the region in every way possible. But average-sized estates were not the unit pattern for settlements in the north. Not small settlers, but big capitalists and men with independent incomes colonized its reaches: Guadalajara judges and officials in the southwest; rich miners, soldiers, and governors north of Zacatecas, Guanajuato, and San Luis; merchants, stockmen, and royal officials from Mexico City, in New León, which was occupied later.

Some of the characteristics already observed in the colonization of the center and south are brought into prominence, notably the part played by powerful individuals. As if to bring contrasts into sharper relief, alongside medieval vestiges appear unmistakably modern elements, whose explanation is in general the lack of native "vassals" to be exploited and the presence of the great mines that made and broke their owners. The initial results were an open economy, relatively more brisk commercial relations, some specialization in each town's activities (mining, agriculture, or livestock), and above all, in the *ricos homes,*

a rarely encountered spirit of enterprise and adventure, even of speculation at times.

GOVERNORS AND JUDGES AS
CATTLE BARONS

Under those worthy representatives of the Spanish monarchy at its
height, Viceroys Velasco I and Martín Enríquez, the Audiencia of New
Galicia presented the appearance of a body on the whole devoted to
His Majesty's service. However, when settlements were to be established at the mines north of Zacatecas, the new Audiencia, it was plain
to see, could neither exercise authority directly from such a distance
nor, especially, shoulder expenses for pioneer expeditions.

One of the discoverers of Zacatecas, Diego de Ibarra, had a young
nephew who, starting in 1554, had undertaken to explore the northern
regions. With the aid of his rich uncle's money and influence, Francisco
de Ibarra succeeded in establishing settlements at various mines. In
1562, by the terms of a special patent from the King, Velasco appointed
him "governor and captain general" of the lands lying beyond the
mines of San Martín and Aviño, except Chiametla (which he was not
granted until 1567). There was much ground to be explored and no
funds available other than hypothetical taxes to be collected for the
Crown in pacified regions. Francisco's territory was named New
Viscaya. His functions were those of any governor or captain general,
fairly vague until the 1573 laws. He did recruit and command troops,
render civil and criminal justice (without having jurisdiction over
appellate cases probably), appoint minor officials, and distribute fields
and estancias, almost always through his lieutenant and relative, Martín
López de Ibarra.

The monarchy was, however, still jealous at this time of its prerogatives, relinquishing as few of them as possible. It forbade the distribution of encomiendas in territories conquered or to be conquered, for
example, in its 1560 instructions to Dr. Morones, who colonized Chiametla. In other places, the King ordered the local royal treasurer
to aid colonizers and pay officials with pacified Indians' tribute, which
had been set aside for the Crown's exclusive use.

Shortly after promulgation of the 1573 laws, the King confirmed young Ibarra's titles and granted him the privilege of designating and appointing his own successor, who would in turn serve for life. This first governor seems to have been neither as independent nor as concerned with personal business as many of his successors. Whether his actions were in response to outstanding moral qualities or to monarchical authority and the climate of the times we cannot ascertain.

Francisco de Ibarra did not misuse his complete economic autonomy. Although in 1574 he was given the same salary as the Guadalajara Audiencia judges—2,000 ducats—it was made clear to him that he must take the entire sum in taxes collected from his territory, in other words from enterprises created by him. In 1571, royal officials in New Viscaya had been formally denied permission to take their salaries out of the Crown's fifth share in New Galicia mines; they had a right only to "revenues produced by the region itself." In his progress reports, Ibarra frequently mentioned his having personally financed the discovery, colonization, defense, and provisioning of mines. Also, he had pacified the Indians and got them to settle down. After founding Durango and Nombre de Dios in 1563, he had supplied the inhabitants with everything that they needed. Finally, he had developed agriculture and livestock raising. Particularly at Durango, he said, he had distributed to colonizing soldiers "cattle, sheep, goats, maize, flour, gunpowder, and other necessary products in large quantities," not to speak of all the tools required for building their houses and "digging canals in order to bring water to the town and irrigate fields and orchards." He ended with the assertion that in under twenty years he had spent 200,000 gold pesos. Most of that sum must have come from his uncle's mines.

Francisco de Ibarra was certainly not as "poor" or as much "in debt" as he claimed; he owned mines and large droves bringing him in 6,000 pesos in income. However, his earnings were small in proportion to his outlay, smaller yet in proportion to his struggles over a period of fifteen or twenty years. The point is that the great explorer's goal was not essentially an economic one.

Later governors and other royal representatives were not always so disinterested, although they, too, were obviously less concerned with wealth for its own sake than with the omnipotence it afforded them. They, like Audiencia members, were often powerful businessmen and rich cattle barons. The most unscrupulous were the ones to put the most money in circulation in the sense that they exploited mines, established rural haciendas, or developed commerce.

The governors were what they were because of the general situation and royal policy. As long as the Crown would not or could not take a hand in the colonizing of the distant north, the task had to be entrusted to men possessing both personal means and local experience. The 1573 laws made many promises to these "rich and powerful" men: a hereditary title of governor (*adelantado*) or captain general, hereditary fortresses, and permission (previously withheld) to distribute encomiendas and lands (particularly to their own children), to take for themselves one-fourth of any new town district, and to turn this share into one or more entails.

Since they were obliged to spend so much of their own money on their office, they naturally sought reimbursement in personal business schemes. Unfortunately, we cannot always tell how much of their fortune was acquired thanks to their office. Sometimes, on the other hand, their title cost them more than it brought in. At all events, most of the early governors were men of merit. When chosen from local mining or landowning groups, they could differ from their peers only in that their appointment opened up new opportunities.

The second governor of New Viscaya, Francisco's uncle, Diego de Ibarra, settled a huge entail on his daughter slightly more than a year after taking office. The entail comprised many rich mines at and around Zacatecas, more than 130,000 head of cattle, the large Trujillo and Valparaíso haciendas, and still other land at Lagos on which great herds of horses grazed (1578). The two main haciendas were located in the western part of the province in a fertile, well-watered zone; even so, they took in eighty-four estancias plus annexed land. The Crown confirmed the title thirty-three years later, when Ibarra's heirs claimed that they could not find the deeds "because they were so ancient." There is more than a remote possibility that the heirs had never had any, their forceful ancestor having simply moved in without leave. All Diego's actions reveal his independent spirit. His lieutenant, Martín López de Ibarra, distributed grants not only to others, but various pieces of land (Parras, in Coahuila) "in the Valley of the Pyrenees . . . to himself." The family's influence made it easy for some of its other members to build up estates; for example, Juan de Ibarra, who was royal treasurer of New Viscaya, owned large agricultural and livestock interests near Durango. In vain did the Guadalajara Audiencia try to make such powerful groups acknowledge its prerogatives.

The third governor, Rodrigo de Río de Losa y Gordejuela, was born in Old Castile, at Puebla de Arganzón, and had accompanied Francisco de Ibarra on his journeys. He increased his vast holdings during his term of office. Between 1587 and 1597, he purchased title to a large amount of land that he had just finished granting others as governor. He also bought in the same period mines, dwellings, and other property. Once, in a single operation, he acquired fourteen estancias north of Nombre de Dios for the sum of 13,500 pesos. Another time, he bought ten estancias from the alcalde mayor of San Martín, who had no right to own them, even less to sell them. He transformed his acquisitions into the Santiago hacienda, lying between Sombrerete and Cuencamé. The hacienda included not only huge droves, orchards, a winery, a water system, and four silver smelters with their charcoal heaps, but also "a tax on all the mine pits in this realm, estimated at over four thousand." His free Indian workers, slaves, mestizos, and retainers comprised a large village equipped with church and chaplain. The governor lived there in his castle—"a palace filled with amenities"—and was renowned for his bounteous hospitality.

Luis de Velasco having quoted some fantastic figures one day, those present expressed doubt that Diego de Ibarra and especially Río de Losa could brand that many cattle every year. Velasco had an official count taken and duly notarized. According to Basalenque, who tells the story, in the year 1586 Governor Ibarra branded 33,000 calves on his haciendas at Trujillo, and Río de Losa 42,000 on his. Río de Losa had not yet reached maximum production, however; a dozen years later he sold over 60,000 head of cattle at one time to a certain Álvaro de Soria of Mexico City, who paid 1½ pesos a head for them. At least, that is the Guadalajara canons' assertion; they blamed the cattle—and tithe—shrinkage in New Galicia on such massive transactions.

Like mine revenues, herds helped to feed many impoverished Spaniards and passing visitors, as well as keep peace among some Chichimeca tribes (who were very fond of meat) and, especially, to supply troops leaving on war or exploring expeditions. Río de Losa was a great traveler and an intrepid explorer, "most competent" (*muy plático*); he had been all over New Viscaya and had taken an active part in Don

Tristán de Arellano's expedition to Florida. One day he even considered the usefulness of discovering the Northwest Passage and colonizing "Great Cathay." In 1589 and again in 1590 the king warmly congratulated him on all his activities: "discoverer of lands" and plain captain in the struggle against the Indians, then lieutenant-governor, and finally governor. As a reward for his services he was made a knight and eventually a commander of the Military Order of St. James, a much envied decoration, which had also been conferred on Diego de Ibarra. His governorship paid him a hereditary income of two thousand pesos.

Francisco de Urdiñola, who was governor from 1603 to 1612 or 1615, was a man like Río de Losa. A Basque hidalgo born close to the French frontier, he went to northern Mexico while still a young man to take an ordinary soldier's part in many campaigns against warring Indians. Having been appointed captain of the Mazapil company around 1582, he acquired mines there and pacified various nomad groups at his own expense. His love of adventure led him to request the King's authorization to trade with "Macao and Canton, China."

Urdiñola's great fortune was composed largely of farms and estancias. He truly had land fever and put together near Saltillo and Río Grande (Aguanaval) five or six enormous haciendas extending over several million acres. They were already partly constituted when he received his governorship; he went on developing them. In 1607, for example, he bought property from a Saltillo citizen that he himself had granted the same year, and received several gifts of land from individuals who must have been dummies; they were probably dependents. Expressions used in certain title deeds lead to the hypothesis that he also may have granted estancias to himself.

Governors traveled like Carolingian kings from one hacienda to another, as land grants and other documents issued in the course of their progress show. They were of course attended by swarms of friends, relatives, and retainers. Almost without exception, governors came from rural areas of Spain—the heart of the Basque country, Asturias, Old and New Castile—where medieval customs had survived, as had the large groups of relatives and intimates so important in Peninsular history. Río de Losa's hacienda near Sombrerete conjured up visions of a patriarchal existence. According to Captain Mange and the Jesuit Pérez de Ribas, his house, "like the prophet Abraham's," was always overflowing with people, among them visiting travelers. The "magnificent hospitality" that this *caballero* lavished on so many friars, soldiers, travelers, and poor people elicited praise from his contemporaries; every passer-by could find in his house "refuge, protection, and a viaticum."

The two Ibarras and Urdiñola were surrounded by Basques. In 1606, the Guadalajara Audiencia recommended that the granting of certain favors not be left to the Governor; "he will distribute them among his relatives and in-laws and will refuse them to anyone else." Urdiñola's close enemy, Lomas y Colmenares, may well have picked Castilians and Andalusians for his escort, whence perhaps the fierce rivalry between the two powers. It is difficult to assess with any degree of accuracy the importance of these loyal groups; they were not bound to the *ricos homes* by any written pledge, and the humble among them have left scarcely any record of personal activity. They are probably carried on New Viscaya census lists as having no visible goods or definite profession; one inhabitant is said to have "no property or means of support," and another "to subsist in the manner of an honorable hidalgo." The more important retainers were lieutenant-governors, factors, or royal treasurers. They were in a good position to become large landowners themselves.

Some of Urdiñola's successors were cattle barons in the northern provinces, like Don Hipólito de Velasco, Marqués de Salinas and successor by his mother to the Ibarra entail, or Gaspar de Alvear, who married Urdiñola's heiress. Others were recent arrivals from Spain, soldiers or nobles without local connections; they do not seem to have kept landed estates. Having made use of local strength in the early days to pacify and colonize the territory, the Crown now wished to vest power in men more easily brought to heel.

The early governors' passage had nevertheless left a permanent mark on land distribution.

In the provinces of New León and New Mexico, a similar process seems to have taken place, except that Carvajal did not possess the Ibarras' moral fiber, or Oñate their cleverness.

Luis de Carvajal y Cueva had obtained in 1579 capitulations for exploring and colonizing a vast area between the Pánuco River in the south and Mazapil in the north, plus two hundred leagues taking him "clear to Florida." The terms were that he should undertake the expedition at his expense and that he should furnish at least one hundred men, including sixty married farmers. In exchange, he should be given the title of governor (obviously under the conditions outlined in the 1573 laws). He set out with a few score soldiers and "sixteen relatives," men, women, and children. There were no mines to be discovered on his route, with the result that Carvajal, to obtain capital, made several expeditions to the Palmas and Bravo rivers; each time, he brought back 800 to 1,000 Indians, whom he then sold in Mexico City—"for all the world as if he had gone out hunting hares or deer." By the time Viceroy Villamanrique had apprised his successor, in 1590, the accused had fled Mexico City, where he had been ordered to appear before the court, and was living scot-free in his remote territory. He was finally caught and jailed by the Inquisition.

After that initial fiasco, New León long remained half-abandoned. Although Agustín de Zavala, a rich Zacatecas miner and knight of St. James, was appointed governor in 1613, he never took up residence in the territory. Not until 1625 did Martín de Zavala, Agustín's son, conclude a treaty with Philip IV: he was to found two towns in exchange for the hereditary title of governor. Don Martín began to colonize in earnest; he distributed cattle and plows, lured settlers with encomiendas, and attracted southern sheepmen with enormous land grants, usually forty or fifty estancias to each applicant. He naturally ran his own businesses, and it would be interesting to know to what extent the existence of his family estates contributed to the influx of large landed proprietors into the northeast.

Plans for the colonizing of New Mexico brought forth, from 1581–1583 on, a large number of powerful candidates, of whom the Crown appeared to make sport for twenty years. Treaties were proposed by rich inhabitants of New Spain, such as Cristóbal Martín, Antonio de Espejo (in the name of "twenty companions"), and Francisco Díaz de Vargas. The most curious offer was made in 1589 by Juan Bautista de Lomas y Colmenares, the powerful miner and landed proprietor of Nieves, north of Zacatecas. He asked for a good deal more than the 1573 laws had conceded: the title of *adelantado* for his family in perpetuity and that of governor-captain general for six heirs in succession, together with all prerogatives pertaining thereto; the right to distribute three encomiendas in perpetuity and any others for six generations; 40,000 vassals in perpetuity, "with the fields, pastures, woods, and water rights of the districts" in which they would be located; the collection of all taxes and duties in the "state" thus constituted; the rank of count or marqués; civil and criminal jurisdiction, and finally twenty-four square leagues of land that the applicant would select himself, reserve for his own use, and enclose ("veinte y cuatro leguas de tierra . . . con término cerrado e rredondo y acotado"). Two final conditions: the whole was to be entailed and a ten-year monopoly granted for the raising of livestock in the region.

The most astounding episode in this drama is Viceroy Villamanrique's acceptance of the stipulations on March 11, 1589. They would have given rise not only to a gigantic latifundium, but to a state within a state and what would have amounted to an autonomous principality. The mere fact that one of these *ricos homes* could dream of making such proposals and a viceroy of accepting them gives us a singularly clear picture of the medieval mentality and concepts of these men: their notion that they could transform themselves from royal governors of the "new kingdoms" of the north into something like powerful feudal lords, masters of the soil in their "states."

Villamanrique's scruples fortunately caused him to refer the offer to his sovereign, although a 1586 cédula had authorized him to conclude individual colonization agreements. The answer, when it arrived five years later, was negative, naturally. That the King's highest representative in Mexico could take seriously an offer so contrary to the modern conception of a sovereign state is nonetheless highly significant.

In 1594, a new agreement was signed with the rich landowner and future governor of New Viscaya, Urdiñola. Lomas was so greatly annoyed that he succeeded in getting the agreement nullified by falsely accusing his rival of a crime. The man finally chosen after many vicissitudes was Juan de Oñate, the grandson of one of the three extremely wealthy miners who had discovered Zacatecas. In 1596, Oñate was preparing to leave "with many relatives and friends," who were in turn "accompanied by their wives and sons," when a rival appeared in Spain. In order to eliminate the rival, Oñate wrote the King that, however powerful someone coming from overseas might be, he could never take along on his expedition so huge a household—so many relatives, intimates, and trustworthy retainers—which was the staff on which a chief must always be able to lean if he would be feared and respected. The agreement with Oñate was in general modeled on the 1573 colonization laws. His further requests had met with firm resistance from the Viceroy: title to an area thirty leagues square and the right to distribute encomiendas either in perpetuity or for six generations. In the end, Oñate proved incapable of overcoming serious difficulties and was replaced a few years later.

The Crown's next step, as it had been in New Viscaya, was to re-establish its authority by appointing outside governors. Its policy explains some apparent inconsistencies, such as Viceroy Guadalcázar's recommendation in 1621 to the governor of New Mexico: "In conformity with the obligations incumbent on you as governor and with the laws of this realm, you may not own cattle estancias or like investments; if certain reports are true and you do own some, you must dispose of them." The daring of such an order is in itself an indication of royal authority's strides forward.

In spite of the 1573 laws, the agreements signed, and the spirit of medieval decentralization that both reflected, not one of these powerful governors and captains-general succeeded in transmitting to his heirs the extraordinary powers vested in him. From a strictly political point of view, the Crown, following the same course of action as in the south after the Conquest, had gradually regained control of the northern territories. From a social and economic point of view, however, the great explorers and powerful governors held on to their acquisitions and left permanent reminders of their coming. Their mines and business ventures were to prove shaky; but the immense rural estates of Río de Losa, Urdiñola, the Ibarras, and the Zavalas, legally established or confirmed by title deeds, have occasionally survived intact down to our time. Even if we limit ourselves to New Viscaya and the border region of New Galicia, we can point to about ten such haciendas, which are among the largest in Mexico.

Unlike many of the governors, the members of the New Galicia Audiencia were not selected locally, nor were they authorized, even tacitly, to possess land or personal businesses in the territory. But if the oidores of the Audiencia of Mexico, under the very eyes of the Viceroy, were able to contravene [royal] orders, what else could be expected in distant Guadalajara? New Galicia's Audiencia enjoyed even greater prerogatives than did that of Mexico City, including land distribution in territories under its jurisdiction. Even before it moved to Guadalajara (1560), it was handing out from remote Compostela deeds for land as far away as San Martín and the recently explored zones north of Zacatecas.

The judges understandably outdid their Mexico City counterparts in the volume of personal business transacted; they sent for their relatives and retainers and showered them with favors. Sometimes they were given permission to take a local bride or, more frequently, to marry their children to local people. Such marriages smoothed the way to acquisition, by relatives or by the judges themselves using proxies, of rich estates, haciendas, and mines. Too much land was hard to conceal, however, with the result that judges often ceded it immediately after purchase. Prohibited from taking up permanent residence in the region, they frequently preferred other sources of profit: estancia sales and resales, various forms of loans, cattle and horse deals, and miscellaneous trafficking. They consolidated their authority, working through the swarms of relatives and dependents which characterize this microcosm of New Galicia. The province was indeed huge in the amount of space it covered; but it was diminutive in all other respects, for its population at the beginning of the seventeenth century had not yet reached 2,000 legal inhabitants, or *vecinos*.

What has been said of the center and south applies equally well here. Such extralegal activities were not always harmful. Some of the Audiencia's licenciados and doctors were extremely energetic men who created haciendas and developed commerce and the livestock industry. Their goal may have been personal enrichment, and justice may have suffered in the process; a poor country's economy was the gainer.

At the beginning, there seem to have been only a few modest examples of trading on influence. Around 1575, one Dr. Alarcón had cattlemen stock his house with meat and candle tallow free of charge. The Guadalajara canons maliciously observe that cattlemen "have never lost a lawsuit yet in this Audiencia's territory." Cases became more interesting by the end of the century. The same canons quote precise facts in 1592. The Audiencia's oldest member, a licenciado named Pedro de Altamirano, appears to have openly taken up residence and shown favoritism to his many relatives and in-laws. He gave one of the choicest alcalde mayor positions, at Sombrerete, to an uncle of his wife, Pedro López de Olivares. The latter then requested ten estancias there in other people's names; the Audiencia, presided over by Altamirano, granted them without question. The estancias were later sold for a high price to the governor of New Viscaya. It would be a good idea, the canons conclude, to send anyone "so passionately devoted to his family to a place where he would have fewer relatives on both sides and fewer household in-laws and dependents."

The most flagrant instance of favoritism was undoubtedly displayed by President Santiago de Vera. This grave doctor of canon law had had a more than honorable career in the Indies before assuming the presidency of the New Galicia Audiencia; he had been a judge in Santo Domingo, crime commissioner in Mexico City, and head of a tribunal in the Philippines. He came to Guadalajara in the closing years of the sixteenth century. In 1602, the chief constable, a regidor named Jerónimo Conde, turned in so circumstantial a report that we cannot doubt certain of the facts, even after making full allowance for exaggeration and malevolence.

[According to his report,] New Galicia's capital city numbered at the time only 160 *vecinos*, all but 40 of whom had jobs in the courts, the Audiencia, the diocese, the cathedral chapter, the municipal government, or the royal treasury. Most of the forty were indigents.

In this tiny, wretched town the aforementioned President has thirty-seven relatives and in-laws, counting his own and his sons' and nephews', plus nine sons, sons-in-law, or grandsons, not to mention cousins' cousins and a host of Spanish friends and dependents of all these people. Said sons, sons-in-law, and nephews, all married if old enough, are constantly in his company; they all live under his roof and in one building; they take their meals around a common board.

The word *criado*, or dependent, as used in the chief constable's report, still has its patriarchal and etymological meaning of "nurtured and looked after."

The President's *criados* were gradually cornering the region's only source of wealth: the cattle and mule trade. They had made a profit of 300,000 pesos in under five years, we are told, and had about 200,000 in capital. One of the most active was Dr. Vera's son-in-law, Fernando Altamirano, who appears to have been truly a promoter. Corregidor at Tonalá, two leagues away, he raised some 10,000 calves near by. He must have sold them for a good price, since he was a partner of Guadalajara's meat contractor. He took merchandise to Mexico City which he let businessmen there have on credit; he collected 15 per cent interest. Lacking minted coins, northern miners obtained an advance from him, then paid him back in a heavier amount of pure silver. He also sold the big mines cattle and mules. All in all, his yearly profits were said to exceed 100,000 pesos.

A nephew, Gaspar de Vera, conducted himself in a similar manner. Having been granted land at Juchipila, he had established there a sugar refinery. As he had been appointed alcalde mayor immediately afterward, he had no trouble in obtaining the requisite Indian helpers through forced labor or repartimientos. He then sold the refinery for 12,000 pesos.

By the time the report comes to an end, we have been given the detailed activities of eighteen of the President's sons, nephews, brothers-in-law, uncles, cousins, or dependents, who had been appointed corregidores or alcaldes mayores at Teocaltiche, Culiacán, Sombrerete, Fresnillo, and Compostela. There they defied regulations by raising quantities of livestock, engaging in trade, and making money in amounts that the report does not fail to mention. Two years later, Licenciado Gaspar de la Fuente wrote to the King while on a tour of inspection:

> *In this realm [of New Galicia] justices are considered to be for the good of a few individuals, not for your vassals' general welfare, as is your intention. Most justices are superflous, located in barren regions or Indian villages, where their presence serves merely to use up what little strength the unhappy natives possess. Most Indian cases can be better examined by their own alcaldes than by Spaniards.*

The picture is complete with the President himself, who in his own house had opened a store selling all the countryside's produce, from grain and butter to the orange blossom extract made at Lake Chapala. His gossip, Licenciado Pinedo, who was the Audiencia's prosecutor, cornered the futures market in unborn mules and growing maize. If we reflect that save for a few straggling mining communities New Galicia had very little in the way of resources or markets, and that most of the 1,500 to 2,000 permanent *vecinos* were poor, especially in the west, we can grasp the almost total domination that a solid, influential family like that of Santiago de Vera could exercise.

After the President's unexpected death three or four years later, charges were filed against at least one of his nephews, Gaspar de Vera, who was convicted of trafficking and other abuses during his term as alcalde mayor. Others must have left the country, since no more was heard of them. Except for the purely speculative ventures, most survived to swell the remaining members' pockets and influence. Diego de Porres, for example, who claimed (like everyone else) to be an hidalgo from Santander's mountains, established a large entail between 1608 and 1619. He must have arrived before Vera; but he took for his second wife "one of the President's cousins," Catalina de Temiño, and was made alcalde mayor of the rich Sombrerete mines, royal treasurer, and chief ensign and ordinary alcalde of Guadalajara. That was more than enough to allow him to become a rich landowner.

The investigation into Porres' fortune revealed that he had got his start selling mules at Zacatecas, San Luis, and Sombrerete. In 1602, Conde asserted that during his term of office at Sombrerete Porres had earned some 40,000 pesos in the mule trade. He probably increased his volume of business after Conde's report, for in 1611 he was reportedly "one of the wealthiest men in the entire kingdom," possessing a house full of slaves, silverware, and jewels, with "tapestries on the beds, silk curtains, portraits, weapons, and horses." Witnesses swore on oath that his holdings were worth 360,000 pesos; they mentioned houses and shops in Guadalajara and rich country estates in particular, such as a nearby wheat hacienda containing over thirty estancias and an irrigation system.

In 1606, the prosecutor complained to the King about a clique of relatives who had gained control of the city government; whenever food supplies had to be laid in, Porres and another landowner named Juan González de Apodaca "would join forces" with them, Porres and Apodaca having a quasi-monopoly over supplies. Apodaca, himself chief constable of the court, owned one of the largest haciendas in the entire west, Cuysillos (Tlala), whose yearly tithe collection alone was farmed out around 1620 for 2,000 pesos.

The following years saw the continued predominance of large family groups headed by officials and magistrates who scattered their favors like manna from Heaven. The Spanish state, conscious of the threat posed by such feudal habits, from time to time attempted to combat them. In a 1608 cédula addressed to the magistrates of New Galicia, the King voiced his disapproval of their having handed out judicial posts to "relatives and dependents," who with complete impunity were engaging in personal business on the pretext that such was the established custom. In stern language the King ordered punishment for offenders even when there was no evidence of spoliation or forcible seizure.

To judge by contemporary letters and accounts of all sorts, the situation remained unchanged. Around 1625, a monk, Fray Juan de Santa María, pointed to several cases of nepotism; the facts were dazzlingly clear, he wrote, and "what I am telling Your Majesty in these lines is as much a fact as the sun shining on our heads!" A miner's report in 1634 is even more circumstantial. The Audiencia's President, Dr. Damián Gentil de Párraga, was able, by inventing a tale to deceive the King, to marry a rich "Creole hailing from Guadalajara," the widow of an Audiencia judge, Doña Leonor de Pareja y Ribera. As a result, the President found himself closely allied with a group of influential citizens who, according to the custom of the country, drank chocolate with him and shared administrative handouts with his household dependents. His son, despite his sixteen years and his still being at school in Mexico City, was the holder of five *corregimientos* or *alcaldías*, including one of the most lucrative at Lagos. In the lad's name, Dr. Gentil dealt in livestock with Mexico City merchants. He owned sixty pack mules and cornered the grain market in order to send prices skyward. The report lists still other misdeeds.

Thanks to their possessing capital in a mineless region, high officials' relatives and familiars were well situated to make money in livestock and settle there. Matters frequently were arranged according to regulations. As early as the sixteenth century, it appears that an honest president, Dr. Orozco, had requested the King's permission for his children to contract local marriages and own estancias and caballerías, in New Spain to be sure; but they were granted land on the edge of New Galicia, at Ameca and elsewhere. They founded a family and were the ancestors of the Tellos de Orozco, landed proprietors in Jalisco. In the seventeenth century, marriages became increasingly frequent between well-to-do Creoles and Audiencia members or their relatives. Audiencia members eventually stopped trying to conceal their estates inside the territory. At the beginning of the eighteenth century, a judge, Dr. Miranda Villaysán, paid His Majesty settlement money in order to clear title to the largest estate in all New Galicia, the adjoining haciendas of

Cedros and Caopas, which comprised 224 cattle estancias (4,000 square kilometers); it is true that they were largely arid land.

Authorized or not, the establishment of such enterprises by judges and their hangers-on was a fruitful achievement in a rather poor region where, without the incentive of big mines, colonizers seem to have lacked initiative. However, after this period of creative activity, which witnessed the founding of the haciendas and the development of the livestock industry, officials' personal, extralegal activities sank to the level of mere speculation and no longer benefited the region at large. By the middle of the seventeenth century, almost all usable land in the New Kingdom of Galicia had been distributed or occupied. That does not mean that all of it was being exploited.

Although exploiting was as a matter of fact still modest in scope, Audiencia members, royal officials, and church dignitaries had all had a hand in it. But their not inconsiderable enterprises were largely confined to the southwest and the Compostela–Guadalajara–Lagos region. North of Zacatecas, other powers held sway whose initiative, activity, and capital derived from different sources: miners, governors, and borderland captains who were also miners.

MINERS AS OWNERS OF RURAL HACIENDAS

In the sixteenth century, all those *ricos homes* who did not owe their start to public office owed it wholly or in part to the mines or, frequently, to trade, never, unlike their fellows in New Spain, to rich encomiendas. Agriculture and livestock, which were to be their subsequent source of capital, did not count in the beginning; they were merely a necessity in order to supply the mines with food. Then agriculture and livestock became a way to invest earned income—a most tempting one, because food and beasts of burden were bringing very high prices in the new mining centers.

The *ricos homes* lived in almost complete independence, far from the Audiencia and farther still from the Viceroy. The Guadalajara prosecutor pointed out to the King in 1576 that the Audiencia had practically no influence at Zacatecas, because of the long distances involved and the insecure state of the roads. Justice officials, he added, had trouble making the rich and mighty obey. Mine owners had been the first to make fortunes, sometimes in a very few years. In 1572, the Englishman Hawks described admiringly some miners' pomp and liberality; they would have an outdoor bell rung at mealtimes to call to their table travelers passing within hearing distance. Other contemporaries mention their luxuries, which were the more noticeable for the poverty-stricken surroundings.

At first, however, the miners found themselves confronted with serious problems. They had to feed their slaves and staffs in a region both empty and hostile. They also needed many oxen and mules for hauling, carrying, and, especially, turning their heavy ore crushers—unless they were fortunate enough to have a river near by. At so enormous a distance from producing centers, food and livestock prices were exorbitant, disconcerting and dismaying contemporaries.

Many miners began as a consequence to add droves and wheat or maize fields to their mining outfits. Since large quantities of charcoal were required for smelting, they also sought to acquire woodlands, which, rather than true forests, were areas thinly covered with scrub; there they installed their charcoal burners. Such was the origin of the mixed type of hacienda, recalling somewhat the big sugar plantations in the south and containing crushers and smelters, woods and charcoal heaps, fields of crops, grazing livestock, slaves, and other workers. Often, when a mine was located in the desert, its hacienda would be established beside one of the few streams big enough to furnish motive power and irrigation. The advantages far outweighed the inconvenience of having to transport ore from some distance—in one case twenty-two leagues—on muleback or in carts. Sometimes rivulets had to be dammed in order to allow at least the washing of the ore and at best irrigation of a few fields.

Very early, wealthy miners like Juan de Tolosa, Diego de Ibarra, Vicente de Zaldívar, and Guerra de Resa acquired land, by grant or purchase, between Fresnillo and Sombrerete and along the Aguanaval River, which, notwithstanding its moderate rate of flow, was also called Río Grande. A series of huge haciendas soon grew up there. Owners often had title to only a few caballerías and estancias, but they occupied in fact vast expanses without anyone's daring to dispute their right. We possess an early seventeenth-century description of one of these haciendas, Medina, "with huge droves of cattle and sheep, irrigated wheat fields, four water mills for smelting and refining silver, an enormous orchard full of all the fruit trees of Castile . . . and especially a great vineyard of many vines and trellises"; its red wine, made on the premises, was quite an acceptable one.

Five leagues farther along, travelers would come across *el asiento del Capitán Loiz* (Río Grande), named after its powerful founder, who was to become Urdiñola's father-in-law. There they would find an endowed vicar in residence, several families of Spanish farmers with their helpers, and four silver mills in neighborly proximity to a couple of flour mills. Some of the other estates on the river did not have crushers or smelters—Casa Blanca for example; but they still belonged to miners in distant Saín, Fresnillo, or Zacatecas. Slightly outside the valley was located the district of Nieves, in a basin where temperatures were higher. By the turn of the century, it was already one man's property, Lomas y Colmenares, Urdiñola's enemy. He had bought up all the inhabitants' workings and made the locality into one vast hacienda; he had his mule-powered crushers, droves, wheat fields, and vineyards (for he, too, made his own wine). Eastward on the road to Mazapil, where nomads frequently attacked, the district of San Juan de Cedros developed in the same way, becoming in the course of the seventeenth century the center of the largest estate in New Galicia, as previously mentioned.

It would be no task to accumulate other examples of silver mining's close link with the great rural haciendas' rise and expansion in the north. Nearly every crusher, smelter, or mine pit had at least one mule rancho, consisting of corrals and wide pastures for work animals. The word *hacienda*, unlike *estancia*, suggests capital invested in land, capital that the *ricos homes* had spent to dam streams, build permanent installations, and buy slaves, animals, and a complete stock of iron implements and wagons.

We occasionally are told the sums that miners paid out to create new haciendas. Captain Pedro de Arizmendi Gogorrón had made a fortune in the mines of San Luis Potosí, where he had been one of the first on the spot. Unlike many others, he did not take his ingots back to Spain, but invested them in the region. He spent more than 80,000 pesos, he tells us, to establish a mining hacienda in the San Francisco Valley, where he built a large dam, twelve furnaces for smelting and one for refining, and an ore crusher; he rounded out his estate with estancias. A large farming hacienda still bears his name. Separate installations had cost Gogorrón another 50,000 or 60,000 pesos apiece. All were, or soon became, mixed-type haciendas. When silver production fell to practically nothing, operations had to be restricted to agriculture and livestock.

The capital of the mighty was also indirectly responsible for the birth of new mining towns whenever one of their prospectors made a discovery. Since the original claim staked out could cover only a fraction of a deposit, miners flocked to it. If the region was particularly dangerous, it was to the rich man's interest to attract settlers and even give them material aid. The Tepezala and Charcas districts, ghost towns after a series of nomad raids, were resettled at powerful individuals' expense in 1573–1574. Ordered by the King to give encouragement, the Guadalajara Audiencia promised the individuals a large number of estancias in adjacent areas; that was also encouragement, to be sure, to grab eventually the rest of the land and the mines themselves.

Some of the most powerful miners and governors were not satisfied with merely adding estancias to the furnaces and crushers which had been the origin of their wealth. Mindful of the universal demand for mules, leather, and flour, and tending to see things on a big scale, they quickly perceived the advantage of mass-producing those items in the best-watered zones, even though the zones might be far removed from their mines. Farm income could not compare with profits from a rich ore deposit, but was much steadier. Besides, agricultural estates could be entailed, thus ensuring their families' perpetuation and delivering them of a source of anxiety.

These great rural estates sprang up in very broad belts surrounding Zacatecas, San Luis Potosí, and Guanajuato. In the west, where there was more water, were Valparaíso with its cool streams and Trujillo with its willow-lined canals; both haciendas sent their wheat to Zacatecas and both were the property of "a single master," Diego de Ibarra's heir. There were many others belonging to powerful miners and soldiers, like Diego de Mesa, Juan de Gordejuela Ybargüen (Río de Losa's heir), and Pedro de Minjares and his son Francisco.

Toward the northwest, at the base of a plateau from which springs poured, were the huge haciendas that Urdiñola with his unflagging energy had begun to establish while still a mere miner and captain in Mazapil: Los Patos (containing a crusher), Castañuela, and Parras. Each one had irrigation canals, vineyards, and wine presses, and was managed by a Spanish bailiff who was one of the Basque's dependents. Toward San Luis Potosí were Bledos (belonging to the miner Ortiz de Fuen-mayor), Zavala (named after Juan de Zavala, another rich miner and merchant), Illescas, Jaral, and Ciénaga de Mata, to mention only the largest. Guanajuato and the Bajío formed a transition zone with the southern regions; mines were not always the chief source of rural capital there.

Several of these haciendas, when entailed, would bequeath their names to powerful ennobled families (Jaral, Valparaíso) or would give rise to large villages and even small cities (Patos, or General Cepeda; Parras; Río Grande, Valparaíso). The process resembles an abridged version of some old Mediterranean province's evolution through the centuries: pastoral age, Roman villa, feudal aristocracy, and finally free city.

To a greater extent than in central or southern Mexico, haciendas constituted new population centers. In the words of a New Galicia inspector writing in 1608, "On every mining hacienda and many estancias there are far more Indians usually than in most villages." The reason was that in the east there were no Indian communities, only nomads, and in the west, communities were scattered and not very large. Lacking repartimientos or other adequate labor services, both mines and rural estates had to use slaves, mulattoes, and free Indians; these last were imported from the south and detained by various means, especially by letting them get into debt. Bishops touring their dioceses, and particularly Audiencia judges, remark upon the "large" villages of *naboríos*, or peons, around the masters' houses. These heavily populated estancias prefigured the classical Mexican hacienda at a date when, in the south, almost no one lived on the land and harvest estancias were still being cultivated by Indian work gangs coming daily from their villages. Northern owners also put to work captive Chichimecas and pacified tribes which they had settled on their estates; they were not good workers.

For want of anyone better, cattle barons had recourse to the motley crews of adventurers and vagrants whom travelers would meet in fear and trembling on the northern highways. When big rodeos or expeditions against the nomadic Indians were impending, owners would collect as many as 300 of these mounted highwaymen, who from vaqueros turned so easily into rustlers.

From their numbers armies were recruited whose function was to repel the Chichimecas or forestall them by driving them back to their lairs in the Bolsón Desert, the plains, and the rugged sierras northeast of Zacatecas. The armies were private, because the King was unable or unwilling to pay campaign expenses. Just as he bestowed governorships on the mighty, he passed out captaincies to rich miners and landowners, without regular pay, naturally. (The royal treasury did assume a share of campaign expenses by maintaining small groups of soldiers in danger spots.) That was another aspect of the monarchy's decentralization policy which benefited the *ricos homes* by letting them become absolute masters on their estates—true lords of the manor.

For several centuries, these honorary captains were one of the most numerous and characteristic social types in the northern provinces. Some had been appointed by His Majesty "captain and chief peace officer of the Chichimeca frontier," for example, Arizmendi-Gogorrón, a miner near San Luis Potosí, who boasted of having spent 5,000 pesos out of his own pocket to try to pin the nomads down. North of Zacatecas and Durango, many alcaldes mayores were also soldiers, probably recruited locally, like one Captain Cristóbal de Heredia, who in 1604 possessed at Indé "four furnaces . . . and a goodly number of mines," as well as a large farm and a horse and mule ranch. In New León, in spite of tardy colonization, the situation had become exactly the same by the middle of the seventeenth century. To take the example of a notable writer, Captain Alonso de León was at one and the same time *justicia mayor* of Cadereyta, cattle raiser and landed proprietor, and scout "in Huasteca, on the Río de Palmas section of the coast, and the road to Florida as far as the River Turbio."

These individuals were so independent at times that some of them handed out grants of land, estancias, and water rights, like Don Jerónimo de Alvarado y Salcedo in 1659. He was chief peace officer and captain of Saltillo; his signature indicates that he wielded the sword better than the pen.

Others were given the official title of "captain and protector of the Indians." Saltillo possessed four captains in 1604 (for twenty-two *vecinos*); of the four, one was chief peace officer and a second was "protector of the Tlaxcalans and Huachichiles." Some soldiers tried to win the nomads over to peace through gentle treatment, ingratiating themselves with gifts of what the nomads liked best: brightly colored clothing, hats, and especially meat. They also tried to settle them in villages, or even on their own estates. Other soldiers, however, repaid their cruelty with even worse brutality, capturing and enslaving them or selling them outside the territory. The result was a constant, merciless warfare, as waged, for example, by Saltillo's founder, Captain Alberto del Canto, whom the Audiencia called to account for various abuses; at large in the back country, he was never caught.

During the seventeenth century, titles and ranks became more diversified. Alongside "captain" appeared "sergeant," "sergeant major," "ensign" (*alférez*) and "ensign major," and finally "general," the holder of the last often being lieutenant to the governor-captain general. Appointees multiplied to so curious an extent that in 1676 there were eleven of them among the fifty-one armed *vecinos* residing in Saltillo. Nomads attacking from the north were not the sole cause of the proliferation, since such titles had been distributed all over Mexico, including the most peaceful zones.

Even at the end of the sixteenth century, it was fairly obvious that not all the many miners and cattle raisers assuming the rank of captain had received their promotion from the King, or, if they had, their title was a purely honorific one. They were often hard-pressed to make ends meet and, in danger zones, keep their estates running. Probably many were like Miguel de Barrassa of Durango, who in 1615 petitioned His Majesty for the titles of corregidor and protector of the natives, having spent twenty or thirty years fighting without pay and at his own expense, "furnishing weapons, retainers, and horses." There was also an odd individual, Captain Pedro Morcillo, who was a scout in the "new district" of Cuencamé near the dangerous Bolsón Desert. Many attacks had come from that quarter, but he had repelled them and headed off others by presenting the nomads with gifts—at his own expense, it goes without saying. From 1569 on, he had patiently put together piece by piece, adding springs to pastures and grants to purchases, a large hacienda, San José, which finally comprised fifteen estancias, thirty caballerías, and an ore crusher. It was eventually absorbed into an even larger estate.

By the end of the seventeenth century, there were almost no northern hacienda owners who were not at the same time captains; every district contained at least a few. Likewise, there was almost always a churchman owning farms or mines who could, if occasion demanded, lead an expedition. These soldiers, mighty or humble, all lived in dwellings topped with battlements and pierced with loopholes. Modest castles of sorts, they have unfortunately left few traces, this stoneless region having usually built in adobe. In their towers' protective shadow the peons and other workers lived, making up, in case of an alert, the main body of troops.

Such intermingling of military, civil, economic, ecclesiastical, and lay functions had been typical of medieval Spain. Conditions arising from the need to wage war against the nomads had revived or strengthened old traditions born of the centuries-long Reconquest.

The *ricos homes* of New Viscaya collected title deeds by exactly the same methods as their counterparts in New Spain, but on a scale commensurate with the region's vastness. Every trait tending to place all property in the hands of a few was exaggerated in the north to the point of becoming a caricature of itself: cattle raising, even more extensive in a semi-arid region without native labor; the independence of the mighty, reaching a new height because their numerous retainers had no definite jobs; the common people's restlessness, verging on nomadism; and, finally, the complicity of Audiencia judges and governors linked in so many different fashions to settlers eligible for grants.

The old conception of grants as rewards for services rendered flourished anew in these regions where private citizens were paying for armies and campaigns. It was only natural to offer them some sort of compensation, and a land grant was one of the few favors costing the King nothing. The individuals who had resettled and defended the Tepezala and Charcas mines after their destruction by nomads were rewarded around 1574 in this manner. One hundred and forty years later, the owner of the Cedros hacienda was granted, in exchange for a very small fee, an area the size of several hundred estancias. His estate was a strategic part of a war zone's defenses; it was also an arid zone.

Many rewards in New Galicia went to Audiencia officials and clerks, who were perhaps badly paid but who were certainly in an excellent position to obtain land grants. A single estate's deeds had been issued in the sixteenth century not only to the Guadalajara town scribe but also to the Audiencia's chief clerk, interpreter, and receiver. The estancias' location beyond Fresnillo shows that they were meant to be sold at once; and they were, to a capitalist who added them to the big Casa Blanca hacienda. Although it is much more difficult to recognize deeds intended for judges and officials who were forbidden by law to possess them and therefore used proxies, some grantees, their friends or dependents, stated explicitly that they were merely agents or go-betweens.

The farther north we go, the more blatant the actions become. Partly owing to Basque solidarity in New Viscaya, Urdiñola, the most enterprising of the Basques, had succeeded in accumulating, even before his governorship, vast estates west of Saltillo. Using his treasurer's name, Juan de Ibarra (who immediately transferred title to him), he obtained in 1587 all the unoccupied land lying between two of his haciendas, "an area approximately six leagues around." Another time, he received outright from Governor Gordejuela Ybargüen's lieutenant the ten or twelve square leagues separating other estates of his. At the time of his death, Urdiñola did not own quite all the land in the region, since his heirs acquired still another estate in 1620; but his haciendas took in almost all the springs and streams in an immense stretch west of Saltillo. What was left was not much more than scorched plain and desert.

Town dwellers, like modest settlers and prospectors, were restless and constantly on the move, selling their allotments and seeking their fortune somewhere else. An estate like Casa Blanca was in 1644 composed of twenty-four estancias and fifty caballerías that between 1561 and 1598 had been distributed to at least twenty different persons. Some beneficiaries must certainly have been fictive, but others were miners who had sold out. The same holds true for Nombre de Dios, Durango, Aviño, and Saltillo. In 1583, Urdiñola succeeded in buying from the latter town's inhabitants a long string of caballerías and estancias in the Pyrenees Valley and toward Patos which they had been given a few years previously. The reason for the sales becomes obvious when we look at the town's census records: in 1604, only five individuals or families out of the twenty-two *vecinos* had been in Saltillo since 1591; of the five, two were an original settler and his descendant. Nearly all the original settlers had moved away, and the other *vecinos* were newcomers.

The title deeds of the great proprietors, however many there might be by now, covered only a portion of the land occupied by their droves. When the King on two occasions, in 1644 and especially in 1697, ordered an appraisal of land illegally occupied in order to sell it to the occupants, it was discovered that haciendas had annexed vast expanses of public land. The land consequently belonged to His Majesty, although it had frequently been occupied "from time immemorial." As we shall see, owners able to pay settlements normally doubled or even tripled their legal holdings. In exceptional cases, the figure was even higher.

A single notable example shows the different aspects of the concentration process in the northern zone: the Ciénaga de Mata haciendas. The only anomaly is that their proximity to the agricultural Bajío brought into play men whose capital was not always derived from mines.

In the last years of the sixteenth century, a plain farmer, Pedro Mateos, became very active in the region bounded by the Bajío, Teocaltiche, and a point beyond Aguascalientes. He probably had friends in the Guadalajara Audiencia, for he and his son Diego obtained numerous grants east of Aguascalientes in a zone exposed to nomad attacks. He showed skill in developing his land and in earning money. "Near his house on the Ciénaga de Mata y Tecuan estancia," he obtained the right to dam a creek and install a large water system for irrigating his fields and to build flour mills especially "equipment for processing silver ore." He probably brought the ore from the Tepezala mines, in which his family had bought an interest. As though not satisfied with his various grants, he acquired others by proxy and in the same region bought still more land near the fort of Las Bocas, particularly from a cleric who had just been given a number of grants that were clearly an act of charity.

This already imposing estate passed to a grandson, Agustín Rincón, who seems to have been as dynamic as his grandfather. He started out in public office and was chief constable in several different towns, then corregidor of Zacatecas, a captain, and finally a general. He was the first military man in a family in which they would be numerous. He continued to enlarge his estates, largely by purchases from small Creole farmers in neighboring San Felipe. By 1645, his strongbox contained deeds to 87 estancias and 180 caballerías located for the most part around Ciénaga de Mata. In exchange for a fair sum of money, His Majesty granted him the intervening pieces.

After Don Agustín's death, the sole heir, a cleric, nearly entered the Jesuit order, which would have thus acquired the vast domain. The licentiate could not make up his mind, however; he finally entailed the estate and settled it on a niece married to a captain, Nicolás Gallardo. Their son, Don José, was the first to bear the name Rincón de Gallardo, which would henceforth be attached to one of the most powerful families in the viceroyalty. We shall return to Don José, who was already the perfect type of Mexican hacendado, a benefactor of the Church and captain of a private army containing "at least five hundred men and a thousand horses when on campaign."

After rounding out his holdings, Don José had to settle once more with the King for his immense latifundium of Ciénaga de Mata. The official surveyor estimated its surface area at 202 estancias, only 100 of which had definite title deeds. Probably as a reward for his military services, the captain paid, in spite of his immense wealth, a mere 2,000 pesos for final recognition of his rights to the 202 estancias (including 19 for sheep) and his 255 caballerías. The nucleus of all that land formed a huge rectangle approximately 75 by 60 kilometers in the relatively fertile and well-watered region of Aguascalientes, San Luis Potosí, San Felipe, and Guanajuato. It had taken only a century to create what was truly a small principality, with its own administration and cavalry, a village and castle at Ciénaga de Mata in the center, a string of subordinate haciendas and hamlets round about, a large lagoon, streams, and mountains.

Some of these great land accumulators were bold men of action; their initiative spurred them to create oases and villages on the forbidding cactus-covered plains. Urdiñola especially was not content with mines and droves; he pacified and settled the nomads and brought irrigation to zones where it had never been seen before; he built, plowed, and planted. Mexico owes to him its grape-growing region around Parras.

Arizmendi Gogorrón appears in some respects a modern industrialist and businessman. He founded a number of mining and mixed haciendas, went into partnership with one Acevedo to do some prospecting, and acquired an interest in many mines which he then developed. He also bought land in the Bajío, where he already owned ten *estancias* (containing almost no livestock in 1615, it is true); he wished to install irrigation on the new land. On a more modest scale, men like Pedro Mateos dammed streams and tilled fields, with their harquebus always within reach.

The great haciendas' creation and expansion were not always guided by purely social and economic considerations. Just as medieval Spain's *ricos homes* had been not so much capitalists as leaders—*caudillos*—some miners and cattle barons were plainly less interested in material possessions for their own sake than for the political power that they imparted. There is no evidence that men who had struck it rich in the mines by pure luck ever progressed, on acquiring huge amounts of land, to a clear realization of what constituted a good investment, of how to calculate profits, or how best to develop the soil. They went on acquiring estates, not to increase their incomes, but to *señorear*, to use a word of the time, that is, to be lord of the manor. In 1585, a Guadalajara judge was already informing the King of men who had grabbed as many as twenty adjoining estancias or a whole string of mines without having the slightest intention of working them. The activities of the great were aimed purely and simply at cornering either all the wealth produced in their region, or the means of producing it, not at creating an environment in which they could produce it themselves. On occasion, they even partially destroyed wealth.

In 1604, the Governor of New Viscaya, Urdiñola, who had shown such a creative spirit himself in all his undertakings, explained to the King that at the new mines large numbers of miners, both rich and poor, had installed extraction machinery, each according to his means. Then,

> *a big miner, backed up with powerful capital or credit, comes along or else one of the miners already on the spot begins to misbehave, and in a district where many crushers and inhabitants are at work, this one individual wants to buy from the others all their mines and machinery, solely for the purpose of adding to his establishment and of keeping the district as a sort of entail for himself and his descendants. There is no question of his increasing production over what he has previously attained with a single outfit. In many*

localities, a grabber, once he has bought out the other inhabitants, razes their buildings in order to drive them all out.

The Governor goes on to cite a number of specific examples in New Galicia and New Viscaya. At Mazapil, three individuals, whom we already know and who surely did not live there, bought up twenty miners' holdings. San Andrés had been reduced to two owners, cousins who had installed agents there. At Nieves, Lomas y Colmenares and his son purchased all five haciendas. The Aviño district had fallen into "one owner's hands, a powerful man," as Mota y Escobar had described him: Juan Guerra de Resa, a big stockman, who at Aviño had his private church complete with chaplain, as well as many Spanish, Negro, and Indian servants.

The most curious instance is the Jocotlán mines. Six different outfits were working there "when Antonio de Carabajal, a miner living in the locality, decided to buy them all and, having bought them, either demolished them or let them go to ruin; he kept his own equipment in operation without increasing the current rate of production." He did the same thing at Chimaltitlán. His complete scorn for full production is not lacking in grandeur.

Urdiñola's report deals only with mines, the royal treasury's sole object of concern because of its one-fifth share in silver production. However, most of the individuals mentioned are also known to us as cattle barons and big landowners. Land grabbing was one of the best ways of eliminating mining competition. For the reasons stated, each strike brought mobs of miners; but if one miner succeeded in cornering all the surrounding land, his neighbors could not feed their beasts of burden or even their Indians and helpers.

We can establish a parallel between mine concentration and the linking of estancias by grant or purchase. The motive was the same: to remain in sole possession without developing. Sometimes, an element of speculation entered into the motive. In 1608, an inspector from New Galicia noted that many Spaniards had obtained estancias and fields "solely to keep others out, or because they think that a time will come when land will be very valuable; in spite of the purpose for which the grants were made, they neither work nor develop them, leaving them deserted. As the land is thought to be private property, no one else requests it or cultivates it." "The same applies to the mines." The inspector concluded that it would be fitting to declare all unoccupied spaces free and available. On the strength of his recommendation, the Guadalajara Audiencia began to distribute land on a temporary basis, so as to be able to repossess it and give it to others if necessary.

Mere legislation could not change a mentality. Moreover, estancias continued to be granted each year, whereas droves (except occasionally sheep) were dwindling everywhere; proof is furnished by the dropping off of tithes and the bishops' and cathedral chapters' repeated complaints. In many huge districts there was soon no more land available, although little of it was being used and the number of inhabitants was infinitesimal.

For many, in short, the goal was to monopolize every source of income in agriculture and mining, lest others become independent or rivals by the same means. The many curried favor with the mighty, getting them to bring influence to bear on their numerous dependents, and sought power, even ennoblement; that was their aim rather than profits, unlike their contemporaries, bourgeois capitalists, in various corners of Europe. These new landed proprietors saw no occasion to intensify production in their mines or on their estates in order to earn more money. They merely wanted to occupy all mine pits, every bit of land, the entire territory if possible, and to reign as overlords. Hence the majority's scorn for efficient output, which so scandalized enlightened eighteenth-century spirits like Father Morfi, and whence finally the particularly extensive form of exploitation on the northern haciendas.

THE MINERS' WITHDRAWAL AND THE CASE OF NEW LEÓN

In the course of the seventeenth century, many powerful miners were ruined and disappeared. The more fortunate tended to withdraw into the south, particularly to Mexico City. As early as 1607 or 1608, Bishop Mota y Escobar remarked of Zacatecas that "among its nobles few are rich and those are all miners; among its middle classes many are rich . . . and they are all merchants keeping shops."

The reason was that nobles and would-be nobles could only be miners, landed proprietors, or officials. As we have seen, their idea of rural property was not conducive to riches. Especially in the mines, production was dropping, first at Zacatecas, then at San Luis Potosí; by 1620 or 1630, the decline was perceptible everywhere.

Many local potentates with no outside investments found themselves saddled with debts larger than their capital; in the mines, disaster had struck as rapidly as good fortune had. Rodrigo de Carvajal, who had wiped out all competition in his district before 1604, was bankrupt four years later, "without credit or resources to tide his enterprises over, these having moreover been attached by his creditors." One of the latter, a merchant, had put Carvajal's businesses back into operation, hoping to recover his money. Meanwhile, Carvajal, it seems, was in a debtors' prison; he still owed the royal treasury for 17,000 or 18,000 pesos' worth of mercury, which the prosecutor was trying to realize out of "haciendas containing mares, mules, and other animals."

Income from droves and farms was inadequate for a business recovery. Also around 1608, the Guadalajara canons asked the courts to retrieve the enormous sum of 30,000 pesos in back tithes owed by the rural hacienda of a "powerful individual" and Fresnillo miner, Diego de Messa. In the same district in 1607, nine enterprises owed the royal treasury a total of over 100,000 pesos. At the time of his death, Juan Guerra de Resa still owed the King 23,000. In San Andrés district, the two chief miners, Martín de Gastellu and Captain Diego de Evila, owed in 1604 "to His Majesty and to private citizens" 30,000 and 80,000 pesos, respectively; the second fabulous sum is quoted as a conservative estimate. To be sure, their haciendas had been partially ransacked by the Acaje Indians.

Miners' debts did not mean that all were bankrupt; but royal officials' comments show that many were on the verge and some who could not pay their creditors were in prison. It was even suggested that, instead of hailing them to Guadalajara, they be kept prisoners at their mines, where they could go on working off their debts. One inspector argued that the high price of mercury, a state monopoly, was at the root of the evil; quoting figures, he proved that His Majesty would be ahead to supply mercury gratis or else supply it on credit, in order to stimulate silver production and indirectly increase the royal fifth. The state was deaf to an argument that called for giving up immediate gain in favor of a considerably larger one in a few years' time. During the first decades of the seventeenth century, the situation rapidly worsened; although we know very little about production rates, there is no doubt that they went far down and did not begin to rise again until the eighteenth century.

Having no labor supply and riddled with debts, the *ricos homes* cut down extraction, abandoned their mines, or went into bankruptcy. Some retreated into their rural estates, where we come upon them again bearing the title of captain, like almost all landowners of the period. Unfortunately, the mining depression had diminished the need for mules, hides, and food. Agricultural expansion consequently seems to have marked time and even retreated in the zones most exposed to nomad attacks. In New Viscaya some estancias were abandoned. Near San Juan del Río, La Sauceda, a large and prosperous hacienda, had been deserted and declared uninhabitable before 1667; in spite of the former thriving state of its eighteen estancias and fifty caballerías, its evaluation had dropped to 5,500 pesos. Other estates were also deserted and their mining equipment partly in ruins. Elsewhere, haciendas were tending to become little self-contained worlds, whereas they had been created largely to produce food and beasts for the great mines.

When public offices began to be sold wholesale, a new opportunity was offered miners and landed proprietors. An odd report of the Guadalajara Audiencia in 1612 deals with "the reasons why permanent offices of chief ensign, chief constable, and regidor must not be sold in New Galicia." Inasmuch as a "permanent official is absolute master of justice, administration, and royal finances in his district," the first thought of those possessing some capital "and fields, droves, mines, or businesses" is indeed to buy one of those offices. Then they can corner commodities and have the whip hand over everyone, particularly "farmers by gaining control of daily workers or repartimiento Indians," fix the price of bread at excessive levels, and in general so conduct their administration as to further their own affairs.

The very rich were not satisfied with these local offices, which they could leave to their relatives and gossips. Money permitting, they liked to buy offices in the capital. In 1609, Juan de Zavala, a San Luis Potosí miner and hacienda owner, was adjudged the office of Mexico City's chief constable for the enormous sum of 110,000 pesos. San Luis was still prosperous at this time; but as the industry's decline set in, migration southward seems to have accelerated. Henceforth, old mining families' descendants, intermarrying with the aristocracy over the centuries, would mostly be found in Mexico City and Michoacán: the

Oñates and Ibarras, the Tolosas and Zaldívars (connected by marriage with the Cortés-Moctezumas), and the Guerra de Resas (connected with the Guerrero de Villasecas).

In the course of the seventeenth century, a few rich Mexico City families and royal officials conversely acquired interests in the northern provinces, usually small ones because of the mining depression which was paralyzing the entire region's economic development. In New León we can observe best of all the subsequent shift in wealth and the final eclipse of the miners in their role as pioneers and colonizers of the north.

For want of mines New León was settled much later than the west. Governor Martín de Zavala seems to have been unable initially to make Spaniards stay fixed. In spite of good land and a fair amount of water, Monterrey was vegetating, its only inhabitants soldiers and adventurers whose chief means of subsistence was the slave trade. There were none of the *ricos homes* who elsewhere in Mexico constituted "the country's backbone."

After the first few decades of the seventeenth century, San Luis Potosí and the other big mines had withdrawn into themselves. The only sources for new enterprise and capital were consequently Mexico City and other prosperous regions in the south. Martín de Zavala tried to attract to his "government" the great flocks of sheep of Querétaro and Mexico City, whose pastures dried up in the spring. The only inducement that he could offer sheepmen for sending their flocks so far through nomad-infested territory was land grants, which he started distributing generously in 1635. Grants to a single person of from forty to fifty sheep estancias became the rule. When the figure fell below thirty, either the recipient was some needy captain in the area or the figure included cattle estancias, two and one half times as large. Exceptionally, more than seventy estancias were granted at one time. The land was not arid plain, but fertile pasture. Probably such immense expanses were a necessity to entice men with whose visions of grandeur we are already familiar.

The texts of the earliest deeds seem to reveal a desire on the part of the Governor to justify grants of such an unprecedented size; he discusses at length the risks of winter pasturing and what benefits the region would derive from the flocks. Flocks were immense, upward of

20,000 or 30,000 head. Each shift of position required a small army of shepherds, mounted and afoot. Led by a majordomo and four or five Spanish assistants, a caravan was ordinarily composed of 70 to 100 Indians or Negroes with their wives and children, plus 100 to 130 pack animals and saddle horses.

Around 1648, Captain Alonso de León wrote that thirteen large flocks moving into winter pasture comprised more than 300,000 sheep. Numbers rapidly increased. Around mid-century, we know the names of fifteen or so sheepmen who had been given or who had bought large sweeps of New León territory. That is the same as saying that the best regions were already occupied, at least nominally. Most of the owners were powerful Mexico City residents. The less important were rich men from Querétaro or Huichapan, Mexico's main sheep-raising zone, located near the capital. The list is instructive.

We find Captain Juan de Espíndola, in 1644 "Treasurer of the Holy Crusade" in Mexico City, and the chief accountant, Juan de Alcocer, who had been treasurer of the same organization the year before; already possessing vast estates in New Spain and the northern provinces, Alcocer purchased from Captain Juan de Zavala the twenty-five estancias that Governor Martín de Zavala had given Juan a few months previously. We also find Captain Antonio de Echaide, who established an entail, and especially his powerful brother, Luis Tovar Godínez, who had purchased the title of "Secretary for Administration and War in New Spain" for 126,000 pesos and had entailed a rich estate in 1643–1644. There are finally Don Juan Francisco de Bertiz, Mexico City's regidor and royal ensign; four members of the Zúñiga family, Don Luis, Don Juan, Don Francisco, and Don Lucas, and Captain Don Diego de Horduña (or Urdune), who owned immense, flourishing haciendas all over Mexico and assembled in New León, by grant or purchase, over 150 sheep estancias. Most, in summary, were rich individuals who resided in Mexico City and had probably never set foot inside the new territory.

There were exceptions. Captain Hernando de Mendiola helped to colonize the region "with his family, household, and property consisting of 30,000 sheep in addition to other livestock." Captain Alonso de León was another of the few stockmen to settle in New León. Arriving from New Spain in 1635 as a plain soldier, he became a *vecino* of Cadereyta and was soon granted thirty estancias there plus an encomienda of more or less stable nomads. After his appointment to the post of chief peace officer and to a captaincy, he founded a family; a century and a half later, one of his great-grandsons, also a captain and a big landowner, was still living in the vicinity. More modest grants were sometimes given to other colonizers and captains or chief peace officers in recognition of services rendered.

The rich Mexico City proprietors' capital funds were no less fruitful for their absence. Captain Alonso de León explains in his account that the flocks' arrival gave the necessary impetus to colonization, attracted merchants, and fostered commerce to some extent. Then, large-scale stock raising was developed and farming haciendas were established; these sold their crops outside the territory, whereas previously only enough wheat had been grown for local consumption. In the past, the Governor had had to send clear to Zacatecas for produce needed in the town of Cerralvo.

Contrary to regions with a mining economy, no rich and powerful class grew up here. In spite of a few large rivers and green pastures, these vast reaches were for a long time simply annexes to the big haciendas of New Spain. Owners were absentee landlords, as we should say today, living 800 kilometers away in the capital, sending their flocks north each year under a major-domo's supervision, and having no other ties with the region than the income derived from their sheep in winter pasture there. If economically such families belong among the northern mighty, the same cannot be said of them socially.

Some of these huge estates were not even used, either because their owners were in no hurry to develop them (being more concerned with grabbing land than with making a profit) or because they were particularly exposed to attacks from warring Indians. For example, Captain Diego de Horduña's 150 estancias were declared uninhabitable in 1677; his heirs had stopped using them and they represented only 1,000 pesos out of a fortune evaluated at 400,000 and consisting almost entirely of land. However, even unworked, these vast expanses remained private estates. They could no longer be distributed among new settlers. Formal title deeds had insured possession; the settlements to be paid the King would soon guarantee absolute ownership. If only potentially, the most derelict were still huge haciendas.

Throughout the northern provinces, finally, the decline of the mines had turned sheep raising into the owners' chief source of income. Immense flocks were ranging over these sparsely settled dry expanses, where boundaries established under official supervision would mark off for several centuries to come properties as big as states.

6.FACTORS LIMITING THE GREAT ESTATES' EXPANSION

The great estates were not the only landed establishments in New Spain. Except in isolated instances, native communities' lands were still intact at the end of the sixteenth century. Since the natives did not own droves, they occupied only a fraction of the soil, even in the densely populated central regions. Their *milpas*, or maize patches, were on the other hand situated in fertile, well-watered valleys. They thus made up in quality for the quantity of ground that they left vacant. In addition, the soil in wooded areas wore out so fast that the Indians had to clear more and more land. (Their temporary clearings may still be seen today in the Huasteca.) As a result, they moved into huge stretches whose ownership would give rise to disputes with Spanish stockmen. Indian communities also had internal enemies, since even before the Spaniards' arrival their noble class had begun to usurp land and reduce many free farmers to the status of *mayeques,* or serfs. This class, too, usually occupied small, fertile tracts because it raised no livestock.

Recognizing the threat implicit in the Spaniards' large droves, some individuals and communities succeeded in having their rights acknowledged to much more land than they were actually cultivating. They were aided in this by the religious orders which, in the sixteenth century at least, were naturally their protectors. In outlying regions beyond the Aztec empire's borders, sedentary tribes were occupying vast areas that they utilized for hunting and gathering wild food as much as they did for farming.

Indian communities were not alone in their opposition to the early large estates. Small Spanish towns had sprung up nearly everywhere; we are referring less to the encomendero communities established shortly after the Conquest than to the slightly more recent towns that had been founded, for strategic purposes, along the roads leading to the far-off silver mines. The second category's inhabitants were almost all farmers and stockmen within town districts, which they frequently had to protect from neighboring haciendas. Many of these towns did not last out the seventeenth century; others, whose sturdy white or mestizo peasant stock possessed greater tenacity than the natives, became centers of active resistance or, later, of counterattacks that sometimes swept big landowners from the region.

Both native and Spanish communities, unless they fell a prey to the big estates, consequently thwarted the latter's continued expansion.

NATIVE COMMUNITIES

When the conquistadors first settled on the new continent, they sought only tribute and, a little later, labor for small-scale placer or pit mining and drove tending. Instead of representing an obstacle for them, the most densely populated zones had attracted them in the beginning, because they needed exploitable native communities close at hand. Then, however, they began to want land, too, in order to make the most of the available labor supply. At the same time, the herds' multiplying had made areas that had been of no interest until then (because they were semi-arid or remote from population centers) suddenly acquire considerable value.

The small but fertile community fields early attracted the Spaniards.

Their droves and crops would have quickly invaded the *milpas* if Luis de Velasco and other viceroys, with continual missionary support, had not immediately taken stern measures. At first, the measures were a hasty response to a state of emergency; that is, they were empirical and purely negative. Soon, however, they began to reflect a rationalized system, which was an adaptation of the Salamancan philosophy to a new, concrete case—the Indies. Government by theologians and law licentiates had now replaced the extralegal powers of the soldiers and adventurers who had conquered the country. For that reason, it is impossible to ignore the powerful legal weapons that could be brought into play to protect the natives and, particularly, their fields. What these weapons were, what new status emerged for the communities, what protective barriers were erected, and what the latter's strong and weak points proved to be are all questions affecting the organization of Mexican society down to the present day.

CIVIL AND RELIGIOUS PROTECTION

As early as the sixteenth century, theologians and philosophers like Matías de Paz (d. 1519) and, especially, Vitoria (d. 1549) had sought in the teachings of St. Thomas and the medieval realists a solution to the big jurisprudential problems that the Spanish Conquest and adminstration of the New World had raised. Their doctrine had influenced, directly or indirectly, most members of the Council of the Indies and many of the missionaries and licenciados sent out from Spain. Important works like *De Indis* and *De Jure Belli* were published. Bartolomé de las Casas passionately espoused the doctrine. Somewhat later, Domingo de Soto reworked and expanded it.

After an initial period of reticence, the monarchy lent its wholehearted support to the new philosophy, thereby discrediting Sepúlveda's theory of the Indian as an irrational being. The philosophy's conclusions were simple, to the point, and fundamental: there existed independently of revealed truth a temporal order of things and a law of nations whose conception was immediately accessible to human reason. Natural law, which was a reflection of divine law and the basis of universal order and harmony, applied equally to all rational beings, Christians or not. ("Jus Gentium aequale est cristianis et infidelibus," Soto says.) Indians accordingly had rights like Spaniards, who, possessing no innate superiority, could in relation to them be no more than their guides. As Vitoria put it, "Infidelitas non est impedimentum quominus aliquis sit verus dominus"—"Paganism does not keep a man from being a true master in anyone's eyes."

These ideas were current by mid-sixteenth century. In Mexico, they found an echo in an anonymous monk's remark to His Majesty that the Indians had true kings and lords, who possessed "a master's rights over his vassals, just as the vassals do over their lands and goods *jure gentium*, because the lord and master's rights that man enjoys over material objects is grounded on neither faith nor charity. Gentiles and idol worshipers are true masters in the same way that Christians are, and proffer the same qualifications." "Contrary to some philosophers' assertions, the fact that the natives worship idols is not in itself sufficient justification" to despoil them. Even the Pope does not have the power to authorize that, "quia nemo dat quod non habet" ("because one cannot bestow what one does not have"). Encomiendas were illegal, the monk concluded, and no person might deprive Indians of their natural right to own possessions, govern themselves, and live in freedom (1554).

Missionaries and jurists took the short step dividing theory from practice when they declared that Indians obviously could not be kept enslaved, except those living *more ferarum* ("like wild animals"), such as the Chichimecas. They were capable of self-government in their own "civilized states" and were fully as well qualified as Spaniards to possess, individually and collectively, both real and personal property. If they were already converts to Christianity, their rights were all the more compelling.

Neither the philosophy's clarity nor the authorities' excellent intentions prevented inconsistencies, blunders, and a good deal of groping when they had to translate them into practicable measures. The first Viceroy complained that in matters concerning the Indians, monks and Council of the Indies members "waste so much time, paper, and ink doing and undoing, issuing contradictory instructions, and changing daily the order of government." The elaborate systems conceived in Spain turned out to need considerable adaptation in view of the American experiment. Also, it was practically impossible, for want of time, to use the new ideas in a constructive fashion, except sporadically as in the two combined villages and hospices that Vasco de Quiroga had founded. The authorities were being confronted with too many emergencies; chaos in many Indian communities made it imperative to forestall exactions and countless other excesses that soldiers might so easily perpetrate in the sixteenth century, particularly when they were conquerors occupying a country whose population was unusually defenseless and docile. Protecting the natives was of course a purely negative way of applying the new ideas; the fact remains that these same ideas were the source of the vigor and energy with which missionaries and jurists set about their task.

The need to defend community *milpas* and estates, though initially a secondary consideration in view of the soldiers' lack of interest in land, did arise early in some regions, Oaxaca, for example. In this rich, populous valley, a small Spanish town, Antequera, had been founded "in the middle of the community of Guaxaca." Native crops naturally took up most of the available soil. Although Spaniards had demanded land repeatedly, the authorities had always refused. When Antequera's public attorneys petitioned for a league of land surrounding the town, because of the "great need of pastures and fields for caballerías, *peonerías*, orchards, and commons," the King merely replied, in 1532, that they should submit a more detailed statement—which was the customary method of gaining time and burying the matter in red tape.

Five or six years later, the same Spanish town submitted another request begging Her Majesty most humbly to allow land distribution, since it had "no fields or estates on which to sow grain." The Queen authorized her representative (or another reliable agent) to make an on-the-spot investigation and, if the Indians would suffer no harm, to "allocate a moderate amount of land for houses, orchards, and crops." Owing to the highest authority's determined opposition, however, the situation had not changed by 1544; and it does not appear to have done so until the shrinkage of native populations during the epidemics—as well as the weak characters of certain viceroys—afforded Spaniards a foothold in the valley. In the meantime, although they still owned no land, they were attempting to raise large herds of cattle and, especially, horses. Around 1550, Viceroy Mendoza had them expelled from the "three valleys"; their loud outcries fell on deaf ears, since, without title deeds, they had no case to lay before the courts.

Spanish crops did not invade native lands on any appreciable scale until the seventeenth century. A more immediate threat was posed by herds, which, twenty years after the Conquest, had multiplied so alarmingly that they had overrun the entire country, respecting neither fields nor boundary posts and forcing the authorities to take emergency measures. The first two viceroys, whom the monks usually kept informed of violations, prosecuted offenders with unflagging zeal. Mendoza set aside two mornings a week for listening to Indians' complaints; Velasco embarked upon a systematic defense of their rights and personally supervised execution of his orders whenever he could. Still, some communities did suffer considerable damage, toward Toluca in the west and Jilotepec in the north; in the east and south around Tlaxcala, Tepeaca, and Atlixco, and much farther away near the hot lands of Colima, New Galicia, and Pánuco. Sooner or later, however, damage was brought within well-defined limits, depending on a given region's degree of obedience to royal authority.

In their mission villages, the monks, too, placed obstacles in the path of Spanish settlers and traffickers. Their aim was to isolate villages from all outside contacts, since they fondly believed that their charges were pure, newly born creatures whom religion must enlighten and Old Europe's Iron Age civilization must not corrupt.

Individual initiative was discernible in the many local, purely empirical measures that solved emergencies, prevented the extortion and incursions incident to the Conquest, softened its blows, and bound up the wounds that it left in its wake. Soon, however, the most ardent monks and the pick of officials (of whom there was no lack under Charles V) were no longer satisfied with defending their wards piecemeal. Behind the fumbling empiricism, we glimpse a rationale, a carefully conceived, concerted plan of action, and some degree of unity; they were certainly present in the organization of mission villages on a large scale (in contrast to the few established previously) and Viceroy Velasco I's lengthy series of Indian ordinances.

Since Indians were rational beings, the argument went, they had similar rights to those of Spaniards; the first step must therefore be to incorporate into Spanish peninsular jurisprudence all their institutions that did not run counter to divine or natural law. The ideal was eventual equality; this implied progressive assimilation, but not, of course, abolition of the existing social hierarchy. Such is the origin of the curiously close association of native and Spanish elements in rural Mexico's present life and institutions.

This lofty scheme was partly conscious and calculated, partly un-premeditated in minds shaped directly or indirectly by Salamanca's and Alcalá's philosophers. Although its manifold aspects cannot be gone into here, we do need to be familiar with a few of the innovations that monks and legists made in transforming the old *calpullis*. Viceroy Velasco I's part was also a capital one, for he consolidated and con-siderably expanded the early missionaries' achievements.

The tendency was to assimilate Indian groups and villages to Spanish municipalities by emphasizing community institutions, in which the two countries seemed to share a common tradition. In order to evangel-ize scattered groups more conveniently, missionaries brought them to-gether in three types of villages, which had to be set up and supplied with food: congregations, assemblies (juntas) and organized ad-ministrations (*policías*). The word *reducción*, designating still another kind of town to which natives were brought to be converted ("re-duced") to Christianity, did not come into general usage until Viceroy Monterrey's term of office (1595–1603); he carried out, somewhat clumsily, a vast operation of this type covering the whole country. Whereas the missionaries were naturally inclined to give towns founded by them the solid municipal framework of a Castilian community, native society, built on *calpullis* that had evolved out of clans, was much better adapted to strong corporate institutions. It may be that the missionaries were more or less conscious of the need to combat native individualism, whose nascent anarchical tendencies were threatening to undermine society's ancient foundations.

As to physical appearance, the new villages were built "in the image of Mexico City," to use the Augustinian Grijalva's expression; the capi-tal itself had been rebuilt in Spanish style. Streets laid out at right angles and a monastery and municipal edifices lining the central square were like a materialization of the nation's order and harmony—the "orden y concierto" so close to the philosophers' and humanists' hearts.

Let the alcalde mayor . . . lay out the town plan, picking first of all the most suitable sites for the church and public square, then the town hall, prison, and community bank, the commons and municipal pastures, and everything else required for the adorning and efficient organization of said town. Let him also make arrange-ments for distributing fields and building lots.

This 1560 ordinance for a new native settlement is the exact replica of one for a "Spaniards' town" with its different municipal institutions. Hundreds of Indian villages were thus established or rebuilt. We can still see them today all along Mexico's roads, even though a large number of public and private adobe buildings have had to be restored many times over.

Innovations were probably not as significant as they might appear at first sight. Former native villages had also contained a great square surrounded by a temple and public buildings. The *barrios*, or quarters, of the new towns corresponded in general to the *calpullis* which had been grouped there either from ancient times or by "congregation" on the missionaries' part. The fields that municipalities rented to their inhabitants for a nominal fee must have frequently been survivals of the allotments distributed to *calpulli* members. And the *sementeras de comunidad*, or community crops designed to subsidize the administration, the vicar's living, festivals, and so on, are curious analogues of Aztec customs. Community property, though organized in the Spanish manner, was sometimes designated in royal orders by the Nahuatl word *calpisca*, or that which belongs to the house of the *calpulli*, or *tecpan*. These and many other examples reveal how closely linked the two traditions are and how difficult it is for us to separate them.

Other institutions were exclusively Castilian, at least in origin; they, too, were inevitably modified in so different an environment. In addition to town administrations (already a mixed type encompassing the former local chiefs), these institutions were: community banks and estancias, and the native brotherhoods and hospitals, which owned estates.

Indian administrations appeared very early in the evangelizing villages. They increased under Velasco I and covered the country by the end of the sixteenth century. A town governor, usually (but not always) the former cacique, was assisted by two ordinary alcaldes, several regidores, and an indefinite number of constables. Usually there were also a bailiff to manage community property, a prosecutor to serve as the vicar's agent for all secular affairs, and various minor officials bearing native titles, whose functions predated the Conquest. Certain judicial responsibilities were vested in the governor, the alcaldes, and the regidores, and were symbolized by wands called *varas de justicia*. The responsibilities and the wands have survived in various parts of Mexico.

Community banks did not exist in Moctezuma's time, but were "invented by the monks," according to Archbishop Montúfar, who severely criticized the institutions. The prelate explained in 1556 that the banks were designed to aid the missionaries and defray various municipal expenses. Their funds were derived from community crops, limekilns, droves, woodcutting, farms run "in collaboration" with Spaniards, or, all else failing, small taxes in currency added to the natives' tribute. Some of the monks worked hard at developing these and still other kinds of enterprises in order to keep money flowing regularly into the tills. (A further advantage was to make communities utilize their district's resources efficiently, thereby depriving Spaniards of an excuse for moving into villages and fields.) At a very early date in the Mixteca, Fray Francisco Marín and Fray Domingo de Santa María planted mulberries to raise silkworms, nopals to breed cochineal insects, and "community orchards." In Michoacán, Fray Juan de San Miguel endowed hospitals with income deriving from community crops and livestock. Districts in the Upper Mixteca specialized in large-scale silk production.

Somewhat later, under Viceroy Martín Enríquez cochineal became an important resource for Indians in Tlaxcala, Tepeaca, Tecamachalco, and Oaxaca. Harvests had risen from 2,000 or 3,000 arrobas to 5,000 by about 1570; they reached 7,000 and even 12,000 six or eight years later. Production was under government supervision, because cochineal was an export commodity and consequently very valuable; an arroba [25 pounds] fetched 25 or 30 pesos in Mexico and much more in Spain.

Early community banks had been almost entirely in the monks' hands (hence Archbishop Montúfar's ire). With the second Viceroy, they had gradually come under civil control; Luis de Velasco had expanded them with the missionaries' agreement, he being their friend. Audiencia judges, as they traveled about on the King's business, created many new banks. The King issued decrees governing their operations; and corregidores or alcaldes were given specific orders to supervise them. Coffers bore three locks whose keys were entrusted to three different members of the municipal government—usually the governor, an alcalde, and the bailiff. This measure was an attempt to avoid abuses, numerous, as we shall see, because of the rich contents of some coffers as early as the sixteenth century.

Luis de Velasco clearly understood that, if banks were not to serve as an opportunity or a pretext to impose new taxes on the Indians, they must be given sufficient investments to enable them to supply communities with the funds needed. The Viceroy gave much thought to the problem. The simplest and most widely adopted solution was community raising of maize, beans, peppers, and tules (used for making cordage). Revenues remained inadequate, however, with the result that authorities had to supplement them with a work tax (thus still avoiding a currency tax).

The Viceroy also organized joint ventures with Spanish farmers, who could furnish the capital that the natives lacked. Velasco reported to Philip II in 1554:

> *The Indians supply land and labor for weeding and harvesting; the Spaniards contribute oxen, plows, carts, and other implements, in addition to their skill. The latter take one-third of the harvest and the former two-thirds, which helps them to pay a part of their tribute and provides administrations with funds. The natives also gain experience in plowing with oxen, sowing, and tilling as we do in Spain.*

The joint ventures, of which several examples exist, appear to have been failures, because the Spaniards endeavored to seize the land in order to keep all the profits.

Another method of filling municipal coffers was sheep and goat raising, whose obvious advantages were that they required little work and few laborers, gave excellent returns, and suited semi-arid regions. Besides, the space utilized created a buffer zone protecting *milpas* from Spaniards' herds, particularly when cattle reproduction reached a crisis around the mid-century. Simultaneously with his orders prohibiting herds and flocks on their way to other pastures from approaching within a league or half-league of many villages, Velasco began granting native communities sheep estancias whose formal title deeds were identical with those given Spanish stockmen, except that they were untransferable. He wrote His Majesty in 1559 that in the course of his trips to the "best parts of the country" in the company of competent monks, natives had been systematically grouped around the churches, "fountains and bridges constructed, roads opened . . . and all villages granted pastures reserved for their own use, as well as commons for the grazing of their animals and those of passing visitors, without harm having been done to their harvest lands."

Documents show that Velasco was not exaggerating. When native authorities in the Upper and Lower Mixteca reported to him that their communities had lands available for sheep raising and that each village applying should be granted one or two estancias, Velasco, in January, 1560, ordered seven provincial corregidores or alcaldes mayores to pace off the lands and give them to the communities with final, inalienable title deeds. The Viceroy's decision must have been prompted by the Dominicans, who were in charge of conversions in the province and, desirous of making the communities' exploitation of their own lands legally unassailable, already had numerous similar achievements to their credit.

During the last five months of the same year, thirty or so native communities and hospitals were granted untransferable estancias with the stipulation that they be stocked with sheep or (more rarely) cattle. Six sheep estancias at one time, an unusual amount for the period, were granted to the village of Zacatlán out of its district. For livestock tending, a work detail was usually formed of a few Indians who were paid from community funds. Income from some droves was large enough to cover not only the municipalities' expenses, but also their entire tribute.

Less frequently, native communities obtained other grants and privileges, such as caballerías for crops; the right to build water mills, inns, or shops on the public square, and licenses to operate weaving mills or mule trains. These were additional sources of revenue. In imitation of Spanish towns, commons were sometimes staked out for "grazing said village's plow, draft, and pack animals." Actually, commons in villages serving as halting places were used almost exclusively by Spanish wagoners and muleteers.

Estancia grants to a community's leading citizens often accompanied grants to the community itself. Inhabitants of Chapa (Jilotepec) received as many as nine in one day; they were all notables (*principales*) save one, who was designated simply as a "native of the locality." Contrary to established custom, they could freely dispose of their title deeds, except that as usual they could not sell them to the Church. In 1579, every Indian in New Spain was authorized to raise three hundred sheep, six yoke of oxen, and four milk cows; he was not obliged to possess an estancia for his animals, from which fact we may infer that there was still plenty of uncultivated land under the Crown's jurisdiction.

Velasco also abolished the old injunction against natives' owning horses. In 1555, for example, thirty-five inhabitants of the city of Michoacán—dignitaries, artisans, and common people—were each granted the right to keep a mare. In other instances, licenses authorized four, six, eight, or more pack horses for one individual. Although until 1597 formal permission theoretically had to be obtained, communities and individuals had long since been given the explicit right to raise horses. The privilege was if anything abused, and the geographical reports drawn up under Philip II and Philip III occasionally indicate native horse estancias. However, the prohibition against [the natives' use of] bits and saddles continued to be enforced, except in nomad-infested regions. Indians were often reported to have been seen riding bareback with only a halter.

While continuing to grant estancias to communities, Velasco extended them to Indian hospitals when requested; one hospital received three at one time. In 1564, after the death of the "father of his country" (so he was called, according to Muñoz Camargo), the rate at which these various grants were handed out slackened. Unfortunately so, because at the same time grants to Spaniards were picking up speed and pushing against the central zone on all sides, although Velasco II and the Count of Monterrey made numerous grants to Indian communities at the turn of the century. The latter inaugurated harvest caballería grants to Indian brotherhoods of many regions. These brotherhoods, bearing such titles as "of the Most Holy Sacrament," "of Our Lady of the Rosary," or "of the True Cross," were not merely religious organizations, but also mutual aid societies.

Native grants, however, never approached the numbers made to Spaniards. Community banks whose funds came entirely from droves and like enterprises remained a minority. One important, if not the most important, source of revenue continued to be a yearly fee added to the tribute; it consisted of a 1½-real head tax up to just before 1580, when it was replaced by each Indian's having to raise a ten-fathom square of maize for the community.

There was more to the problem than favoritism shown to the Spaniards. The Indians frequently took little interest in estancias and sometimes neglected to exploit them entirely. When Spaniards requested grants within a native village's district, the village frequently opposed the grants on the grounds that they would be prejudicial to its welfare. That was often true, but generally the land requested was not being used. Around 1567, the Viceroy, the Marqués de Falces, seized the opportunity to force Indians to choose between two alternatives: exploiting and stocking a given plot within a definite period of time (three to six months) or letting it go by default to Spanish petitioners. In view of communities' lack of initiative and resources, the method was somewhat brutal; but it does give an idea of the problem's complexity.

The commons, village estancias, and buffer zones turned out to be inadequate protection against encroaching Spaniards' droves and crops, at least in the central regions. In 1567, the Marqués de Falces also had to prohibit Spaniards from tilling fields closer than 500 varas to villages and maintaining estancias closer than 1,000. In a vast country where the terrain is often hilly and the soil dry and poor, these minimum distances of 420 and 840 meters seem too niggardly to have allowed communities any kind of independent existence, particularly when we remember that a single cattle estancia covered one square league. Velasco I had shown a better understanding of minimal needs in pushing Spanish droves back to a league or half-league from many villages. Although later ordinances fixing the dimensions of commons and village domains were much more favorable to the Indians, these boundaries proclaimed in 1567 became the general rule. There was to be one modification: in 1687 the King raised the minimum distance to 600 varas (504 meters), which came to be known as the "legal area" belonging to native villages. It was a bare minimum, but some communities were eventually confined within it—when they were not completely absorbed by neighboring haciendas. Others put up more resistance. The Tlaxcalan communities that Velasco II founded in the north are a special case, because of their privileged status; elsewhere, however, ordinary villages took up the cudgels in their own defense, thanks either to their municipalities' greater initiative or, especially, to the tutelary regime firmly entrenched in evangelization zones.

Noble-minded friars and humanists like Archbishop Juan de Zumárraga had sincerely believed that teaching the Indians a trade and making them live like civilized beings in villages, whose squares and streets were well laid out "in the manner of Castilian towns," would suffice to raise their moral and material standards in a very short time and "quickly bring them riches." Missionaries soon realized that institutions, however excellent, would take longer to transform the natives than they had planned.

Innumerable documents tell us that many Indians ran away from these new, well-regulated towns and either went back into their mountain fastnesses or became vagrants. Epidemics, previously unknown, periodically thinned the ranks of villagers enjoying the benefits of civilization and spread over the entire country, notably under Viceroy Martín Enríquez. Notwithstanding native governors' and alcaldes' insignia of office, Spaniards flouted their authority. Governors and alcaldes themselves dipped hands into community tills—unless their corregidores had arrived ahead of them. Except in Michoacán, Indians hardly ever used their hospitals; only too frequently, "the Lord knows how," local caciques spent the funds. Community estancias were sometimes empty of cattle, or they were leased for nominal rents to Spanish stockmen who subsequently refused to give them up. Indians also had an extremely vague conception of real estate; both individuals and communities would recklessly give away their land for small sums often squandered on drunken sprees and useless objects.

As late as the nineteenth century, parish priests, criticizing a recent law authorizing the division of native community property, insisted that formal action should be taken to prevent Indians from selling public lands, because "they have so ancient and inherent a propensity to sacrifice their possessions for spot cash, resembling the man in the fable whose goose laid golden eggs, but who killed it in order to get at its insides."

Generalization could easily lead to exaggeration, however. Numerous Indian groups, particularly in Michoacán, showed considerable aptitude for self-government and self-defense under conditions that appeared completely strange to them. It is no less certain that many other unfortunate natives fell victims to might's being right. Having previously been sheltered by their *calpullis,* that advanced kind of clan, they were hardly prepared to have to calculate, plan in advance, and take the initiative in affairs transcending their customary narrow sphere of interest. Livestock raising, of which they had been ignorant, remained outside that sphere. Far from wishing to grow rich, they had a hard time grasping the idea of earnings or profit; as Velasco II related, they sowed only what was strictly necessary for their sustenance, unless forced to sow more. Money was for them something to be enjoyed immediately, usually in the form of alcohol. It was no easy task for a people lacking centuries of evolution to catch up with our sixteenth century in a few years—or even decades, for that matter.

The newly arrived Spaniards, flushed with their success at arms, were going to take brutal advantage of a primitive nation's inexperience. The most generous laws would be powerless to alter that fact; they could only be applied universally, vigilantly, and unceasingly, as the missionaries quickly came to realize. Insofar as isolation was still feasible, the missionaries cordoned off their communities. Bishop Zumárraga and many others had believed initially that natives would profit by the example of carefully selected Spanish families ("married farmers") living in their midst. Experience dashed the friars' hopes. They inspired royal cédulas forbidding Spaniards to stay in Indian villages more than two or three days and had the measure enforced wherever practicable, that is, in less frequented and less fertile regions. For the missionaries, the Conquest's true purpose had been, not Spanish colonization, but conversion of the heathen. Some missionaries went so far as to assert that they themselves were the only Spaniards needed in Mexico and that a stop should be put to all other immigration.

At the same time the missionaries were restricting their charges' contacts with the outside world, they were supervising every detail in the running of the newly established institutions. They gradually substituted their personal authority for the old *calpullis'* collective discipline, which the Conquest had already seriously undermined. As to lands and, especially, individual family allotments, both religious and civil authorities made a fresh start under Castilian jurisprudence, but they soon found themselves back in the native tradition. Whereas they had hoped for a while to make over to each *macehual*, or community member, some kind of property of his own, they ended by giving him merely the usufruct, since his allotment was strictly untransferable. In addition, the *macehual* was under obligation to cultivate it; the same requirement had been attached to his *tlamilpa* when his overseer had been the clan's elder (*hermano mayor*). This could not have been simply the missionaries' acknowledgment of or return to pre-Conquest conditions. Although the *calpullis* had not gone out of existence (many traces of them are still found today), they had by then inevitably been thoroughly transformed into communities that the missionaries, paternally but firmly, had displaced, partially deprived of their traditional authorities, endowed with new institutions, and converted to Christianity.

Immediately after the Conquest, the land distribution system was somewhat disorderly and confused. Accordingly, Viceroy Mendoza, and especially his successor, Velasco I, redistributed many allotments. At Metepec in 1550, for example, each Indian was given 40 fathoms of ground surrounding his house, as well as a long parcel 30 by 200, if he was a notable, or 20 by 200, if he was a common *macehual*. At Tula, lots distributed the same year measured 40 by 200. Allotments were comparable in size in other regions, that is, three or four hectares. Legal ownership was frequently vested in the community. Although individual cultivators received the land "personally, for themselves, their children, and their descendants," they paid the community bank a very modest tax or rent, the *terrazgo*. This fee came to be purely a symbol, a means of acknowledging the community's retention of title. Sometimes, however, no fee was collected; but it was made clear that the land was untransferable and must be kept partially or entirely under cultivation, on penalty of confiscation. At San Juan Teotihuacán, for example, recipients enjoyed only the usufruct of the lots given them.

Indians were also granted perpetual holdings on the estates of nobles, to whom they paid a small quitrent. Franciscans persuaded the nobles at Huejotzingo to grant commoners possessing no land "with a gift deed and a contract irrevocable for all time." The stipulation was made that out of each 80 by 20-fathom parcel grantees would cultivate in perpetuity for the donors an area 20 fathoms square; that amounted to collecting a fourth share of the crops.

In all the above instances tenure was untransferable and cultivators had the usufruct for as long as they and their descendants worked the land. No better method could have been devised of avoiding purchase, grabbing, or spoliation by Spaniards, provided that a close watch was kept to ensure the carrying out of the contractual obligations. In their villages, the missionaries were ideally situated for keeping such a watch.

The many orders requiring Indians to work their land or see it confiscated complete the curious parallelism between the Spanish land distribution system and the old *calpullis'* rules. Rarely, it must be admitted, did Spanish laws and instructions cite institutions dating from before the Conquest; the return of civil and religious authorities to such institutions undoubtedly developed by force of circumstances and half-unperceived. Following the Conquest, natives had developed a dangerous tendency to drift away from their villages, thus avoiding an excessively heavy tribute and personal labor services to which they were unaccustomed. The first two viceroys, Velasco especially, endeavored to lighten and regulate officially the Indians' duties; at the same time, they took measures, backed by the monks, which, it was proposed, would eliminate vagrancy and put half-deserted fields back under cultivation. After a visit to Jilotepec in 1555, the Viceroy decreed: "Let every Indian in the province be made to sow annually a 30-fathom square of land." Numerous other orders around 1563–1565 were calculated to make Indians work their *milpas* and stay settled down. Somewhat later, each native was obliged to cultivate at least 60 fathoms of land, 50 for himself and 10 for the community. In New Galicia, too, each one had to sow a 50-fathom square and keep six hens and one rooster.

Viceroy Martín Enríquez, whose fondness for detail in execution corresponded admirably to Philip II's minutely worded instructions, set up a permanent service of "sowing officials," who supervised Indian sowing; "cochineal officials," who watched over the harvest and official prices; inspectors for Mixteca silk, and even "chicken officials," who made certain that every Indian family was raising a specified amount of poultry. Velasco II abolished some of the posts when they proved to be an additional burden on the Indians.

Once the period of groping and contradictory legislation was over, that is, by mid-century, these many measures applying to specific cases, groups, or regions tended to converge and reflect a policy formulated by the second viceroy and echoing the missionaries' attitude in their conversion villages, as well as the Crown's, which had been largely inspired by the missionaries. In order to prevent recurrence of the mishaps that we have mentioned and counteract the universal improvidence that communities showed in new situations, a trusteeship was instituted, buttressed by constant, minute supervision. The trusteeship attained its perfect expression in the missions. An Augustinian quoted by Robert Ricard wrote in 1579 that the missionaries looked upon their charges "as fledglings in the nest, whose wings . . . will never grow enough to allow them to fly by themselves"; the missionaries "are their parents, advocates, and representatives, their supporters and defenders, shields and protectors, their doctors and nurses, who take adversity's blows in their stead." Fray Juan de Grijalva added that the missionaries were judges who reconciled adversaries and "punished wrongdoers like stern fathers, even for offenses having nothing to do with ecclesiastical law." One could not be shocked by the missionaries' point of view, he concluded, since Indians needed guardians their whole life through. The Jesuits were conducting their missions in the northwest in about the same manner, long before their system had reached its acme in Paraguay.

One seventeenth-century Augustinian prior in Michoacán not only administered his monastery's rural holdings, but also supervised work in the fields "for the Indian community as well as for individuals." He saw that everyone in the village did his sowing for institutions at the proper time, for the hospital one day, for the church another, a third for the corregidor, and a fourth for the bank. When community labors were done, "he then made sure that each did his own sowing; he knew the amount necessary, and if one of the Indians was a lazy sort, he would drag him from his house and make him go to work; he was a father in both senses of the term." It can be readily perceived that the monks treated their *macehuales* as if they were minors and they, the monks, were their guardians, watching over them, defending them, and administering their property. Such protection and coercion could be exercised only indirectly over Indian nobles and caciques, who, as freemen, were often able to dispose of their possessions. The nobles and caciques were the chink in the armor, as the encroaching hacienda owners were quick to realize in pursuing their advantage.

The missionaries' quasi-absolutism aroused resentment, even wrath, in some official quarters and, especially, in Spanish merchants and settlers who had been ejected from villages where they had planned to trade or increase their holdings. Archbishop Montúfar complained of the religious orders' "intolerably highhanded dealings." Viceroy Martín Enríquez observed in 1580 that the missionaries wished to "exercise spiritual and temporal authority in all villages . . . [as a result] they are customarily on bad terms with justice officials and other Spaniards." Hence in New Spain the often-mentioned warring factions: on one side, the monks, and on the other, the conquistadors and landed proprietors.

Turning now to civil authorities, we note that the higher the echelon, the more loyal was the support granted the missionaries' protective practices. The Council of the Indies' decisions were usually influenced by the religious orders; and royal legislation in the sixteenth century greatly favored the natives. They came to be regarded as "wretched people," in Solórzano Pereyra's phrase, meaning that they were incapable of fending for themselves. In the seventeenth century, instructions were issued in the name of their perpetual "minority," and they occasionally referred to themselves as "poor minors." The consequence was that theoretically they could not transfer property without their guardians' consent.

Practice was more important than theory, however. Silvio Zavala remarks that the Indians had at their disposal "a broad, well-organized channel of communication for defending their rights and bringing their complaints to the Viceroy's attention," who was unstinting in "protection and favors." In the National Archives of Mexico, thousands of decrees are preserved arising from Indians' individual complaints, particularly in regard to land. Most sixteenth-century viceroys appear to have listened personally to native grievances; we have already mentioned Mendoza's having set aside two mornings a week for the purpose. After spending five years in New Spain, Hawks noted in 1572 that Indians "receive most favorable treatment from justice officials" and that they did not hesitate to cover twenty leagues on foot to register their complaints; "a complaint is immediately accepted, and the Spaniard, even if he is of noble blood, is sent for at once and fined or imprisoned according to the justice's decision." Hawks's observation is confirmed by other evidence, at least for regions near the capital.

The increasing Spanish population and the resultant pressure of business forced the Viceroy to delegate a share of his responsibilities. In the early seventeenth century, the Count of Monterrey changed his opening phrase in orders from "The Indians of . . . have reported to me that . . ." to "Licenciado X . . . , His Majesty's prosecutor for this Royal Audiencia, in the name of the natives of . . . , has reported to me that . . ." Mention is even made of an "attorney general for Indians in New Spain," whose job it was to receive and transmit complaints. In addition, the Viceroy's decision was often based upon an opinion prepared by one of the Audiencia's lawyers who had been charged with examining the case.

In 1574, a Tribunal for Indian Affairs (*Juzgado General de Indios*) was created within the Audiencia; this special court's origins and functions remain somewhat obscure. At the turn of the century, documents refer to its having an assessor, who was generally a lawyer, a member of the Audiencia or crime commissioner, and counsel for the Viceroy, as well as an "attorney for the general defense of the natives of this kingdom," whose mandate was to lend the natives assistance and keep an eye on their lawsuits. In principle, sales of any significant amount of community property could not be concluded until the assessor had reported favorably. Lawsuits were probably handled with dispatch and were usually settled in the natives' favor.

Some provinces had been given Indian protectors by the terms of a 1542 royal order. The office was suppressed forty years later, owing to the extra expense for the natives, and was reëstablished at the century's end. On the local scene in the sixteenth century, supervisory positions were heaped one upon the other and many different titles were handed out: "chief constable for protecting the Indians," "defender," and, particularly in the north, "protector." For lack of funds to pay decent salaries, however, the positions were frequently either given to powerful miners and landowners or added to local justice officials' tasks. Corregidores and alcaldes mayores were responsible for good management of community banks and even had to make up themselves any shortages caused by the Indians' neglecting to collect community taxes; in the seventeenth century, some banks were rich and collected fees in currency. These royal officials, however, often sided with the Spanish settlers—whose agricultural, mining, or commercial pursuits they shared—against the Indians; they could not be expected to live on several hundred pesos a year, their salary in the seventeenth century as in the early days.

In the seventeenth-century Audiencia, bureaucracy was rampant and legal procedures became increasingly snarled in red tape. An eloquent example is the Nexapa Indians' request for authorization to establish an estancia in an unused portion of their district; they wished to graze their five hundred head of cattle there. In 1626, Viceroy Cerralvo answered their petition with a writ of execution, which he sent to the local alcalde mayor with instructions to take the necessary steps. "In accomplishment of which," the Viceroy then wrote,

General Don Diego de Burgos took said steps and submitted a certified copy of his report to the government. I ordered the file to

be turned over to Dr. Don Juan González Peñafiel, His Majesty's
prosecutor in this Royal Audiencia, and to Dr. Cristóbal Sánchez
de Guevara, the attorney for Indian affairs. I added their replies
to the file and forwarded it to Licenciado Juan de Medina Bargas,
a lawyer of said Royal Audiencia, requesting him to make a report,
which he has made. Inasmuch as I have gone through the file my-
self, the findings in the report are favorable, and General Don
Diego de Burgos's investigation shows that no harm will be done
to third parties, by these presents I do authorize and grant permis-
sion to the Indian community of said town of Nexapa to make free
with the land that it owns at Niçalamal and to establish there an
estancia for its five hundred head of cattle . . . Dated at Mexico
City, August 21, 1634 . . .

For this trifling affair of a one-estancia grant that would allow a native
village to graze its cattle on its own land, a general, two doctors, and a
licenciado had to undertake investigations and draw up reports. Only
then—eight years later (or more, since we do not know the date of
the original request)—did the Viceroy feel empowered to make a decision.

The above matter did not directly concern defense of the Indians.
Viceroy Cerralvo and his successor, Cadereyta, both very active men,
did expedite all business connected with abolition of the repartimiento
system. Absorbed in carrying out that program—which would free
all workers—perhaps they did not see the lowering cloud that was
taking shape over the natives' lands. The courts, at any rate, were much
less expeditious in cases of this kind. The reason is that ability to "en-
tangle a lawsuit," as the vicar Arregui put it in 1621, was considered to
be an indispensable attribute for Spaniards in the Indies. If a case was
not open-and-shut and started out badly for a landowner, and the landowner had a little influence, he could almost always find in the welter
of laws and court procedures some means of dragging it out or giving it
a new twist. If the verdict went against him, he could usually manage
to defer execution.

The protective laws were extremely important. Missionaries, as well
as altruistic "defenders" and justice officials, who were actively assisting

the Indians, could brandish them as legal weapons in the fight against encroachment and make litigation particularly risky for their adversaries. The government, after all, was in the hands of jurists. In 1607, Viceroy Montesclaros deplored the fact that immense stretches of land were being left unutilized because of the natives' systematic opposition to grants to Spanish settlers; they could always find missionaries, the Viceroy stated, to testify in their behalf and support their claims in court. Slightly later in New Galicia, Indians would often send one or two men to live in deserted villages; their sole purpose was to maintain the fiction of a community in the eyes of the law and prevent Spaniards from declaring the land unoccupied or ownerless. The only reason natives were willing to continue to assume tributes and work services owed by deserted villages was that they knew that they could count on effective protection of community lands.

Today, the Mexican government's humanitarian measures have preserved the hunting grounds of the more primitive tribes, such as the Huicholes. When one observes how much pressure is brought to bear by neighboring peasants and stockmen, who consider the hunting grounds so much wasted grazing land, one has a fuller appreciation of the difficulties which beset the early conservation laws. More powerful means than those available to the viceroys would have been needed to contain land invasion on all fronts at once.

Defense measures seem to have been effective wherever missionaries were in direct control, although sometimes to the detriment of economic expansion. In addition, as Robert Ricard has pointed out, the missionaries' success stored up trouble for the future. Their paternalistic regime, treating their Indian wards like perpetual minors, preserved them from any contacts with Spaniards or the life of the country. Because the regime was a convenient one, it stopped evolving, either through incapacity or dislike for change. Like some employers and heads of state, the missionaries were convinced that they would go on forever. When they disappeared, the Indians did not know how to come of age and were at a loss to defend themselves; they withdrew into isolation, and many were stripped of their land.

There may well have been no satisfactory solution. The trusteeship must at least be credited with having protected a large amount of community land over a period of several centuries, until the 1856 laws provided for its division and frequently brought about its loss.

SETTLERS' ENCROACHMENTS

Human malice so perverts everything that it changes the very shields designed to protect these poor people into weapons for attacking them.
—VICEROY THE MARQUÉS DE MANCERA, 1673

Missionaries and civil authorities could not assume full responsibility everywhere. Sometimes Indians were not masters in their own villages, Spanish farmers, stockmen, and traders having settled among them, particularly in the vicinity of Mexico City, Puebla, and the other chief Spanish towns. Elsewhere, Spaniards had succeeded in acquiring land and were investing in improvements; they were making inroads on caciques' personal estates, which had never received the same protection as community lands. The missionaries themselves had sometimes encouraged mixed settlements, for example at Atlixco, since they preferred seeing Spaniards work the soil to seeing them remain idle on Mexico City's main square in expectation of some royal handout—which the Indians would pay for in the end. The viceroys generally followed the same policy.

The rate of infiltration varied according to locality. In the Puebla region, not only had Spanish farmers occupied all untilled land, but many of them had married caciques' daughters. From one point of view, the results might appear excellent; but from another, as the tide swelled it became impossible to protect fully communities near by. In the Puebla region alone by the end of the sixteenth century, Spaniards by the score were living in close proximity to the natives around Cholula and Huejotzingo, and by the hundred around Atlixco, Tepeaca, and Tecamachalco. The questions that arise for us are the following: By what means, legal or otherwise, did the intruders gain access to native lands? What was the sequence of events and what were the protecting authorities' reactions? What, finally, was the significance in terms of the formation of the great estates?

A curious, little-known fact often helped Spaniards to acquire land in the heart of native districts. Before their coming, there already existed a marked trend toward the constitution of estates beneficial to the nobility and detrimental to the old clans. The confused situation growing out of the Conquest accelerated the trend for a time. While the newcomers were showing little interest in land, the native aristocracy was busy gaining possession of the estates that had formerly belonged to Moctezuma and the temples. More seriously yet, it took fields away from the *calpullis*, especially after these had been decimated by epidemics. The usurpation's chief consequence was to transform free Indians into a kind of serf or perpetual tenant farmer. The nobles, having lost nearly everything else in the Conquest, thus sought to reestablish morally and materially their position, which was somewhat compromised.

There being a limit to Indian taxes and labor services, it soon became apparent that the quantity collected by caciques was just that much less for Spaniards. (Also, with the development of livestock raising, land was acquiring some value.) The conquistadors awoke to the situation in the second third of the century; they viewed it with alarm, but took advantage of it to acquire a large amount of land for next to nothing.

At Huejotzingo, near Puebla, native chieftains had appropriated a big expanse of land under cover of the serious dissensions that had troubled this large village. One of them, in the first flush of his newly acquired prosperity, started to "live high," as contemporary accounts state; whenever he went out, he was preceded by a Spanish pageboy who carried his gloves. The chieftains had Antonio de Mendoza confirm possession; the Viceroy had "just arrived and was eager to help the Indians." When he did become aware of his mistake, it was too late. However, he informed his successor, who, with the help of the local Franciscans, succeeded in 1554 in having part of the expanse distributed to *macehuales* for a nominal fee. Another part was unfortunately being rented to Spaniards. The first two viceroys endeavored to have usurped land returned to its rightful owners wherever and whenever they could. More often than not, restitution was doubtless impossible, either because title had already been confirmed or the land had been broken up into lots and sold.

Following President Fuenleal's similar animadversions in 1532, Martín Cortés, overstating his case perhaps, wrote some thirty years later (1563) to Philip II: "Native dignitaries have usurped all the land formerly belonging to Moctezuma and worked for his benefit; they have arbitrarily added it to their estates." Likewise, they had seized land originally owned "by the devil [Huitzilopochtli] and his priests." They had auctioned off a portion of each category to their communities. Pedro de Ahumada, reporting to the Audiencia in 1559, observed that village chiefs and nobles had seized such "vacant" estates and other fields worked by the community at large "on their own authority, without anyone's knowledge or opposition"; then, "in the Mexico City region they sold them to Spaniards."

The native authorities' most serious offense was abuse of their power in order to take *calpulli* land, which they then made *mayeques* work. According to Martín Cortés again, over 100,000 Indians in New Spain had been reduced to serfdom in this manner. At about the same time, an Audiencia judge and learned jurist, Vasco de Puga, wrote an even more circumstantial letter to the King stating that notables were despoiling poor *macehuales* and communities of their land and then forcing free Indians to cultivate it with the status of sharecroppers (*terrazgueros*); that meant that they had to give their new masters a large share of the crops (at least half, Vasco de Puga asserted) and perform various services for them. As missionaries invariably showed favoritism to native chiefs, Vasco went on to say, abuses frequently arose when old villages were moved or new ones were founded; caciques would divide the land among themselves, one taking the north, another the south, a third the east, and a fourth the west. Then, they would tell the *macehuales* that they "have to become their *terrazgueros* and pay any rent that it is their pleasure to charge them." When native farmers were unwilling to accept the degradation of working as serfs or permanent sharecroppers, a cacique would pay a visit to the Viceroy, proceeding with sly caution, and, thanks to the writ that he obtained from the Viceroy, he would have a formal title deed drawn up in his name —a colored map of his so-called estates—and order the recalcitrants to pay up or get out.

Caciques' misbehavior was only one aspect of the disorder and confusion that the Conquest had created in native communities. Zurita asserted that the men who stole or grabbed land were not really the former local aristocrats, but rather upstart chiefs who had taken the aristocrats' place more or less illegally; they were serfs who had rebelled against their masters and seized the latter's estates. Caciques' complaints against commoners were quite frequent on this score.

One thing is certain: Viceroy Velasco in his wisdom regulated, cut down, and even abolished many of the *terrazgueros*' fees. His successors followed his example. On the other hand, native authorities had been made responsible for collecting tribute; when epidemics wiped out a large part of the population, caciques who were town governors often had to make up the difference from their own pockets pending a census adjustment. At the same time, Spaniards were gradually wresting away all the fees and other sources of profit normally accruing to these ousted overlords. For all these reasons and many others besides, the native aristocracy was in a bad state before the end of the century; its decay was visible everywhere. As a result, the fields that its members had succeeded in grabbing were of little value; their recent acquisitions went the way of their old estates—sold for a song as soon as the conquistadors began to take an interest in land.

With the development of livestock and, somewhat later, sugar cane, Spaniards discovered new inducements to own land. In need of workers, they looked for day laborers (*gañanes*) among the former serfs and free Indians who had been deprived of their fields. Nobles' and caciques' private estates were often the wide breach through which the newcomers were able to slip into village districts.

The first land to be occupied was usually of the category legally available after the Aztec empire's fall: estates having originally belonged to Moctezuma, to temples, or to chiefs fallen in battle. Soon, however, such niceties were ignored and settlers made no attempt to discriminate origins or kinds. Land's being "untilled" seemed sufficient justification for municipalities to appropriate them, while for individuals, purchase, often for practically nothing and by intimidation, appeared to be an excellent way to gain legal title. As early as 1530, high Audiencia officials had seized native land, justified by purchase or other pretexts. The Crown ordered the purchases invalidated. President Fuenleal recommended to the King that each Spaniard be restricted to two caballerías and allowed no more "either by purchase or donation or by any other means whatsoever." Otherwise, the President went on to say, Spaniards, paying little or nothing, would shortly invade the estates of both native nobles and communities without opposition from a docile, submissive race. He was a good prophet.

Crown policy, though well intentioned to the Indians, vacillated for a long time. Because they were freemen, native nobles and chiefs could not be prevented from disposing of their property as they saw fit. At the same time, provision had to be made for Spanish farmers who, it was planned, would live solely on the proceeds of their toil. Las Casas had already attempted the experiment, and the second Audiencia was attempting it again at Puebla. Bearing this in mind and also wishing to encourage the planting of Castilian fruit trees and crops, the Queen in 1535 formally authorized all Spanish residents of the towns and cities of New Spain to buy "any estates whatever" from the natives, provided that the natives sold them of their own free will in the presence of a town scribe and an ordinary alcalde. The next year, the presence of an Audiencia judge was also required, but this was a condition practically impossible to fulfill and remained a dead letter. Big farmers and cattle barons put the authorization to good use. A royal order of 1539 gave Peralmíndez Chirinos, a powerful inspector, blanket permission to "buy from any Indian in New Spain, lord or commoner, a freehold . . . before an Audiencia judge." The same permission had already been given to Hernán Vaca and Lope de Saavedra.

Purchases from caciques and native landowners were quite numerous by this time; we know only those cases submitted to the Viceroy for investigation or confirmation. Many other purchases were not legalized until one hundred years later, at the time of the settlements with the King. A large number of these early acquisitions, often for paltry sums (as investigations and resales show), were made by Spaniards in their encomienda villages, particularly since authorities were reluctant to make outright grants in areas where the grantee was also the Spaniard in charge of the Indians. Pérez de Bocanegra's haciendas on his Acámbaro–Apaseo encomiendas were partially composed of holdings that he had bought from his Tarascan vassals at a very early date. Authorities had been obliged to deal severely with encomenderos like Diego de Ordás, who at Calpa had had his tribute paid in the form of land, especially that of Indians killed by the epidemics.

Acquisitions had grown larger in size by mid-century, notably in regions where sugar refineries were established; as many as ten caballerías were purchased at one time. When buyers requested official confirmation of title, the Viceroy would have the local alcalde mayor verify the petitioner's statement that the Indians were selling the land "of their own free will and pleasure." An affirmative report was not always a disinterested one. According to Zurita, Spaniards were able to gain control of some *calpulli* lands legally, because of collusion with justice officials and the fact that a few lots were momentarily lying fallow.

As early as the second half of the century, Anáhuac villages were "cramped" and "hemmed in" by Spanish fields, as New Spain bishops in 1565 and a few years later Judge Zurita and Viceroy Martín Enríquez noted. A 1570 report mentions by name certain high officials whose estates had crept up to the very thresholds of huts in villages like Tenayuca and Tultitlán near Mexico City; the Indians were "so fenced in that they cannot sow or keep an ox or any other sort of livestock." Ill-tended droves were particularly destructive, overrunning everything; a 1553 cédula paints a somber picture of the Jilotepec region, laid waste and practically deserted thanks to Mexico City stockmen's criminal negligence.

Encroachments, when not resulting from ill-advised grants, usually were parcels sold heedlessly by native dignitaries, who often possessed vast estates. After a few sporadic defense measures at the local level, the highest authority tried to control individual transfers and keep them within bounds. A royal order dated June 23, 1571, authorized sale of real estate on condition that it should be at public auction, notice to be proclaimed each day for a period of at least thirty days following justice officials' recognition of the seller's property rights and the feasibility of alienating them without major inconvenience to himself or others. Movable personal property of any importance (as distinguished from real estate) need be proclaimed only during a period of nine days preceding the auction.

The several verifications and thirty proclamations by town criers having proved quite expensive, permission was granted in 1572 to omit these formalities when transfers involved sums of less than thirty pesos. Actually, the corrective was a serious error, since Indians usually sold off their land in small lots. It was canceled in 1603 and all Indian land, irrespective of value, had once again to be sold at public auction. Then Spaniards started to circumvent regulations by taking long-term leases; the auction and verification provisos were consequently extended to cover the leases.

All these requisite formalities were really carried out at the end of the sixteenth century and in the seventeenth, at least for important transactions. Such respect for the law is proof of the authority exercised by Spain's judicial apparatus, in spite of its cumbersomeness. Hacienda archives are filled with interminable notarized reports of the thirty legal proclamations by town criers and the subsequent auctions and winning bids.

The system was obviously an improvement, for natives were at least assured of selling their land for its full value in conformity with the law of supply and demand. Nevertheless, they were exchanging solid real estate for cash, which they rarely knew how to handle; frequently the cash went to cover back tribute payments and other debts. When an Indian, as it often happened, wished to sell land in order to satisfy his creditors, the alcalde mayor could hardly formulate an unfavorable opinion, especially if the creditor was the royal treasury.

The Tepeaca region is a typical example. Many Spanish farmers and bourgeois of Puebla, who had bought a good deal of land from the Indians at the turn of the century, possessed estates in Tepeaca. Sometimes the community itself would sell, say, three caballerías for 1,500 pesos (the land having been purchased ahead of the sale) "in order to pay its tribute." More often, sellers were caciques whose apparently wretched plight contrasted with their magnificent names, which they had borrowed from the viceroyalty's great families. One cacique, Don Tomás de Tapia, saw his land gradually being invaded by Spanish farmers. According to an Indian witness, instead of spending what little money he had on lawsuits, he decided to sell two caballerías. The proceeds would feed him and his family and satisfy his creditors, who did not let a day go by without taking him to task and molesting him. Another Indian aristocrat, Doña María de la Cruz y Luna, was a widow whose parents had left her "many plots and quarters" along with "many debts"; she herself had had to borrow money. Without a penny to her name and saddled with debts, she could not operate all her estates or defend them against an excessive number of invaders who "might well remain in possession." The best thing for her to do, she concluded, was to sell the land that was being wrongfully occupied. A third, Don Fernando de Guzmán, had inherited the title of cacique (*cacicazgo*) and various properties from his "parents, grandparents, and ancestors," as he declared in 1607 with some pride. Now he was poor and in debt and desirous of selling a caballería on which Spaniards had settled against his will. This wretched cacique was also responsible for tribute collection; he had been obliged to sell a parcel of land for twenty pesos in partial settlement of a loan of "sixty pesos that I had had to pay at Atlixco for the tribute of Indians who had died or fled the missionaries' roundup."

Other native notables voiced the same complaints over having to sell their land in order to avoid its becoming a total loss. Several years later, the Bishop of Puebla on a tour of his parish was greatly afflicted by "the decay of these poor Indian lords and nobles, stripped of lands and vassals, dissatisfied, impoverished, discouraged, and deprived of all that God and *natural law* had bestowed upon them." This graphic description applies to the native aristocracy's plight in many regions, where its heavily mortgaged estates were being devoured piecemeal by creditors, village loan sharks, and Spanish neighbors especially. Many haciendas owe their origin to the ruin and pressing needs of the local notables.

Some notables, on the other hand, were able to maintain their position and even improve it in little frequented zones where the missionaries were powerful. The caciques of the Upper and Lower Mixteca, for instance, owned in the seventeenth century thriving orchards and large droves. Their wills sometimes mention houses furnished with escritoires, paintings, and silver-incrusted weapons. At Yanhuitlán, one of them lived in a chateau with vaulted halls, baronial fireplaces, porticoed courtyards, and a bull ring. In Chiapas, too, some native chiefs led a sumptuous existence.

There were exceptions, however, particularly in the central zones crowded with Spanish settlers. The greater the number of small white or mestizo farmers and landowners in a region—the swarms between Puebla–Atlixco and Tepeaca–Tecamachalco, for example—the earlier and speedier the disintegration of individual and community estates. The phenomenon was repeated in the nineteenth century, when small white rancheros, no more reasonable than their ancestors, moved down from Jalisco into lower Michoacán, pushing the Indians out of their communities and seizing their lands by virtue of an imprudent law. The cause was the same in both instances: rapidly multiplying families in need of living space. It was also probably easier and less expensive for modest sixteenth-century settlers to buy a few *milpas* and fields on village outskirts than to obtain a grant from the Viceroy for an untilled caballería or a distant estancia.

These small farmers had originally been settled on their holdings by the second Audiencia and the missionaries, who had wished to develop agriculture and provide Spaniards with means of subsistence other than the tribute and encomiendas which were crushing the Indians. At its inception, the measure was a felicitous one; in the long run, it proved to be a boomerang and the Indians suffered just the same.

After the small settlers came the great landowners, who also bought much land from the Indians in order to round out their huge viceregal grants. They were all the more willing to buy as the state was gradually withdrawing their work repartimientos; the best way to obtain day laborers and peons was to deprive Indian villages of their fields. Not only individuals, but communities, frequently sold their lands, protection laws notwithstanding. When Indians owed back tribute, the state had the unfair advantage of being both the plaintiff and the not so impartial judge. Communities' real estate constituted their only liquid asset (when not their sole asset, liquid or otherwise). Consequently, they had to sell off blocks of land to reimburse His Majesty's "chief accountant for mercury distribution and tributes in New Spain" or pay the fee for an inspector's coming at their request to take a recount of the number of villagers owing tribute or to settle "back tribute and services due the King for those who have died or departed, or are old and unable to work." Likewise in the nineteenth century, when community lands were divided, the new owners had to sell lots to pay taxes.

When sales were negotiated legally, they had of course been investigated by "His Excellency's assessor in the Tribunal for Indian Affairs." However, this viceroy's counsel sometimes authorized rash ventures, such as the transfer of fields situated at debtor villages' doorsteps. His task was not an easy one, especially if the creditor was the state itself, constantly in need of money since the late sixteenth century.

In spite of the 1603 ordinance, little or no attempt was made to supervise transactions involving small sums. As we have seen, most Indian land was sold in this way. One hacienda at Coyoacán, near Mexico City, was made up entirely—except for one block—of tiny pieces sold for 2, 4, 8, 11, or 14 pesos. Regular or not, the purchases were all confirmed by the Viceroy in 1641. Civil authorities responsible for protecting the Indians also seem to have tolerated the sale or donation of community estancias when they were "not stocked with cattle." In the course of the seventeenth century, villages, hospitals, and notables lost many of the grants, mostly untransferable, that they had received from the two Velascos or other early viceroys.

There appears to have been almost no supervision in the Marqués del Valle's state, even though it contained several of the richest, most densely populated regions in New Spain. Spaniards there were uncertain who should make them grants, the Viceroy or the Marqués; pending the settlement of a long, drawn-out lawsuit, they received land from both sources. It was easier for them to evade a moot question altogether and buy land directly from the Indians, however fictitious their rights to the coveted areas might be. Purchases were very heavy, especially in the cane-growing region of Cuernavaca, in Oaxaca, and, sporadically, around Tehuantepec. Legal formalities were flouted to a greater degree than elsewhere, it seems, probably because royal authority was weaker. Land was bought for trifling sums and sold immediately afterward for from six to eight times the purchase price. In the marquisate as in other regions, the slate was wiped clean and irregularities were forgotten when His Majesty, starting in 1643, exchanged new title deeds for settlement fees.

In sedentary Indian zones the great epidemics furthered the Spaniards' advance into community lands. Epidemics ravaged New Spain in 1531, 1545, 1564, and 1576–1577; the last one, the most terrible of all, wiped out entire hamlets. In 1588, the Tlaxcala, Tepeaca, and Toluca regions were visited once again. And the turn of the century brought a new series of outbreaks, which were aggravated by Viceroy Monterrey's ill-advised gathering of Indians for conversion. The epidemics then seem to have abated, except in New Galicia and areas which either had been colonized late or contained less compact Indian groups. Perhaps by that time the natives had built up a resistance to European diseases. To judge by a study made in El Salvador, the native population appears to have leveled off and even begun to increase in the course of the seventeenth century.

In the early years of that century, however, many villages were half deserted. The number and size of Spanish purchases may well have been due to communities' weakened resistance, since for the time being they had more land than they could use. Besides, in the periods between head counts, tribute based on larger numbers was burdensome for survivors. In sales of this period, mention is sometimes made of fields "belonging to deceased Indians."

According to the laws of Castile, property of persons dying without an heir reverted to the Crown. In the Indies, legislation left land in this category partially to native communities, in order to enable them to pay their tribute; the rest was the King's to give as he saw fit, a fact which explains grants made of depopulated village sites—unless the Indians defended them by maintaining the fiction of an inhabited village. Settlement inspectors, out to find irregular titles requiring payment of fees to the King, discovered that villages and their caciques had ceded much Crown property of this sort.

The Oaxaca region and Cuilapan in particular constitute a typical case. Around 1645, one of His Majesty's representatives criticized nearby haciendas' title deeds in these terms: "It has been ascertained that all the land sold by notables and inhabitants of these towns, villages, and quarters did not belong to them, but to Indians dying without heirs." The representative added that the sellers had invoked the necessity of paying their tribute. The solution for Spanish settlers in the locality, usually rather modest landowners, was to pay fees to the King varying between twenty and several hundred pesos and thus to legalize innumerable acquisitions made for the most part between 1605 and 1620.

In very hot and semi-arid zones where natives were scarce, each purchase involved, not a few fields or caballerías, but immense spaces. In 1638, the Jesuit college at Pátzcuaro bought at auction, for a mere hundred pesos, a huge unbounded territory in lower Michoacán toward the Pacific Coast. The bill of sale's seven Indian signers were the sole survivors of a deserted village who consequently owed back tribute for the village. In the next century, a claimant representing the original purchaser wanted to fix the estate's boundaries at Zacatula and the Balsas River in the south and the "Colima hills" in the north—several hundred kilometers apart.

Almost without exception, villages could never recover land absorbed into haciendas. When the native population began to increase again, villages naturally found themselves in cramped quarters. Nothing could be done, since in the meantime most of the purchases had been validated by settlements with the Crown, including purchases that were quite baldly usurpations of native rights. The Crown's new measure to raise money meant that it had unwittingly let financial needs take precedence over its traditional role as champion of the Indians.

In addition to purchases by hacienda owners, imprudent viceregal concessions completely closed in some villages as early as the sixteenth century. Owing to uncertainty over distances and the total lack of surveys, even rough ones, the boundaries of an estancia were not always definitely known. When a grantee subsequently paced off his square league—stepping high and wide—it would often turn out to include a portion of community fields. In 1568, the King wrote his Audiencia that a series of villages, Chapa (Jilotepec) among them, had complained of being encircled by grants. Three years later, Martín Enríquez made the same observation. Viceroy the Count of Monterrey seems to have been particularly hardhearted in automatically approving every request for fields still lying fallow three or six months after the request. In the Huatusco region, a series of sheep estancia grants made by various viceroys took in *calpulli* lands and even native hamlets; protests from five villages resulted in their obtaining merely the legal minimum of 600 varas (503 meters) around each village.

Along with their fields, communities often lost their water for irrigation, particularly important in a country that is rainless six months of the year. There was no equivalent for water rights in the precise, general regulations governing the use of land, with the result that settlers tried to divert springs, rills, and even rivers at low water (when fields were parched). Authorities did give natives some protection by forcing restitution, reapportioning *surcos* (the unit for measuring water), and putting monopolists in jail. But there were probably more wrongs and plundering left unrighted than there were corrected.

The contest over water rights was especially bitter in the semi-arid stretches of the north. The few permanent Indian villages were, first, settlements that Velasco II had founded with families transplanted from Tlaxcala and, second, clusters of straw huts (*rancherías*) and encampments whose purpose was to keep the Chichimecas from roving. In the beginning, the villages had been respected, since the Tlaxcalans were needed to help fight the nomads and the intention was to coax the Chichimecas into becoming sedentary farmers. When the local situation was somewhat improved, however, neighboring landowners began to evince "envy and greed"; they attempted to grab village lands at any cost—the huge expanses that they already possessed notwithstanding —and to reduce the Indians to the status of peons on their estates. In order to reach their goal, as Father Morfi shrewdly observed, they had first to wipe out a town's government, thereby depriving it of its privileges. Then they could seize its land and water with impunity. Throughout the seventeenth and eighteenth centuries, many little settlements whose population was Chichimecan or mixed were gradually absorbed into adjacent haciendas. Some Tlaxcalan towns successfully resisted their powerful neighbors' attacks, for example, Saltillo's Indian suburb, San Esteban de Nueva Tlaxcala, whose carefully irrigated green orchards still stand out in vivid contrast to the dry, treeless pastures surrounding them. The community of Parras, which did not possess a town charter, was stripped of everything except its gardens; but its natives did keep most of their water, despite the maneuvers of Urdiñola's heirs (the largest landowners in the north) and Gaspar de Alvear while he was the all-powerful Governor of New Viscaya (1615–1618).

Among the Indians imported from the south, these natives of Tlaxcala definitely showed the greatest skill in resisting big sheepmen and hacendados who wanted to force them into peonage. They obtained royal injunctions, went to court over their privileges, and cleverly played on the kindly feelings of certain of their titular protectors, for example, the rich miner Arizmendi Gogorrón, who defended their estates at Tlaxcalilla, Mezquitic, and Agua del Venado.

Land fights and spoliations in some regions (on which we are naturally better documented) should not conceal from us the relative tranquillity of other regions, where protective measures were efficacious and native villages often remained in possession of more land than they could work. At the capital's gates, there were communities still owning good land in the mid-nineteenth century—a proof of the old system's validity.

It is not yet possible to ascertain the exact proportion of villages in New Spain and the northern provinces that were reduced to the 600-vara legal minimum in relation to those able to conserve adequate fertile land. We need to know more about local and regional conditions, the situation in the eighteenth century, and the effects of the 1856 laws. The fact that the latter could still result in considerable reapportionment would seem to indicate that in the sixteenth and seventeenth centuries numerous communities had succeeded in holding large amounts of land.

The seventeenth-century native communities, in summary, offered a passive resistance that blocked to a point the great estates' expansion. Frequently protected by their inability to transfer title (because of their status of permanent minors), but in other instances whittled down or actually invaded, communities remained, for lack of strength or skill, purely on the defensive. Yet in the twentieth century, these same communities, having dwindled to still smaller dimensions, were to supply, to a much greater extent than the peons and other estate dwellers, the revolutionaries who would destroy the haciendas.

CREOLE COMMUNITIES

As Justo Sierra has pointed out, the most insignificant Spanish town [in Mexico] was not merely some houses and a church assembled around a square, but an institution. The title of *town* or *city* meant that a community had a right to a *cabildo*, or municipal council, some degree of administrative and judicial autonomy, and various other advantages, which became progressively less real as the monarchy became more absolute. They remained important, however. A large mining center like Zacatecas had to wait thirty years to be elevated to such a dignity; in the meantime, its inhabitants could not even sit in council unless they were called by the local royal corregidor.

The central square, containing a town hall, a prison, a pillory, and a gallows, was visible evidence of a community's prerogatives. It also had its own fields and pastures—the *ejido* and *dehesa* for work and meat animals, usually an expanse of several square kilometers. The limits assigned to a town and its inhabitants were quite often a four-league square, in conformity with the 1573 colonizing ordinances. In the north, it was larger as a matter of custom, measuring six leagues at San Miguel. San Felipe had a square ten leagues to a side used for plowland and sheep estancias, and encompassing another of four leagues restricted to orchards and crops; in 1605, an Audiencia judge came to stake out boundaries "two leagues in each direction" from the town center. At Aguascalientes (founded in 1575), the same official bounded in 1644 a one-league *ejido* surrounding the town. The *vecindad*, or rank of burgher, usually included rights to a few caballerías and, occasionally, to a sheep or cattle estancia. These moderate concessions were theoretically freeholds and tended as a result to form accretions of small farmers and middle-sized landowners, at least in the north central zone and settlements whose late founding precluded encomiendas. A town's judicial functions, finally, meant that it had recourse against powerful neighbors' attacks or royal officials' encroachments upon its prerogatives.

Few towns of this type still existed in the middle of the seventeenth century, and they were widely scattered. There were none at all in some of the richest zones, such as the Marqués del Valle's state, where they were not wanted for jurisdictional reasons. The main cause of their scarcity was communities' internal weaknesses. (Threats from without had not yet arisen, owing to the obvious advantage for big landowners in having certain unpopulated regions colonized.) Practically from the inception of most towns, a handful of rich individuals succeeded in gaining control, legally, of the municipal government, paving the way for future monopolizing. We have seen what happened at Puebla; rich encomenderos acquired the position of regidor, which allowed them to grant themselves land in the new town's district or have existing titles confirmed. Officials were naturally more independent still in remote towns, whose councils, in the face of some opposition from the Viceroy, were long able to distribute caballerías and even livestock estancias. In Compostela, for example, municipal magistrates allocated themselves blocks of land between 1570 and 1575 and one regidor had himself given a caballería "carved out of the town *ejido*." A similar abuse had occasioned Viceroy Velasco's wrath during his visit to Puebla in 1557. At San Felipe, seizure of community lands had assumed even more serious proportions.

Although the title of alcalde was not purchasable, it was often the perquisite of a family or an oligarchy not always residing in the locality. Some towns had involuntarily prepared for such intrusions by selling *vecindades sin asistencia*, that is, full freeman status, including the right to own land, but without the usual obligation to take up residence. This emergency measure to raise money for irrigation or other projects led at New Salamanca to the installation of major-domos by rich hacendados living in Mexico City and other localities. The hacendados possessed more than one *vecindad*, and nothing prevented them from occupying municipal offices that empowered them to defend their interests in several regions simultaneously. At Nombre de Dios, a landowner named Andrés de Rojas, father of the chief constable of the same name and close friend of the chief peace officer, had succeeded at the turn of the sixteenth century in cornering all the high positions for his relatives, friends, and gossips, some of whom did not even live in the town. It was good business for the family, since the town council distributed irrigation rights. A similar state of affairs may be surmised in New Spain communities.

In most towns founded by private citizens after 1573, the predominance of a few rich individuals was made a certainty when the King provided for granting a founder one-fourth of the town district. The provision was carried out for Martín Rolín Varejón, "permanent corregidor and . . . founder" of Lerma (sometime after 1611), for Captain Tovar Guzmán at Cadereyta in 1641, and others, to judge by frequent references to the 1573 colonization ordinances.

Some small communities were constantly threatened by dispersal, especially in the northern provinces, where many people preferred to live on outlying estancias. Consequently, municipal regulations required every *vecino* to own a house in town and live in it at least during the principal feast days. The requirement was only fairly well observed.

The same mentality was reflected in big landowners' relations with white and mestizo communities as with native communities: to take away their lands and thus obtain badly needed vaqueros, stewards, and harvest overseers. They used all the means at their disposal, without too great a concern for legality. Guillén de Lampart, an official surveyor in Michoacán at the time, observed that "less powerful farmers" lost heart on seeing "the rich man take over their [fields] without a right." The same tactics were employed as for native communities in the north, namely, depriving a town of its legal status—hence of its liberties and judicial authority and its right to inalienable community property and a district reserved for *vecinos*—and then annexing its lands.

In the second half of the seventeenth century, the corregidor of San Juan de Coscomatepec, a powerful captain by the name of Cano Moctezuma, had joined forces with the region's big landowners in order to destroy the small town of Córdoba. When suit was filed against a bachelor at law for usurping some community land, the conspirators succeeded in the course of the trial in having the Audiencia strip Córdoba of its rank of town and reduce its district to a one-league square; they argued that the King had never confirmed the town's charter (specious logic, since the King almost never did confirm charters). The corregidor, acting in the Audiencia's name and backed by his militia, then tried to prohibit the election of alcaldes. The citizens, however, showed considerable spirit in defending their liberties and even sent an attorney to Spain. In spite of the Audiencia's having handed down a new judgment confirming its previous one, the Council of the Indies decided in favor of the town, and by a royal decree of March 17, 1680, restored all its prerogatives. The next year, another cédula forbade any further molesting.

Elsewhere, towns were undermined from within when landowners cornered all the positions of authority. At Asunción de Aguascalientes in 1644, an Audiencia judge, who had come in the capacity of official surveyor to collect settlement money for land and water rights, discovered that "the mighty and divers individuals, on the pretext that they had wheat and other cereals growing, were stealing water from the main [irrigation] ditch, which they had pierced in various spots; as a consequence, poor people were starving and said settlement was not increasing." A half-century later, the situation had become worse; after an exhaustive investigation, the alcalde mayor (unlike the royal official in the Córdoba affair) took sanctions against several influential men who had diverted nearly the entire town water supply into their own estates. Meanwhile, many small growers of "peppers, melons, and squashes" helplessly watched their fields and gardens dry up, and even monasteries and convents had no water "for their kitchens." The monopolists were two ordinary alcaldes (one of whom was a big merchant), several regidores, a "provincial of the brotherhood," a licenciado who was an ex-alcalde mayor, and some captains. They were all, a town attorney wrote, "individuals whose water needs should be satisfied ahead of the poor's, because of the offices that they hold; [after all] they are justice officials and regidores . . . if the poor were starving, it was because they were poor."

These "destitute pepper growers of the Triana quarter," however, were determined to defend themselves, with the result that every day brought its exchange of dire threats and blows resulting in wounds. Whence arose "temporally and spiritually, most serious inconveniences" and much "giving of offense to God," the local curate, a bachelor of canon law, affirmed. The curate had so wholeheartedly embraced the poor's cause that in his fervor he swore that on some occasions the church had been without holy water.

In order to put a stop to the daily brawls between rich and poor, and at the request of several witnesses, including another bachelor of canon law, the parish vicar, and the alcalde mayor, Captain Don Hernando Delgado y Ocampo, forbade the powerful landowners to sow wheat requiring irrigation. In spite of their threats and insults and their request for an injunction, the Audiencia confirmed the alcalde mayor's decision in 1704 and even went farther, ordering their wheat fields destroyed without delay by putting cattle out to graze in them. The royal official then instructed the Indian alcalde of the San Marcos de Aguascalientes quarter to collect as many animals as he could and turn them loose in the fields. The order was executed before his eyes. That was the final episode in a protracted dispute whose proceedings omit none of the pungent details that remind us, 150 years in advance, of the great Mexican novelist Mariano Azuela's *Los Caciques*.

Such favorable court decisions were no deterrent to the hacienda owners' steady advance through purchase or other legal means. In some communities, the *vecinos'* poverty and lack of initiative made their task easier. San Felipe, probably out of carelessness, had stopped electing its municipal authorities. "For this reason, its land, district, and *ejidos* have been usurped by neighboring hacendados, who have occupied every bit of ground up to the roof gutters of the houses." The inhabitants did not know where to "plow or pasture their cattle, for the hacienda hands drive them out [of their former land and back to the village] where they are starving to death." In 1729, community representatives made reference to the long evolution that had led to this deplorable state; they declared that their town was now almost deserted and no longer had a council to defend its interests.

By their neglect, the *vecinos* had played into the landowners' hands; the latter could now say that the locality did not qualify as a town, since it had no municipal council. Using the same stratagem as the would-be destroyers of Córdoba, they also argued that it never had been a town, since the King had not ratified its founding.

The Audiencia's prosecutor nevertheless rejected the landowners' claims on the grounds that their title deeds were null and void. San Felipe, it appeared, had issued the deeds illegally:

In violation of the tenor of its charter, as well as of the law, the town had embarked upon so wholesale a distribution that in the end it had given all its land away, including land that should have been reserved for ejidos, *municipal pastures, and local commonage. This carelessness gave rise to the surrounding* hacenderos' *unjust occupation, which by now has reached the town gates.*

The title deeds were doubly illegal, since they had been issued by the council, the alcalde mayor, or the ordinary alcaldes without once having been submitted to the Viceroy for confirmation—a flagrant violation of a law dated January 10, 1589. Consequently, the Audiencia ordered hacienda hands and farmers expelled from the *ejidos,* notably those coming from Ciénaga de Mata. The hacendados were, however, firmly entrenched in the rest of the district, from which they must have subsequently mounted a counteroffensive and recovered the lost terrain, if we are to believe Father Morfi, who, passing through the region in 1777, observed that "this town is extremely wretched, for it possesses no land."

Fights between hacienda owners and Creole or mestizo communities took place all over the country in the seventeenth century, for example, in New León, between local settlers and absentee sheep raisers acting through their bailiffs, or near Mexico City, at Lerma, impoverished and half-abandoned because of its having been deprived of its land; its four-league district had been gradually devoured by the Marqués del Valle and other hacienda owners. The plight of small farmers not belonging to any town or city was still more serious—almost desperate. Near Parras, Urdiñola's powerful descendants (soon to become the Marqueses de Aguayo) and the Indian community of San Esteban de Tlaxcala were quarreling over irrigation rights. Both parties possessed formal title deeds and could lay their case before a court; but the Creole farmers in the area were unable to obtain water except by purchasing it, at exorbitant rates, from one party or the other. They were at either party's mercy to keep their stunted grapevines and fruit trees—their sole means of subsistence—alive. These small farmers were particularly numerous in the Bajío; when Salvatierra was founded in 1644, they crowded into the town to become *vecinos.*

The region of Lagos and Los Altos de Jalisco presents a peculiar problem. Its small landowners bear today the same names as the modest stock-men of the early seventeenth century: Macías, Anda, Padilla, Ornelas, Torres, Isaci, Aranda. Yet the big haciendas seem to have divided the entire region among themselves. The small, unencumbered rancho of our day is a relatively recent phenomenon, dating from the end of the eighteenth century at the earliest and usually from the nineteenth. It is possible that the rancho represents the old holding, or rented land, which had later split away from the big estate. If so, the ranchero would have unintentionally avenged his Creole ancestors who, after having been reduced to the status of sharecroppers and tenant farmers, thus regained their independence a century or so later.

PART III ■
The Trend Toward Stabilization

7. THE GREAT CHURCH ESTATES

GENERAL CAUSES AND THE AUTHORITIES' ATTITUDE

The first missionaries to arrive in New Spain were almost without exception apostles whose sole, burning desire was to spread the Gospel.

We are shown them walking, lonely and undefended, over the rocky roads of the vast country to which they were bringing tidings of Christ. Many were men of learning whose influence is to be explained by civil authorities' and viceroys' realizing that when they spoke out, they were not trying to further their own petty interests. They naturally, and passionately, protected the Indians against encomenderos or settlers ready to prey upon the helpless. In the opinion of some conquistadors, they acted like dangerous revolutionaries, preaching racial equality from their pulpits and inciting natives to shake off the semi-illegal yoke of the encomienda. Such are the reasons for their great prestige and the scope and speed of their "spiritual conquest," which Robert Ricard has described.

The magnitude of their success was in itself a danger. The Indians, with the overwhelming gratitude characteristic of the weak and humiliated, offered their saviors lands, legacies, and other gifts. The temptation to acquire worldly goods was a strong one, not for personal enrichment certainly, but to ensure a monastery or an order the material security that would spare it from living precariously on alms or government subsidies. The Franciscans alone generally resisted. In addition, the great mendicant orders were not the Church's only representatives in Mexico; where there were no missionaries, there was secular clergy. Not having the same reasons as the monks for despising this world's treasure, secular clerics not attached to a vicarage sometimes behaved in quite unedifying ways. Tithes increased yearly with the growth of crops and droves. Contemplative orders established convents into whose coffers the dowries of well-to-do Creoles' daughters were soon flowing.

Then, a recently founded religious order, differing from all the others, implanted itself in the country: the Society of Jesus. After founding schools in the cities (at the close of the sixteenth century), its members gradually pushed on with their chain of missions into the huge northwestern territories. The Society soon complemented its rigid internal discipline with a solid economic organization, which its rule did not forbid. At the very time when the other orders' zeal was showing signs of abating, the Society's high principles and the undeniable superiority of its educational system won for it powerful friends among the nobility and the rich Spanish or Creole miners and merchants whose sons were attending its schools. Twenty or thirty years after the Jesuits' arrival (1572), few wills were being drawn up that did not provide for them generously; their novices were being recruited from the wealthiest families, and innumerable gifts and endowed masses were bringing them in large sums of money.

In this relatively poor country, the improvidence and wastefulness of encomenderos, as well as that of miners' and high officials' heirs, amazed contemporaries. "This country's children are so prodigal that they spend every cent they own," the Mexico City administration remarked in 1637. The same document contains a denunciation of the monasteries' wealth. The Church was merely managing its fortune with greater skill. As in medieval Europe, its branches constituted the only closely knit organizations in Mexican society. Its individual representatives were usually the best educated and most capable members of that society. And, finally, it had tenure in the form of mortmain.

Much of the Church's money went for construction, as shown by the countless monasteries and convents, churches and chapels, whose towers and cupolas betray the smallest Mexican village's presence to a traveler still some distance away. Buildings and altarpieces were all very well, but they were not productive capital assets. If the orders, which collected no tithes, did not wish to remain dependent on private charity or royal subsidies, they would have to assure themselves a regular income by investing to advantage sums coming their way. For those seeking stability and security rather than big profits, there was only one possible investment, land.

The dazzling wealth of some miners had not prevented the Church from being wary of the industry that had made it for them; by the end of the sixteenth century, shrewd men could sense approaching disaster. The decline of the mines was an accomplished fact a few decades later, just when the Church's land investment program was going into full operation. In 1637, Mexico City's municipal government ignored the mines completely in listing present sources of revenue: "There are in this realm only six types of investments [haciendas], namely, housing, farm lands, flour mills, sugar refineries, and cattle and sheep raising." The municipality went on to say that all six were gradually being monopolized by religious orders, which already owned one-third of investments; they should be prohibited from establishing haciendas or accepting gifts, and a stop should be put to all sales from which they would benefit.

Nothing proved of any avail against Spanish and Indian donors' irresistible piety or the clergy's perspicuity, knack for organization, and close understanding with the monarchy (on all matters save this one). Besides, flimsy legal barriers could not be expected to withstand the onslaught of the clergy's capital at a time when the country needed ready money and the clergy needed opportunities for investment.

The problem of determining the exact date at which Church estates sprang into being, as well as their earliest forms, is a very complex one. Great differences of principle and method—sometimes of opinion—quickly developed between regular and secular clergy, missionaries and contemplative orders, Franciscans and Jesuits, or prebendaries and clerics not attached to a vicarage. Regardless of the many shapes that Church property assumed, however, it did evolve in conformity with a few general norms, which authorities stressed in passing from a negative attitude to a tolerant one and, finally, to legal recognition of Church property rights.

Although the King in 1538 had authorized churches and vicars to have provisional use of estates and revenues formerly belonging to native "idols" and their temples, he had also forbidden, on the occasion of granting the Viceroy the right to distribute lands in his name, the eventual transfer of any such lands "to a church, monastery, or ecclesiastic" (October 27, 1535). Caballería and estancia deeds issued by the viceroys after 1542 invariably bore such a clause, stating further that violation would result in the deed's nullification.

The monarchy's goal was doubtless a double one. From an economic and social point of view, it wished to ward off the threat that ecclesiastical mortmain, with its monopolistic tendencies, had traditionally posed to landed property—ever since the early Middle Ages, in fact. To a lesser degree, the monarchy, in a spirit anticipating the Council of Trent, took its moral and religious guardianship (*jus patronatus*) in the Indies quite seriously; by forbidding clerics to acquire rural estates, it wished to spare them concerns alien to the Church's spiritual mission.

The viceregal administration did not hold steadfastly to the rule, however, since it occasionally granted an estancia to some particularly needy convent, monastery, or college, for example, in 1550 to the nuns of "Our Mother of God" and Holy Cross College in Mexico City or, in 1560, to the monastery of St. Dominic in Nexapa. Likewise, Augustinians and Dominicans accepted from the Indians a few gifts and legacies of land on which they raised sheep or built flour mills; they claimed that they were less interested in profits than in setting a good example to Spanish settlers. In any event, acquisitions were still insignificant in 1558, when Viceroy Velasco wrote Philip II:

> It cannot be rightly said that [the friars] seek to acquire worldly goods. To my knowledge they have none of their own at present; their habit is made of rough homespun and their diet is so frugal as barely to support life. Whenever they find that their possessions are in excess of their daily needs, they immediately give them to the poor. The same cannot be said of the secular clergy.

The secular clergy nevertheless kept a jealous eye on the few infractions benefiting the monks; their strictures were harsh, because monastery lands were exempted from the tithe. In 1560, they were in-strumental in the dispatch of a royal cédula reminding the provincials of the orders of St. Dominic and St. Augustine that under no circumstances were they to accept temporal goods (as they had begun to do). Land grants to help needy monasteries were thenceforth made to the Indian communities, with the stipulation that accrued income should be used to "sustain the monks" in their care of souls. In 1562, another cédula ordered the monks to dispose of all the possessions, estates, and businesses that they might own in native villages. A second clause in the same cédula, however, opened a sluice gate that could never again be closed: Orders were authorized (in compensation) to accept gifts and legacies from Spaniards within Spanish town districts. In the next few years, the Dominicans and Augustinians—but not the Franciscans—set about con-stituting their first landed estates. Prior to 1569, secular prelates pointed an accusing finger at their large acquisitions in the fertile Atlixco and Otumba valleys, then around Mexico City and Puebla. The acquisitions elicited a new series of royal injunctions in 1569, 1570, 1576, and 1579. Confirming the previous prohibitions, they apparently had no greater success, despite some degree of intervention by the viceroys; in various regions monasteries now owned lands that, obviously, pious donors had sold, deeded, or bequeathed to them.

Although Church grants practically ceased under Martín Enríquez (1568–1580), they became more numerous than ever with some of his weaker successors. Velasco II was patently tolerant in his views, for he gave lands or confirmed their titles to Dominican and Augustinian monasteries, the convent of St. Catherine of Siena at Oaxaca, and Jesuit colleges, among others. This was the time when the Jesuits were be-ginning to acquire vast estates and obtain official confirmation for them; in 1581, an Audiencia decision, which was ratified in 1583, exempted Jesuit lands from the tithe, even lands that had been leased out. In 1580 and 1597, the Audiencia reaffirmed the prohibition against selling real estate to orders, but at the same time it authorized charitable donations of all sorts. Whether the authorities wished the religious orders to own landed estates or not, they had, by the end of the sixteenth century, bowed to the inevitable.

The secular clergy, who had so vigorously denounced their rivals' property, went about obtaining theirs in a different fashion. Although churches and chapels generally possessed little land of their own, they did enjoy large endowments deriving for the most part from fees paid by rural haciendas. No law prevented these mortgages from multiply-ing indefinitely; and they were the steadiest, safest kind of income. Be-sides, the secular clergy collected tithes on all Spanish holdings, less the two-ninths that the Crown took for its share, by virtue of the powers that the Pope had relinquished to it in the New World.

Individual clerics, vicars, and high church officials frequently pos-sessed, in their own names, estates or mines in their parishes. Neither the original royal prohibitions nor the limitations imposed by the Council of Trent seem ever to have been enforced, even partially. The reason is probably the tithe's unproductiveness in regions still only sparsely settled by Spaniards. The Council of Mexico (1585) drew up detailed regulations for all clerical activities; but it devoted only a short para-graph to the question of real estate exploitation, which, in fact, it tol-erated. The royal government, in its capacity of patron of the Church in the Indies, adopted for its guiding policy the Council's most impor-tant resolutions.

Prelates on inspection tours saw nothing wrong with instructions such as these, issued by the Bishop of Guadalajara in 1648: Churchmen are strictly forbidden to engage in trade, that is, "to buy or sell more than is necessary to maintain their house and family and keep their har-vest haciendas, droves, mills, and mines in good condition, *these latter occupations being permitted them* because of the difficult living conditions in the country and the inadequacy of ecclesiastical reve-nues."

The rapid development of Church property did elicit some protests. At the early date of 1599, Gómez de Cervantes claimed that "half of New Spain is in the hands of monks and Theatines [Jesuits]," who had so many endowments, houses, rentals, and, especially, rural estates that "what land they do not own is parsimoniously measured out for us in feet." The remedy must be a sweeping one; otherwise, the entire coun-try would soon be under their control. The phenomenon was wide-spread—indeed, common to all the Indies—for in 1608–1609 the Vice-roy of Peru, the Viceroy of Mexico, and all the Audiencias in the Americas were ordered to furnish information about the rapid cornering of land "by the religious orders," which, it was declared, owned a third of the estates, thanks to endowed masses, novices' dowries, legacies, and purchases. Also, each viceroy was asked whether it would not be ap-propriate to "reduce the number of monasteries and convents in [your] district." It had taken only twenty or thirty years to reach this state of affairs.

Honest officials still entertained some doubts about the validity of ecclesiastical title deeds. An Audiencia judge on a tour of inspection in New Galicia, the Licenciado Paz de Vallecillo, refused in 1607–1608 to confirm title to monasteries', convents', or individual clerics' estates, because the original grants had forbidden sale or transfer to any members of the Church. He admitted to His Majesty that he had never seen the clause enforced or the land in question declared forfeit and unoccupied; there were many such holdings, and he did not dare to make any innovations without specific instructions; to have done so would have caused "grave concern throughout New Spain and New Galicia."

It was already difficult, if not impossible, to take decisive action. A favorite argument against change was that in some regions it would "kill agriculture." Nevertheless, the King twice again (in 1609 and 1619) reaffirmed previous cédulas and forbade religious orders to acquire any new real estate. Still later, the celebrated jurist Solórzano Pereyra, when he was Council of the Indies prosecutor, unhesitatingly called for the law's enforcement and insisted that resultant litigation should not be allowed to drag on for a century, as sometimes happened. However, while this thorny question was being debated in Spain, the Crown, short of money, urged its Viceroy to proceed with the collecting of settlement fees—which special tax would allow all landowners to legalize their numerous defective title deeds.

The Church, possessing badly needed ready cash, was naturally requested to pay what it owed the royal tax collector along with the others. In 1643, Dominican provinces, Augustinian monasteries, Poor Clares, and the brothers of the St. Hippolytus Hospital in Mexico City came to terms. They were followed, somewhat later, by Jesuit colleges. Infrequently, reservations were timidly voiced over the proceeding's outcome; but settlement fees had made reform even more difficult, since they would have had to be returned. A 1655 decision, although it required religious orders to pay a harvest tithe henceforth, effectively removed the last restrictions to the growth of Church estates.

These estates were not disturbed again until the Society of Jesus was disbanded. The consequences of that measure transcend the question of Jesuit real estate, however important such real estate may have been in New Spain's social and economic development.

THE THREE EARLIEST ORDERS

As Marc Bloch shrewdly observed, ecclesiastics may well have all belonged to the same class in the eyes of the law; they did not all belong to the same class in society. Perhaps to a greater extent in the Indies than in the Old World, innumerable singularities differentiated men, communities, and institutions within the Church. Prelates and the great orders' provincials were rivals, as were Creole monks and Spanish immigrants or some missionaries and rich prebendaries. In a body so huge and overflowing with vitality, varying monastic rules, living conditions, social backgrounds, mentalities, interests, and degrees of wealth—not to mention imponderables like the quality of morals or faith—gave each individual or group its peculiar physiognomy and character. Among the many elements making for this diversity, the attitude toward worldly possessions was one of the most significant. A word of caution, however: moral decadence was not always the concomitant of riches, as the example of the Jesuits will show.

The Franciscans, on the other hand, will always be honored for having scrupulously observed a particularly severe part of their rule; theirs was the only order in the seventeenth century to abstain from acquiring large estates. As far as we know, the order itself owned no land, although some of its communities in outlying provinces did have a few droves and fields.

There were local abuses, to be sure. In Avalos, notably at Zacoalco (Jalisco), Franciscans in charge of Indian welfare had leased pastures to eastern stockmen who were wintering their flocks there. According to a 1608 report by the Guadalajara prosecutor, they had also distributed positions on Indian town councils, dictating duties and disbursements, and interfered with the running of the public jail. "The way in which they order their charges about shows that they [act as if they were] . . . all mighty." In New Galicia, other Franciscans derived profit from hospital lands on which Indians, working for the hospital without pay, raised wheat, maize, and sheep. The fact remains that, unlike the other orders, the Franciscans did not attempt to acquire title deeds. Without such legal support or authorization from their superiors, their unwarranted occupation of a few pieces of land was destined to be short-lived, at least in the seventeenth century. The farming and handicraft ventures associated with several Franciscan missions in the north may be explained by the absolute necessity of producing consumer goods locally, since they were not to be had for the asking in those barren regions. In well-watered valleys in New Mexico and other northern provinces, the remains of mission enclosures, mills, stables, and workshops reveal that the missions were small economic and social units comparable to the haciendas.

The Franciscans' selfless fervor and vow of poverty inspiring all their actions were no longer, by the late sixteenth century, as unsullied as when they had arrived. Although they had escaped the land fever, they were somewhat contaminated by the spirit of lucre. Whereas their earliest missionaries had refused payment even for the saying of masses, by the close of the century, they, like other orders, were known to have allowed Indians to disinherit their families in order to have masses recited for the good of their individual Indian souls. The Franciscans were also accused of having occasionally had an ulterior motive in visiting the dying: to persuade them to draw up wills in their favor or to obtain, at least, "a horse or a mule" to pay for last offices and burial. As early as 1588, the King forbade wills of this type; but there is abundant proof that the practice continued.

The Dominicans had acquired some land very early. With their purchases and, especially, donations, they built a string of estates the most important of which was probably their great sugar plantation and refinery at Cuautla–Amilpas, where they used Negro slaves in the sixteenth century. Unlike many Augustinians and Jesuits (particularly), they do not appear to have cared much for farming; instead of operating their own estates, they often leased them out, for example, their haciendas at Tlalnepantla.

For the Augustinians, who liked sumptuous altarpieces and places of worship, rural haciendas seem to have represented essentially a means of supporting their churches and missions. Fray Diego Basalenque, the order's chronicler, relates how one of their saintly monks, Fray Diego Magdaleno, requested permission to leave his priory—"the best in the sierra"—because the region offered no investment opportunities and he was reduced to living on what his charges' toil and sweat brought in. In other words, his moral imperative was almost the exact opposite of the Franciscans'.

Fray Diego Basalenque takes pleasure in describing at length the [Dominican] sugar *trapiches* and large refineries, flour mills, sheepfolds and mule ranches, and various haciendas established by members of his order. Dominican estates were, in fact, numerous and were often considerable undertakings. If one compares Fray Diego's account with those of other orders' historians, one cannot help being struck by his keen interest in agricultural and livestock expansion and his constant quoting of figures for wheat production, cattle raising, and the real value or revenues of the different estates.

Estates belonged to either an individual monastery or one of the Augustinian provinces; they were found all over New Spain, around Mexico City, Puebla, and Oaxaca; in Huasteca, and, especially, in Michoacán. One of these estates near Tlalnepantla, it appears, was the site of Mexico's first grain silo, which was installed experimentally in 1580. Some Augustinian missionaries were devoted farmers and felt a deep, abiding love for the countryside, like the one who created the order's biggest hacienda, San Nicolás, near Yuriria. In 1583, one of the generals waging war against the Chichimecas had given the friars land there. A prior had undertaken some preliminary work. Then, toward the close of the century, one of the monks was entrusted with completing it. The monk built a dam across a river and dug an irrigation ditch several leagues long to water an area capable of yielding 50,000 fanegas of grain annually. He also built two large flour mills and purchased more land, which he placed under cultivation. One of his successors "bought an adjacent hacienda, for 5,000 pesos, solely to avoid the bother of having neighbors in too close proximity." The successor later established a mule ranch in the vicinity.

At the turn of the century, San Nicolás owned 400 work oxen and 150 pack mules used for transporting crops to market. Its wheat production was 10,000 fanegas (5,500 hectoliters), and its net income was 6,000 pesos. The 120 Indians that it sustained (*indios de ración*), free laborers and muleteers, formed the embryo of the present-day village of San Nicolás. Twenty-five "rich and powerful men," tempted by the estate's prosperity, offered the monastery a handsome endowment in exchange for permission to found a town there. The best lawyer in Mexico City was set to study the project, but the interested parties could not reach an agreement. San Nicolás' appraised value was some 100,000 pesos, a rather exceptional sum for an estate containing no sugar refinery. Thanks to such revenues, the order was able to acquire, a few years later, the splendid golden reredos in nearby Salamanca.

Fray Diego Basalenque shows us one of San Nicolás' monk farmers riding off from the monastery around midnight, as soon as he had finished saying matins, in order to reach the hacienda (two or three leagues away) in time to lay out the day's tasks for the workers. In the nineteenth century, some hacienda owners likewise arose at two in the morning in order to wake their peons at sowing, harvest, or shearing time. Sometimes mission villages were governed in the same manner; the example of the Michoacán father who saw that his charges did their sowing on fixed days immediately comes to mind. Such paternalism could obviously lead to abuses, for example, when monks needed labor for their own estates.

THE SOCIETY OF JESUS

The Jesuits were undoubtedly the greatest farmers of all. Many of them were agronomists, and the Society's colleges owned the best-operated, most thriving estates in the viceroyalty. Only the order's professed house vowed to live strictly on alms.

The first Jesuits did not reach New Spain until 1572. The three great orders and the secular clergy had long since apportioned among themselves the task of converting the country. Consequently, the new arrivals settled in Mexico City and other towns, initially at a loss to know what activities they should pursue. Their itinerant missions, of which there were several, did not seem to have much future. Remarking that young Creoles' education was being neglected and that the instruction in religious seminaries was inadequate, the Society hit upon the idea of founding colleges. At the same time, it sent missionaries northward into the desolate stretches of far-off New Viscaya. The Jesuits were thus able not only to avoid incurring the other orders' enmity, but to win the secular clergy's favor, which stood them well in the early days. The natives, too, seem to have liked them. The Society was the cleverest of all the orders in finding rich benefactors, such as the famous "Croesus" of New Spain, Alonso de Villaseca; this dry, matter-of-fact businessman, taciturn and of a forbidding appearance, handed over to the Society, before his death in 1580, sums totaling 224,791 pesos (according to his somewhat disgruntled grandson, whose entail had decreased in value). In particular, he founded the Jesuit college in Mexico City with 40,000 pesos in the form of 41 ingots of silver. He had enough money left to bequeath his daughter a large estate.

Villaseca gave the Jesuits advice that was worth more to them than all his gifts, in the words of a Jesuit who had known him: The best investments for supporting their colleges were "half-completed rural haciendas." The haciendas' unfinished state would keep the sale price low, and the Jesuits' improvements would turn them into valuable assets. Villaseca's own fortune offering proof of his business acumen, the Society followed his recommendations to the letter. Because of the colleges' utility, Viceroy Martín Enríquez closed his eyes to what took place; he even granted the Society many favors in the gruff, offhand manner of its earlier benefactor.

In 1576, the Jesuits' first college, St. Peter and St. Paul in Mexico City, acquired for less than 20,000 pesos a large estate situated a few leagues to the north, on which sheep were being raised. The fathers made it into the Santa Lucía hacienda, the most important one of its kind, it seems, in all the northern Indies. The college went on to buy or constitute other estates and sugar refineries that were even larger than Santa Lucía.

Additional Jesuit colleges were quickly established in many localities. There were sometimes initial difficulties, but the fathers would soon overcome them by making an appeal to wealthy merchants or clergymen. At Puebla, for example, Melchor de Covarrubias, a Creole cochineal merchant, helped them to found the College of the Holy Ghost and then left them most of his fortune (1587–1592). As Covarrubias had recommended, the college invested most of its 72,800-peso bequest in land. Besides farming haciendas, the Puebla Jesuits owned, in 1603, a flock of 40,000 sheep.

The big college at Tepotzotlán received in 1604 benefactions from an opulent Mexico City trader, Pedro Ruiz de Ahumada, who had been an elector of the merchants' guild in 1594. His statue may still be seen in one of the college chapels; he is depicted as a knight wearing a ruff and breastplate, with his plumed helmet at his side. Thanks to its founder's generosity, the college was able to acquire, in 1608, the large Santa Inés domain, comprising 35,000 sheep, as well as harvest lands. The college's numerous haciendas all prospered, with the result that in the eighteenth century, having become a seminary, it could afford to adorn its church with five golden reredos, one of the richest sets in the entire New World.

Most of the powerful merchants of Mexico City, Puebla, or the big mining camps became at one time or another the Jesuits' friends and benefactors. Alvaro de Lorenzana, whom a contemporary described as "one of the richest men ever to be seen in this kingdom or anywhere else" (his liquid assets alone were said to total 800,000 pesos), not only served as patron of the Convent of the Incarnation and endowed eight cathedral prebends in Mexico City, but appointed the Jesuits executors of his will and, naturally, did not fail to remember them therein (1651). Martín Ruiz de Zavala, a member of the northern family whose miners and merchants were nearly all outstanding Church benefactors, supplied funds for the founding of the college at San Luis Potosí in 1620.

The landed aristocracy was not so generous, probably because it had less money; its entails were, by definition, indivisible and often in a bad state. It welcomed, moreover, alliances with the rich merchant class. Because of so much intermarriage, it is hard for us to determine to which category certain benefactors belong, for example, a powerful man like Juan de Chavarría.

The secular clergy, too, answered the Jesuits' appeals most generously. Clergymen's fortunes were more modest than merchants', to be sure; but the most insignificant prebendaries usually had good incomes and, owing to their vow of celibacy, fewer heirs. In the early days, vicars, canons, and ordinary clerics—even prelates and wealthy cathedral chapters—bestowed upon the Jesuits a striking number of gifts and legacies. The Guadalajara chapter endowed the town college; somewhat later, a local archdeacon did the same for Durango. At Puebla, Bishop Mota y Escobar bequeathed land and income for the founding of a second college (1625). A Puebla canon was the Society's benefactor at Vera Cruz. Many caballerías, estancias, and cash donations came from plain clergymen, country vicars, and small-town prebendaries. Good relations were unfortunately impaired when the Jesuits asserted that they were exempted from tithing; the dispute culminated in an extremely violent controversy with the venerable Bishop of Puebla, Palafox y Mendoza.

The Society converted its pesos and countless gifts (often of a very humble sort), purchases, and exchanges of land into huge estates and flourishing haciendas. The process is a curious blend of calculation, spontaneity, skill, and force. The Society's temporal activities approach the grandiose; starting from scratch, it soon had the largest flocks of sheep, the finest sugar plantations, and the best-managed estates, not to speak of the undisputable superiority of its colleges and missions.

Firm self-discipline and high moral standards were at the root of the disinterestedness, even the love of poverty, which members of the order revealed in their pursuits. The large sums that they gathered in were spent, not on individuals, but on the betterment of the order; consequently, every peso was made to count. Thomas Gage, a shrewd but ill-disposed observer, might well, in the early decades of the seventeenth century, show Jesuits fawning on the rich and influential; but he could not show them, as he did members of other orders, personally leading lives of ease, riding richly caparisoned mules, or gambling away their substance. The Society, in a sense, did just the opposite of the Franciscans who, as an order, were still poor a century after their arrival, but who, as individuals, sometimes were sufficiently self-seeking to arouse comment.

For a period when the Church was still prohibited from buying, if not from owning, real estate in the Indies, the Jesuits systematically built up their rich estates in an amazingly short time and without difficulty. Relying on their powerful backers and lawyer friends (many of whom had attended their schools), they did not allow obsolescent clauses in title deeds to deter them from attaining ends that they felt justified the means: maintaining their colleges—of whose usefulness there was no question—and aiding their missions in the remotest, most forsaken parts of the viceroyalty. They showed so peculiar a skill in handling men, whether Spaniards or Indians, and so keen a business sense in acquiring, managing, and utilizing to the utmost their worldly possessions that an Italian, Gemelli Carreri, remarked, apropos of the northern missions, that the Jesuits were "more ingenious than the other missionaries in looking out for themselves."

Their abilities showed to advantage in their achievements in the region between Mexico City and Pachuca. Midway, near Tecama, the Mexico City college bought, in 1576, five estancias containing 18,200 sheep and eight Negro slaves; it made the purchase with 17,000 pesos in endowment funds. For greater safety, the bill of sale, dated December 4, was cleverly made out to Juan de Monsalve Cabeza de Vaca, who on

December 23 donated the property to the Jesuits. A separate document affirming the latter's rights stated that Monsalve "really and truly concluded said purchase . . . in the name of the Society of Jesus' college in this town and with its money, which had been furnished by the college's founder, Alonso de Villaseca."

The estate was the one already mentioned, named in honor of St. Lucy, whose feast day (December 13) was being celebrated at the time of the purchase. Its flock of sheep very quickly reached 50,000, and numbered 60,000 by 1602. Its annual income at this later date was greater than the original purchase price, since the fathers had continued to acquire land for grazing and farms: unimproved land, neighboring haciendas, and many estancias and caballerías (after 1582), including a 12,000-head sheepfold. The estate gradually surrounded all the villages located in the twelve-mile plain between Santa Lucía and the Pachuca mines—Acayuca, Atlica, Tolcayuca, Tezontepec, and others. Purchases and donations continued through the seventeenth century, with the result that by 1670 the college owned most of the large plain extending from the mining camp [Pachuca] to Lake Texcoco.

Many of the estate's title deeds did bear two restrictive clauses: no sale to the Church or any of its members and no transfer for the first four years. Both were honored in the breach; in fact, some titles were transferred a few days or months after issuance, the devout recipients having felt impelled to show their "great regard for the Society." Still, precautions had to be taken to prevent literate Indians (*ladinos*, who, like wily peasants everywhere, had already picked up a smattering of law) from complaining about or contesting transactions. They were sometimes given trifling gifts on the eve of a father's coming to fulfill the ceremonies of occupation, whose practically irrevocable nature we have already described. In 1582, a representative of the Mexico City college noted in his report that he had taken care of "the little matter of the Indians in [the village of] Acolman" by giving them eighty pesos—thirty in silver and fifty in ornaments for their church—"lest they register a complaint, rightly or wrongly."

Various caciques gave estancias (untransferable in principle) to individual clergymen who, within a short time, sold them to the Mexico City college. However, the Jesuits, unlike many laymen and other orders, left ample breathing space around native communities.

As some of the above examples make obvious, colleges frequently used friends and third parties for delicate negotiations in which they preferred not to figure directly, seeing that they had no legal right to own land. In 1594, a man was granted two sheep estancias. Two years later, he made them over to the Society. In 1607, acting as if he still owned them, he requested the Viceroy's permission to use them for cattle. He was clearly a dummy for the real owner, the College of St. Peter and St. Paul. In spite of opposition from an Indian municipality and two encomenderos, the local alcalde mayor approved conversion of one of the estancias. Actually, the fathers did not scruple to raise horses and mules on land officially reserved for sheep, even when permission was denied them.

In many regions, the Society did not attempt to conceal the fact that, acting through proxies, it was obtaining needed land from the Viceroy. Documents drawn up by the Jesuits contain statements like this one concerning the college at Pátzcuaro:

> *The title deeds for these two sheep estancias and caballerías were obtained, in the name of Rodrigo Vásquez, from Viceroy Luis de Velasco on March 13, 1591. The acts of occupation were accomplished on May 9 of the same year. Said Rodrigo Vázquez transferred title on the 13th of the same month in the presence of the notary. The papers are all in the safe.*

The Jesuits had no monopoly on such irregularities. However, their greater zeal and method in bridging the gap between theoretical inability to own any land whatsoever and the actual acquisition of vast holdings gave rise to the greatest variety of legal subterfuges; some of them were curious, even unexpectedly comical. The viceregal administration could hardly continue to feign ignorance. It acknowledged the holdings' existence on several occasions; in 1581 and 1583, for example, it confirmed their exemption from the tithe. The authorities' tolerance was also tacit admission of the great services rendered by Jesuit colleges, which charged no tuition. The Jesuits' rural estates, furthermore, were self-supporting—except for their northern missions —unlike other orders whose revenues were not so flourishing. Favors granted the Society by local major and minor officials show that, by the turn of the century, it enjoyed considerable standing throughout New Spain.

All the Society's blocks and parcels of land—large or small, purchased or donated, tilled or fallow—were grouped according to region and made into large, prosperous estates at a tempo depending on the region. Like some medieval monasteries, colleges spent generous sums on equipping their estates with the best livestock and farm implements available, stout outbuildings (still in use today), and, especially, plentiful crews of Indian day laborers, and even Negro slaves on their sugar plantations. They plowed and seeded the best land, leaving arid or less fertile expanses for sheep pastures. Needless to say, in regions where encomiendas existed, the new haciendas' limits were completely outside the encomiendas.

Some colleges' estates formed compact masses; others were located in more than one region. Around 1670, for example, the seminary at Tepotzotlán, north-northwest of Mexico City, owned large haciendas in its home territory; but it also had holdings around Colima, Sombrerete, and other New Galicia localities. Dispersal was sometimes due to chance donations. At other times, it was deliberate, as in Colima, where certain colleges had acquired winter pastures for the immense flocks in which they specialized. The Tepotzotlán seminary obtained a royal order allowing its tens of thousands of migrating sheep to graze on all the fallow and stubbled fields in New Spain "without anyone's gainsaying."

Complementary holdings appear to have been often grouped in accordance with a plan, which would supply a given religious community with some of all the country's diversified products. That is probably the explanation of colleges' many exchanges, sales, and resales until they had exactly the land that suited their purposes.

Although estates were to keep on growing, they were already large by the middle of the seventeenth century. The College of St. Peter and St. Paul in Mexico City possessed the richest. Its Santa Lucía y Nuestra Señora de Loreto hacienda was one of the biggest sheep-raising centers in the Indies; it was surrounded by a string of smaller farms and estancias, also the college's property. The college possessed besides three sugar refineries, among the most important in the country: one at Jalmolonga (Malinalco) and two in the Marquesado del Valle, at Chiconocelo (near Cuautla) and Suchimancas (near Yautepec); this last was bought in 1639 for 82,000 pesos and considerably expanded. The College of St. Anne, also in Mexico City, owned a large refinery at Tiripitío, in Michoacán, while the Oaxaca college owned one at Santa

Inés, in addition to a smaller one (*trapiche*) at Nexapa. Aside from their properties in New Galicia, the other seven main Jesuit colleges in New Spain possessed all sorts of estates, particularly sheep haciendas, which they sometimes operated in conjunction with textile mills.

Except at Mexico City and Puebla, each college or seminary was administered by no more than four to eight brothers. In 1653, the order's total membership—including Guatemala and the northern missions and ordinary regulars and novices—was only 336.

Unlike many private landowners, the Society was interested, not in cornering all the land in a given region solely to eliminate competition, but in operating its enterprises at maximum efficiency. If it would support colleges and missions that were growing in importance daily, it had to keep constantly increasing its revenues, capital investment, and assets. The Jesuits tried to organize land exploitation on a rational basis. An anonymous father of the Pátzcuaro college makes some curious observations about various haciendas, including the "plowland at San Antonio." An agriculturist of many years' experience, he notes what crops and livestock are best suited to different kinds of soil, as well as the safest and most profitable types of farm contracts. "In that spot," he says, "no more than eight fanegas of maize should be sown, and the crop must be cultivated with great care."

Around the end of the sixteenth century, the Society's General in Rome, Father Claudio Acquaviva, did not think it beneath him to have special instructions drawn up for New Spain. He dealt not only with such questions as the proper way to celebrate Mass or what relations should be with vicars residing on rural haciendas, but also the appropriate conduct to observe with servants and farm hands, agrarian economy, and even the best method of planting and cultivating sugar cane. He especially advised provincials and rectors to follow local farming practices: "Experience is the mother of science," and no individual must take it upon himself to invent clever new agricultural methods.

A century later, a provincial who later became rector of St. Peter and St. Paul, Father Ambrosio Odón, drew up operating ordinances for the sugar mills belonging to this "Colegio Máximo."

The most complete document of the sort which we possess, however, is the "Instructions to Be Observed by Brothers in Charge of Administering Rural Haciendas." The *Instrucción*, issued in the second quarter

of the eighteenth century, summarized and completed previous ordinances; it thus codified the experience that the Jesuits had accumulated
in 150 years of farming in New Spain. The text is a long one—twenty
chapters—regulating in minute detail every phase of hacienda administration: spiritual, moral, social, economic, and technical. Granted that
the instructions formulated in more precise, systematic language many
practices common to all big estates, irrespective of ownership, they also
gave the finishing touches to certain rules and attitudes peculiar to the
Jesuits.

First, as could be anticipated, the moral and religious duties of the
religioso campista, to himself and to his servants, both free laborers and
slaves: all hacienda members should say their prayers in common, cate-
chism should be taught according to prescribed practices, and all girls
twelve years of age or older should be housed in a separate school. An
administrator should always treat his charges gently, as if he were their
father and they were his children. The instructions stress particularly
the treatment of slaves. The administrator should never "utter threats
of maces, handcuffs, chains, or iron collars," lose his temper, or "imitate
the tyrannies of other refineries' secular administrators, who keep slaves
languishing in prison cells and are too free with lashings"; otherwise,
the brother would be guilty of "grave sins against charity." On the
contrary, he should "secretly seek out sponsors who would intercede
on their behalf" in order that he might be able to pretend to relent, and
then release prisoners, who would owe him a debt of gratitude. The
foregoing would appear to echo the Jesuits' long pedagogical experience.
It naturally did not apply to their free workers, whose only punishments were extremely light ones. These workers must be paid on time
and should never be advanced money with an ulterior motive in mind.

The Society's tact is particularly noticeable in the instructions governing relations with other Spaniards: vicars, justice officials, neighboring landowners, mendicant friars, and travelers. Except for the
hacienda's Jesuit chaplain (if there was one), all its members were restricted, generally speaking, to such business or hospitable relations as
good breeding and courtesy required. The reason is the number of
parasites who tried to attach themselves to the Society's prosperous
haciendas.

Instructions for technical operations were more detailed; but at the
same time, they allowed for some flexibility in execution. Deep furrows

were recommended for wheat and other cereals. Sugar plantations should be as specialized as possible, limiting themselves to growing cane and refining sugar. Rules were also laid down for the mills that wove all the brothers' clothing, for cattle and sheep raising, and even for water mills. Special attention was devoted to bookkeeping and record filing. Each administrator was charged with having his clerk keep as many as eight sets of books for the estate under his responsibility: a rough and a clean copy of cash receipts and disbursements, and ledgers for "sowing and harvesting," hiring workers, keeping account of their wages, general inventories, land and water deeds, and debits and credits. The order's rigid discipline made application of every rule a certainty. To judge by what is left of its archives, its workers seem to have been better treated, its accounts better kept, its livestock and equipment of better quality, and its sugar refineries' production above average; these last sold 20,000 to 24,000 loaves (200 to 250 tons) without speeding up the output per worker. St. Anne's College, for example, purchased San Juan Zitácuaro and its livestock annexes for 89,000 pesos; it spent 84,000 pesos more on improving buildings and land and buying pack animals, boilers, and entirely new equipment.

We can still appreciate today the excellent qualities of the Jesuits' construction, since they used stone and bricks instead of adobe. The sugar refinery of Jalmolonga, once among the largest in the country, still rears its powerful bulk, its great domed church, and its narrow turrets above the foliage of a cool valley near Malinalco. Santa Lucía hacienda, north of Mexico City, still rises out of a plain as dry as those in Castile; rebuilt in 1592, according to the date on the façade, it is vaulted throughout—from its chapel, observation tower, and huge sheep-fold to the smallest rooms opening off its two patios and barnyard.

So much concern with haciendas and Mammon made individual brothers and even college communities run the risk of forsaking the ways of the Lord. Some administrators had to be expelled from the order for violating their vows, in particular the vow of chastity. Mexico City canons were only too eager to claim that the Jesuits had had themselves granted the vicarage at Tepotzotlán in order to be able to expand their big temporal interests in the region without outside interference. It was, of course, a question of the pot calling the kettle black, since the secular clergy were annoyed to see so much rich land escape the tithe.

Nevertheless, the "most sumptuous college" and novitiate at Tepotzotlán also had its shops, "where all sorts of things are sold publicly—quarters of mutton and meat to town inhabitants and natives"; there was in addition a chocolate factory operated by a large number of Indian women. A 1645 royal cédula condemned these activities and directed that they cease at once.

The order's provincial purchasing department traded in cattle on a large scale. More shocking to some, the College of St. Peter and St. Paul alone bought or sold more than 500 Negro slaves (carried on their books as "items") in the course of the seventeenth century. The same establishment's purpose in 1582 was perhaps less selfish in buying a band of captive Chichimecas who had been condemned to twenty years of forced labor.

Transactions such as these were the logical, inevitable outcome of exploiting haciendas, droves, weaving mills, and sugar plantations. The Bishop of Puebla, Don Juan de Palafox y Mendoza, in 1647 scathingly denounced the Jesuits' accumulated wealth in a letter to the Pope. He considered it indecent that two colleges should own 300,000 sheep, as well as cattle, and that the Society itself should own six large sugar plantations in New Spain worth 500,000 to 1,000,000 pesos apiece and bringing in incomes of as much as 100,000 pesos, prosperous haciendas four to six leagues across, besides factories, shops, and slaughterhouses, and that it should carry on trade with China by way of the Philippines. The Bishop felt that each day its power bred more power and its riches more riches.

The author's tone was vituperative. In his indignation, he failed to add that the Jesuits' personal lives were plain and frugal and that their money went primarily for offering a superior kind of education free of charge. The figures that the Bishop quoted were not exaggerated, however; one sugar refinery was worth 700,000 pesos in the seventeenth century. Some of the Society's arguments in rebuttal were not very convincing; for example, it claimed that colleges had small endowments or even "live in straitened circumstances." The debts that it was constantly pleading were essentially fees due on property recently acquired or loans designed to improve its haciendas and cover the costs of its numerous sturdily constructed buildings. It methodically paid the fees and repaid the loans; but at the same time it incurred new ones by acquiring more land and making more improvements. Over a thirty-four-year period, St. Peter and St. Paul's spent 380,000 pesos to amortize 176 loans, fee payments, and mortgages; in the same period, the college contracted new debts "for the outfitting of its haciendas and plantations." Actually, the Society's holdings never stopped growing and were larger than ever in the eighteenth century.

The wealth of most of the colleges cannot be doubted, although their estates' earning power was hampered by inadequate markets. The Jesuits undeniably carried on various economic and commercial activities. Just as undeniably, their striving for worldly possessions was a way of strengthening the order's independence, social influence, and political power.

The whole Society, still a youth among orders, had kept the vitality and powerful self-discipline drilled into it by its founders, as witness the wonderful missions in New Viscaya and Lower California. In 1621, the vicar Arregui, who was familiar with the New Viscaya missions, extolled "the saintly zeal of the Fathers of the Society of Jesus, whose ministry in these regions, as well as the example they set, are worthy of eternal praise." Although much information about the missions is lacking, we do know that those founded by Father Kino served, on a temporal plane, as important farm and livestock centers in the vast northern provinces.

To a greater extent than the other orders, the Jesuits, in their task of converting the natives, were concerned with improving living conditions and developing the missions' economic activities. Father Kino taught various native tribes in the northwest how to raise cattle; they owned immense herds, and he, not a single cow. Avoiding the medieval Templars' errors, the Jesuits did maintain, in the seventeenth century, a perfect balance between their worldly pursuits and their order's spiritual aims. Furthermore, their understanding of economics, their business sense, and their efficient exploitation of landed property struck a relatively new and discordant note in the Indies, where so many hidalgos and cattle barons were disdainful of economics.

LATER ORDERS

By the end of the sixteenth century, other orders, as well as communities of nuns, had arrived in Mexico.

Rubbing elbows with the Franciscans in their gray-blue habits, the black-robed Augustinians and Jesuits, and the Dominicans clad in white, many different monks and sisters trod the streets of seventeenth-century Mexico City, Puebla, and other cities and towns. There were numerous Discalced Carmelites; friars of the Order of Mercy, of St. João de Deus, St. Anthony the Abbot, and the Hospital of St. Hippolytus, as well as the new branches of the Order of St. Francis and various uncloistered nuns. Some were poor and lived on alms—not all, however, since the King complained in 1655 that too many monks were seen "in beaver hats" and "silken hose," riding on muleback or in carriages.

Nunneries increased to such an extent that by the close of the sixteenth century there were twenty-two in Mexico City in comparison with twenty-nine monasteries; all, according to the pious Italian merchant Gemelli Carreri, "were extremely rich"; Carreri also stated that "both power and wealth are in the hands of clergymen." The same situation obtained in other localities, for example, at Puebla, where there were ten nunneries and seven monasteries, plus six colleges and numerous churches and hospitals. Only six leagues away, at Atlixco, an unpretentious town of wealthy farmers, there were five more monasteries and two churches around 1660.

Except for the Franciscans and a few mendicant nuns, all orders eventually owned rural haciendas, or at least endowments and annuities; but not all were as rich as Carreri claimed. Soon after the arrival of the Order of Mercy, its members were given a hacienda at Colima, the Zacualpan mines, and gifts of money or land by Basques and other miners at San Luis Potosí; in a short time their estates were in operation. At San Angel, the Carmelites had one of the finest orchards in the country, planted with 13,000 trees and bringing in yearly the same number of pesos. The Brothers of St. Hippolytus established a large sugar plantation at Oaxtepec, in the Marquesado del Valle. In addition to the communities of monks, there were many Spanish, Indian, and Negro brotherhoods, which penetrated to the smallest villages, where they normally possessed revenues, droves, or fields.

Communities of nuns were particularly numerous, because their usual task was to provide an education for girls, who stayed with them until marriage. Nunneries also became the sanctuary of portionless daughters, plentiful in a country where there were frequently fifteen or twenty children to a family. Rich widows and pious donors remembered these penniless girls in their wills, leaving convents endowments, lump sums, or real estate to care for them.

Other nunneries, however, required of their novices a dowry of at least a specified sum, for example, 3,000 pesos in the Augustinian Convent of St. Lawrence in Mexico City. Yet these sisters cannot have been badly off, since their patron, Captain Juan de Chavarría—"a man of great substance," according to Guijo's diary—had showered them with favors. As a result of the practice, certain convents were to all intents and purposes reserved for high Creole society; in them, each nun had personal serving women or companions. A number of Immaculate Conception convents quartered several hundred of these servants. The cloister rule was so lenient that civil and religious authorities sometimes had to intervene and ban performances of plays and concerts, or too assiduous lay visitors. In Mexico City, the Convent of the Incarnation was richly endowed by Alvaro de Lorenzana, whose generosity seemed boundless; the convent owned haciendas as far away as New Viscaya. St. Agnes' Convent had received from Don Diego Caballero and his wife two large sugar refineries in the Marquesado, as well as estancias, houses, and the sum of 30,000 pesos. Blessed St. Joseph's founder had endowed the convent with an income of 2,000 pesos.

This last convent belonged to the Order of the Immaculate Conception. The Order's oldest convent, named after the Order, had difficulty making ends meet in the early decades of the seventeenth century; then, two captains in succession made it substantial donations. The Carmelites of St. Joseph, too, were poor in the beginning. Not until the end of the seventeenth century did another captain, Don Esteban Molina Mosquera, and his wife present them with more than 400,000 pesos. Thanks to their patrons' generosity and the marriage portion of 4,000 pesos required of entrants, they were able to build a luxurious convent and arrange for a tidy investment income.

Benefactors were motivated by both piety and emulation; considerable prestige was attached to being the hereditary patron of a convent, college, or hospital. The church of the establishment bore the founder's coat or arms; after his death, it harbored his tomb and statue. In following generations, his descendants would continue to be honored with marks of special consideration.

Hacienda administration raised problems for those possessing no business sense or particular liking for the job. Nuns' communities consequently hired bailiffs to manage their interests; but bailiffs were often neither zealous nor loyal. Not wishing to see their estates go to ruin for lack of competent attention, many convents would rather have held mortgages on haciendas belonging to others, when haciendas were good investments and well managed. Not only convents but, especially, cathedrals, churches, and brotherhoods preferred perpetual rents or annuities, which, regardless of cattle prices or the state of the harvest, brought in fixed incomes at regular intervals.

LAND RENTS OF THE REGULAR AND SECULAR CLERGY

In the sixteenth and seventeenth centuries, there were several kinds of rents (*censos*) in the Indies. First of all, there was the nominal quitrent that certain lands paid in perpetuity; arising in medieval Europe, where it had originally been linked to labor services (*corvée*) carried out on the lord's estate, it had gradually absorbed the *corvée* and become purely pecuniary. Such was the rent that the Marqués del Valle made a stipulation in all land grants in his state.

In the latter half of the seventeenth century, when the rural hacienda had taken final shape, the archaic quitrent, with the *corvée*, was suddenly revived. Big landowners gave Indians small pieces of land, or tenements, in exchange for an extremely low rent. The real and unavowed purpose was not income, but labor to work the master's enterprises.

Rents collected by the Church in the Indies were of a different sort. They represented the final stage in the five-centuries-long evolution just described. However, the revival of the archaic throwback meant that in Mexico, paradoxically, all the stages of the institution were present simultaneously.

Under the influence of a nascent capitalism, some rents, especially ecclesiastical ones, were rapidly divested of their original function and characteristics. Probably lacking cash, pious donors would place a perpetual lien on one or several of their haciendas in order to endow some church or convent. The lien usually represented the income, at 5 per cent, on a principal that was not paid the beneficiary, nor could it be claimed by him; but the principal was in his name. Many parents made these arrangements for daughters entering convents; a dowry of 3,000 to 4,000 pesos, for instance, represented an annual income of 150 to 200 pesos taken from the revenues of a rural estate or rental property. The convent, in a manner of speaking, owned stock in the undertaking.

Dr. Fernando de Villegas, Rector of the University of Mexico, decided in 1610 to found a convent for the Order of the Immaculate Conception, which his eight daughters and mother-in-law could then enter. He gave a permanent endowment of 2,000 pesos to be taken from the earnings of his twelve harvest haciendas, cattle estancias, and orchards. The endowment corresponded to a capital investment of 40,000 pesos —nearly a third of the total value of the donor's property. Subsequently, the convent (of the Blessed Virgin) had to return a large portion of the endowment to one of Villegas' sons, who had argued that his father had had no right to place such a heavy encumbrance on an entail that had been settled on him.

Some religious communities found these arrangements so convenient that they applied them to their own real estate. The operation was in that case presented as a kind of sale; the sum realized by the sale was then, partially or entirely, put back into the property to provide the source of income. Henceforth freed from management worries, the investor collected each year 5 per cent of the value of the property ceded. However, the purchaser had the option of acquiring full title to the property by reimbursing the principal, provided that the contract stipulated that the lien was redeemable. Such transactions also attracted unattached women, orphans who were minors, and everyone else who found it difficult to manage property.

There were drawbacks. Whereas incomes remained invariable, some properties increased in value, particularly as more land was brought under cultivation and prices in general followed an upward trend. On the other hand, an estate could suffer financial reverses and payments would cease; that was a frequent occurrence, owing to social and economic instability in the Indies. The Society of Jesus bought one huge hacienda, which had been completely abandoned, for a mere 500 pesos; the Poor Clares of Mexico City were supposed to be receiving income on 2,000 pesos of its capital. Payments must have been sporadic, to say the least.

For many religious communities, such rents were the favorite means of investing dowries and gifts of cash. In fact, they were the only means for those wishing to avoid estate management; interest-bearing loans were still strictly forbidden. The third Council of Mexico in 1585 fulminated against any kind of usury. The King invoked existing injunctions on several occasions, most notably in 1608, when he promulgated for Spain, and then extended to all the Indies, a decree forbidding "lending money at interest, with the exception of money invested in a profit-and-loss venture."

We may legitimately wonder what real difference there was between a 5 per cent loan and these annuities. The fact that the principal could not be called in at a given time is not a telling argument, since, if the need arose, the principal could always be recovered by selling the annuity to another investor. Landowners willing to pay an annuity in future years in exchange for spot cash were no rarity in Mexico. For example, hard-pressed heirs, often prodigal sons, whose entails tied up all their property, could have recourse to what amounted to a mortgage. The word was actually used in some deeds of trust, which made clear that such and such a sum was a "lien against said haciendas, mortgaged to provide income."

Just as a modern Frenchman would not buy a farm or rental property without a visit to the mortgage registrar of the local prefecture, would-be hacienda owners consulted the records of property liens which were kept, from 1546 on, in the Mexico City town hall, in order to be sure that they could have clear title.

Landowners other than prodigal sons had worthier motives. The Jesuits, especially, sold annuities, redeemable at their discretion, which allowed them to obtain temporary capital for improving and enlarging their estates. When a representative of the College of St. Peter and St. Paul accepted several entrance dowries from the Convent of the Incarnation, he specified that the money was restricted to "equipping the haciendas and sugar refineries of said college." The transaction thus worked to the advantage of both parties. By the middle of the seventeenth century, the convent just mentioned was the Jesuits' creditor to the sum of 45,000 pesos; many other convents had also invested in their enterprises.

Jesuit colleges were continually shuttling back and forth between paying off such obligations and contracting new ones, depending on whether they possessed idle capital or needed additional capital. Their books contain records of all their transactions of this sort, which ended by their having nothing to do with land held for rents. The word for rent (*censo*) tended to disappear with the institution. Finally, colleges often received plain deposits against which they could draw and on which they paid 5 per cent interest until the deposits were reimbursed.

By conceiving of capital investment in the modern sense of the term

—in order to improve their estates and increase the latter's efficiency—
and thanks to their metamorphosing the ancient institution of the land
rent, the Jesuits and some others circumvented and rendered inoperative the traditional prohibition against lending at interest. Churchmen
had originally been responsible for the prohibition; churchmen were
the first to awake to reality and the need for progress.

To an even greater extent than the regular orders, the secular clergy
enjoyed endowments deriving from mortgages of the sort described.
Very few of the dying neglected to add to their will a clause providing
for masses to be said for the repose of their souls. They felt that there
was no better way of pleading their case with the Almighty than a perpetual endowment. Literally thousands of these special endowments,
called *capellanías* (benefices), were placed as liens not only on rural
haciendas and estates, but on houses, stores, and factories as well.

A benefice theoretically provided the living of a cleric whose sole
obligation was to recite yearly a specified number of masses for the
dead person's soul. The endower's heir was usually the patron of the
benefice; that is, he made sure that stipulations were carried out and, if
the will had not designated a priest as beneficiary, appointed one to
serve for life.

In the sixteenth century, *capellanías* were not very large, ordinarily
representing a principal of 2,000 pesos or less, which furnished an income of some 100 pesos. When prices rose, incomes were inadequate
even to help provide a living for a cleric. Consequently, benefices became somewhat more substantial in the next century, yielding incomes
of several hundred pesos.

That was still not much. Yet many individuals were allowed to take
holy orders because they satisfied the minimum requirement of possessing a single benefice of the old type, which went on paying only 100
pesos a year for two centuries. In 1637, the Mexico City municipality
asked that no priest be ordained whose income was under 300 pesos (*la
congrua sustentación*—"the competent sustenance"). The municipality
explained that a swarm of priests had only one 100-peso benefice purchased for the same sum; the cost of living demanded an income six
times that amount, and there were probably 6,000 priests in the principal
dioceses of New Spain who could not live decently, and their numbers
should be reduced.

The number of endowed masses increased constantly, and the burden borne by landed property grew heavier and heavier; rising prices and the consequent depreciation of older liens could not keep up with the rate of growth. Since *capellanías* were perpetual and not redeemable, soon almost every hacienda was mortgaged to some degree. As early as the end of the sixteenth century, Gómez de Cervantes complained that very few of New Spain's inhabitants escaped paying tribute to the Church in the form of endowments. A little later, it was quite customary for real estate to be mortgaged up to a fourth or a third of its value. Some haciendas were sucked dry by the number and size of their rents; when they were sold, the legal owners received only the tiny portion corresponding to their equity. The real masters of the soil had turned out to be the mortgage holders, that is, primarily the Church as represented by the two branches of its clergy.

A stop had to be put to the crazy spiral sometime. There was no appropriate legislation; but, instinctively, laymen found a compensatory solution. Endowers had long preferred to bequeath *capellanías* to sons, grandsons, or relatives in the priesthood. The trend became more pronounced. In addition, since descendants—"the elder taking precedence over the younger, and a male over a female," according to the set formula—had the bestowal of the living, they tended to choose with increasing frequency a member of their own family, even one still in swaddling clothes. Therefore, the income remained within the family and supported relatives who had taken, or would eventually take, holy orders.

The descendants often went one step further. They did not consider it an insult to their forebears' memory to keep the endowment and simply pay for the prescribed number of masses. The saving was appreciable. By such devices as these, families tended to recover their expenditures.

Priests were being produced in ever larger numbers, with the result that, however much income from real estate went to the clergy, many priests had only their one benefice worth 100 to 300 pesos, inadequate even for a rural existence in the seventeenth century. The reason they persisted in taking orders was that in so devout a society the clergy enjoyed an extremely favorable civil status and incomparable prestige. On the other hand, there was scarcely any other calling open to boys with a propensity for study and speculative thought, hence the large number of bachilleres and licenciados among vicars and unattached clerics. While many monks had lost their early zeal by the seventeenth century, the moral and intellectual level of the priests seems to have improved, doubtless thanks to the excellent education the Jesuits were giving them. For clerics unwilling to accept the responsibilities of a parish and regular duties, there were still other inducements. In its request of 1637, the Mexico City municipality insinuated that a life without worries, the esteem of one's fellow men, freedom from manual labor, and a secret hankering after a state of semi-idleness were considerations not without bearing on many a Creole's decision to be ordained.

The above advantages may well have made the unattached clergy-man's lot an enviable one; they did not feed him. All those endowed with a single *capellanía* of the old type and having no personal income had to find supplementary means of eking out a living. That is why there were two or three priests among the operators of any fair-sized mining camp. Around 1641, the San Luis Potosí district alone contained, in addition to its four prebendaries, *forty-one* unattached clergymen, many of whom obviously lived off mines or farms supplying the mines with produce.

Priests preferred farming, probably because the occupation was more in keeping with their rank. The priest-farmer was one of New Spain's stock social types. Either he was rounding out the income from a *capellanía* by farming or he had been ordained "a título de patrimonio," that is, by virtue of his possessing an estate that could ensure him a living befitting his station. In the small Spanish town of Lagos, where seventy *vecinos*, mostly stockmen, had been living in 1610, we find, in 1648, not only the prebendary, but five or six unattached clerics, including two licenciados combining a *capellanía* with various fields and droves; a deacon "ordained by virtue of a *capellanía* founded by his maternal grandmother on a cattle hacienda belonging to him"; two bachilleres, of whom one was in practically the same situation as the deacon and the other was the owner of a flour mill; and a third bachiller who, though a native of Lagos, resided in Michoacán, where he possessed a *capellanía*.

In most outlying regions we find a similar state of affairs. These priests and university graduates naturally had broader horizons than the average country farmer; as a consequence, their estates were usually better managed. Travelers and geographers tell us, for example, of "an honorable, most devout clergyman" who lived on his estancias in the remote Tehuantepec region; he raised livestock with the aid of a few Negroes, and he proudly exhibited to Father Alonso Ponce [in 1588] the maize he had just harvested, whose stalks (though not cut close to the ground) were over twenty feet long.

In New Galicia, Father Arregui was, as late as 1620, the sole farmer in the warm, fertile Tepic region. In lower Michoacán, near Tamazula, the best hacienda at the end of the sixteenth century belonged to a clergyman; a big spring on his land first flowed over a milldam and then provided irrigation for large fields of wheat and vegetables and, especially, a fine orchard filled with riches: apples, pomegranates, oranges, olives, even water cress, mint, and ginger. Usually these gardens were the monks' rather than the secular clergy's specialty; they were veritable nurseries supplying European plants to the surrounding regions.

Many priest–farmers in the New World led a life similar to that of one vicar in a remote village in New Galicia, who operated a self-sufficient estate containing cattle, sheep, and poultry; he had a saddle horse and hunting dogs too, as well as his crops, and grain and maize, which he ground into flour and meal in his own small mill. As soon as Mass was over, he would doff his cassock and tend to the chores.

Vicars living this kind of life were more subject to censure than un-attached clergymen; yet many sixteenth-century prebendaries did raise cattle or even carry on trade inside their parish boundaries. Definite reforms were carried out after the Council of Trent, to judge by the reports of bishops bent on stricter observance in their dioceses. The Council's recommendations, to be sure, were adapted to the American environment; and ecclesiastical authorities continued to tolerate such activities, at least in outlying or poor regions like New Galicia.

Abuses were naturally frequent in a country whose size made supervision difficult. According to various inspectors, prebendaries misused their authority by making Indians work their lands. Vicars' wills often mention droves and slaves. The Licenciado Maldonado, holder of a parish in the Huasteca, owned at the time of drawing up his will, in 1635, many head of cattle and sheep, "twenty saddle mules, ten or twelve broken-in horses, . . . eight cedar chests equipped with locks . . . used to contain the cacao and cloth paid in tribute," a complete set of silver dishes, and horse trappings whose flaps were made of Cordovan leather. He manufactured candlewicks with the help of a few slaves. The sums that he mentioned owing, or owed to him, make us suspect that he also engaged in trade.

Near Saltillo, an ecclesiastical judge, the Bachiller Pedro de la Serda, brandishing "the mailed fist of canon law," had absorbed into his hacienda land and streams belonging to the Tlaxcalan Indians. When the latter's captain-protector came to force restitution, the bachiller had ridden up with "his harquebus slung across his saddle" and an armed Negro retainer; in a menacing tone, he forbade the captain to go any farther. It took five years and the intervention of the Bishop's official inspector in 1640 to bring the misuser of benefit of clergy around to confessing his sins and making amends. Even at that, he had to be threatened with major excommunication. He was made to pay the Indians a heavy indemnity.

At Guadalajara, canons and prebendaries owned fields and droves, mines, and various other enterprises. Their frequent absences from their posts on personal business were in violation of holy Tridentine rules, the Audiencia declared in 1606. Such conduct was exceptional, however, in the Mexico City and Puebla dioceses.

These black-frocked farmers, stockmen, and miners were a familiar sight in Creole society, as they jogged about on their mules. If they were plain bachilleres, the mules bore simple harnesses; if they were licenciados, doctors, or prebendaries, the mules were bedecked with colored trappings.

The primary source of cathedral chapters' incomes was the tithe—one-quarter to each chapter—collected in their diocese on Spaniards' droves and crops. Tithes did not amount to much during most of the sixteenth century. In the entire archbishopric of Mexico City, they represented less than 10,000 pesos around 1550; they reached only 35,000 to 40,000 at the end of the century, and some 90,000 in 1668. Because of the Puebla bishopric's agricultural resources, tithes were almost exactly double there, rising in the same period form 67,000 pesos to 200,000. In the Michoacán diocese, they approximated Mexico City's; but everywhere else they were considerably lower—even at Oaxaca and Guadalajara. The rise had lagged behind agricultural expansion, because so much land belonged to tithe-exempt religious orders.

Cathedrals supplemented tithe income with numerous land rents and some, but not much, harvest land, droves, and rental properties. The King was referring to such investments in 1643, when he requested the primate to take out *juros* (a kind of treasury bond) instead of acquiring annuities on rural estates and other private property, which were subject to risks. The King argued that the Church would further its own interests, as well as the Crown's, by advancing the Crown the money it needed. To judge by Gemelli Carreri's figures for the end of the seventeenth century, revenues from *capellanías* and land fees were large: a total of 300,000 pesos for the cathedral of Mexico City, divided between the Archbishop (60,000 pesos) and a group of fifty-two canons, dignitaries, and chaplains.

Bishops quite frequently belonged to the Spanish or Creole aristocracy and consequently had personal fortunes. Few of them, however, led the princely life of some European prelates. That does not mean that they did not have a palace corresponding to their elevated rank, with swarms of servants, pages (under the orders of a page master), confidential secretaries, and relatives, as old Spanish custom warranted. We also catch a glimpse in travelers' accounts of more unassuming bishops, devoted to their studies and spending more than their incomes on alms and good works. In 1639, His Majesty took the trouble of congratulating the Archbishop of Mexico City on his having sold his silver and books to aid the poor during a serious maize shortage. Many episcopal palaces seem to have had a special dining hall where the poor were fed and at the same time were edified with pious readings.

The Jesuits distributed alms generously; the different convents gave free meals to anyone knocking at their doors between specified hours. Orders like the Brothers of St. João de Deus and St. Hippolytus maintained numerous hospitals. Bishops' palaces were always filled with travelers and visitors; while, for village monasteries, hospitality was a sacred duty that has persisted to this day in remote pueblos. The many brotherhoods fulfilled the function of modern mutual aid societies.

A natural balance, somewhat medieval in flavor, was thus struck between what society gave the Church and what it received in return. Revenues from rich haciendas, dwellings, rents, and alms did flow into the Church's coffers; but they were returned in the form of charity, education, advancement of knowledge, and literary and artistic works. In the seventeenth century the Church's temporal power in New Spain was equaled only by its spiritual power. The marks are still visible today, in the imposing monuments, the religious fervor of so many country dwellers and Indians, and, perhaps by reaction, some Mexicans' present anticlericalism.

8.THE HACIENDA AND ITS MASTERS

In the early sixteenth century, the boundaries of the great estates were ill-defined and shifting. Estancias, mingled indiscriminately, could not impart more than usufruct rights, as distinguished from actual ownership. In the spaces between legally granted caballerías, large areas were left unoccupied. Title deeds were frequently sold several times over for prices so cheap that they clearly indicated the low value of land.

By mid-century, landowners had begun to come into contact with one another in zones that were thickly populated either because of their rich soil or their proximity to the capital. Some owners secured their estates against dismemberment by entailing them. The first properties to possess well-delineated boundaries and an easily identifiable social organization were harvest estancias (smaller than the grants for cattle or sheep) and sugar plantations located in fertile zones. They were composed of carefully measured caballerías; their labor was supplied by Negro slaves, crews of requisitioned Indian workers, or, in the north, imported resident peons. On estates specializing in livestock, however, operations were still of the extensive sort, that is, thinly spread over vast stretches that had been estimated by eye or paced off on horseback; the minimal surface area of a cattle estancia was 1,760 hectares. Grazing rights being held in common, a cattle baron could not keep his neighbors off his land. Not until the seventeenth century did a more compact kind of estate appear and property rights become better defined.

Not until then did the word *hacienda* take on its modern meaning. At the beginning, it had designated liquid assets, and was used for any sort of real or movable property. People talked of "migrating sheep haciendas"—flocks with their shepherds—as well as of "Indian haciendas," which were every native's maize patch, hut, and handful of utensils. The word was even extended to cover "mining haciendas" alongside "harvest and livestock haciendas." All these acceptations were current in the seventeenth century; but used without a modifier, the term was tending to mean, specifically, a rural estate. The reason was that haciendas, by virtue of their size, more often than not combined caballerías and livestock estancias into one estate; at the same time, their significance in the country's economic life was increasing.

The final stage in the word's evolution was not accomplished until the eighteenth century, the golden age of the hacienda. The Andalusian *cortijo* was never adopted in Mexico. Although the *cortijo* (the Roman *curtis*) and the inchoate hacienda had elements in common, the Peninsular word was too closely identified with olive groves, which were almost completely lacking in the Indies. *Estancia* and *caballería*, because of the growing popularity of *hacienda*, were gradually divested of their specific meanings and ultimately restricted to units of measurement: 1,750 hectares (cattle estancia), 780 hectares (sheep estancia), and 43 hectares (caballería). Originally, they had not only designated surface areas, but also implied varying degrees of property rights: the caballería, actual ownership of the soil (with reservation of commonage, which was fairly well observed), and the two kinds of estancias, with no more than preferential, or usufruct, rights for the grazing of one's own sheep and cattle. As a matter of fact, Spaniards often ignored the distinctions as early as the sixteenth century, exploiting their grants as they saw fit. The crux is the date at which the law sanctioned this trend toward indiscriminate use of land; for then, plain grazing rights were turned into vested property rights and stockmen passed from *de facto* to *de jure* possession of the soil.

No over-all plan had been established, it has been pointed out, for land distribution. Spaniards chose their plots at random, as Viceroy Martín Enríquez remarked, for reasons of personal convenience or unusual fertility. Between plots, large expanses were left vacant, which neighboring farmers and stockmen annexed. Nearly all holders of title deeds had moved into such surplus land (*demasías*). The most powerful had, naturally, taken the lion's share; an official surveyor in Michoacán reported as early as the first half of the seventeenth century: "Those who have a right to one [plot] are occupying six." The surplus land thus usurped was Crown property; it could be taken back and redistributed at the King's discretion. In addition, many title deeds contained irregularities arising from illegal transactions between Spaniards, grants made by municipalities, or Indian purchases not authorized by competent authority; as to royal confirmation of viceregal grants, very few deeds bore proof of having satisfied that requirement.

From a juridical point of view, most of the country was being occupied unlawfully. The King would have to act eventually, if only to acknowledge an accomplished fact. Once he had made his decision, there was no lack of jurists or attorneys, in the unwieldy bureaucracy governing New Spain, to carry it out.

Farmers and stockmen, however, were less concerned with these technicalities than with another, more pressing problem. Since the end of the sixteenth century, the state had been progressively reducing Indian communities' labor services. Landowners were wondering how to replace them. Negro slaves were expensive and insufficient in number. Silvio Zavala has studied the solution that landowners hit upon: serfdom through debts. When this institution was fully developed, each estate's complement of *gañanes*, or peons, constituted a capital asset.

CONSOLIDATION OF THE GREAT ESTATES: SETTLEMENTS OF TITLE

At the end of the sixteenth century, the Spanish monarchy was beset with serious financial difficulties. Though already hard-pressed by his creditors, Philip II had ventured upon an ambitious European policy which required a constant search for new sources of revenue. In Mexico he increased taxes, created new ones, gave greater impetus to the sale of public offices, and sharply raised the price of mercury—eventually causing mining production to fall off. Land settlements were one of the expedients designed to fill his coffers. Royal legists argued that, since unoccupied expanses were Crown property, His Majesty could sell new grants, as well as land held illegally.

The King wasted no time; in 1581, he asked his Viceroy whether it would not be possible to sell or lease *dehesas*, pastures reserved for the exclusive use of the holders; he also inquired whether a special tax might not be levied on every farmer and stockman in the country. A halfhearted attempt at compliance during the Villamanrique regime having ended in failure, the next Viceroy, Luis de Velasco, advised against the project on the grounds that it would force meat prices up, meat being the only cheap commodity in the New World. The King evidently took no heed, since two extremely important royal cédulas, in 1591, laid down the principles of settlement fees.

In his first cédula, the King recalled that he was master of all the land in the Indies; although it had been his pleasure to make grants to both Spaniards and Indians, certain individuals either had usurped many parcels or were holding them under false pretenses, "with spurious or invalid title deeds that have been issued by unauthorized agents." Consequently, he was ordering universal restitution of land seized illegally. Indians should be left the amount necessary for their subsistence.

In his second cédula, His Majesty made provision for a general amnesty—at a price. Instead of "punishing" his vassals and confiscating their property, he would be satisfied with a "convenient settlement," which would be used to launch a mighty Indies fleet capable of protecting the coasts and merchant shipping against pirates. Then, the Viceroy, after setting aside a generous share of land for Indians and town commons, could "confirm [all the rest] and issue new title deeds" on behalf of irregular land holders. Those whose title deeds were already in order could obtain "such clauses and guarantees as they saw fit to request." Fees would henceforth be charged for distribution of unoccupied lands. As for the die-hards who refused to pay a fair settlement, the royal treasury would confiscate all their lands not adequately covered by title deeds.

Weighty principles were involved. In exchange for a handful of pesos to be thrown into the bottomless pit of military expenditures, the Crown seemed to be deliberately running the risk of sanctioning land grabbing, officially recognizing pasture appropriation, and putting the final seal of approval on large estates. The Crown was apparently willing to sell its inheritance for a mess of pottage. However, Spaniards in the Indies were not so farsighted. For them the law meant only one thing: at a time when land was almost worthless and income from farms and livestock was exiguous, they had to pay a new tax. They resisted, not actively, but with the force of inertia.

They were successful up to a point. At least, Viceroy Velasco, in hopes of deferring execution as long as possible, protested to the King on several occasions that it was practically impossible to collect settlements on any scale:

> *Most of those holding land without legitimate title deeds are so poor and wretched that they have never known any other kind of life than the one into which necessity has forced them; all their worldly goods consist of a plot or two purchased from Indians or acquired without title, on which they have knocked together their humble dwellings and which they work with the help of an Indian from some repartimiento or other. To take away their land (there is no question of their being able to make a settlement) would be tantamount to depriving them of their livelihood.*

Velasco's recommendation was to limit settlement fees to the rich and those who would request confirmation of their own volition. If absolutely necessary, and in spite of the general poverty of the country, he concluded, the administration could manage to squeeze an amount equivalent to the settlement tax from new land grants (1592).

The Viceroy soon afterward had difficulties of another order to report. First, many of the surveys for detecting encroachments were going to cost more than the land was worth. Second, many illegal holdings had passed through three or four hands; appraisal of the holdings and defense of Indian claims filed against them would overload the Audiencia's judges, prosecutor, and Indian protector with litigation. The government in Spain, however, found an answer for both objections (and many others besides). The Council of the Indies remained optimistic and urgently recommended that as large a sum as possible should be obtained "through adroit, gentle treatment."

The time was not ripe for wholesale operations. With Velasco, settlements were the exception rather than the rule. At most, he occasionally added to new title deeds a clause warning grantees that they would eventually have to pay a sum whose total was not stipulated. Nevertheless, in this matter, as in a few others, the state exhibited remarkable tenacity. It had finally succeeded in abolishing almost all the labor services condemned by the theologians; after fifty years of dogged effort, it also collected its settlements. The Council of the Indies never let the question drop. The slow, steady progress, in the seventeenth century, toward implementation of the 1591 cédulas offers a curious example of the qualities and defects of Spanish bureaucracy, which, for all its clumsiness, did command obedience.

Constantly goaded by instructions from the King, Viceroy Monterrey decided in 1601 not to grant Spaniards any more land unless they tendered in exchange a promissory note for one-fourth of the land's value. The administration was able to credit itself, on paper, with small sums like 12, 30, or 50 pesos. Two years later, the total having reached 15,000 to 18,000 pesos, officials proceeded to collect. Then, in 1606–1607, the first new grants to be settled for spot cash appeared; they were for either hospitals and convents (theoretically ineligible) or irregular Indian purchases and usurped expanses (*sobras* and *demasías, malos títulos*). Twenty-five years after the tax's proclamation, the only income—a meager one—that it had yet furnished the treasury came from these settlements paid on new land grants as a preventive measure. Furthermore, the tax was not collected consistently; grants made by the New Galicia Audiencia do not appear to have been taxed otherwise than sporadically. (A precedent had been established in 1605, however, whereby grantees would pay a third, a half, or the whole of the real value in order to create a public works fund for Guadalajara.)

The Council of the Indies was steadfast in its resolve to develop the new source of revenue. A royal cédula of 1615, confirmed the following year over the Viceroy's objections, did not beat about the bush; it ordered all new grants to be sold at public auction and constrained the successful bidders to have their title deeds confirmed by the King within a three-year period. No attempt was made at this time to conceal the tax behind a settlement fee which had not worked to advantage. Besides, the necessity of having to obtain confirmation from Madrid—

extremely difficult in practice—left the door open to future settlement fees. The Viceroy, in carrying out the order, found himself faced with so much opposition that he had to mitigate its severity and make exceptions; feeling ran high in a country where, as Viceroy the Marqués de Guadalcázar explained to the King, grants had traditionally been made without charge in order to reward services or colonize danger zones. A few capitalists did put the auctions to good use, acquiring enormous amounts of land in one or several operations: 12, 16, or 24 estancias and 30 caballerías, chiefly in the Huasteca.

In 1629, the Crown issued orders for a vast undertaking; on its completion two years later, it had brought in 112,000 pesos. It consisted of auctioning off 650 caballerías in the most fertile zones—fields suitable for sugar cane or wheat at Cuautla, Atlixco, Oaxaca, and Toluca—and 30 estancias in the heart of the sheep-raising region of Querétaro. They must have been idle land (*demasías*) or expanses confiscated from Spaniards, since presumably none of the areas mentioned had had any unoccupied space for a long time.

As a parallel measure, authorities urged farmers and stockmen to request confirmation of their title deeds (nearly always inadequate or irregular). From 1613 or 1618 on, after the 1591 decrees had been repeatedly proclaimed in town squares, a few individuals began to offer larger sums than before for official recognition of their rights to estates ordinarily constituted by purchases from natives. However, these were still voluntary contributions, and they were not very numerous.

In 1631, the King's orders grew more specific: Spaniards having usurped lands could retain them by paying a moderate fee in compensation; otherwise, all such lands would be sold at auction. Mexico City authorities were still applying delaying tactics. The slowness of the mails and the red tape resulted in an interval of at least two years between a viceroy's remonstrances and Madrid's urgent confirmation of instructions issued. In 1636, two new cédulas reaffirmed those of 1591 and urged the Viceroy to proceed without further demur to collect settlements for constructing the mighty fleet, which still existed only on paper.

Public opinion was now prepared to accept the measure; and the Viceroy could no longer elude his sovereign's orders. They were implemented chiefly during the Count of Salvatierra's term of office (1642–1648), more than a half-century after the first cédulas had been issued. Having begun in 1638 under Viceroy Cadereyta, collections reached their peak between 1642 and 1645. However, they were not completed until long afterward: for New Spain, not until 1675–1676, and for New Galicia, not until 1697–1698, following another cédula in 1692. Remote provinces like New Viscaya, still sparsely settled and under attack from the nomads, were to "settle with His Majesty" slightly later. By the end of the century, haciendas seem to have been in possession of their final title deeds throughout most of the country.

Enforcement did encounter a lively resistance in some quarters, particularly in Spanish farming communities. They were poor and had little to gain, since, in regions like the Bajío, there had been few irregular purchases made from Indians. As the argument of Celaya's public attorney ran in 1643, the allotments distributed to the town's inhabitants had been uncleared land.

> *What value they have now is solely the result of farmers' skill and perseverance, for the land was certainly not worth much originally; in the early days, an allotment [vecindad] comprising 2½ caballerías could be bought for 50 or 60 pesos. If some areas within the town district are still undistributed or some title deeds are defective, the land, nevertheless, belongs by right to the town, which was granted full title to its four leagues, with no restrictions whatsoever.*

The farmers of the fertile Atlixco Valley, near Puebla, a quite different region, had unlawfully occupied neither land nor free space, since they had kept a jealous eye on one another. They protested that the King's project could be justified only "in regions where the land's cheapness had induced hacienda owners to annex uncleared fields and Crown territory."

Both communities' arguments were sound ones. Each, notwithstanding, had to pay a settlement of 20,000 pesos, plus costs—which were not low—these in addition to the individual fees paid by a few big landowners in the district. They were compelled to settle, owing to a convenient arrangement of the King's which caused the vacillating to make up their minds in a hurry; a royal commission (or sometimes a single commissioner) of "justice officials charged with land and water surveys" would be dispatched to a town. The commission would perform its functions with the usual pomp and ceremony—at the town's expense, of course. On the one hand, citizens were normally not very eager to have their titles searched, and on the other, they could count on having to pay out several thousand pesos in surveying costs before there was any question of settlement fees. Celaya learned that fact to its sorrow; after handing over 6,000 pesos to two surveyors, it decided to cut its losses—"fruitless expense"—and settle with the royal treasury at once.

The measure was a success in the administration's opinion; as a result, impending visits by royal commissions were widely publicized. It was a kind of blackmail, since a survey was never completed anywhere. Both hacienda owners and townships preferred to pay immediately fees arbitrarily assessed in exchange for final title to their land—whose manner of acquisition usually did not brook investigation anyway. Pseudo-surveys were first instituted in the richest, most densely populated zones: around the capital (Tacuba, Chalco, Tlalnepantla, and so on) and Puebla and Atlixco, particularly Tepeaca, where farmers, having bought a considerable amount of Indian land, paid out no less than 30,000 pesos. Then, the surveying teams swept on in one direction to the Bajío and in the other to cane-growing regions in Michoacán and the Marquesado del Valle (after the 1628 decision had confirmed the Crown's rights to all its unoccupied areas). Next, stockmen on the Atlantic slopes as far north as Huasteca, including Valles and Pánuco, were instructed to pay the tax, as well as those dwelling on the San Luis Potosí plains. Finally came the turn of the scattered inhabitants of the Pacific Coast—Colima paid only 600 pesos. In the north, even the far-off enclave of Nombre de Dios had to settle accounts with the treasury, while New Galicia, with mines idle and business at a standstill, was thoroughly ransacked and forced to contribute some 40,000 pesos.

The biggest landowners, especially those with interests in more than one region, made individual settlements. They comprised captains, rich farmers, justice officials, magistrates, merchants, encomenderos, and canons. For example, the lump sum of 1,500 pesos that the King and town authorities had agreed upon for Santiago de los Valles, in Huasteca, covered only fifteen *vecinos* (most of them poor residents probably); eight cattle barons paid personally much larger amounts to have their holdings in this huge district confirmed. One of them was Villaseca's heir; a second was alcalde mayor in Querétaro; and others were hacienda owners from the latter town, including Doña María de Castro y Betancourt, a widow who, although not the richest of the lot, possessed twenty-seven estancias in four valleys, named respectively Maize Valley, Valley of France, Valley of the Wolves, and Valley of the Parrots.

Settlements revealed the large estates' predominance all over the country. A case in point is Izúcar (Matamoros), south of Puebla and Atlixco in a region differing greatly from Huasteca. It paid the treasury 12,000 pesos; the same year, large haciendas and plantations situated within its limits, along the Atoyac River, were individually assessed sums totaling five or six times that amount. They were given, however, twelve years in which to pay, instead of the customary two installments.

Private landowners had to pay for more than land rights, as conditions in the region just mentioned will show. Water rights were even more closely scrutinized and taxed accordingly, particularly since a few individuals, both laymen and ecclesiastics, had often cornered them all. When the natives of the region and their attorney in the Audiencia protested, the Audiencia alleviated injustices somewhat by returning slightly more than half of the water rights to the communities robbed; the rest was divided among the haciendas and refineries. The biggest of the refineries received the large volume of "twelve units [*surcos*], which it needs," the Audiencia decision stated, "because of the unusual size of its water wheels and factory, its abundant production, numerous cane fields, considerable equipment, and irrigation requirements." When the time for settlements came, however, the refinery owner, Alonso de Toro, had to pay the King 18,000 pesos—1,500 per *surco*—in order to acquire his permanent rights.

Religious orders, too, made individual settlements for their estates, which were already huge. Title deeds issued in the King's name gave legal sanction to this real estate, which had been merely tolerated before, but was now declared to be untransferable and indivisible—even before the lawsuit of the Council of the Indies prosecutor contesting the Church's right to own property had been brought to a verdict. Only a few title deeds referred to the lawsuit and hesitantly stated that their validity would depend on its outcome. In 1644, many individuals and communities—dignitaries and plain clerics, Jesuit colleges, Dominican provinces, Augustinians, and Poor Clares—paid their money and obtained their confirmations.

The Order of St. Dominic was authorized to hand over 4,685 pesos for estates in two of its provinces, including 1,185 for the Coahuixtla sugar plantation, founded partly on land that the Indians of Anenecuilco (near Cuautla–Oaxtepec, in the Marquesado del Valle) had donated around 1580. This little hamlet's *calpullis* were soon to be invaded, from the north and east by the Coahuixtla plantation and, from the west, by an hacienda belonging to the Brothers of St. Hippolytus' Hospital in Mexico City. In 1643, the last mentioned had paid a huge settlement of 6,500 pesos for this one hacienda alone. The two plantation sites are today the hamlets of La Hospitalidad and Coahuixtla. The Jesuits, too, had acquired a plantation in this rich region. Although they declared that they had enjoyed their water rights "from time immemorial," in 1643 it cost them 3,500 pesos to keep their considerable volume of 10 *surcos*, and 700 pesos more to retain possession of lands "settled for with the community of Amilpas" (Cuautla).

Throughout the Cuernavaca–Cuautla region (the most important sugar-producing center in all Mexico), owners settled with the King for sums ranging from 800 to 4,000 pesos and upward. They had either bought their lands from the Indians or leased them from the Marqués del Valle; the indispensable water for their machinery and cane fields (which required irrigation) they had simply taken. In other words, there is little doubt that their title deeds were not in order. Frequently, as we have just seen, water rights were returned to natives at the same time an estate's title deeds were confirmed.

It is clear that the Viceroy did not confer definitive possession for a certain sum with his eyes shut. Either the local justice official's opinion was sought or a special inspector, often a member of the Audiencia, was commissioned to investigate the case. If Indians registered a complaint, their special attorney, too, was brought in. Unfortunately, natives did not always understand the exceptional importance of the proceeding, in the sense that it would make spoliations and other abuses irrevocable. It was generally quite easy to pull the wool over their eyes; their "natural fecklessness," in the words of one inspector, did the rest. Besides, it was physically impossible for the Viceroy and his most trusted officials, however well-intentioned, to examine closely the hundreds of files reaching their desks at the same time. As a result, injustices were committed. What was really serious was that injustices no longer arose from the law's ignorance of *de facto* situations; the law, owing to the peculiar, definitive nature of settlements, itself was sanctioning injustices. In a country governed by jurists, this was a commitment pledging the word of future generations.

Typical results could be observed in the native community of Huatusco, near Orizaba on the warm Atlantic slope. By paying a settlement of only 200 pesos, the heiress to eight sheep estancias, not contiguous, but all in the community's district, spared herself, in 1643, a visit from the royal surveyor. In future litigation with the Indians, her receipt was to serve as justification for having occupied all the intervening spaces (*sobras*) as well, and hence nearly the entire district. The Indians were eventually reduced to their legal 600 varas measured from their church tower.

Many other thefts, whose effects could still be observed at a fairly recent date, seem to have been made legal by the settlements. In any event, immediate advantages and future possibilities far outweighed, for contemporaries, an occasional amputation of native property. A divergent view would be surprising, when the Crown was demanding a maximum yield from the tax and its native policy had other goals in mind, particularly the abolition of repartimientos. There was, as yet, no clear picture of the eviction threatening the Indians. Besides, there may well have been a correlation between the gradual reduction of requisitioned labor and the encroachment on native lands; landowners had quickly realized that the best way to obtain "free" (in a qualified sense) workers was to deprive communities of their fields. Not possessing our hindsight, contemporaries did not come to realize the pressure that the great estates' new legal status could exert on native communities until trade had picked up, population had increased, and more land had been brought under cultivation.

Title confirmations exchanged for settlement fees thus covered a multitude of sins. They not only wiped out irregularities of all sorts, but completed original grants with new, explicit concessions. We may judge by the experience of eight Jesuit colleges in New Spain; for the modest sum of 7,000 pesos, they received from the Viceroy, in His Majesty's name, blanket approval and confirmation of

> *all title deeds proceeding from sales, purchases, grants, or donations which their said haciendas, lands, sugar plantations and refineries* (trapiches), *watercourses, houses, . . . [and] pastures may possess; any and all defects and irregularities that may affect said deeds and purchases are made good by these presents, which grant anew said possessions, including parcels held in excess of title and other surplus lands.*

Similar formulas were used for other farmers and stockmen. The following frequent abuses were all forgiven: irregular acquisitions from Indians (except in cases where complaints had been filed or injustices were flagrant); purchases of title deeds before the end of the four-year period dating from issuance; unauthorized grants by municipalities (even to nonresidents); and the use of harvest caballerías for grazing lands, or vice versa.

Settlements were also the means whereby hacendados could legally appropriate half the unoccupied lands between them and their nearest neighbors. However, early settlements were less important in this respect than a new series imposed in the second half of the seventeenth century, when excess lands were settled for on a massive scale, the authorities having threatened to sell at auction all portions of estates held without specific title. In 1697, the Rincón de Gallardo family legalized the equivalent of eighty-seven estancias on their immense Ciénaga de Mata hacienda.

The new privileges were more extensive yet. Settlement fees gave formal title to all the springs on estancias, as well as the right to enclose woods and pastures. The Jesuit college at Pátzcuaro owned an enclosed estate consisting of two estancias and four caballerías. They claimed that they had previously received permission to establish an enclosure; and in any event, their having already walled in 3,600 hectares became perfectly legal after their settlement in 1645. The same year, Don Agustín Rincón de Gallardo was granted the right to seed his grazing lands, establish water catchments and irrigation ditches, and raise either sheep or cattle as he wished. In the same manner, a New Galicia landowner was given permission in 1697 "to sow in whatever parts of said estancias he will, whatever grain he will, without any limitations."

Such clauses, current in title deeds exchanged for legal settlements, imply a thorough transformation of land rights, that is, the progressive disappearance of the old restrictions, especially the three categories of grants, henceforth interchangeable at owners' discretion. Caballerías and the two types of estancias were emptied of all meaning except surface measurement. To be absolutely certain, of course, we should have to see how jurists interpreted the new regulations in eighteenth-century lawsuits. Nevertheless, the regulations are couched in precise terms in post-settlement title deeds, and we may safely assume therefore that true property rights had taken the place of the original usufruct rights, as the latter had been exemplified in the early estancia grants. The old notion of grazing lands held in common had vanished without a trace. Both legally and actually, the great estates had assumed their final appearance. Far to the north, Anglo-Saxon stockmen, too, owned great droves; but, generally speaking, their never having obtained the same rights as their Mexican counterparts meant that ultimately they would be driven out by farmers and settlers.

Financially, settlement fees, as one manifestation of a cumbersome fiscal system, had different consequences, fortunately not so lasting. Except possibly in the capital city, minted silver was scarce. The "great shortage of reals" was a frequent complaint, even in mining districts, where many outfits were heavily mortgaged—a paradoxical situation for a country that was flooding Europe with precious metals. Owing to inadequate markets and the great distances separating southern and northern zones, as well as the unsafe roads, most estate owners were land-poor. Their lack of money shows up in the trifling sums they could afford to pay the King, unless they happened to possess a large sugar plantation or particularly well-located farming haciendas. As it was, title settlements drained a good part of rural Mexico of badly needed capital. Following a report from the prosecutor for New Galicia, the King acknowledged in 1647 that "farmers' cash reserves are so depleted that, to the great dissatisfaction of my vassals, trade in that city [Guadalajara], as well as in Zacatecas and other towns, has been halved."

The settlement tax could not have been levied at a more unfavorable time; droves had shrunk and the mines' decline had brought business practically to a halt. Except for a few influential individuals and rich convents or monasteries, the country definitely seems to have been impoverished by the measure. The hardest hit were modest farmers in Creole communities and even more modest white or mestizo free lances, who had struck out on their own and were trying, with the help of one or two Indians, to make a living off small parcels of land purchased irregularly. As Velasco I had foreseen, some of their ranchos (the word was already in use) were confiscated for taxes and sold at auction. The deterioration of some entails and landed estates in the second half of the century is in all likelihood also attributable to settlements, since so many seemingly thriving haciendas were already mortgaged to the hilt for perpetual rents and endowed masses; settlements were calculated on the basis of an estate's full value. The advantages accruing from the new title deeds were not of a kind that would bring about an immediate increase in revenues. Here, too, some real estate was confiscated and some incomes were attached.

Although at times big landowners found themselves in a precarious position, their estates remained nevertheless essentially intact, chiefly because liens for endowments or entailing precluded division or transfer of title. Money was raised by increasingly frequent marriages between rural aristocrats and rich merchants' progeny.

To sum up: The settlement tax constitutes one of the most important events in the seventeenth century. Its consequences were far-reaching. The country was impoverished, to be sure; but at the same time, the great estates attained their definitive boundaries and were ensured continuing, even heightened, predominance. The new title deeds were like a Magna Charta for the rural hacienda; its status had been strengthened and its territory considerably enlarged.

STABILIZATION OF WORK SYSTEMS: DEBT PEONAGE

The great estates' physical coming of age, in the course of the seventeenth century, was accompanied by a corresponding evolution in their social structure, which was also consolidated in that century. For early hacienda owners, labor supply was a much more vital question than land rights, since the Crown was persistently cutting down, and even trying to abolish entirely, native communities' work services. Estates could not continue to exist without hands. Except for expensive

Negro slaves, the only available source was free Indians; but they had to be induced, first, to come to work and, second, to stay fixed. Owners hit upon a solution that was unique, but whose origins differed greatly according to each region's peculiar geographical conditions and human environment.

In the vast, sparsely populated northern provinces, inconsistencies were rife. The classical hacienda, with its theoretically free workers, appeared there much earlier than in the south; yet alongside, estates were to be found harking back to the most primitive times in New Spain. Near the New León border, for example, citizens of Saltillo settled on their estates—probably not for long—groups of nomads (Huachichiles, Rayados, and Nacahuans) whom the Governor had entrusted to them. The groups were officially designated as encomiendas; in exchange for a specified tribute, the citizens were to teach them "everything concerning our holy Catholic faith." One Juan Navarro placed a few of them on his harvest hacienda. As early as 1591, consequently, Saltillo farmers had more labor than they needed and could raise a large amount of wheat for sale to Zacatecas and other mines. Nomads made poor workers, however, and often attempted to escape. In any event, their numbers did not increase.

Spaniards also tried to recruit workers in the Tlaxcalan colonies that Velasco II had founded in the north. That was probably the reason why some owners established haciendas in close proximity to the colonies; one of Urdiñola's estates, Mota said, was situated "so near the village of Parras that it seemed to form a part of it." The Tlaxcalans, however, had been granted special privileges of which they were very jealous. Spaniards had to handle them with tact, for their help was needed to ward off nomad attacks. Not only did they supply little labor, but at least one of their towns, Santiago, was a haven for workers fleeing Spanish farms. To the northwest, especially in the better-watered San Bartolomé region, repartimientos of Concho Indians survived for a long time; twice a year, at sowing and at harvest time, they would come to work on the haciendas. Spanish farmers supplemented them with free Indians, usually about ten to an estate, who lived on the estate and were paid a monthly salary of four pesos.

For want of sedentary Indians, labor was harder to find along the boundaries of New Galicia and in the San Luis Potosí area. In the west, on the large Valparaíso hacienda, "a few wild Indians come down from the sierra of Tepic to hire themselves out" (probably not of their own free will). Farther eastward, haciendas were located in dangerous frontier zones or hundreds of kilometers inside nomad territory; there, it was practically impossible to find repartimientos, except occasionally for building projects. In the agricultural region of Nombre de Dios, for instance, the authorities wrote in a 1608 geographical survey: "There are neither repartimientos nor encomenderos, because the Indians do not pay any tribute. As this is a war zone and we need the Indians' services, we deemed it more prudent to continue to treat them well." Such services were remunerated at the rate of five or six pesos a month; Spaniards received three or four hundred a year.

In the early seventeenth century, the five or six middling estancias in the Zacatecas district (semi-arid and approximately five leagues wide) were employing some 200 Spaniards, Negroes, and Indians. The Indians were "serving voluntarily and earning 50 to 60 pesos a year." They were restless and wandered from jobs in the mines to jobs in the fields or on the range. They were mostly Mexicans and Tarascans, with some Indians from Juchipila in addition; that is, all were imported from the south. A few big haciendas had succeeded in pinning down a sizable number of their workers (especially by letting them run up debts), with the result that the *hacienda de gran población*, or classical hacienda with resident peons, came into existence earlier than in the south. Around church and manor, a "swarm of free Indians" were housed, together with mulattoes and slaves (particularly in the Durango region).

The different work systems that had permitted colonization of the north gradually resolved themselves into one. The seminomads in New León disappeared in the course of the seventeenth century. Acting on orders from Madrid, the Guadalajara Audiencia in 1671 abolished repartimientos and obligatory labor services for the natives of the western sierra. There thus emerged from local divergences a single system in which workers who were theoretically free, but were actually in a kind of debtors' prison, furnished the labor necessary for hacienda operations.

In those coastal areas, which were torrid, remote, or unsafe, and in which white settlers were consequently scarce, land had been distributed in unusually large blocks—generally later than on the central plateaus. There the native population seems to have shrunk more than elsewhere. Repartimientos were naturally smaller, perhaps also because tribes were smaller at the outset. With the exception of a few sugar and cacao plantations, the areas contained only vast cattle and sheep ranches utilizing for the most part Negro slaves, plus some free mestizos or mulattoes. The hacienda long remained rudimentary in these areas, though it ultimately reached the same stage of evolution as in the rest of the country.

The central plateau region is the most suitable one for observing the transition from the harvest estancia, run with repartimientos or work crews from native villages, to the classical hacienda with its resident peons under the master's authority and protection.

On central Mexico's temperate plateaus and in its warm valleys, several types of rural enterprises were to be encountered at the turn of the seventeenth century: harvest estancias (*de pan llevar*), limited in surface area and restricted to a few rich, densely populated regions like Atlixco; mixed estates, much larger and less localized, on which crops were subordinate, in varying degrees, to livestock; and, finally, sugar refineries with their annexes, cane and maize fields, droves, and woods. The latter, in the very first years of the century, were reduced to using Negro labor, with a sprinkling of free Indians; their special repartimientos had just been abolished. On the other kinds of estates, the disappearance of village work crews was more gradual. However, thanks to the combined efforts of the Crown and the theologians over a period of fifty years, all repartimientos for farmers, too, were suppressed in 1633. The goal of complete freedom for Indian workers seemed to be in sight, as the Viceroy progressively cut down native communities' obligations. Then, to compensate for the sudden dearth of labor, a curious phenomenon [debt peonage] developed, which the authorities could not or would not stop in time.

Immediately after the Spaniards' arrival, the words *naborío* and *laborío* had come into use. They had quickly become synonyms for *gañán*, or the native worker who, in contradistinction to the repartimiento, or requisitioned, worker, voluntarily hired himself out. *Gañanes* had usually settled on the Spaniards' estates. A conflict had then arisen between native communities and employers, who had not been willing to let free workers return to their villages when their turn came to serve on repartimientos. By the close of the sixteenth century, *gañanes* had become quite numerous around Mexico City and Puebla; local farmers were using them to supplement workers furnished by repartimiento judges. In 1584, Spaniards in Tepotzotlán, Cuautitlán, and elsewhere had asserted that they could not get along without the free workers, whose "main job," they said, "is to sow, cultivate, and harvest crops." The viceregal administration had understandably been glad to foster their employment.

By the end of the sixteenth century, however, the Franciscan Jerónimo de Mendieta pointed out that the system had taken a disquieting turn. Farmers who treated their workers well had "twenty, forty, even sixty or eighty, perhaps more." The fact that they treated them well did not prevent the farmers from considering their workers as personal property and denying them permission to leave at will. Mendieta had been Indian trustee for the monastery at Tepeaca, in a region colonized by Spanish farmers. In connection with his work there, he said an Indian came up to him one day and stated that, after having served voluntarily on an estate recently sold, he had wished to return home to cultivate his own plot of ground. He owed money to neither the former master nor the new one; but an agent of the latter was trying to force him to accept an advance that would place him under obligation to continue to work on the estate.

"Father," the Indian said, "help me; I do not want to remain a prisoner there!"

The Franciscan sent for the agent, a Portuguese, and inquired whether the Indian owed him or his employer money. The man said no, but that the Indian, inasmuch as he was a laborer on the estate, owed the estate his services.

"On what grounds and by virtue of what obligation?"

"Because the old owner sold him along with a certain number of other laborers. And besides [in reply to another question], it is the custom for all owners of haciendas, workshops, estancias, and droves to sell their workers along with their establishments."

"What? Are these Indian laborers and servants free, or are they slaves?"

"Small matter. They belong to the hacienda and must serve on it. This Indian is my master's property."

The agent would not listen to any other argument. Thanks to Fray Jerónimo, the laborer was liberated by the local magistrate. Without his intervention, Fray Jerónimo concluded, the Indian would very likely have been sent back to the hacienda "like a stray cur to his master." That the Spanish farmer would take the case to court indicates that the custom had sufficiently taken root for him to believe that he was in the right.

In 1601, and again in 1609, the King formally prohibited mention of Indians in documents concerning sales or donations of lands, haciendas, or any other enterprises where Indians might be working; their status of freemen, he declared, protected them for detention against their will. Mentions did become more discreet; but the practice of selling them along with property continued nonetheless, as bills of sale frequently show. At Tepeaca again, a small hacienda comprising fewer than six caballerías was sold in 1614. At the same time were sold: "the right to the Indians who may have fled" and—listed between "brood mares" and "plows"—"sixteen Indian laborers, plus three females, together with the debts they may have contracted." Throughout the seventeenth century, bills of sale refer again and again to *naboríos*, *laboríos*, and *gañanes*, "who have received money to [make them] serve." Effective opposition was extremely difficult, because this illegal serfdom was a spontaneous reaction on the part of farmers to the steady drying up of their sources of labor. Besides, settlers were naturally inclined to take advantage of their Indian workers' trusting docility; the latter were too often ignorant of their rights, as well as of the measures enacted in their behalf. These poor wretches were offered money, which they took and spent at once; as they could never pay it back, they were bound to the soil by their debts. Some masters, when the occasion arose, went so far as to refuse to be reimbursed.

As early as 1560, Viceroy Velasco prohibited advance payments for work, merchandise, or anything else, in order to prevent such payments from being used to justify forcible detention of Indians or "giving them away as chattels." Many similar orders were published in the years following (for example, in 1561 and 1566). In 1589, even that fundamental institution, the initial payment designed to attract new natives to estates, was restricted to one peso; the maximum was raised to six pesos in 1600. Loans were, however, too ingrained and widespread a practice for hacienda owners not to find ways of circumventing laws that aimed at their abolition; the debt system went on expanding. It was first perfected in weaving mills (*obrajes*), which were usually small rural factories with their own pastures and flocks of sheep. As early as 1590, *obrajes* possessed the prototype of the famous *tienda de raya* (commissary store) that would subsequently appear on haciendas; there, as Viceroy Villamanrique wrote his successor the same year, Indians could buy on credit "shoes, hats, stockings, and other objects at exorbitant prices; as a result, they never get out of debt and die like prisoners after spending twenty years or more in one weaving mill."

An inspector would occasionally impose fines and reforms; for example, Dr. Santiago de Riego, in 1596–1597, ordered debts outstanding in various textile mills uniformly reduced, the largest to 24 pesos and less serious ones to 2 to 6 pesos. However, as soon as the august visitors had turned their backs, affairs reverted to their former state. Authorities in Spain finally grew alarmed, particularly since Mexican fabrics were beginning to outsell Spanish ones in the Indies. At the turn of the century, crippling measures were taken against the textile industry, which never fully recovered. The measures did not affect the debt system's progress on rural haciendas.

In 1609, the Crown mounted a new and vigorous offensive against it. Once again, all advance payments for the purpose of detaining Indians were forbidden on the pretext of the Indians' permanent minority. Then, in a series of specific orders the viceroys attempted to eradicate the practice, which, by this time, had become current among farmers and stockmen. In particular, any detention on the pretext that workers owed money was henceforth declared illegal. However, legislation was powerless in the face of landowners' determination to compensate for the elimination of personal services—to say nothing of the Indians' timidity and credulousness. Opposition was forthcoming from some nongovernmental quarters; encomenderos and native communities looked with disfavor upon the emptying of the villages for the haciendas' benefit, since they found it difficult to collect tributes and community fees from their Indians who were living on the haciendas. Conflicts frequently arose. Yet hacienda owners quickly awoke to the benefits that they could derive from making to the royal treasury or encomenderos an advance payment on the tribute owed by laborers on their estates. They thus turned the tables on the King, using His Majesty's financial interests as a tool against his liberal Indian policies and neatly outflanking his prohibition of advance payments. Each individual's tribute, of course, represented only a small sum; but it was enough to keep an improvident laborer momentarily in debt to his master and, indirectly, to the Crown, since in all villages under the Crown's jurisdiction (rather than encomenderos'), the individual native was, in the royal treasurer's eyes, a taxpayer. Between 1630 and 1650, the viceroys authorized Spaniards to detain for four months workers who could not pay them back their tribute.

When repartimientos were finally suppressed altogether, labor became so scarce and so valuable that authorities were frequently obliged to take stern measures against owners who had lured *gañanes* to their estates from neighboring estates by promising or advancing them more money. Measures like these made the authorities run the risk of unduly hampering the Indians' right to circulate freely. From the point of view of native emancipation, however, such restrictions, which circumstances had necessitated, were trifling in comparison with the vast strides forward accomplished since the beginning of the century. The perseverance of two viceroys in succession, Cerralvo (1624–1635) and Cadereyta (1635–1640), had resulted in the extirpation of many abuses, ensuring for the Indians a much greater degree of self-determination and, to use the phrase current in a large number of specific orders, the "protection of native liberties." During this period, the Tribunal for Indian Affairs (*Juzgado General de Indios*) invariably vindicated Indians who wanted to change masters or jobs, provided that they paid the year's tribute in their villages. The Christian principle of the unrestricted right to work was applied to a greater extent than ever before, perhaps to the maximum compatible with the environment. The sovereign, as well as high officials, wrestled with their consciences in order to be sure that they were treating the natives fairly. There is something moving in such marginal annotations to cédulas as this one:

> It is my will and desire that you shall give me satisfaction, in my eyes and in the eyes of the world, as regards the treatment of these vassals of mine . . . It is my bounden duty to order you to consider the slightest infractions of the rule as grave abuses, for they go counter to God's and my will and bring about the total ruin and destruction of these realms whose natives enjoy my highest esteem. I will have them treated in a manner befitting vassals who serve the Crown's interests so meritoriously and have contributed so greatly to its grandeur and luster. I, the King [1632].

The benefits that a firm, undeviating policy had so painfully won were placed in jeopardy around 1641–1642 by the writs of Bishop Palafox y Mendoza, Inspector General, and later Viceroy, of New Spain.

By authorizing a number of farmers to detain their workers for debts, the nature or amount of which was not specified, the Bishop set a dangerous legal precedent. He was, paradoxically, the author of a famous work in defense of the Indians.

This serious about-face coincided with the settlement fees, and hence with a time when negotiations of great delicacy made it imperative not to provoke hacienda owners. Palafox's successor, Salvatierra, to whom the task of levying the tax fell, could hardly resume the struggle for Indian liberties; once again, the Crown's own financial policies had frustrated its efforts on behalf of the natives. Then, a rapid turnover of viceroys, including some quite mediocre ones, sealed the doom of Indian reform. In spite of the Jesuits' opposition and the civil authorities' occasional invoking of the natives' sacred right to work wherever and whenever they chose, and in spite of the authorities' reminders of legal restrictions existing before 1642, debt peonage crept slowly—and irrevocably—into more and more haciendas. By the end of the seventeenth century or the beginning of the eighteenth, it was common practice to refer to *gañanes* or *naboríos* as estate property, in conformity with a custom so firmly established that it would have been a breach of etiquette to question it. Especially, the increasing numbers of Indians being born on the haciendas, and designated as Creoles, were regarded as naturally bound to the land.

Masters paid all their laborers' tributes, advanced them money, clothed them, gave them medical attention when they were ill, and thus kept permanent debts accumulating which, it appears, they finally stopped totting up altogether. Nevertheless, they were quick to ascertain total outlays whenever they wished to retrieve workers who had been improperly lured to other haciendas.

The proprietors of the largest haciendas, while utilizing money advances and perpetual debts to procure needed labor, had other means at their disposal. One convenient procedure was to take the Indians' own land away from them, thus obliging the Indians to work for hire, or to become sharecroppers or farmers on the great estates, capable of supplying sufficient manpower in seasons of heavy field work.

The method was neither new nor peculiarly Spanish, since we know that the native aristocracy had already hit upon it. Before the Conquest, many serfs (*mayeques*) were probably former freemen who had lost their fields to nobles (*pilli*). After the Conquest, we know for certain that caciques had taken advantage of the confusion to absorb "despotically" much land into their estates, forcing a number of free farmers (*macehuales*) to become their tenants (*terrazgueros*) and pay them rent. The caciques had lost their tenants quite rapidly, either because Spanish authorities had suppressed, or strictly controlled, the various fees and services owed by Indians (in order to prevent interference with tribute payments to encomenderos or the King), or because the caciques' estates had passed, wholly or in part, into the hands of Spanish farmers and stockmen.

We know of no specific instance in which the transfer of a cacique's estate also explicitly involved the transfer of tenants. However, since mention of Indian workers was forbidden in bills of sale and they would have had no reason to leave an estate when it changed hands, certain examples lead us to believe that this pre-Hispanic filiation was, indeed, part and parcel of the hacienda system. In 1540, the King had confirmed a Spaniard's title to an estancia of several hundred hectares acquired from Hernán Pérez de Bocanegra who, in turn, had purchased it from caciques and other Indians at Copala, in Michoacán. There is evidence that in 1554–1555, the estancia contained four native hamlets of about 100 huts in all, inhabited "before and after purchase," and that all the estate dwellers worked for the master. In spite of some opposition from the native community controlling the hamlets, the King had reaffirmed the master's rights on condition that he should exercise over the Indians residing on the estancia "no dominion or other jurisdiction" except by virtue of his owning the land on which the Indians were living of their own free will.

In the same manner as the former caciques, Spaniards would speak of their *terrazgueros;* whether they held them in perpetuity we cannot determine, owing to the absence of written labor contracts. One Fernando de Villegas, owner of the Asunción hacienda at Chalco, wrote in 1610: "I possess 100 *terrazgueros*, who pay me each year a rental fee in maize delivered to the Mexico City municipal granary." At the beginning of the seventeenth century, there were so many Indian laborers that not all of them could conceivably have been *gañanes*, that is, workers drawn to the haciendas after these were constituted. For the time being, moreover, *gañán* and *terrazguero* were not synonymous terms, and would not become so until all peons had been deprived of their freedom of movement and usually obliged to take up perpetual residence on the haciendas.

Spaniards had been trying for a long time to create new sources of income and labor by leasing parcels of land to natives. Before 1535, President Fuenleal had stigmatized those who were stripping Indians of their fields and then leasing them back at exorbitant rents. In 1542, the Viceroy served an injunction on an estancia owner in Tlaxcala for that very offense; the Viceroy had been told that "you have been seizing and occupying [Indian] land all around said estancia, which you then, in exchange for work and tributes, distribute to your slaves and other Indians who come there." Likewise, encomenderos at Colima enticed natives to their farms and then demanded tributes of them. It would be fruitless to attempt to determine the exact juridical sense of the fees imposed on these menials. The vocabulary employed by viceroys and inspectors alike was somewhat shaky; "tribute" and "rent" (*terrazgo*) were sometimes used interchangeably. When the value of real estate increased, the terms tended to take on more precise meanings.

Around the end of the sixteenth century, those skilled agronomists, the Jesuits, suggested holding lands jointly (*a medias*) with the Indians —a most profitable venture, according to them; they also advised buying up all available land in a given region in order to ward off intruders. The early hacienda owners, in fact, distributed parcels to Indians less to make a profit than to assure themselves of adequate labor for their own fields. The method was, after all, a franker one than debt peonage. Consequently, land seems to have been transferred for nothing, or rather, for nominal fees designed to retain title. The seventeenth century must have originated the many small perpetual tenements, paying a peso a year, characteristic of eighteenth-century haciendas. In the north, where labor was scarce and land was plentiful, some owners (in a manner reminiscent of lords in medieval Europe who granted charters to new cities and burgs in order to people their domains) even gave away title to estancias to be used for founding villages of free workers.

In addition to settling modest tenements on *terrazgueros*, large haciendas, which had swallowed smaller farms in the vicinity, often leased their outlying portions to small ranchers able to supply landlords with a few services when needed. These adjuncts, or ranchos, appeared toward the end of the seventeenth century and rapidly multiplied in the eighteenth. In this acceptation, the word *rancho* is American and, more specifically, Mexican. Actually, its meaning was always a little vague, since it also designated small freehold estates, similar to the medieval alodiums, which were gradually dying out in New Spain. The word's growing popularity does appear to have coincided with the appearance of the small ranches located just within the boundaries of big haciendas. However, *rancho* is found as early as 1563, and also in the first years of the next century, in the sense of a hut or temporary shelter, or else the cabin or fold constructed by shepherds, including migratory ones. Deriving from this original meaning, the word kept a derogatory connotation whenever it referred to a small independent holding. By the end of the seventeenth century, the connotation had disappeared; a rancho was, quite plainly, the act of settling (*ranchearse*) on land belonging to another and, by derivation, the land itself, that is, the small holding rented from a great estate.

At about the same time as the rancho appeared, social relationships on the haciendas grew more complex. Between the Spanish masters and the Indian workers, increasing numbers of mestizos and mulattoes took their assigned ranks. Some of them were detained for debts along with free workers and peons, whereas it is scarcely conceivable that there had been mestizos among the members of the former repartimientos. Also, the hacienda gradually drew into its sphere of activity segments of the rural population heretofore quite distinct, for example, farmers from Creole communities, who show up as peon overseers, cowboys, and farm hands, or else as humble ranchers on the hacienda's annexed lands.

THE HACIENDA AS A NEW SOCIAL AND ECONOMIC UNIT

The seventeenth century witnessed not only the haciendas' acquisition of their definitive land rights and their adoption of the system of serfdom through debts, which settled the fate of peons and sharecroppers (wherever workers were not Negro slaves), but also their growing into semi-independent economic units. They were, in fact, new rural communities governed by the owner or his major-domo.

In the northern provinces, so barren of resources that Spaniards possessed only what they had brought with them or created for themselves, the isolated haciendas dotting the enormous landscape were from their inception microcosms striving for as great a degree of self-sufficiency as possible. Aside from the haciendas' ore crushers and smelters—when they possessed them—they usually contained a dam, an irrigation system, charcoal heaps, wagon trains, a flour mill, workshops, and, especially, huge flocks and herds. The decline of the mines, in the seventeenth century, further emphasized the economic autonomy of these small population centers.

The largest sugar plantations, although located in a quite different kind of region—rich, densely populated, and reasonably close to main thoroughfares or Mexico City and Vera Cruz—quickly assumed similar characteristics. In addition to their carefully irrigated cane fields, they needed pastures for their pack animals, as well as for the cattle and sheep supplying a large Indian and slave community with meat, leather, and wool. They also had fields of maize and broad forests for firewood. As early as 1580, the owners of Orizaba–Tequila listed, among their refinery's appurtenances, "cane and other fields, woods, commons, slaves, livestock, implements, harvest and cattle estancias and sheepwalks, and all outbuildings." Another plantation inventory, one of the detailed kind drawn up by lawyers, shows us, first, a farm containing eight yoke of oxen (at Ystapa), a flour mill, grazing land for 1,520 head of cattle (at Alcusingo), and, especially, an estancia (called Pozuelo) filled with 27,924 sheep—and, second, the refinery itself, with its factory buildings, carpenter shop, and smithy; its cane fields; 35 oxen and 181 pack or draft mules and their Negro convoy captains and drivers, as well as 88 saddle horses, and, finally, swarms of Negro slaves (72 men and 44 women for refinery operations alone), and repartimiento Indians (the institution not having yet been abolished).

Many plantations, like the ones just mentioned or Santísima Trinidad, near Jalapa, were huge conglomerations of holdings whose diverse functions were complementary to one another. This was not difficult in a country such as Mexico; the long slopes in the high plateau region permit, according to the degree of altitude, a wide range of growing conditions and crops. Other plantations were less sprawling, notably in and beyond the rich Cuernavaca–Cuautla depression, largely because their own numbers kept them from spreading indefinitely. These last were frequently harvest or livestock estancias whose better portions had been intensively irrigated and planted with cane, which grew profusely; one big refinery plant or several smaller ones (*trapiches*) were built for sugar production, while the estancias' remaining portions were utilized for maize and livestock. Such mixed estates, whose main income was derived from their sugar, customarily extended over a few thousand hectares, in conformity with their title deeds to one or more estancias. They were not large, as plantations went, but a plentiful supply of water and intensive farming methods made them significant enterprises employing scores of slaves and large numbers of peons; they were out-fitted with workshops and contained big droves and hundreds of pack animals. In 1665, for example, a moderate-sized plantation in the Cuerna-vaca district, San Salvador Miacatlán, owned 35 slaves, 170 oxen used for plowing or hauling, 98 mules for turning the *trapiche* machinery, 50 saddle or draft horses, and several hundred brood mares. Slightly later, another plantation in the same district, though not among the largest, possessed no fewer than 506 work oxen, including 378 needed for wagon trains; owing to the long distances separating plantations from consumer and distribution centers, haulage was an item of primary importance in a plantation's operating budget. In more remote regions, such as southern New Galicia, small refineries, operated with a hand-ful of slaves, were no more than a belated addition to harvest and live-stock haciendas.

The trend toward self-sufficiency was combated by the Jesuits who, in the name of efficient operation, tried to keep to a minimum crops other than cane (such as maize, wheat, or beans) on their plantations. At their great Jalmolonga sugar plantation they sought water rights and purchased a large number of fields from the natives throughout the first half of the seventeenth century; but, unlike other proprietors in the region, they did not add vast estancias to their holdings. They doubtless wished to specialize operations and make intensive methods pay greater profits by keeping their various kinds of haciendas—sugar refineries, wheat farms, sheepfolds—strictly separate.

Another mixed type of hacienda, mentioned several times previously, was a sheep estancia run in conjunction with a weaving mill (*obraje*). Before the end of the sixteenth century, Fray Alonso Ponce had de-scribed one such hacienda (Huamantla, Tlaxcala) as *muy gruesa*—"very large": four leagues from a village, one huge building housed the looms and two others the water and fulling mills, while roundabout, large flocks of sheep grazed, as well as "many head of cattle used to feed the numerous employees, who also enjoy the services of a vicar." In the seventeenth century, whereas cattle reproduction was on the wane, sheep began to multiply rapidly again. The huge herds of 30,000, 50,000, or 100,000 head of cattle were a thing of the past; Jesuit colleges, however—as we know—owned immense flocks of sheep. Sheepmen in Mexico City, Puebla, Querétaro, Aguascalientes, and Zacatecas frequently possessed flocks of 30,000 to 50,000 head. Toward the end of the century, Captain José Rincón de Gallardo had 100,247 sheep on his Ciénaga de Mata haciendas, in comparison with 6,288 head of cattle and 2,710 horses; his entail, on the other hand, had title deeds to 67 cattle estancias and only 18 sheep estancias. The richest landed proprietors were clearly, first, plantation owners, and second, sheep raisers; significantly, the latter were the ones who colonized New León around mid-century. The cause of their prosperity was probably the huge quantities of wool still needed by Mexican weaving mills; in contrast, cattle raisers had lost their main markets, owing to the decline of the mines (formerly great hide consumers) and the small tonnage and irregular crossings of shipping fleets, which in former times had sailed away to Spain filled to the gunwales with hides.

The decline of silver production seems to have had more far-reaching consequences on the hacienda's economic structure than merely the closing of the hide market. The mines were the "sinews" of colonization, as contemporaries said. At the time of maximum exports to Spain (about 1600), silver made up two-thirds to three-fourths of the value of ship's cargo; consequently, it was the chief exchange item in the country's import-export balance of credits, the one permitting the inflow of vitally needed European products. When silver grew scarce, trade with Europe declined proportionately; even internal trade slowed down appreciably. The small mining camp (*real de minas*) was not able to survive in a vacuum; it had to import mercury from Almadén, in Spain, and it had to have an export market for its silver. Partially dependent on a mining economy (since the mines were great produce consumers), agriculture and livestock raising had owed their vitality to the mines' vigorous activity in keeping goods flowing through the domestic circuit—as long as the mines had flourished.

Commercial channels were very precarious in a large, underpopulated, and underdeveloped country whose badly laid-out roads were unsafe and whose transportation system was slow and difficult. When large numbers of miners deserted their mines and smelters, the flow of products was partially blocked; neither sugar production, not much of which was exported, nor the weaving industry, which did export cloth to South America, was sufficiently developed to take the preponderant place of the precious metals in the country's economy. Because of high transportation costs and lack of diversified farming from one region to the next, each region withdrew into isolation. Except in zones that were either particularly rich or close to the capital (such as Atlixco or the Bajío), farms lost a part of their markets in the second half of the seventeenth century, especially for wheat. Whereas wheat had been the main crop on the former harvest estancias operated with repartimientos, it was relatively unimportant on many haciendas. Owing to the rapid growth of the Creole, mestizo, and Indian populations, its place was taken by more extensive plantings of maize, beans, and maguey, or agave, for making Mexico's national drink, *pulque;* all these crops were for local consumption. Like wheat, hides sold badly, in their case because of the inaccessibility of overseas markets. In 1638, the General of the Jesuits remarked in a letter to the Provincial of Mexico City that "hacienda produce is a risky investment; some years the yield is bad, while in other years it may be good, but it fetches low prices and lacks outlets."

With the exception of a few years when shortages created some inflation, food prices in the seventeenth century, as a matter of fact, leveled off and even dropped. The depression was widespread, affecting not only maize and wheat (and, of course, bread), but also sugar, meat, and leather. In the north, ore crushers and smelters disappeared from the haciendas. All over the country, the trend toward self-sufficiency was accelerated. The trend did not have merely economic implications, but social ones as well.

Abolition of native work services wrought considerable changes in the functioning and structure of the various types of haciendas. Sugar plantations were the first to lose their repartimiento crews, early in the seventeenth century. Then, in several phases, work gangs were removed from farms. Meanwhile, the use of slaves and, especially, indebted *gañanes,* tenants, and peons had been pursuing a parallel evolution, gradually increasing as requisitioned labor declined and finally disappeared.

As long as sugar refineries and, ultimately, haciendas remained on the right side of the law, they were no longer under the jurisdiction of the repartimiento judges, hiring commissioners, or other royal officials concerned with labor distribution under the old system. Slaves were chattels, and peons came under the master's authority (the chaplain's, too, if there was one), which was delegated to a few Spanish and mestizo overseers: the bailiff, the captain of the work crews, and—on sugar plantations, where the use of natives in refinery operations was forbidden—the supervisor of the cane fields (*cañaverero*). Whereas under the repartimiento system crews of constantly changing Indians had come and gone and resident laborers had usually been reduced to the minimum, seventeenth-century haciendas lodged their *gañanes*, *laboríos*, and peons in small cabins clustered around the church and mansion; some Indians were allowed to live in their own villages, provided that they were close. If the estate was a very large one, perpetual tenants (*terrazgueros*) dwelt on their allotments some distance away from the center, while rancheros occupied the perimeter.

For tasks requiring a rapid pace, owners generally used Negro slaves. In industries where the output per worker was high, such as sugar refineries and weaving mills, the labor force was essentially composed of them. However, they were also used on many big estates alongside native peons, particularly in the rapidly expanding sheep-raising industry. Large haciendas would normally own 10, 15, or 20 slaves. In 1683, Don José Rincón de Gallardo had "144 of all ages," distributed among the six haciendas and various ranchos comprising his huge Ciénaga de Mata latifundium. His helpers must have been many times more numerous than that figure shows, since, when he was appointed a captain, he offered to place at the King's disposal a private army of at least 500 mounted soldiers recruited on his estates. On sugar plantations, the proportion of slaves was, naturally, much higher; the smallest refinery (*ingenio*) in the Marquesado del Valle usually had several score. In the seventeenth century, as many as 200 or 300 were employed on the larger ones; in 1653, Suchimancas, near Cuautla, owned 230 of all age groups. Besides a plantation's Indian settlement (*real de indios*), or small cluster of peons' huts, there was the slaves' stockade (*real de esclavos*), pierced with only one opening. A good idea of the quality of construction may be obtained from the description of one stockade on a Yautepec plantation, which contained five adobe buildings appraised at 10 pesos, plus thirty-six cabins whose total value was under 9 pesos (1699).

Hacienda owners supplemented their supply of slaves and *gañanes* with day laborers hired in nearby villages; villages, as we have learned, were often confined to such exiguous spaces that their inhabitants had to earn an outside living. For two reals a day, these laborers would help harvest or work on the ambitious projects that owners sometimes undertook: irrigation ditches, aqueducts, buildings, and dams. The various crews of Indians and Negroes were directed or supervised by captains and corporals, who were whites, mestizos, mulattoes, or freed slaves—although they, too, were sometimes being detained for debts. A sampling of functions and types of estates gives us the general overseer (*mandador*), the cane field supervisor and guard (*cañaverero*, *guardacañas*), the *cañaverero*'s counterpart on a cacao plantation (*cacaguatero*), the hunter (*tirador*), and the mining overseer (*barequero*). Many were mounted—a sign of superiority over the rabble afoot, or peons. (Along with its ordinary meaning, *peón* has kept in some regions its etymological meaning of "pedestrian.") Most cowboys, especially the cowboys' corporal (*caporal de la vaquería*), were chosen from the ranks of these excellent horsemen. Their salary varied greatly, according to region and functions; in the seventeenth century, it was sometimes as low as five or six pesos per month. When overseers did not live in the midst of the fields or on the outlying ranchos, they were lodged in small adobe dwellings in the shadow of the master's house, which, as we know, was frequently fortified.

Hacienda owners afforded a measure of protection to their men, who, in turn, made up their small armies in times of danger. Most regions were threatened in one way or another: the northern provinces by nomad attacks, the coasts by pirate landings, and nearly all parts by skirmishes with cattle thieves or even highwaymen and bandits. Around 1611, the road to Toluca was still infested with brigands who, only ten leagues from Mexico City, were making a practice of committing "murders and other atrocities." As the Franciscan Mendieta observed before the end of the sixteenth century, farmers also watched over their *gañanes*' welfare, treating them much better than they did repartimiento Indians, who were lent them for such limited periods that no personal relationship could spring up. They defended their *gañanes* against the many exactions and foul tricks thought up by caciques and white, mestizo, or mulatto traffickers residing in native villages. Before debt peonage had established itself as an institution, owners had been obliged to try to detain day laborers on their estates; after they possessed their own *gañanes*, these free peasants from the outside became a precious source of auxiliary labor that it would have been hard to replace. By the end of the seventeenth century, owners of big haciendas had supplied their peons with a commissary store (*tienda de raya*), which supplied their every need and chalked up the purchasers' debts. The stores were either a benefit or an instrument of oppression, depending on whether owners sought to help their workers or increase their own profits. With the exception of sugar refineries and textile mills, which had ready markets, owners could not increase their profits by very much. There was no point in accelerating workers' pace and expanding production beyond the limits set by the absence of outlets and a financial system still in the doldrums. As a result, the owners' authority over their workers was often paternal rather than calculating. Workers may have led a humdrum existence, with little hope of betterment; but they were protected from the misfortunes and bad harvest years that might have befallen them as independent peasants—no mean consideration in a country of light and intermittent rainfall.

Hacienda masters enjoyed considerable discretionary powers in the dispensing of justice to their workers. They could make free to a certain extent with their slaves, as faces branded "Marqués del Valle" or "Doña Ysabel de Villanueva" showed. They could punish and jail their slaves at will; sugar plantation inventories often list handcuffs, iron collars, and "chain prisons"—the latter quite complicated, to judge by their description. In 1671, the San Salvador Miacatlán *trapiche* itemized four such chain prisons and five pairs of handcuffs—three for women and two for men. In the eighteenth century, the Jesuits' *Instrucción* cautioned their administrators against imitating prevalent practices. Church authorities strove to limit masters' tyranny and relieve the plight of these wretched slaves. Of course, it was to a master's interest to treat his slaves well in order to keep his enterprises running smoothly. Theoretically, the Church had accomplished a good deal in the matter of mixed marriages: When a Negro married an Indian woman, their offspring were born free like the mother. In fact, however, a master or, rather, his bailiff, had abundant means at his disposal to coerce slaves into marrying bondwomen; he could then claim the issue as chattels.

Whereas the institution of slavery, as long as it did exist, implied masters' vested rights in the dispensing of justice, many, less understandably, took it upon themselves to punish and imprison their peons also. Their conduct could be partly explained by the Indians' status of permanent minors. A master could even obtain from the Viceroy a writ prohibiting justice officials from visiting his hacienda, except to investigate complaints or statutory offenses. Culprits were handcuffed or thrown into hacienda jails; such transgressions of authority sometimes spurred civil and ecclesiastical authorities to action. Abuses were particularly frequent in the northern provinces, where many masters were military men called upon to exercise the functions of chief peace officer (*justicia mayor*) in their districts. As captains of private armies raised on their estates, they were obliged to discipline their own men. The master of Ciénaga de Mata, José Rincón de Gallardo, was commissioned a "captain of cuirassiers" in 1693; his commission explicitly granted him the right to "punish the disobedient." The previous year, Don José had been authorized to pursue, imprison, or deliver to higher authority "thieves and brigands plying the highways" in the vicinity, as well as those guilty of civil or criminal offenses; for all such cases he possessed powers similar to an alcalde mayor's, namely, to conduct hearings and provide substantiation for the eventual judgment. This is another aspect of the *de facto* and *de jure* decentralization in the seventeenth century which we have already encountered.

From the religious point of view, the largest haciendas and sugar plantations formed independent parishes; they had their resident vicar, who was usually fed and given a salary by the master—300 pesos a year at the Orizaba plantation, plus perquisites, naturally. A vicar's presence was fully justified, since these large estates contained veritable villages; around 1610 or 1620, Bishop Mota y Escobar, while on tour in the Jalapa region, confirmed, on two large plantations lying side by side, 80 children on one and 183 on the other, "mostly Indians and Negroes." The great northern estates also frequently had a chaplain or a vicar whose living was paid from the estates' tithes; masters prided themselves on having obtained a vicar, because of the considerable prestige attached. Smaller haciendas were visited at more or less regular intervals by the vicar or curate of the nearest village, who celebrated Mass in a chapel constructed by the master and consecrated by the bishop.

Chapels, some small and others large enough to qualify as churches, were usually the best furnished and most decorated buildings on the haciendas, containing reredos, paintings, chasubles, crosses, reliquaries, and other sacred objects (often made of solid silver). In the seventeenth and, especially, the eighteenth centuries, some were even sumptuous, as a visit today would prove. Religion was at the very center of hacienda life. The hacienda was generally under the protection of the Virgin or a patron saint or, if the master was ambitious, of God the Father or the Most Holy Trinity. In 1727, the Count of Miravalle invoked the protection of the following, in order that they might watch over his estates:

First, Monsignor St. Joseph, as administrator.
Second, Monsignor St. Anthony of Padua, as bailiff.
Third, the Venerable Señor Don Juan de Palafox, as corporal.
Fourth, St. John of Nepomuk, as adjutant.
Fifth, the Blessed Souls in Purgatory, as cowboys.

The Count did not neglect to beseech the Virgin's special blessings. Twice a day, peons and slaves would join the master or the bailiff in the chapel for morning prayers and evensong and the recitation of the Rosary.

The master's house was located near by, usually fronting on a large square at the hacienda's center. Such houses are described in detail in numerous seventeenth-century inventories. Surviving examples usually have been enlarged or altered (in the eighteenth century) or refortified (in troublesome times during the nineteenth and twentieth centuries). On the large haciendas, the master's dwelling was a large stone structure built around several patios, including one off which his apartments opened through an arched passageway. The apartments were furnished with canopied beds, arms, and great chests for storing personal effects, jewelry, and the silver plate so common in Mexico. Gargoyles and carved capitals decorating this part of the house did not appear in appreciable quantities until the eighteenth century. There was sometimes a private oratory in addition to the chapel. The walls were hung with paintings: Flemish landscapes and, especially, religious subjects, such as the twelve apostles, the saints, the Virgin Mother, or, rather, the

Virgin of each great shrine, down to and including the Virgin of Peña de Francia, near Salamanca.

Outbuildings were usually grouped around a second patio. Stables were large, because mounts were cheap and hacienda owners were great horsemen. The heavy wooden and leather saddles ornamented with silver were kept there, as well as the caparisons, chaps, leather jackets, and huge spurs which comprised the riding paraphernalia so vital in a country whose urban centers were several weeks' journey away. In flat country, owners also used big mule teams; Captain Rincón de Gallardo had no fewer than forty-four carriage mules at Ciénaga de Mata, not to mention a much larger number used in the estate.

Some sugar refineries and older houses had a second story, perhaps partly for defense purposes; but usually buildings were one-storied, with high, vaulted ceilings. Battlements, ledges, parapets, observation towers, and dovecotes were not always adornments, even in the central areas, where banditry was not completely wiped out and the hostility of some native communities occasionally culminated in uprisings. As a result, window openings remained narrow for a much longer time than in Spain; eighteenth-century Mexican buildings, with their thick walls, recall the massive ones of sixteenth-century Castile. From time to time, a loggia or outside gallery would anticipate a later, more carefree period.

There is a further point of comparison that might be established. Although bleaker and reflecting a rougher sort of life, these hacienda dwellings remind one of the Andalusian *cortijos* and other houses in southern Spain, which in turn closely resemble certain buildings in North Africa and other Mediterranean regions. The floor plan of the Roman villa, built around one or more colonnaded courtyards, is common to all. Not only the architecture, but estate organization as well, calls forth memories of the Roman empire. The Negroes, peons, and Indian tenants resemble the slaves, colonists, and native farmers on the latifundia of Rome's provinces; and the hacienda masters, like the Roman estate owners of the Byzantine period, enjoyed an authority over their people which went considerably beyond economic relations. Many European peasant communities were founded on former Roman villa sites. In eighteenth-century Mexico, some peons succeeded, with the King's backing, in forming free villages; and hacienda owners feared that more would follow their example.

The hacienda may be regarded, then, as the fruit of an encounter between conquerors of Mediterranean stock and a less fully evolved population, the encounter having taken place in an environment that was temporarily cut off from normal trade channels. It is even legitimate to imagine that portions of the Late Roman empire presented similar conditions when, in the fourth century, commercial activity slackened and life became centered in the great rural villas.

THE FORMATION OF A LANDED ARISTOCRACY

In the seventeenth century, the true owners of haciendas were families and lineages, rather than individuals. Some estates were owned jointly by a number of relatives and, therefore, could not be divided; many others were entailed, so that individual owners could not dispose of their property, which remained indissolubly linked to a family name, a pedigree, or, sometimes, to a title.

Encomenderos and high officials—the first groups to possess steady incomes—had striven to obtain hereditary tributes and offices for their families. They had been impelled by the same strong sense of blood ties and duty to one's progeny that later Spaniards displayed in wishing to ensure their lines' preëminence by entailing their estates. The latter succeeded where the former had failed; while the King had insisted on repossessing encomiendas and selling offices to each generation in succession, he saw no objection to the formation of great entails or to families of rich landed proprietors. On the contrary, he considered them a help in maintaining order and defending the state. Consequently, the Crown granted requests for entails whenever it was proved that the petitioner was an honorable man possessing enough capital to settle an entail on his eldest son without disinheriting his other children.

The first known entail dates from 1550 and was granted to "one of the first conquistadors," Gonzalo Cerezo, who had become the Audiencia's chief constable and had taken part in the New Galicia expedition "with many retainers, relatives, friends, and supplies." Then, entails were infrequent until the last third of the century. A few big encomenderos and stockmen like Juan Gutiérrez Altamirano and Hernán Pérez de Bocanegra (1562) were followed by a number of rich miners: Diego de Ibarra, Cristóbal de Oñate, Alonso de Villaseca (1566–1568), and, quite a few years later, Lomas y Colmenares from Nieves, and Pedro de Minares from Sombrerete (1588). Entails increased considerably at the end of the century and especially in the next, in the regions of Mexico City and Puebla, Vera Cruz, Querétaro, Oaxaca, Valladolid (Morelia), Guadalajara, and the northern mines. Whatever the source of their fortunes, landed proprietors aspired to link their name with a domain and create a large rural aristocracy like that of southern Spain. In particular, the sons and grandsons of conquistadors knighted for their military feats felt that they had a right to special consideration.

The peculiar mentality of proprietors is reflected in the phraseology of entail deeds.

> *Let all interested parties know by these presents that . . . we [husband and wife] were agreed to make and constitute an entail on behalf of our eldest son, considering that possessions divided and apportioned dwindle and disappear. Whereas if they are bound together and made indivisible, they remain and increase, the holder's cousins and relations may be succored in their time of need, houses and families are ennobled and lineages are rendered illustrious and preserved for posterity, and those who enjoy the income from such entails are more inclined to defend and protect the nation and city in which they reside and to serve their rightful King and master, in peace as in war, as both divine and natural law require of them, whereby the Lord Our Master is served and His Holy Gospel exalted. And inasmuch as it is both lawful and just to establish an entail, we most respectfully requested, and received, permission of His Majesty, King Philip.*

Certain clauses in the deeds were designed to guarantee accomplishment of the pact-making ceremonies that were customary between suzerains and vassals. The heir to the Mota-Portugal entail was enjoined to pay "feudal homage in accordance with the laws of Spain," and to swear before a knight that he would honor and obey all the clauses of the deed. Around 1628, the founders' grandson,

> *Captain-Sergeant major Don Cristóbal de la Mota y Ossorio . . . placed his clasped hands between those of the aforementioned Don Manuel del Castillo y Móxica (knight of the Order of St. James and ordinary alcalde of Mexico City) . . . and paying feudal homage*

once, twice, and thrice, in accordance with the laws of Spain, swore
to respect and carry out said stipulations attached to his entail.

Entailers seeking titles willingly exercised military functions. The
army tradition had been preserved in the families of the conquistadors,
who, having received their coats of arms, felt themselves superior to
settlers arriving after hostilities had ceased. Even later, favors and land
grants had gone primarily to reward military services. When prepara-
tions were being made for the conquest of New Mexico, the Governor
of New Viscaya, Río de Losa, advised authorities to use individuals
willing to serve without pay—"always providing that His Majesty may
grant them noble rank, hereditary encomiendas, estancias, and other
lands." The most influential tried to obtain membership in one of the
military orders, which conferred a noble's privileges, including a title
held for life, as well as exemption from most ordinary obligations, such
as the tithe. In 1588, a number of Mexicans, among them Don Nuño de
Chávez Pacheco de Córdoba y Bocanegra, who owned the great
Acámbaro–Apaseo hacienda and whose son was to become Marqués
of Villamayor, purchased from someone at Court habits for a spurious
Order of St. George. By the middle of the seventeenth century, New
Spain possessed twenty-six Knights or Commanders of St. James and
seven of Calatrava, who constituted the cream of the aristocracy. The
King also rewarded outstanding services with the titles of Regimental
Commander and Hereditary Governor (*adelantado,* as in *Adelantado de*
Filipinas). The conqueror of Florida, Don Tristán de Luna y Arellano,
was given the hereditary title of Marshal of Castile, which remained
attached to one of the largest entails in the country.

Captaincies were much more easily come by. They multiplied in an
odd fashion in the seventeenth century, not only in the nomad-infested
northern provinces, but in the best-pacified regions, such as Puebla,
where in 1697 at least eighteen out of twenty regidores were captains.
(The alcalde mayor was a general.) Many other hacienda and plantation owners in the region had the same title. The reason was that ever
since Viceroy Cerralvo's days, an infantry battalion and a company of
cavalrymen had been stationed there. Likewise, Mexico City, around
the middle of the seventeenth century, possessed a battalion consisting
of 12 companies (each composed of 120 men), commanded by captains
who were all influential individuals, largely Creoles, and either nobles

or entail holders; a few were rich merchants. Obviously, they all served without pay; they may even have paid their soldiers from their own pockets. In any event, these captains who were also large landowners were one of the seventeenth century's characteristic social types.

Private armies were no rarity in Mexico. In the sixteenth century, Alonso de Villaseca had helped the Audiencia quell a riot by galloping up at the head of two hundred riders, all of whom were his retainers and familiars. The Marqués of Villamayor and others later indulged in the same derring-do. Toward the end of the seventeenth century especially, these brave men were given official military rank—for example, in 1693, the powerful hacienda owner and alcalde of Lagos, Don José Rincón de Gallardo. The year before, he had offered to aid the Viceroy to extricate himself from a difficult situation "with all the horses and men needed from his haciendas; he would take to the field at any time and at his expense, as he had done several times before, notably against the South Sea pirates." The Viceroy appointed him captain of cuirassiers "of the militia battalion of the Kingdom of New Spain," since Don José had promised to muster "at least 500 men and 1,000 horses . . ." in case of need. The Viceroy made quite clear to Don José, "You will do so at your own expense and will use volunteers, seeing that you will receive nothing from the royal treasury."

For over fifty years, encomenderos, settlers, and stockmen had been the rivals or adversaries of the missionaries. In his diatribes, Jerónimo López had accused the fathers of telling the Indians that they were Spaniards' equals, teaching them Latin and science, and considering them to be always in the right and Spaniards always in the wrong. Later, the Church had changed its attitude somewhat on acquiring large estates and admitting to its ranks many Creoles and children of hacienda owners; not only the Church seems to have changed its attitude, for seven of Jerónimo López' thirteen grandchildren were allowed to enter the Church. At that time, the former rivalry between colonists and clergy was transformed into a new one between Spaniards and Creoles, within the Church and throughout society.

Rich merchants, miners, and, especially, large landowners not only had ceased opposing the Church but were its munificent benefactors; they founded many *capellanías*, colleges, and convents. Don José Rincón de Gallardo was the patron of five churches and monasteries. At the risk of some repetition, let us recall that benefactors were perhaps less

concerned with ensuring their souls' eternal salvation than with further-
ing the interests of their families and descendants. The livings accompanying endowed masses were often reserved for "priests of the lineage,"
while bestowal of livings was otherwise vested in founders' descendants.
In addition to the benefits in connection with burial rights, founders
of convents and colleges were entitled to a place of honor in all religious
ceremonies and to have admitted to the establishment, without fees or
dowry, a specified number of novices or pupils. Most of these advantages were hereditary; they were even made a part of entails. The founding of a rich convent was either a family's chief claim to glory or an
important steppingstone on its way to nobility.

Some entail holders, all of whom already had their coats of arms,
succeeded in obtaining from the King a title besides. Not to mention
the special case of the Marqués del Valle, early in the seventeenth
century, individuals, usually scions of younger branches of noble Spanish
houses, were rewarded for their good services (notably military) with
the title of count or marqués. At the close of the same century and in
the following one particularly, His Majesty, short of funds, did not
hesitate to sell these titles to men of lesser rank who had the money to
purchase them.

One of the oldest, most curious instances is the Marquesado de
Villamayor, which was conferred upon the grandson of Hernán Pérez
de Bocanegra y Córdoba, the big farmer and cattle baron who had
founded an entail within his encomiendas at Acámbaro–Apaseo. Don
Francisco Pacheco de Córdoba y Bocanegra's maternal grandfather had
been the famous northern conquistador, Francisco Vázquez de Coronado, who had served as Governor of New Galicia before the creation
of the Audiencia at Guadalajara. Pacheco-Bocanegra himself had served
the Crown, having fulfilled the functions of corregidor in some of the
richest regions in Mexico. He received a pension of 3,500 pesos from the
King and claimed that he was related to several great Spanish families.
After an Audiencia investigation, he requested, and was granted, the
rank of marqués. By 1625, the full title of his son, Don Carlos Colón de
Córdoba Bocanegra y Pacheco, had become "Marqués de Villamayor,
Governor General of the Kingdom of New Galicia, Lord of Los Apaseos
and the Entail, and Encomendero of Acámbaro." He was, indeed, "Lord
of Los Apaseos," for he possessed the permanent encomienda for the

locality, in which his largest haciendas were also located. In addition, he had his private army; he rushed to the defense of the Viceroy, the Marqués de Gelves, during the 1625 riots. That same year, the second Marqués of Villamayor moved to Spain, where his family seemed to prefer to live, leaving their entail and fortune in administrators' hands.

The eminent services of the two Velascos were twice rewarded. In 1609–1610, Luis de Velasco II, a big encomendero and landowner in spite of his functions, was made Marqués of Río Pisuerga; in 1616, a younger branch of the Velasco family, which would ultimately unite the two branches' entails (before the century's end), was given the title of Counts of Santiago Calimaya. Because of their many aristocratic connections, the heirs of the first Count of Santiago (Don Fernando Altamirano y Velasco), in addition to the two branches' entails, came into possession of others throughout the country; they were probably the most powerful hacienda owners in the viceroyalty. Although each unit constituted by the first masters of the soil was large in itself, great family estates were rarely in the hands of a single individual; as in medieval Europe, inheritances and wedding portions kept adding to families' holdings new units in various parts of the country.

Two other early titles were those of the Counts of Montezuma (1627?), descendants of the Aztec emperor who had intermarried with Spaniards, and the Counts of the Orizaba Valley, first granted, at the beginning of the seventeenth century, to Rodrigo de Vivero, a powerful man who had held high offices in the Philippines, Tierra Firme (New Granada), and New Viscaya (where he had spent over 30,000 ducats during the campaign against the Chichimecas). In New Spain he was the encomendero of Tecamachalco and the owner of the great Orizaba plantation, as well as of estates in five or six different districts.

By the end of the seventeenth century, titles had markedly increased. The King had sold some at high prices to men who had acquired large fortunes by various means; many were big Spanish landowners. Other and more interesting titles represented the culmination of a long series of efforts, going back to the sixteenth century, whereby family estates had progressed from small holdings to large entails and were finally raised to counties and marquisates: the López de Peralta family becoming the Marqueses of Salvatierra, the Estrada Carbajal family the Marqueses of Uluapan, Urdiñola's descendants the Marqueses of Aguayo, and Christóbal de Oñate's the Counts of La Mejorada and Santa Rosa.

The most noteworthy example of a family's rise was that of the López de Peralta family, descendants of the conquistador, Jerónimo López. He and his son of the same name had patiently created a large estate, most of which was eventually entailed and settled on the founders' great-grandson, Gabriel López de Peralta. By such action, the family became noble in fact if not by law; letters patent conferring the title of Marqués of Salvatierra were not issued until 1708, in recognition of Don Gabriel's having donated, in 1644, much rich land for the founding of Salvatierra (named after the Viceroy then in office). In addition, Don Gabriel had claimed, but had not been given, a share of the royal sales tax (*alcabalas*) and, especially, the office of corregidor to be held in perpetuity by his family; that would have amounted to making him lord of the town [of Salvatierra], but would scarcely have pleased its new farmer citizens.

These recent aristocrats, who were already encomenderos, big landowners, and town founders—often all three in the same locality—must have accumulated considerable power, particularly in view of the monarchy's decentralizing process. Nevertheless, their authority derived not from their titles but from the functions that they exercised simultaneously.

The functions were those of regidor or alcalde of a town, corregidor or alcalde mayor of a province, or one of the many offices that the King sold in the seventeenth century. Among the alcaldes mayores of Puebla, for example, we find all the great names of New Spain society. Creoles, on the other hand, rarely occupied the highest positions, which the King preferred to save for Spaniards.

Although the actual work connected with their functions was frequently accomplished by lieutenants or agents acting in their name, aristocrats were obliged to keep town houses, in conformity not only with the obligations of a citizen (*vecino*) but also with Castillian and, especially, Andalusian tradition. The wealthiest usually had houses in the capital also. Toward the middle or end of the seventeenth century, handsome dwellings were erected there, with fronts of *tezontle* (a deep-red volcanic stone), spacious arcaded patios, and fountains, walls, and floors covered with tiles from Puebla. In Mexico City and the larger towns, houses gradually shed their fortified appearance. Some hacienda owners possessed mansions in several towns; the least rich were content with one house, emblazoned with their coat of arms, in the village closest to their estates. Many even spent part of the year on their haciendas, in manor houses that were their chief dwellings and, at times, veritable palaces.

As a class, they were great travelers, constantly moving about between the capital, towns where they held municipal positions, and their various haciendas, which were often far apart; or else they would be off on business connected with their military rank or royal office.

The aristocrats' favorite pastimes were riding and bullfighting. In the sixteenth century, viceroys had encouraged these inclinations in order to keep them in fighting trim, and perhaps also to provide an outlet for their turbulence and "divert them from the pitfalls and other opportunities [for mischief] that idleness ordinarily engenders" (Count of Monterrey, 1596). Nearly every Saturday, Velasco I would ride out with 80 or 100 horsemen drawn from the ranks of high society to his country house at Chapultepec, where they would break lances (made of reeds—*correr cañas*) with one another and fight wild bulls imported for the purpose from Chichimeca territory. Later, no fiesta was complete without equestrian feats, tournaments, and bullfights (usually on horseback). The greatest fiesta took place on the feast day of St. Hippolytus, celebrating the anniversary of the fall of Mexico City (August 13). The same kind of fiesta was held on the larger haciendas; around 1620, the rich owner of Santísima Trinidad plantation, near Jalapa, felt that the most fitting way to receive his Bishop was to ride out to meet him "with a large body of horsemen," who showed off their riding skill; the worthy prelate, the Creole Mota y Escobar, in order to conceal his amazement ("with mouth agape") at such wondrous exploits and not to be outdone, felled a bull with a single shot through the neck. The art of bullfighting was still rudimentary upon its arrival from Spain; in the sixteenth and seventeenth centuries, a typically Mexican style began to develop, involving the use of the crescent-shaped billhook (*desjarretadera*) to hamstring (*desjarretar*) bulls while still on the run, as well as the various feints and passes characteristic of *jaripeo* (riding the bull) and *charrería* (horsemanship) which are so close to the heart of old Mexican society.

This emerging Mexican aristocracy resembled the nobility of Andalusia in two respects: both were half-urban and half-rural; both were devotees of horsemanship and bullfighting. Unlike the closed castes of

Europe, however, the noble class in Mexico was still receptive to outsiders. The King was selling titles; conquistadors' descendants and sons of old Creole families were not reluctant to wed the daughters of rich merchants who, in turn, were eager to contract alliances with the landed aristocracy. In 1673, Viceroy the Marqués de Mancera noted: "In these provinces, generally speaking, the caballero is a merchant and the merchant is a caballero; I see no major objection to that, but rather, a convenience from the political point of view." As the Viceroy also remarked, many entails and patrimonies were going downhill; nobles' incomes had withered away in the seventeenth century, owing to the decline of the mines and the lack of markets for farm produce. The haciendas not only had been forced into economic isolation but were being drained by mortgages, perpetual rents, and endowed masses. It is scarcely astonishing, then, that each class should seek its advantage, the aristocracy by marrying money and the merchants by investing their profits in land and acquiring noble sons-in-law.

In the seventeenth century the hacienda's agrarian economy permeated every aspect of business life, in the same way that the hacendado, or hacienda owner, influenced all other types and classes of Creole and Spanish society save the highest officials, who insisted on maintaining close ties with the mother country. The return to the soil helped revive in Mexico certain medieval institutions and customs recalling the patriarchal existence of Biblical times. During the same period, however, other and more modern traits came into being that served to emphasize the bewildering complexity and diversity of this land.

SUMMARY

Under an enlightened viceroy like Luis de Velasco I (1550–1564), it had begun to look as if Mexico might one day evolve into a new kind of state founded on the principles of Christian humanism. The Crown, gradually reëstablishing its authority, wished to rule the country in strict accordance with divine and natural law. The conquistadors, impelled by motives harking back to feudalism, had tried to turn their encomiendas into fiefs; they had failed. Nor had their captains been any more successful in their attempt to carve out principalities for themselves. The Viceroy, the jurists, and their missionary allies had wrested from them the perquisites of government and had thereby regained the initiative. Many among them dreamed of achieving a Christianity as pure as the early Church's, with a rational "order and concert" reigning in all spheres of the nation's activity—political, social, and economic. Humanists like Zumárraga and Vasco de Quiroga, as well as missionaries fired by scholasticism's renovation, had already founded utopias among the Indians.

Then came the series of setbacks at century's end. When the missionaries went into the field, they found that the Indians did not always measure up to expectations. It also proved practically impossible to keep cattle reproduction within reasonable limits and thus to prevent herds from destroying native villages. Colonists abused the Indians, and unscrupulous merchants exploited them—another problem which the authorities and missionaries never really solved. And no human agent could have stopped the great epidemics from decimating or wiping out many native communities. After the failure of their ambitious undertaking around 1600, when Indians were relocated in special villages (*reducciones*) for purposes of conversion, the missionaries lost all their illusions. However, the missionaries' theories, inspired by the doctrine of natural law, did have one signal accomplishment to their credit: they made the Indian, as the King's vassal, equal to the Spaniard in the eyes of the law. At any rate, the Crown did its best to put such a philosophy into practice. The King considered himself personally responsible for his Indian subjects' welfare, as witness his moving marginal annotation to a 1632 cédula, whereby he made the Viceroy personally answerable to him and to the world. Thanks to a powerful bureaucracy made up of lawyers who were capable of carrying out an admirably unswerving policy, two important reforms were accomplished: the encomienda was reduced to no more than the right to collect a tax regulated by the government, and the repartimiento was progressively abolished.

Might, unfortunately, often won out over right. Exploitation of the Indians assumed many guises; as soon as it was stripped of one, it would find another allowing it to elude the law. The Spanish missionary state could find no better way of protecting its charges than to declare them permanent minors who were prohibited from transferring their lands and were subject to everlasting guardianship.

The discovery of the silver mines in the sixteenth century had stimulated trade and the flow of goods, developed a favorable attitude toward profit-making ventures, created large fortunes, and given rise to speculation.

Here, too, the story is one of partial failure. In the early decades of the seventeenth century the silver boom collapsed, smothering in its passage the first stirrings of a barely nascent capitalism. Land became the sole source of income. By the end of Philip II's reign, the Crown was faced with retrenchment because of the depletion of its reserves and increasing financial difficulties; consequently, it let rich private citizens shoulder certain categories of public expenditures. The trend became more pronounced under the last Habsburgs.

By that time, the cattle barons' steady encroachment on grazing lands had culminated in the creation of great estates and latifundia. (The event did not necessarily set a pattern for the future, as the experience of other Spanish colonies would show.) Light and intermittent rainfall, as well as a loose-knit kind of colonization adapted to the continent's scale, had created a favorable environment. Royal land grants had traditionally (ever since the Spanish Reconquest, in fact) been considered a reward for military services and part of the spoils of war. In New Spain, they were also distributed as favors, sometimes to influential citizens who deserved well of His Majesty and, at other times, to widows, orphans, and penniless heirs of the conquistadors. The families lost no time in selling land that they could not afford to exploit themselves. As a result, almost all grants ended in the hands of the moneyed classes: big encomenderos, royal officials, and, somewhat later, miners, wealthy merchants, monasteries, convents, Jesuit colleges, and individual clergymen.

Ecclesiastical mortmain coupled with the religious orders' vast holdings and the formation of indivisible, untransferable entails brought about a gradual stabilization of estate boundaries. The settlements with the King made any backward move unthinkable. In exchange for the special tax, the King had replaced all defective title deeds with new ones transforming the usufruct rights of the old estancias into definitive owner rights. The hacienda had acquired full legal status. In a country governed by lawyers, this was a decisive step.

While the great estate was taking on its final form—the hacienda—the mines had become half-deserted, trade had come virtually to a halt, the Spanish merchant fleet had dwindled and its sailings had grown erratic, royal authority seemed to have become more remote, and the country had been withdrawing further and further into isolation. Local life became centered in the hacienda, which had evolved independently of the encomienda. In spite of their long-standing privileges, some free villages of Creole farmers were devoured by the great estates. Others were paralyzed. A few, however, resisted and won out. Most native communities survived, protected by a paternalism that refused to change with the times; but they had lost so much of their land that the villagers could earn a living only by hiring themselves out to neighboring hacienda owners.

The largest estates were self-sufficient. The big sugar refinery, the plantation, the harvest estancia, and the smelter with its farm annexes supplied nearly all their own needs. They had their crops, their flocks and herds, their wooded areas, their flour mills, forges, and workshops. Each had its church and chaplain or vicar. Naïve drawings show us their donjon keeps, watchtowers, and other defenses.

Toward the close of the seventeenth century, decentralization of authority placed new powers in the hands of landed proprietors who, legally or illegally, set themselves up as dispensers of justice and captains of private armies entrusted with local policing, repelling coastal pirates, or combating the barbarous Chichimecas in the northern provinces. Proprietors were surrounded by swarms of relatives, retainers, gossips, and familiars; their influence was gauged by the size and importance of their households. Only one city, Mexico, broke the monotony of an otherwise standard pattern; the capital was like a limit set to the countryside's encroachment and a purchase point for a government that ran the risk of seeing the rest of the vast country slip from its grasp.

Hacienda owners naturally did everything in their power to obtain a vitally needed, permanent supply of labor. Theoretically, the peon was free to come and go; in practice, he was detained for his debts, which he could never satisfy. Although his lot was not a happy one, there were certain compensations. He was protected from the crop failures and other misfortunes that often befell the free farmer. The small amount of money in circulation, communication difficulties, and lack of markets spared him the brutal exploitation to which workers in other colonies were subjected. Speeding up output was of no use when harvests were hard to dispose of, and maize, wheat, and even sugar had little value outside a few favored zones.

The landed proprietor's peculiar mentality was not conducive to thinking in terms of efficient production. He acquired land, not to increase his earnings, but to eliminate rivals and hold sway over an entire region. His scorn for extra profits sometimes went to such lengths that he destroyed perfectly good equipment on land recently purchased. Merchants and administrators of haciendas or plantations belonging to religious orders (especially the Society of Jesus), on the other hand, were constantly on the lookout for ways of augmenting their revenues. Thanks to their clever handling of a traditional institution, the land rent (which meant their adapting to modern conditions), they were able to evade the prohibition against interest-bearing loans. Their capital served to bring abandoned areas under cultivation, build large sugar refineries, expand sheep raising, and finance weaving mills. As in Europe, the Church's estates were better managed and more prosperous. The absence of adequate markets, however, set a limit to their rising incomes as well.

There was nothing rigid about the hacienda system. Custom, founded on bold deeds, often preceded the law; sometimes the two were inextricably confused. Diversity verged upon imprecision, even vagueness, at times. In the Marquesado del Valle—a truly feudal state within a state—no one knew exactly the respective prerogatives of the King and the Marqués. There, as elsewhere, the Crown and its vassals did not appear disturbed by ambiguous situations which interminable lawsuits brought into sharper relief or which the lawsuits even created on occasion. Within the boundaries of the great estates, too, a complex social hierarchy grew up, bringing with it the development of a new set of juridical conditions. We can catch no more than a glimpse of the different categories of peons that must have existed. In all likelihood, they were scarcely less varied, in their subtle relationships to their master and to one another, than the serfs of Europe. Even less well documented is the part played by the groups existing on the fringes of the creeping haciendas—the modest independent and semi-independent farmers, who were Indians, mestizos, or Creoles and remind us inevitably of the medieval tenement holders.

We have frequently had occasion to recall the Middle Ages in our summary thus far. In addition, the hacienda owners who were also captains, the missionaries, the priest-farmers, and the licenciados of canon law—the most characteristic types of Creole society—put us in mind of the Spanish Reconquest, on which clerics and soldiers had left so original an imprint. The huge family circles made up of relatives and intimates, the tug exerted by blood ties and one's ancestry, and the feuds or rivalries between families also bring us back to Mediterranean shores. Likewise, the "rich and powerful men" who, particularly in the north, concentrated in their persons economic resources, military functions, and judicial powers may be compared to the *ricos omes* of Castile. They constituted an aristocracy in fact; some succeeded in obtaining titles. The state of the Marqueses del Valle, finally, is a pale replica of the Duchy of Burgundy.

The survival and revival of ancient institutions—a thousand years of history gathered into one spot—make Mexico a happy hunting ground for the historian. Yet colonial Mexico should not be regarded merely as a depository for archaisms that were passing out of existence in Europe—even in the northern provinces, where the absence of a stable Indian population made the civilization created by Creoles and mestizos resemble medieval Europe more closely than that of the rest of the country. The white man developed new customs and original social types; or, if the types may not be considered absolutely original, they were so thoroughly transformed by the American environment as to make their European origins unrecognizable. The most popular personage in Mexico today is probably the *charro*—that amazing horseman with his broad sombrero, his heavy spurs, and his saddle and costume decorated with silver. Although a trained eye might occasionally recognize an accessory going back to Andalusia or the Orient, the *charro* no longer has much in common with his counterparts overseas.

Ethnical differences are, of course, much more profound than the social transformations of Europeans. In the central and southern plateau regions, the old native civilizations have survived. All over the area, ancient customs and institutions hang on tenaciously in village communities. Even today, their strangeness strikes the most superficial European observer; there is no need to belabor the obvious. The fact is that there were, and to a certain extent still are, several Mexicos: the Mexico of the Creoles or mestizos and the Mexico of the full-blooded Indians. The latter were unchanging and unchangeable, withdrawn into themselves, a world apart from the foreign invaders and their descendants (though supplying them with labor and tributes); and they possessed fully as varied and complex an internal organization as the white men. Ever since the disappearance of the great missionaries of the early days, the problem has remained the same: to "incorporate the native" (to use the consecrated expression) into the nation without sacrificing his personal identity; for he has remained on the fringes of the economic, political, and social life of a country having evolved into a modern state.

Under cover of New Spain's isolation from the rest of the world, a period of equilibrium was reached in colonial Mexico's development which, at the end of the seventeenth century and the beginning of the eighteenth, doubtless constituted the heyday of the rural hacienda.

Already, however, there were signs of a new mining boom. Money had begun to flow freely again. Land was no longer the only source of revenue. With the Bourbons and the period of French influences, new ideas began to trickle into Mexico. The great estates came under attack; enlightened men like the Franciscan Morfi, around 1770, and, somewhat later, Bishop Abad y Queipo claimed that they were hindering the country's continued development. The great entails and a still powerful nobility kept the old framework intact, nevertheless, although it was tottering or had partially collapsed in other parts of the vast Spanish empire.

In the nineteenth century this archaic equilibrium would be upset again and again; the insecurity resulting from civil wars would turn the haciendas back into fortresses and refuges. The twentieth century would witness the final breaking up of the great estates. In spite of unavoidable errors in execution and the economic and social disturbances attendant upon so radical an upheaval, this was the decisive step which placed rural Mexico on the threshold of modern times. The next step will surely be, thanks to the building of schools and roads, the Indians' integration into the life of the Mexican nation—still young as nations go.

SELECTIVE
BIBLIOGRAPHY

Editor's Note: Limitations of space have made it necessary to reduce M. Chevalier's extremely lengthy (and extremely valuable) bibliography to those items immediately pertinent to the theme of his book. Scholars will find the amended and amplified bibliography in the Spanish translation, *Problemas agrícolas e industriales de México*, Vol. VIII, No. 1 (Mexico, 1956).

Alamán, Lucas, *Disertaciones sobre la historia de la república mexicana desde la época de la conquista*, 3 vols. (Mexico, 1844–1849).

Alessio Robles, Vito, *Coahuila y Texas en la época colonial* (Mexico, 1938).

———, *Francisco de Urdiñola y el norte de la Nueva España* (Mexico, 1931).

Amaya, Jesús, *Ameca, protofundación mexicana* (Mexico, 1950).

Arlegui, José, O. F. M., *Crónica de la provincia de NSPS Francisco de Zacatecas* (Mexico, 1851).

Arregui, Domingo Lázaro de, *Descripción de la Nueva Galicia*, ed. by François Chevalier (Sevilla, 1946).

Bandelier, Adolph F. A., *On the Distribution and Tenure of Lands . . . Among the Ancient Mexicans* (Cambridge, Mass., 1880).

———, *On the Social Organization and Mode of Government of the Ancient Mexicans* (Cambridge, Mass., 1890).

————, and Fanny R. Bandelier, *Historical Documents Relating to New Mexico, Nueva Vizcaya, and Approaches Thereto, to 1773*, 3 vols. (Washington, D. C., 1923–1937).

Barlow, R. H., *The Extent of the Empire of the Culhua Mexico, Ibero-Americana: 28* (Berkeley and Los Angeles: University of California Press, 1949).

Basalenque, Diego, O. S. A., *Historia de la provincia de San Nicolás Tolentino de Michoacán . . .*, 3 vols. (Mexico, 1886).

Borah, Woodrow, *Early Colonial Trade and Navigation Between Mexico and Peru, Ibero-Americana: 38* (Berkeley and Los Angeles: University of California Press, 1954).

————, *New Spain's Century of Depression, Ibero-Americana: 35* (Berkeley and Los Angeles: University of California Press, 1951).

Bosch García, Carlos, *La esclavitud prehispánica entre los aztecas* (Mexico, 1944).

Carrera Stampa, Manuel, "Las ferias novohispanas," in *Historia mexicana*, Vol. 2, No. 7, pp. 319–342 (Mexico, 1952–1953).

Carreño, Alberto María, *Cedulario de los siglos XVI y XVII: El obispo don Juan de Palafox y Mendoza y el conflicto con la Compañía de Jesús* (Mexico, 1947).

Cartas de Indias (Madrid, 1877).

Cervantes de Salazar, Francisco, *Tres diálogos latinos* (Mexico, 1875).

————, *Crónica de la Nueva España* (Madrid, 1914).

Céspedes del Castillo, Guillermo, *La Avería en el comercio de Indias* (Sevilla, 1945).

Chamberlain, Robert S., *Castilian Backgrounds of the Repartimiento-Encomienda* (Washington, D. C., 1939).

Chavez Orozco, Luis, *El obraje, embrión de la fábrica* (Mexico, 1936).

Chevalier, François, "Signification sociale de la fondation de Puebla de los Angeles," in *Revista de Historia de América*, No. 23, pp. 105–130 (Mexico, June, 1947).

————, (ed.), *Instrucciones a los Hermanos Jesuitas Administradores de Haciendas* (Mexico, 1950).

Cook, Sherburne F., and Simpson, Lesley Byrd, *The Population of Central Mexico in the Sixteenth Century, Ibero-Americana: 31* (Berkeley and Los Angeles: University of California Press, 1948).

Dávila, Garibi, *La sociedad de Zacatecas en los albores del régimen colonial* (Mexico, 1939).

Decorme, Gerard, S. J., *La obra de los jesuitas mexicanos durante la época colonial, 1572–1767*, 2 vols. (Mexico, 1941).

Donación de bienes a la Compañía de Jesús en el siglo XVI . . ., ed. by Luis Vargas Rea (Mexico, 1947).

Dorantes de Salazar, Baltasar, *Sumaria relación de las cosas de la Nueva España . . .* (Mexico, 1902).

Fernández de Echeverría y Veytia, Mariano, *Historia de la fundación de la ciudad de Puebla de los Angeles* . . . , 2 vols. (Puebla, Mexico, 1931).

Fernández del Castillo, Francisco, *Tres conquistadores y pobladores de la Nueva España: Cristóbal Martín Millán de Gamboa, Andrés de Tapia, Jerónimo López* (Mexico, 1927).

Gage, Thomas, *A New Survey of the West Indies* . . . (London, 1648, but many editions).

García Icazbalceta, Joaquín, *Obras*, 10 vols. (Mexico, 1896–1899).

García Pimentel, Luis (ed.), *Descripción del Arzobispado de México, hecha en 1579, y otros documentos* (Mexico, 1897).

Gómez de Cervantes, Gonzalo, *La vida económica y social de la Nueva España al finalizar el siglo XVI*, ed. by A. M. Carreño (Mexico, 1944).

González Navarro, Moisés (ed.), *Repartimiento de indios en Nueva Galicia* (Mexico, 1953).

Guthrie, Chester L., "Colonial Economy, Trade, Industry and Labor in Seventeenth Century Mexico City," in *Revista de Historia de América*, No. 7, pp. 104–134 (Mexico, 1939).

Humboldt, Alexandre de, *Essai Politique sur le Royaume de la Nouvelle Espagne*, 2 vols. (Paris, 1811).

Instrucciones que los virreyes de la Nueva España dejaron a sus sucesores, 2 vols. (Mexico, 1873).

Konetzke, Richard (ed.), *Colección de documentos para la historia de la formación social de Hispanoamérica, 1493–1810* (Madrid, 1953).

Lancaster-Jones, Ricardo, "La hacienda de Santa Ana Apacueco," in *Boletín de la Junta Auxiliar Jalisciense de la Sociedad Mexicana de Geografía y Estadística*, Vol. IX, pp. 149–178 (Mexico, 1951).

León, Alonso de, *Historia de Nuevo León, con noticias sobre Coahuila, Tejas, y Nuevo México.* . . , ed. by Genaro García (Mexico, 1909).

López de Velasco, Juan, *Geografía y descripción universal de las Indias desde el año 1571 al de 1574*, ed. by Justo Zaragoza (Madrid, 1894).

McBride, George M., *The Land Systems of Mexico* (New York, 1923).

Maza, Francisco F. de la, *Código de la colonización y terrenos baldíos* (Mexico, 1893).

Mecham, J. Lloyd, *Francisco de Ibarra and Nueva Vizcaya* (Durham, N. C., 1927).

Mendieta, Jerónimo de, O. F. M., *Historia ecclesiástica indiana*, ed. by J. García Icazbalceta, 4 vols. (Mexico, 1945).

Mendizábal, Miguel Othón, *La evolución del noroeste de México* (Mexico, 1930).

Miranda, José, "La función enconómica del encomendero en los orígenes del régimen colonial, Nueva España, 1525–1531," in *Anales del Instituto Nacional de Antropología e Historia*, No. 17, pp. 1–26 (Mexico, 1944).

——, *El tributo indígena en la Nueva España durante el siglo XVI* (Mexico, 1952).

Moreno, Manuel M., *La organización política y social de los aztecas* (Mexico, 1931).

Morfi, Juan Agustín, O. F. M., *Viaje de indios y diario del Nuevo México*, ed. by Vito Alessio Robles (Mexico, 1935).

Mota y Escobar, Alonso de la, *Descripción geográfica de los reinos de Nueva Galicia, Nueva Vizcaya, y Nuevo León*, ed. by J. Ramírez Cabañas (Mexico, 1940).

Noticias varias de Nueva Galicia: Intendencia de Guadalajara (Guadalajara, Jalisco, 1878).

O'Gorman, Edmundo, *Catálogo de pobladores de Nueva España: Registro de informes de la Real Audiencia, último tercio del siglo XVI, principios del siglo XVII* (Mexico, 1941).

Ojeda, Hernando de, O. P., *Libro tercero de la historia religiosa de la Provincia de México de la Orden de Santo Domingo* (Mexico, 1897).

Orozco, Wistano Luis, *Legislación y jurisprudencia sobre terrenos baldíos*, 2 vols. (Mexico, 1895).

Ots Capdequí, José M., "Las instituciones económicas hispano-americanas del período colonial," in *Anuario de Historia del Derecho Español*, Vol. XI, pp. 211–282 (Madrid, 1934).

——, *El régimen de la tierra en la America española durante el período colonial* (Ciudad Trujillo, Santo Domingo, 1946).

Palomino y Cañedo, Jorge, *La casa y mayorazgo de Cañedo de Nueva Galicia*, 2 vols. (Mexico, 1947).

Parry, John H., *The Sale of Public Office in the Spanish Indies under the Hapsburgs, Ibero-Americana:* 37 (Berkeley and Los Angeles: University of California Press, 1953).

Peña y Cámara, José de la, *El Tributo. Sus orígenes. Su implantación el la Nueva España* (Sevilla, 1934).

Pérez de Ribas, Andrés, S. J., *Crónica e historia religiosa de la Compañía de Jesús en Nueva España . . . hasta el año de 1654*, 2 vols. (Mexico, 1896).

Ponce, Alonso, O. F. M., *Relación breve y verdadera de algunas cosas . . . que sucedieron al padre fray Alonso Ponce . . . en Nueva España*, 2 vols. (Madrid, 1872–1873).

Powell, Philip Wayne, *Soldiers, Indians & Silver; The Northward Advance of New Spain, 1550–1600* (Berkeley and Los Angeles: University of California Press, 1952).

Rea, Alonso de la, O. F. M., *Crónica de la Orden de N. Seráphico P. S. Francisco, Provincia de S. Pedro y S. Pablo de Mechoacán en la Nueva España* (Mexico, 1802).

Ricard, Robert, *La conquête spirituelle du Mexique. Essai sur l'apostolat et les méthodes missionaires des ordres mendiants en Nouvelle Espagne, de 1523-1524 à 1572* (Paris, 1933).

Robles, Antonio de, *Diario de sucesos notables (1665–1703)*, 3 vols. (Mexico, 1946).

Sandoval, Fernando B., *La industria del azúcar en Nueva España* (Mexico, 1951).

Sarabia, Anastasio G., *Apuntes para la historia de la Nueva Vizcaya*, 2 vols. (Mexico, 1941).

Sauer, Carl O., *Colima of New Spain in the Sixteenth Century, Ibero-Americana:* 29 (Berkeley and Los Angeles: University of California Press, 1948).

Simpson, Lesley Byrd, *Studies in the Administration of the Indians in New Spain, Ibero-Americana:* 7, 13, and 16 (Berkeley and Los Angeles: University of California Press, 1934, 1938, 1940).

——, *Many Mexicos* (Berkeley and Los Angeles: University of California Press, 1957).

Solórzano y Pereyra, Juan B., *Política indiana*, 5 vols. (Madrid, 1930).

Soustelle, Jacques, *La vie quotidienne des Aztèques à la veille de la conquête espagnole* (Paris, 1955).

Taylor, Paul S., *A Spanish-Mexican Peasant Community: Arandas in Jalisco, Mexico, Ibero-Americana:* 4 (Berkeley: University of California Press, 1933).

Tello, Antonio, O. F. M., *Libro segundo de la crónica . . . de la Santa Provincia de Xalisco* (Guadalajara, Jalisco, 1891).

——, *Libro tercero* (Guadalajara, 1942).

——, *Libro cuarto* (Guadalajara, 1945).

Thompson, J. Eric, *Mexico Before Cortez* (New York, 1933).

Torquemada, Juan de, O. F. M., *Monarchía indiana*, 3 vols. (Mexico, 1943).

Vaillant, George C., *The Aztecs of Mexico: Origin, Rise, and Fall of the Aztec Nation* (New York, 1941).

Vázquez de Espinosa, Antonio, *Compendio y descripción de las Indias Occidentales* (Washington, D. C., 1948).

Velázquez, Primo Feliciano, *Colección de documentos para la historia de San Luis Potosí*, 4 vols. (San Luis Potosí, 1897–1899).

——, *Historia de San Luis Potosí*, 2 vols. (Mexico, 1947, 1948).

Villaseñor y Sánchez, José Antonio de, *Theatro americano; descripción general de los reynos y provincias de la Nueva España y sus jurisdicciones . . .*, 2 vols. (Mexico, 1746–1748).

West, Robert C., *The Mining Community in Northern New Spain: The Parral Mining District, Ibero-Americana:* 30 (Berkeley and Los Angeles: University of California Press, 1949).

Zavala, Silvio, *La encomienda indiana* (Madrid, 1935).

——, "Orígenes coloniales del peonaje en México," in *El Trimestre Económico*, Vol. 10, pp. 711–748 (Mexico, 1944).

——, y José Miranda, "Instituciones indígenas en la Colonia," in *Métodos y resultados de la política indigenista en México* (*Memorias del Instituto Nacional Indigenista*, Vol. 4, pp. 29–112) (Mexico, 1954).

Zurita, Alonso de, *Historia de la Nueva España* (Madrid, 1909).

——, *Breve y sumaria relación de los señores y maneras y diferencias que había entre ellos en la Nueva España*, ed. by J. García Icazbalceta (Mexico, 1941).

GLOSSARY

ABIGEO. Cattle thief.

ACORDADA. Decision of a court; the court itself.

ADELANTADO. Royal governor.

AGOSTADERO. Summer sheep run.

ALCABALA. Sales tax.

ALCALDE. Mayor of a town.

ALCALDE MAYOR. Royal magistrate, governor of a province (Alcaldía mayor); virtually equal to Corregidor.

ALFÉREZ. Ensign; corresponds roughly to second lieutenant.

ALGUACIL. Constable.

ALHÓNDIGA. Public granary.

ALTEPETLALLI (Az.). Common land.

ARRELDE. Weight of approximately four pounds.

ARROBA. Weight of 25 pounds.

ASIENTO. Contract; site of a building or estate.

AUDIENCIA. In New Spain, the supreme tribunal, consisting of a Presidente and four associate justices (oidores).

Az. = Aztec

Avería.   A kind of obligatory insurance tax levied on vessels to cover damage to merchandise.

Ayuntamiento.   Town council; also called Cabildo and Regimiento.

Bachiller.   Corresponds roughly to our Bachelor of Arts, but carried more dignity and privileges, such as benefit of clergy.

Baldío.   Uncultivated or abandoned land.

Barbacoa (Arawak).   Bed frame, house frame, or frame for roasting meats over a fire.

Barrio.   Section of a town; ward.

Caballería.   Agricultural land allotted to a caballero; about 100 acres.

Caballero.   Horseman; knight; gentleman.

Cabildo.   Same as Ayuntamiento.

Cacicazgo.   Office of a cacique.

Cacique (Arawak).   Chief; feminine form, cacica.

Calpixqui (Az.).   Major-domo; overseer.

Calpulco (Az.).   Community (big) house.

Calpulalli (Az.).   Lands belonging to a calpulli.

Calpullec (Az.).   Elder.

Calpulli (Az.).   Town district occupied by separate clan; corresponds to Barrio.

Capellanía.   Ecclesiastical benefice.

Carga.   Load; *carga de hombre*, 50 pounds; *carga de mula*, 200 pounds.

Caudillo.   Political or military chieftain.

Cédula.   Royal decree; in New Spain, a decree issued by the Council of the Indies over the King's signature.

Censo.   Income from a perpetual mortgage.

Centecpanpixqui (Az.).   Captain over twenty men.

Charrería (from charro).   Horsemanship.

Chichimeca (Az.).   Loose term applied to all nomad Indians; literally, wild men. Las Chichimecas: land occupied by them.

Ciuacóatl (Az.).   Lieutenant or viceroy.

Coa (probably Arawak).   Digging stick, usually with a flint point.

Compadre.   Godfather. The relationship (compadrazgo) between compadres was (is) very strong.

Composición.   Composition; payment made to Crown to clear land title.

Congregación.   In New Spain, a native community forcibly set up by the Crown; same as Reducción.

Criado.   Servant, not necessarily a domestic, but one who serves.

Criollo.   Creole; white born in New Spain.

Contador.   Royal accountant.

Corregidor.   Royal magistrate, governor of a province (corregimiento).

Cuadrilla.   Squad.

Dehesa.   Vacant or abandoned land; same as Baldío.

Demasías.   Surplus lands.

DESJARRETADERA. Curved blade mounted on a long staff; used for hamstringing cattle.

DUCADO. Ducat; coin worth eleven reales or tomines, or 1⅜ silver pesos (*q. v.*).

EJIDO. Common land of village or town.

ENCOMENDERO. Proprietor of an encomienda.

ENCOMIENDA. A kind of trust, whereby the crown granted to a conquistador the right to the tributes of a native community, in exchange for benefits, such as the support of a priest, indoctrination, and so on.

ESTANCIA. Grant of land for running sheep or cattle; an *estancia de ganado mayor* (horned cattle) measured 3,000 pasos de Salomón to a side, or one square league, approximately 6.76 square miles; an *estancia de ganado menor* (sheep) covered ⅘ square league, or about 3 square miles.

GANADO. (mayor, menor). *See* Estancia.

GAÑÁN. Day laborer; peón.

GARROCHA. Pointed stick used for driving oxen.

HACENDADO. Proprietor of an hacienda.

HACIENDA. In New Spain, a large rural estate.

HATO. Flock of sheep; also, personal belongings.

HEREDAD. Farm.

HIDALGO. A lesser noble; gentleman.

INGENIO. Large sugar mill, operated by water power.

ITONAL. (or Ytunal) (Az.). Plot of land. *See* Tlatocatlalli.

JARIPEO. Bull-riding.

LADINO. Spanish-speaking Indian; also, a rascal.

LEGUA. League, 2.6 miles.

LICENCIADO. Academic degree one rank higher than Bachiller.

MACEHUAL (Az.). Peasant.

MACUILTECPANPIXQUI (Az.). Captain over a hundred men.

MARAVEDÍ. A fictitious unit of value by which all coins were measured. *See* Peso.

MAYEQUE. (Az.). Serf bound to the land.

MERCED. Grant.

MESTIZO. Offspring of Spanish and Indian parents.

MILCHIMALLI (Az.). Land reserved for supply of army.

MILPA (Az., milpan). Cultivated plot, usually of maize.

MOSTRENCO. Unbranded cattle; *bienes mostrencos*, unclaimed goods; our word "mustang" evolved from this.

NABORÍA (Arawak). Free worker; also called Naborío and Laborío.

OBRAJE. Textile mill.

OIDOR. A member of the Audiencia.

OREJANO. Unbranded cattle; same as Mostrenco.

PANIAGUADO. Dependent, hanger-on.

PASO. Pace; the Paso de marca, or Paso de Salomón, 3,000 to the league.

PEÓN. Laborer; same as Gañán.

PEONÍA. Agricultural land allotted to foot-soldier (peón); usually ⅕ the size of a caballería.

PESO. The Spanish dollar, or piece-of-eight; that is, eight reales, or bits. The silver peso contained 278 maravedís; the gold peso, or castellano, 450 maravedís.

PEYOTE (Az., peyotl). The hallucinatory drug distilled from the buttons of the mescal cactus; the cactus itself.

PILALLI (Az.). Lands of nobles.

PILLI (Az.). A noble.

PIPILTZINPILLI (Az.). Sons of nobles.

POCHTECA (plural of Az. pochtécatl). Merchants.

PRINCIPAL. Indian noble.

PULQUE (Az.). Fermented juice of the *Agave americana,* or century plant.

RANCHERÍA. Any unorganized group of native houses; a village.

RANCHO. Farm, smaller than a hacienda; also, camp.

REAL. A bit, ⅛ peso; also, silver coinage. (2) A camp; *real de indios, real de esclavos.*

REAL DE MINAS. A mining community, incorporated under the Crown.

REALENGO. That which belongs to the Crown; here, lands.

REDUCCIÓN. *See* Congregación; also used for a mission settlement.

REGIDOR. Alderman, member of the town council, or Regimiento; some were elected, others held their offices in perpetuity (*regidores perpetuos*).

REGIMIENTO. Town council, or Ayuntamiento.

REPARTIMIENTO. A weekly allotment of Indian labor.

RESIDENCIA. An investigation, or trial, which officers had to submit to upon leaving office, or even during tenure.

RICO HOME. In Castile, a grandee; in New Spain, a rich or powerful man.

SEÑOR. Lord; Señorío, his domain.

SOBRAS. Same as Demasías.

SURCO. A furrow; here, a unit (undefined) for measuring water.

TECPAN (Az.). Palace.

TECPANTLALLI (Az.). Palace lands.

TECUTLALLI (Az.). Estate of a noble.

TECUTLI (Az.). Noble; lord.

TEPIXQUI (Az., tlapixqui). Guardian; in army, a lower officer.

TEQUÍO (Az.). Work stint.

TEQUITLATO (Az.). Foreman; "straw boss."

TERRAZGO. Ground rent; quitrent.

TERRAZGUERO. Renter, or sharecropper.

TIENDA DE RAYA. Hacienda store.

TLACATECUTLI (Az.). Noble.

TLAMILPA (Az., tlallimilli). Cultivated land.

TLATOCATLALLI (Az.). Estate of a lord (tlatoque).

TUNA. Fruit of the nopal, or prickly pear.

VAQUERO. A cowboy; "buckaroo."

VARA. The Castilian yard of about 33 inches, 5,000 to the league.

VARA DE JUSTICIA. Wand of justice, carried by all officials as a badge of authority, the length of the vara determining the degree.

VECINDAD. The rights of a Vecino.

VECINO. Citizen; member of a municipal corporation.

VEEDOR. A royal inspector, attached to the Audiencia.

VIANDANTE. Vagabond; migratory worker.

VILLA. A municipal corporation one step below the city; most Spanish communities in Mexico were organized as villas.

VISITADOR. A royal visitor, appointed by the King (the Council of the Indies) or by the Audiencia; the Visitador frequently had the terrifying power of executing justice by his own hand; usually, however, he laid his findings before the higher authorities.

YAOTLALLI (Az.). Land seized from the enemy.

INDEX